I0874846

AI Solutions for Detecting Cyber-Attacks in Information Systems

Mohammed Amin Almaiah
https://orcid.org/0009-0008-9785-485X
University of Jordan, Jordan

IGI Global
Scientific Publishing
Publishing Tomorrow's Research Today

Vice President of Editorial Melissa Wagner
Director of Acquisitions Mikaela Felty
Director of Book Development Jocelynn Hessler
Production Manager Mike Brehm
Cover Design Jose Rosado

Published in the United States of America by
IGI Global Scientific Publishing
701 East Chocolate Avenue
Hershey, PA, 17033, USA
Tel: 717-533-8845 | Fax: 717-533-7115
Website: https://www.igi-global.com E-mail: cust@igi-global.com

Copyright © 2026 by IGI Global Scientific Publishing. All rights reserved. No part of this publication may be reproduced, stored or distributed in any form or by any means, electronic or mechanical, including photocopying, without written permission from the publisher. Use of this publication to train generative artificial intelligence (AI) technologies is expressly prohibited. The publisher reserves all rights to license its use for generative AI training and machine learning model development.

Product or company names used in this set are for identification purposes only. Inclusion of the names of the products or companies does not indicate a claim of ownership by IGI Global Scientific Publishing of the trademark or registered trademark.

Library of Congress Cataloging-in-Publication Data

Names: Almaiah, Mohammed Amin, 1986- editor
http://id.loc.gov/rwo/agents/n2024031943
Title: AI solutions for detecting cyber-attacks in information systems / edited by Mohammed Almaiah.
Description: Hershey, PA : IGI Global Scientific Publishing, [2026] | Includes bibliographical references and index. | Summary: "The main objective of this book is to systematically cover all essential aspects of AI solutions for cybersecurity attacks, with a focus on reporting on cybersecurity security issues and cybersecurity threats as well as the latest research results, and real-world deployment of AI as security countermeasures"-- Provided by publisher.
Identifiers: LCCN 2025002885 (print) | LCCN 2025002886 (ebook) | ISBN 9798337318073 h/c | ISBN 9798337318080 s/c | ISBN 9798337318097 ebook
Subjects: LCSH: Computer security http://id.loc.gov/authorities/subjects/sh90001862 | Computer networks--Security measures http://id.loc.gov/authorities/subjects/sh94001277 | Artificial intelligence--Security measures | Digital forensic science http://id.loc.gov/authorities/subjects/sh2018000110 | Computer crimes--Investigation http://id.loc.gov/authorities/subjects/sh85029493
Classification: LCC QA76.9.A25 A4154 2025 (print) | LCC QA76.9.A25 (ebook) | DDC 005.8--dc23/eng/20250428
LC record available at https://lccn.loc.gov/2025002885
LC ebook record available at https://lccn.loc.gov/2025002886

British Cataloguing in Publication Data
A Cataloguing in Publication record for this book is available from the British Library.

All work contributed to this book is new, previously-unpublished material.
The views expressed in this book are those of the authors, but not necessarily of the publisher.
This book contains information sourced from authentic and highly regarded references, with reasonable efforts made to ensure the reliability of the data and information presented. The authors, editors, and publisher believe the information in this book to be accurate and true as of the date of publication. Every effort has been made to trace and credit the copyright holders of all materials included. However, the authors, editors, and publisher cannot assume responsibility for the validity of all materials or the consequences of their use. Should any copyright material be found unacknowledged, please inform the publisher so that corrections may be made in future reprints.

Table of Contents

Detailed Table of Contents

Many governmental and private organizations and institutions seek to keep pace with the technological development in their business to provide an electronic system that provides all the services and information customers need at any time and in any place, and also to save effort and time on it, through the use of cloud computing services and the services it provides for these institutions and organizations through the "payment-for- service" services and system management services provided by the service provider or by the user, or both. Despite the availability of cloud computing service, there are challenges and obstacles faced by the organization and service providers, and the most important of these challenges are issues of information security and privacy because of the negative impact on the client and the organization of breaches and tampering with this data. As a result, new models and analyses are needed to deal with the ever-increasing volume of data. Hence, this study came about to clarify the security challenges of big data.

The current research proposed a decentralized-based framework to augment the prediction and diagnosis of cardiovascular diseases using IoT & blockchain. IoT devices are used for real-time data collection as part of the framework, allowing for continuous monitoring & higher precision in determining potential health risks. Patient data is stored securely & tamper-proof with blockchain, which can build confidence & transparency in the system. Also, by decentralizing data processing & decision-making, the proposed work eliminates single points of failure & enables better scalability in large-scale healthcare applications. The design captures predictive analysis in real-time for early intervention, better health data & patient dynamics, enhanced health outcomes, & streamlined health data with secure access for patient empowerment. Thus, with many systematic synergies derived from the aspects of IoT & blockchain, it can be stated that disease management can be revolutionized & integrated into recent healthcare systems by combining advanced predictive analytics & robust security mechanisms.

This research investigates the efficacy of deep learning models, specifically Convolutional Neural Networks (CNN) and Long Short-Term Memory (LSTM) networks, in the context of crime rate prediction. By combining the spatial feature extraction capabilities of CNNs with the temporal sequence learning strengths of

LSTMs, we developed a hybrid CNN-LSTM model. The l results demonstrate that the CNN-LSTM model significantly surpasses traditional predictive models, including ARIMA and standard neural networks, achieving a remarkable accuracy rate of 97.8%. Furthermore, the incorporation of multiple LSTM layers not only enhanced predictive accuracy but also optimized the training process. These findings highlight the potential of advanced neural network architectures in developing robust predictive systems for crime forecasting. The study concludes with recommendations for future research focused on hyperparameter optimization to improve model performance and reliability further, thereby contributing valuable insights for proactive crime prevention and effective law enforcement strategies.

With cyber threats becoming more complex, Cyber-Attack Detection Systems (CADS) are crucial for identifying and preventing attacks. However, traditional methods often fail to detect advanced threats accurately, leading to problems with accuracy, scalability, and reliability. This chapter presents an ensemble-based machine learning framework, referred to Adaptive Weighted Voting Ensemble (AWVE) Model, that leverages the strengths of multiple models to enhance the detection and classification of cyber-attacks. By combining diverse predictive techniques within a unified system, the ensemble approach achieves improved performance, overcoming the shortcomings of individual models. The framework is evaluated using the NSL-KDD dataset, a well-known dataset for network intrusion detection research, to assess its effectiveness in identifying and categorizing various attack types. The results demonstrate that the ensemble framework achieves superior detection rates and classification accuracy across different attack categories while maintaining low false positive rates.

The research tackles the constantly changing realm of cyber threats, drawing comparisons to an insistent and opportunistic cyber-zombie adversary. Through an in-depth analysis, we dissect the tactics of this digital threat, encompassing malware, phishing, and social engineering, while drawing parallels to the relentless siege of a zombie attack. Organizations must implement robust countermeasures to strengthen defenses against an impending zombie attack, including intrusion detection systems, strengthening authentication processes, and equipping employees with the awareness and skills to combat cyber-zombies. It will help secure the systems and data against isolated attacks and the persistent and multifaceted threat landscape. Experimenting within a virtual environment is essential for identifying and comprehending the potential threat posed by a zombie attack. Adopting a proactive stance in preparing for a persistent onslaught is crucial for building resilience and safeguarding against continually evolving cyber threats.

The rapid wave of growth in information systems has led to millions of new attack surfaces have been created by these devices due to the rapid development of information technologies but have left many systems vulnerable to sophisticated forms of cyber-attacks as well. Modern warfare finds it increasingly harder to qualify in today's presumably automatized world, which further implies that automated systems need to be developed. The aim of such technology is to assist a user in considering and assessing huge datasets containing indicators of suspicious behaviour and even taking actions against emerging threats. This chapter outlines the use of cutting-edge technologies in the Host-Based Intrusion Detection Systems, including ML algorithms, deep learning for networks and natural language processing.

This chapter explores unconventional approaches to enhance the capabilities and security of Artificial Intelligence and Vedic Scripture enabled sustainable Medical Cyber Physical Systems (MCPS) to achieve secure healthcare. We discuss overview, types, challenges and opportunities of using Cyber Physical Systems, powered by AI, in healthcare sector, including device coordination and communication, data integrity and patient privacy. Additionally, we review existing research and literature to demonstrate the effectiveness of Medical Cyber Physical Systems in improved healthcare delivery while addressing privacy restrictions. Through this research, we aim to gain a deeper understanding of Cyber Physical Systems, their vulnerabilities and exploration of unconventional ideas, that contribute to the ongoing evolution of secure and efficient AI-enabled MCPS and their ability to transform the health industry.

Cyber-Physical Systems (CPS) represent a critical convergence of computational algorithms and physical processes, enabling smart infrastructures across industries such as energy, transportation, healthcare, and manufacturing. However, the integration of digital and physical components exposes these systems to unique security challenges that can lead to severe physical and economic consequences. This work focuses on Cyber-Physical System security, aiming to protect the delicate intersection where digital control meets the physical environment. By leveraging advanced machine learning techniques, including bi-stacked Gated Recurrent Units (GRUs), this approach enhances the detection and prevention of cyber-physical attacks through effective analysis of sequential sensor and control data. Coupled with feature selection using Particle Swarm Optimization (PSO), the methodology prioritizes relevant system attributes, improving anomaly detection accuracy.

Digital and Information Forensics plays a critical role in today's data-driven world by enabling the discovery and interpretation of electronic evidence amidst vast and complex digital environments. As digital technologies proliferate, cybercrimes and security breaches have grown more sophisticated, necessitating advanced forensic methodologies to detect, analyze, and attribute malicious activities. This field integrates diverse techniques such as data acquisition, preservation, analysis, and presentation to ensure the integrity and admissibility of digital evidence in legal and investigative contexts. By unveiling hidden truths within digital footprints, Digital and Information Forensics not only combats cyber threats but also supports organizational security, regulatory compliance, and justice. Continuous innovation and ethical vigilance remain essential to address emerging challenges, maintain public trust, and uphold privacy rights in an increasingly interconnected world.

The rapid use of cloud computing services for processing, storing data, and deploying applications has raised serious security issues. Traditional security measures are further insufficient against the complex and constantly changing cyberthreat landscape. This study investigates the incorporation of machine learning methods into cloud security architectures to strengthen threat detection and mitigation. The chapter outlines the state of cloud security and the evolution of cyber threats and the benefits of machine learning in strengthening cloud security measures, such as improved accuracy and adaptability, while also addressing the challenges and limitations, including algorithmic complexity and data privacy concerns. Ethical considerations and potential risks, such as biases in algorithms and the misuse of AI technologies, are critically examined. The chapter concludes with recommendations for deploying machine learning-based security solutions in cloud environments and classifies future research directions to address ongoing and emerging challenges.

The next step in Internet development is the Internet of Things (IoT), which gives everyday things the ability to be smart and interactive, facilitating the growth of mobile and electronic health apps for ambient assisted living (AAL). Cloud computing approaches are essential for successfully deploying and maintaining these applications because they offer vast storage capacities and high computational capabilities. To enhance remote healthcare monitoring, this study suggests a novel

Preface

Welcome to AI Solutions for Detecting Cyber-Attacks in Information Systems, a comprehensive compilation edited by Dr. Mohammed Almaiah. In the rapidly evolving digital era, the integrity and security of information systems have become fundamental pillars of modern society. With the exponential growth of connected devices, cloud infrastructures, and data-driven applications, cyber-attacks have grown in both sophistication and frequency, threatening critical infrastructures, enterprises, and individuals alike. Conventional security mechanisms are no longer sufficient to combat these dynamic and intelligent threats. This urgent reality has paved the way for the integration of Artificial Intelligence (AI) into cybersecurity systems as a proactive and adaptive defense mechanism.

The book AI Solutions for Detecting Cyber-Attacks in Information Systems is conceived in response to this pressing global challenge. It explores how AI through its diverse branches such as machine learning, deep learning, neural networks, natural language processing, and evolutionary algorithms can transform cyber-attack detection, mitigation, and prevention. By combining theoretical frameworks, algorithmic models, and practical applications, this volume provides a comprehensive understanding of how AI can enhance the resilience, agility, and intelligence of cybersecurity infrastructures.

This book is designed to serve a broad audience of researchers, academicians, practitioners, students, and policymakers who are interested in the intersection of artificial intelligence and cybersecurity. Each chapter offers unique insights into AI-driven intrusion detection systems, anomaly detection in network traffic, malware classification, phishing detection, and intelligent threat modeling. The contributions collected herein not only present current methodologies but also highlight emerging research directions, including explainable AI, federated learning, adversarial robustness, and quantum-safe AI security systems.

By presenting both foundational knowledge and advanced developments, AI Solutions for Detecting Cyber-Attacks in Information Systems aims to bridge the gap between research innovation and real-world implementation. The book aspires to inspire future research collaborations and guide the design of next-generation intelligent defense frameworks that will protect our increasingly interconnected world.

I would like to express my sincere gratitude to all the authors, reviewers, and editors who contributed their expertise to make this volume possible. Their scholarly commitment and innovative thinking have greatly enriched this work. I also extend my appreciation to the academic and professional communities who continuously strive to advance the frontiers of cybersecurity research through the power of artificial intelligence.

It is my hope that this book will not only deepen readers' understanding of AI-based cybersecurity solutions but also encourage continued exploration into the design of intelligent, adaptive, and trustworthy information systems for the future.

ORGANIZATION OF THE BOOK

In " **Security and privacy challenges and opportunities for e-government services in big data"** by *Mohammad Rasmi Al-Mousa, Ala'a Saeb Al-Sherideh, Ali Abu Zaid, Yousef Hazzaimeh, Nawaf Alshdaifat, Mohammad Aljaidi, Qais Al-Na'amneh and Hind Talafha.* Many governmental and private organizations and institutions seek to keep pace with the technological development in their business to provide an electronic system that provides all the services and information customers need at any time and in any place, and also to save effort and time on it, through the use of cloud computing services and the services it provides for these institutions and organizations through the "payment-for- service" services and system management services provided by the service provider or by the user, or both. Despite the availability of cloud computing service, there are challenges and obstacles faced by the organization and service providers, and the most important of these challenges are issues of information security and privacy because of the negative impact on the client and the organization of breaches and tampering with this data. As a result, new models and analyses are needed to deal with the ever-increasing volume of data. Hence, this study came about to clarify the security challenges of big data.

In "**IoT-Blockchain Decentralized Framework for Predicting Cardiovascular Disease**" by *SHAHNAZEER C K, SURESHKUMAR G, SHINZEER C K, Avinash Bhagat, Ajay Shriram Kushwaha.* The current research proposed a decentralized-based framework to augment the prediction and diagnosis of cardiovascular diseases using IoT & blockchain. IoT devices are used for real-time data collection as part of the framework, allowing for continuous monitoring & higher precision in determining potential health risks. Patient data is stored securely & tamper-proof with blockchain, which can build confidence & transparency in the system. Also, by decentralizing data processing & decision-making, the proposed work eliminates single points of failure & enables better scalability in large-scale healthcare applications. The design captures predictive analysis in real-time for early intervention, better health data & patient dynamics, enhanced health outcomes, & streamlined health data with secure access for patient empowerment. Thus, with many systematic synergies derived from the aspects of IoT & blockchain, it can be stated that disease management can be revolutionized & integrated into recent healthcare systems by combining advanced predictive analytics & robust security mechanisms.

In "**Harnessing CNN-LSTM Fusion for Enhanced Crime Forecasting and Temporal Pattern Analysis**" by *K.Ramalakshmi, L.Krishna Kumari, R.Rajalakshmi, P.Sivakumar, R.Meena Prakash.* This research investigates the efficacy of deep learning models, specifically Convolutional Neural Networks (CNN) and Long Short-Term Memory (LSTM) networks, in the context of crime rate prediction. By combining the spatial feature extraction capabilities of CNNs with the temporal sequence learning strengths of LSTMs, we developed a hybrid CNN-LSTM model. This model was rigorously tested using crime data from India spanning the years 2001 to 2013. The experimental results demonstrate that the CNN-LSTM model significantly surpasses traditional predictive models, including ARIMA and standard neural networks, achieving a remarkable accuracy rate of 97.8%. Furthermore, the incorporation of multiple LSTM layers not only enhanced predictive accuracy but also optimized the training process. These findings highlight the potential of advanced neural network architectures in developing robust predictive systems for crime forecasting. The study concludes with recommendations for future research focused on hyper parameter optimization to improve model performance and reliability further, thereby contributing valuable insights for proactive crime prevention and effective law enforcement strategies.

In "An **Ensemble Framework for Effective Detection and Classification of Cyber Attacks Using Machine Learning**" by *NAVEENKUMAR MAHAMKALI, Krishna Siva Prasad Mudigonda.* This chapter presents an ensemble-based machine learning framework, referred to Adaptive Weighted Voting Ensemble (AWVE) Model, which leverages the strengths of multiple models to enhance the detection and classification of cyber-attacks. By combining diverse predictive techniques within a unified system, the ensemble approach achieves improved performance, overcoming the shortcomings of individual models. The framework is evaluated using the NSL-KDD dataset, a well-known dataset for network intrusion detection research, to assess its effectiveness in identifying and categorizing various attack types. The results demonstrate that the ensemble framework achieves superior detection rates and classification accuracy across different attack categories while maintaining low false positive rates.

In "**Navigating the Maze of Network Security: Threats, Strategies, and Countermeasures"** by *Ajay Kumar, Keshav Sinha.* The research tackles the constantly changing realm of cyber threats, drawing comparisons to an insistent and opportunistic cyber-zombie adversary. Through an in-depth analysis, we dissect the tactics of this digital threat, encompassing malware, phishing, and social engineering, while drawing parallels to the relentless siege of a zombie attack. Organizations must implement robust countermeasures to strengthen defenses against an impending zombie attack, including intrusion detection systems, strengthening authentication processes, and equipping employees with the awareness and skills to combat cyber-zombies. It will help secure the systems and data against isolated attacks and the persistent and multifaceted threat landscape. Experimenting within a virtual environment is essential for identifying and comprehending the potential threat posed by a zombie attack. Adopting a proactive stance in preparing for a persistent onslaught is crucial for building resilience and safeguarding against continually evolving cyber threats.

In "**Deepfake Detection System**" by *Anushree Deshmukh, Kalyani Nakul Satone, Ankush Hutke, Sunil Wankhade*. The use of advanced AI algorithms is growing daily, resulting in increasingly realistic fake videos with facial superimposition that are being produced by Artificial Intelligence, as these videos involve well-known people, their behavior can have severe consequences. Therefore, to stop the rapid spread of Deepfake it is of extreme importance to identify it first. The proposed method has two approaches: Image based, and video based. An image-based approach uses Haar cascade classifier for feature selection and CNN for classification whether the input image is real or fake. Video based approach uses a novel Residual Network based model that learns inherently distinct patterns that change between a real video and a Deepfake. An Inception Residual Network Version 2 has been trained by the proposed model to successfully differentiate Deepfake videos using different features of a frame-based approach. This work shows our model can be used to accurately identify Deepfake faces in each image and video source. This study presents a unified solution to solve the data classification problem.

In "**Adoption of Artificial Intelligence Techniques for Enhancing Host-Based Intrusion Detection Systems**" by *Tarun Kumar Vashishth, Vikas Sharma, Sachin Chaudhary, Rupak Sharma, Puneet Chauhan, Brijesh Kumar Sharma*. The rapid wave of growth in information systems has led to millions of new attack surfaces have been created by these devices due to the rapid development of information technologies but have left many systems vulnerable to sophisticated forms of cyber-attacks as well. Modern warfare finds it increasingly harder to qualify in today's presumably automatized world, which further implies that automated systems need to be developed. The aim of such technology is to assist a user in considering and assessing huge datasets containing indicators of suspicious behaviour and even taking actions against emerging threats. This chapter outlines the use of cutting-edge technologies in the Host-Based Intrusion Detection Systems, including ML algorithms, deep learning for networks and natural language processing.

In "**Artificial Intelligence and Vedic Scripture Enabled Sustainable Medical Cyber Physical Systems for Secure Healthcare**" by *Sachin Sharma*. This chapter explores unconventional approaches to enhance the capabilities and security of Artificial Intelligence and Vedic Scripture enabled sustainable Medical Cyber Physical Systems (MCPS) to achieve secure healthcare. We discuss overview, types, challenges and opportunities of using Cyber Physical Systems, powered by AI, in healthcare sector, including device coordination and communication, data integrity and patient privacy. Additionally, we review existing research and literature to demonstrate the effectiveness of Medical Cyber Physical Systems in improved healthcare delivery while addressing privacy restrictions. Through this research, we aim to gain a deeper understanding of Cyber Physical Systems, their vulnerabilities and exploration of unconventional ideas that contribute to the ongoing evolution of secure and efficient AI-enabled MCPS and their ability to transform the health industry.

In "**Cyber-Physical System Resilience Leveraging Deep Learning for Enhanced Security**" by *Usharani Bhimavarapu*. This work focuses on Cyber-Physical System security, aiming to protect the delicate intersection where digital control meets the physical environment. By leveraging advanced machine learning techniques, including bi-stacked Gated Recurrent Units (GRUs), this approach enhances the detection and prevention of cyber-physical attacks through effective analysis of sequential sensor and control data. Coupled with feature selection using Particle Swarm Optimization (PSO), the methodology prioritizes relevant system attributes, improving anomaly detection accuracy.

In "**Leveraging AI and Machine Learning in Digital Forensics**" by *Usharani Bhimavarapu*. Digital and Information Forensics plays a critical role in today's data-driven world by enabling the discovery and interpretation of electronic evidence amidst vast and complex digital environments. As digital technologies proliferate, cybercrimes and security breaches have grown more sophisticated, necessitating advanced forensic methodologies to detect, analyze, and attribute malicious activities. This field integrates diverse techniques such as data acquisition, preservation, analysis, and presentation to ensure the integrity and admissibility of digital evidence in legal and investigative contexts. By unveiling hidden truths within digital footprints, Digital and Information Forensics not only combats cyber threats but also supports organizational security, regulatory compliance, and justice. Continuous innovation and ethical vigilance remain essential to address emerging challenges, maintain public trust, and uphold privacy rights in an increasingly interconnected world.

In "**Securing Cloud - Leveraging Machine Learning for Threat Detection and Mitigation**" by *Deepa Nehra, Karanbir Singh*. The rapid use of cloud computing services for processing, storing data, and deploying applications has raised serious security issues. Traditional security measures are further insufficient against the complex and constantly changing cyberthreat landscape. This study investigates the incorporation of machine learning methods into cloud security architectures to strengthen threat detection and mitigation. The chapter outlines the state of cloud security and the evolution of cyber threats and the benefits of machine learning in strengthening cloud security measures, such as improved accuracy and adaptability, while also addressing the challenges and limitations, including algorithmic complexity and data privacy concerns. Ethical considerations and potential risks, such as biases in algorithms and the misuse of AI technologies, are critically examined. The chapter concludes with recommendations for deploying machine learning-based security solutions in cloud environments and classifies future research directions to address ongoing and emerging challenges.

In "**Enhancing Security Remote Healthcare Monitoring Through IoT-Integrated Cloud Architecture**" by *Dena Abu Laila, Qais Al-Na'amneh, Mohammad Aljaidi, Sajeda Slnweran, Ayoub Alsarhan, Ahmad Saleh Alhazaimeh, Omar Altamimi, Khaled Maabreh*. The next step in Internet development is the Internet of Things (IoT), which gives everyday things the ability to be smart and interactive, facilitating the growth of mobile and electronic health apps for ambient assisted living (AAL). Cloud computing approaches are essential for successfully deploying and maintaining these applications because they offer vast storage capacities and high computational capabilities. To enhance remote healthcare monitoring, this study suggests a novel architecture that combines cloud computing (CC) technologies and the Internet of Things (IoT). Latency reduction is one of the requirements for computing systems that can allow healthcare operations to be completed. Because fog computing uses only low-end computers, mobile phones, and personal devices, it can offer lower latency than cloud computing. Our suggested architecture unifies all components into a single cloud-based system, unlike typical IoT systems that rely. The architecture has been implemented into practice and tested with Cisco Packet Tracer.

In "**Decoding Digital Evidence and Evaluating and Usability in Digital Forensics**" by *Ayoub Alsarhan, Dena Abu Laila, Mohammad Aljaidi, Qais Al-Na'amneh, Yara Al-dbeisi, Khaled Maabreh, Ahmad Saleh Alhazaimeh*. An essential component of cybersecurity is digital forensics, which includes retrieving and analyzing data from digital devices. X-Ways Forensics, Autopsy, and FTK have gained prominence among the various tools available due to their unique capabilities and widespread use. This paper provides a detailed analysis of these two tools, comparing their features, usability, performance, and application in digital forensic investigations. By examining these tools, we aim to highlight their strengths and weaknesses, offering practitioners insights into the most suitable tool for various forensic scenarios. The results are intended to guide the selection of the best instrument for a given set of investigation requirements.

CONCLUSION

The evolution of cybersecurity in the era of digital transformation has underscored the critical role of Artificial Intelligence (AI) as a cornerstone of modern defense mechanisms. Throughout this book, AI Solutions for Detecting Cyber-Attacks in Information Systems, we have examined how intelligent algorithms, data-driven analytics, and adaptive learning models are redefining the boundaries of cyber protection and risk mitigation. The chapters collectively demonstrate that AI is not merely an enhancement to traditional security systems, but rather a paradigm shift—one that enables proactive detection, contextual awareness, and autonomous response to complex and ever-evolving cyber threats.

In the ever-evolving landscape of AI solutions in cybersecurity for information systems, our edited reference book, “AI Solutions for Detecting Cyber-Attacks in Information Systems” seeks to provide a comprehensive resource for practitioners, researchers, and academics alike. Throughout the chapters, our esteemed contributors have delved into various facets of AI methods for threat detection, risk prevention, AI and machine learning for enhancing cybersecurity of detection, prevention, and risk management, mitigating security risks in different types of information systems on enhancing the privacy and security of these systems.

As we conclude this preface, we extend our sincere appreciation to all the authors who have contributed their expertise and insights to this volume. It is our hope that “AI Solutions for Detecting Cyber-Attacks in Information Systems ” will serve as a valuable resource for years to come, inspiring further exploration and innovation in the ongoing mission to secure our information systems using AI solutions.

Mohammed Almaiah
University of Jordan, Jordan

Chapter 1
Security and Privacy Challenges and Opportunities for e-Government Services in Big Data

Mohammad Rasmi Al-Mousa
https://orcid.org/0009-0008-3034-7693
Zarqa University, Jordan

Ala'a Saeb Al-Sherideh
Zarqa University, Jordan

Ali Abu Zaid
Zarqa University, Jordan

Yousef Hazzaimeh
Zarqa University, Jordan

Nawaf Alshdaifat
Applied Science Private University, Jordan

Mohammad Aljaidi
https://orcid.org/0000-0001-9486-3533
Zarqa University, Jordan

Qais Al-Na'amneh
Applied Science Private University, Jordan

Hind Talafha
https://orcid.org/0009-0001-2226-028X
Applied Science Private University, Jordan

Ahmad Saleh Alhazaimeh
King Abdaulaziz University, Saudi Arabia

ABSTRACT

Many governmental and private organizations and institutions seek to keep pace with the technological development in their business to provide an electronic system that provides all the services and information customers need at any time and in

DOI: 10.4018/979-8-3373-1807-3.ch001

2026, IGI Global Scientific Publishing. Copying or distributing in print or electronic forms without written permission of IGI Global Scientific Publishing is prohibited. Use of this chapter to rative artificial intelligence (AI) technologies is expressly prohibited. The publisher reserves all rights to license its use for generative AI training and machine learning model development.

any place, and also to save effort and time on it, through the use of cloud computing services and the services it provides for these institutions and organizations through the "payment-for- service" services and system management services provided by the service provider or by the user, or both. Despite the availability of cloud computing service, there are challenges and obstacles faced by the organization and service providers, and the most important of these challenges are issues of information security and privacy because of the negative impact on the client and the organization of breaches and tampering with this data. As a result, new models and analyses are needed to deal with the ever-increasing volume of data. Hence, this study came about to clarify the security challenges of big data.

INTRODUCTION

E-government was established to provide a better life for citizens by providing precise information and better service to facilitate their transactions and related government procedures and their negative effects on them, whether financially or morally (Narayanan & Kannan, 2024). Big data technologies shorten the development phase, enhance construction, increase production, and satisfy customers (Thanganadar & Raman, 2024). With the advancement of technology, cloud computing services have become available to all components of the country, including institutions, companies, factories, and organizations (Ali & Shehab, 2023), to provide the best service to the customer by providing three types of cloud computing: Infrastructure as a Service (IaaS) that provides the highest level of flexibility and administrative control over access to devices and resources, in addition to space for storing big data. The second type is a platform as a service (PaaS). This service helps you focus on efficient application deployment and management, so you don't have to worry about resource procurement, capacity planning, software maintenance, patching, or any of the undifferentiated heavy lifting involved in running your application. The third type, Software as a Service (SaaS). This service provides the product in its full form and is managed and operated by the service provider only. Big data is present in most of our daily activities. The term "big data" was created to describe multiple, huge amounts of data that are difficult to control and deal with using traditional systems. Data is the most valuable thing in all sectors, and it is necessary for organizations to perform their daily work, so it is very necessary to deal with it. With this data correctly maintained and its security, integrity, and confidentiality maintained, the safety and confidentiality of data is a priority for government institutions and is the basis on which it is based because of the information it contains for the state and the citizen, so care must be taken to ensure that it is stored in protected places and to prevent its sharing and protect it from unauthorized threats (Jain et al., 2016).

Cloud computing, security and challenges (Addula et al., 2025; Alshinwan et al., 2025); Albinhamad et al., 2025).

Figure 1. A birds eye view of cloud computing

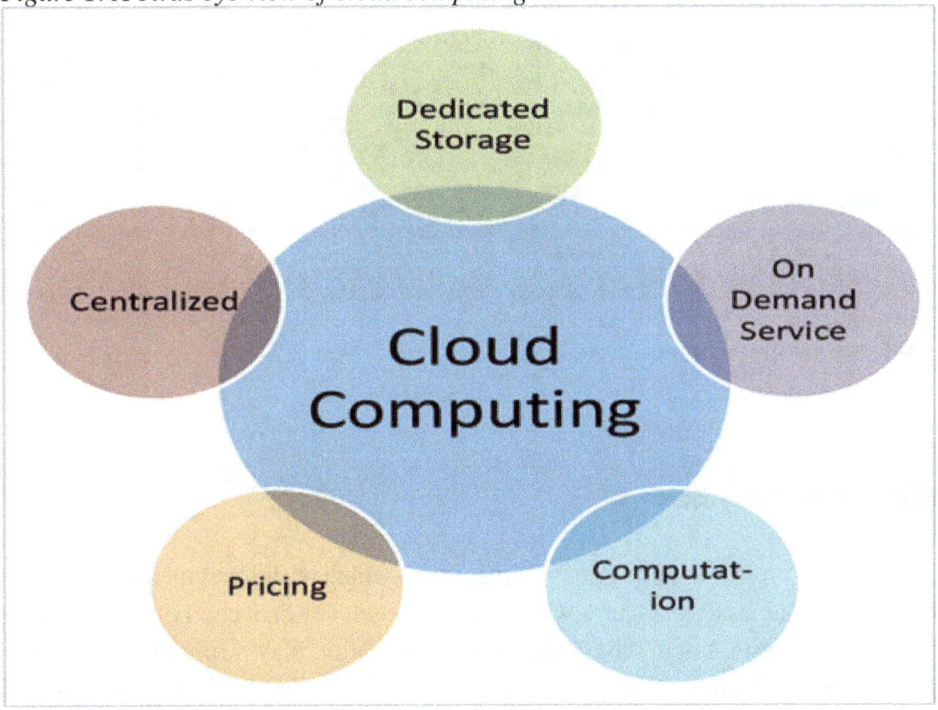

(Bello et al., 2021)

Figure 1, illustrates the types of cloud computing such as public service, hybrid service, Community Service, and private service, and also a clarification for deployment models such as PaaS, SaaS, and IaaS finally, the characteristics of cloud computing such as self-service, flexibility, ubiquitous and shared pool.

In Figure 2, an illustration of the types of cloud computing, The SaaS is used in an explanation of how to manage systems in e-services, either by user or by service provider. In this case, the service provider is the first and last responsible for system management.

Figure 2. Types of cloud computing (red hat)

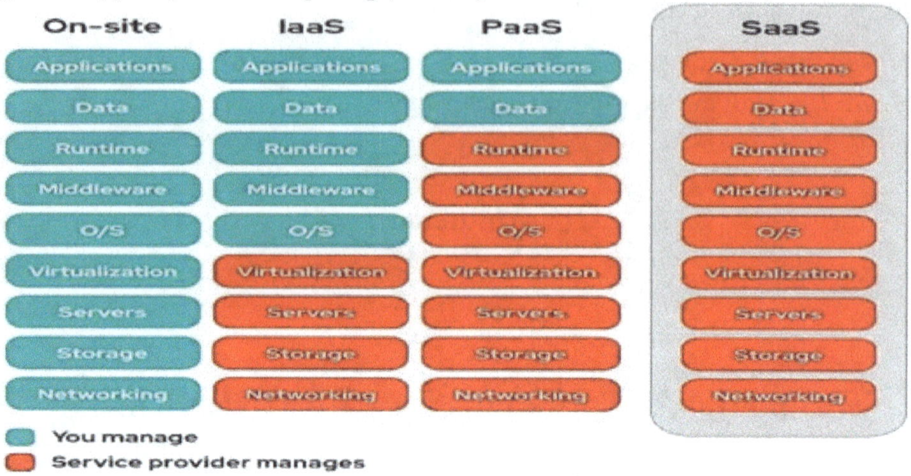

Big Data Lifecycles

"Big data" refers to large data volumes, with which traditional methods are difficult, if not impossible. Over a while, large amounts of data can be accessed and stored for analysis. Large data volumes of information play a role in information processing applications (Zaman & Rani, 2022). The value of data is determined by how it is used. The concept of "big data" is the idea of storing, processing, and disassembling huge amounts of information (such as Zetta bytes) that are incomprehensible to traditional database management systems. Processing big data on categories using parallel algorithms are used in semi-structured or incomplete data management. In addition to well-structured data sets, data places, data warehouses, data management, and data pre-processing are all categories of big data (Hasan et al., 2022). Governments can use big data in their systems for improving operations, providing excellent customer service. Database systems are usually built on relational databases and consist only of large datasets, whereas storage systems can accommodate a wide range of data types. Big data processing places a great demand on basic computing architecture.

Figure 3. Big data classification

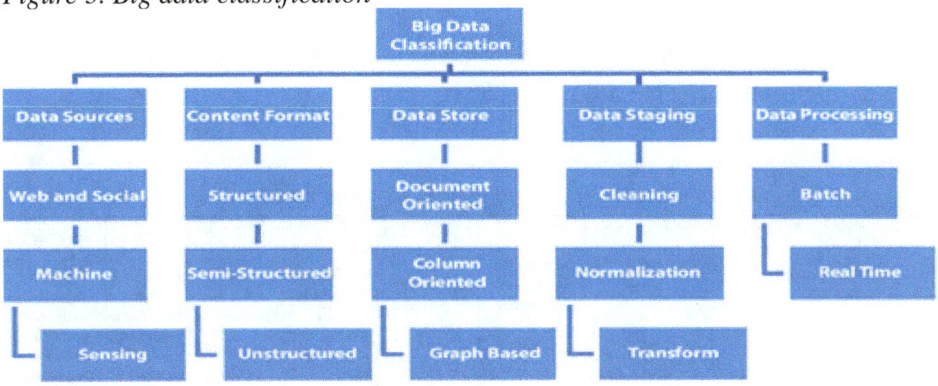

(Zaman & Rani, 2022)

SUMMARY AND DESCRIPTION OF THE PROBLEM

One of the big concerns with big data is exploring the best way to store the enormous amounts of information properly and securely to preserve privacy from tampering and theft (Ali, 2024), (Al-Shareeda et al., 2024). The volume of data saved in company data centers and on company datasets is increasing rapidly. Such datasets are expanded at an incremental rate over time, which making it completely difficult to manage.

Governments have a tendency to be reticent to use big data technology. Uncertain controversies which constrain e-Governments have made some denounce, e-Governments services (Almaayah and Sulaiman, 2024), (Alsahaim and Maayah, 2023). That can create significant obstacles that must be resolved as quickly as possible. In this study, this research will explain the challenges and obstacles in information security and privacy and explain some appropriate solutions that were collected and explained in previous studies.

Objectives

The main objectives of this research are to discover and provide scientific researchers, practitioners and decision makers to include and incorporate the e-government and big data with the issues of privacy and security in big data, identify some privacy issues, and provide explanations proposed by previous studies.

Solutions

In this study, a set of solutions were collected from previous studies to solve these problems effectively based on table 1.

Table 1. Clarification of some solutions from previous studies

prefix	citation	increase the number of staff cyber security experts	crypto and separation of data	verification of identity and permission	end-point protection	monitoring and reporting in real time	making use of big data security technique like IBM and other techniques
1	Wang et al., 2022	√	√	√			√
2	Davies et al., 2022	√	√	√			√
3	Owida et al., 2021	√	√	√			√
4	Yuan et al., 2022		√	√		√	√
5	Wimpenny et al., 2022		√	√		√	√
6	Li et al., 2017		√	√		√	√
7	Abesamis & Caramancion, (2022		√	√			√
8	Usmani et al., 2022			√			√
9	Santhosh & Minni, 2022		√	√			√
10	Ujjan et al., 2022				√	√	√
11	Park et al., 2022				√	√	√
12	Sewak et al., 2021	√	√	√	√		√
13	Comite, 2022			√		√	√
14	Praveen et al., 2022			√		√	√

Discussion

In the table above, the best-fitting solutions are identified for the challenges of specificity and relevance, respectively. The need for modern and advanced technologies that work to maintain the security, privacy and the sensitivity of the data for the user came in 100% of previous studies. Verifying the user's identity and entry permission and making sure of their authenticity by 87%. Importance of encrypting data with finest encryption algorithms that are difficult to decrypt is 60%. Monitoring data transmission in the network, and tracking any changes or modifications in its values 53%. Increase in the number of cyber security experts 27%. Endpoint protection 20%. This is an indication for necessity of preserving data privacy at all stages from beginning to end.

RELATED WORK

This research examines the links between information security awareness, expertise, and actions, as well as their relation to safety, among individual people in 4 countries. The findings show that while web users are aware of cyber threats, they only take the most basic and easy-to-implement precautions. The study results also indicate that higher levels of cyber expertise are related to higher levels of cyber sensitivity, regardless of participant country or identity. Furthermore, awareness is linked to security features, but not to the data they are willing to provide. Finally, findings show variances between the two countries studied that affect the communication of sensitivity, expertise, and actions. The findings, effects, and suggestions of the apps for effective authentication mentoring are presented and analyzed (Zwilling et al., 2022).

This study is titled “Identity-based general population data integrity validation scheme in cloud service via blockchain.” In this article, we present a fresh approach to building the traditional authentication scheme using blockchains. The architecture of the proposed scheme is based on personality-encrypted data, which eliminates the complicated management policies required by a secure channel. The blockchain's properties also ensure that labels are not created. Different memories, on the other hand, could cause the relevant data handed back by the parties involved who participate in public audits to become out of alignment; thus, a limited data architecture log is presented to address this issue. The benefits of audit trails include not only ensuring accurate and soft deployment. Among suggested methods, but rather to demonstrate the TPA's ignorance as needed. Furthermore, the reliability of our strategy has been rigorously demonstrated. At last, a sequence of assessment methods shows that our method is both effective and viable (Yuan et al., 2022).

This research is titled “Zero trust in an edge computing environment: a blockchain-based practical scheme.” Edge computer processing automates data processing capabilities for the consumer, offers flexible and effective cloud infrastructure for smart buildings, and introduces numerous safety problems. A digital certificate method and interactive authenticator of computing and communication endpoints with a distributed record are proposed to solve the challenges of fuzzy boundary data security and interactive identity verification inside the smart building edge cloud servers. To begin, a digital certificate method of multiple verifications is created between both the network edge base station and the detecting port to achieve perfectly acceptable permission and remote access in cloud applications. Second, depending on the personal information and actions recorded in the log (also on a chain), the quantitative measurements of probability value, accepted data transfer, and trust management are performed. The updates are finished, as is the threat intelligence tracking. At last, sub-agreement and conformance auditing in the verification process is realized using the enhanced RAFT consensus protocols. The performance of the proposed model shows that somehow this method can satisfy the criteria of strong authentication validation in an edge computer system while also being accurate and effective (Li et al., 2022).

The term of this study is "A Quantitative Evaluation of End-Point Intrusion Detection Systems against Enhanced Systemic Cyber Threat Attacks." Cyber-attacks pose a difficult task for blue teamwork because they execute numerous attacks over extended periods, making control activities and identification difficult. We use a variety of attack types in this paper to assess the effectiveness of EDRs and other end-user cyber security in detecting and avoiding APIs. Our findings show that there continues to be a clear gap, as modern end-user security measures are unable to detect and log the majority of the threats identified in this study. Furthermore, we explain methodologies for tampering with EDR remote monitoring suppliers, enabling an attacker to conduct a stealthier attack (Karantzas & Patsakis, 2021).

The title of this study is "People in South Africa Have Access to Online Government Services through Library Resources." The research investigates the impact of research published in Namibian academic institutions in urban, semi- urban, and sparsely populated areas to examine accessibility to e-government services through library services. As a result, the survey was based on the theory that the location of the library would impact access to online services. For information gathering, the study also used a design with questionnaires distributed via electronic mail. The study sample consisted of all 65 community academic libraries, 64 of which were involved in the research, and the units that were analyzed were academic libraries' employees, 75 of whom responded to the survey. According to the research results, the e-government services that consumers accessed Users can download, and the library services include completed employment types, employment records, and reporting. The obstacles do include a lack of library workspaces, unstable Internet interoperability, and slow Web access (i.e., low upload speed). The research suggests that research be carried out to gather user perspectives that could also reveal what all these many reasons are (Nengomasha & Shuumbili, 2022).

CHALLENGES

Lack of Privacy

Many governments' institutions and organizations provide data to the user safely and correctly to maintain the flexibility and efficiency of the system, but there are many concerns related to security and privacy when using government services (Chaudhari & Das, 2020; Al-Naami et al., 2021, Al-Sherideh et al., 2018,).

Data Loss or Leakages

Data and information are lost and leaked for many reasons, the most important of which are strangers who try to tamper with and steal hackers, who are usually either an employee of the cloud, the organization or the service (10, Tarawneh et al., 2024; Singh & Pandey, 2020; Al-Sherideh et al., 2023).

Data and Service Availability

The service provider stores user data in the cloud in various locations that may be far or near (Sharma et al., 2021). In the event of any problem that may affect this hosting server, this may lead to the loss of user data. In the event of a power supply failure or a hard disk failure, the user cannot access his data (Chang et al., 2020; Al-Mousa et al., 2022).

Lack of User Control

The user can't control the cloud when using the SaaS. The management here is only done by the service provider, as he bears the responsibility for storing the data. The cloud appears to conflict with user-centered control: when using a SaaS platform, the service provider is responsible for storing the data, so the user's control becomes very limited (Akande et al., 2013). The user faces a problem retaining control over his private data and accessing it in the cloud (Nishad et al., 2016; Al-Sherideh et al., 2024).

Lack of Accepted Standards

Organizations may face disputes with the service provider, during which payment for the service is delayed, or poor service from the service provider. Here, the system is stopped by the service provider, and the data is locked up and fully controlled (Sharma et al., 2021).

Lack of Customer Trust

The citizen relies on the state to provide many services. Trust is based on technology and self- experience, and it is more general than security. Personal data is stored ultimately in the cloud and with full control of the service provider (Lu et al., 2022). The user's lack of control over his data leads to suspicion and mistrust (Khan et al 2022; Alshdaifat et al., 2022).

Authentication and Authorization

Software is considered incomplete if authentication, authorization, and access control are not provided (Xu et al., 2022). If the user violates any of the conditions that the service provider has prepared, the service provider or service provider must delete the user's account (Parast et al., 2022; Owida et al., 2022; Iqtait & Mohamad, 2019; Mohamad et al., 2018).

Loss of Governance

When using the cloud computing service, the software will be controlled and managed by the service provider, and it will in turn solve all security-related problems facing the system. In this case, it is necessary to prepare a binding agreement for both parties (Al-Momani et al., 2024; Alsuhimat et al., 2019; Iqtait et al., 2018).

RESULTS

4Frequency of Proposed Solutions

The review of previous studies revealed that the most widely recommended solutions to big data security and privacy challenges in e-government services are modern encryption methods, identity verification and access control, and real-time monitoring. Figure 4 illustrates the comparative frequency of solutions identified across 14 reviewed studies.

Figure 4. Frequency of proposed security solutions in reviewed studies

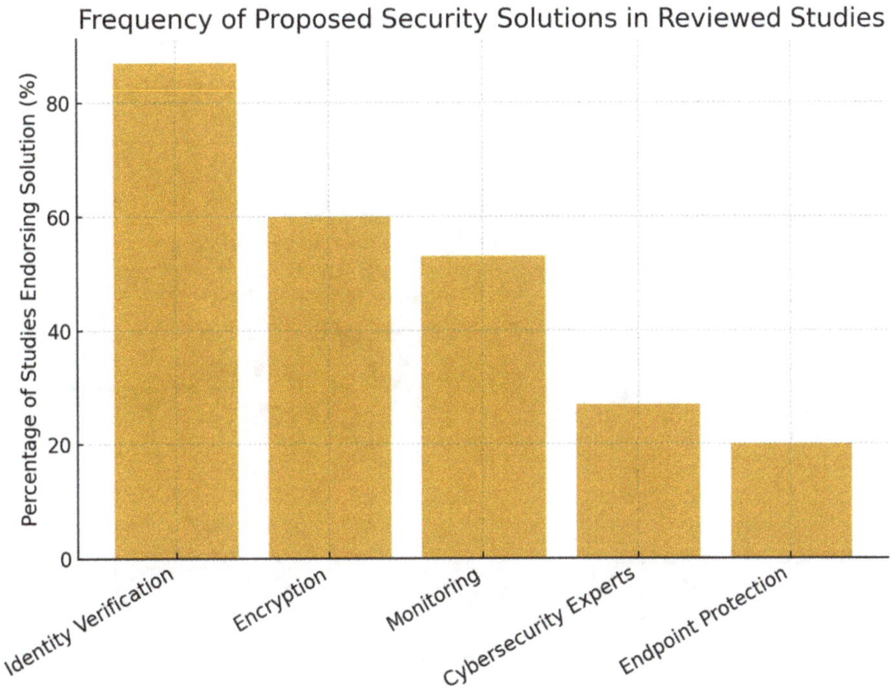

Prioritization of Security Mechanisms

The findings suggest that data privacy protection throughout the entire lifecycle is a consistent theme across all studies. Figure 5 presents a prioritization model that ranks the proposed solutions according to their relevance and frequency.

Figure 5. Prioritization of big data security mechanisms for e-government.

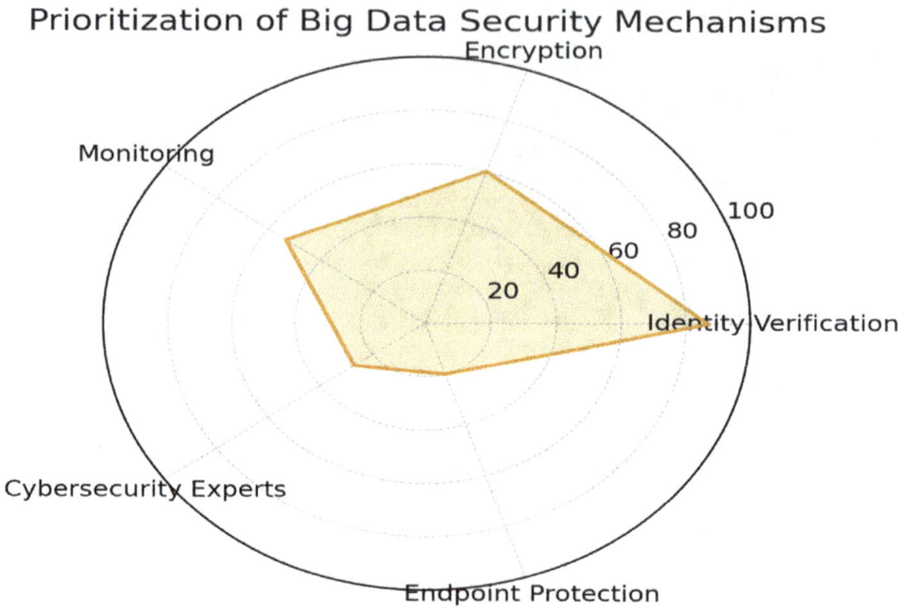

Integrated Security Framework Proposal

Based on the synthesis of solutions, an integrated security framework is proposed (Figure 6). It combines technical measures (encryption, access control, monitoring) with organizational strategies (cybersecurity training, governance policies) to provide layered protection.

Figure 6. Proposed integrated framework for securing e-government big data systems

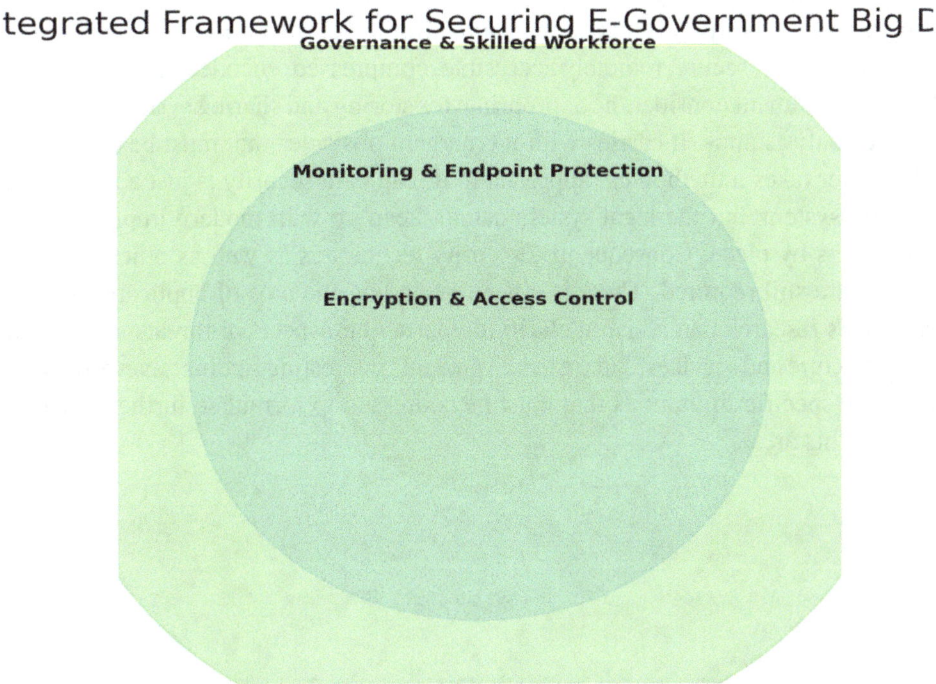

Discussion of Results

The results confirm that most challenges in e-government big data security are technical in nature, yet their sustainability depends on organizational readiness. While encryption and identity verification provide the first line of defense, governments must also invest in building cybersecurity expertise and governance structures to ensure long-term resilience.

These findings reinforce the notion that privacy-by-design and multi-layered defense architectures are indispensable in e-government contexts where sensitive citizen data is at risk. Moreover, the relative neglect of workforce and endpoint security in prior studies suggests an urgent need for future work that considers the human factor alongside technical innovation.

CONCLUSION AND FUTURE WORK

The first and most important aspect of big data is security. As the storage capacity and computing infrastructure become more affordable, and online services become more integrated, secure, remotely accessible, compressed, encoded, and compliant. SaaS environment consider the appropriate for storing and sharing systems and predictive analysis apps. It carries with it emergent obstacles that must be discussed. This paper takes a methodical approach to it. Big data security is just a rule, not a security system, but the legal system cannot keep up with modern improvements and differs by place. Consequently, security techniques as well as other methodologies are still required. There is a need extending the area of application in big data. This research can assist in clarifying particular aspects of threats in big data infrastructure and services. This research presents interesting findings. Nevertheless, there are specific limitations that must be addressed to formulate further research work in this area.

ACKNOWLEDGEMENT

This research is funded by the Deanship of Research and Graduate Studies at Zarqa University /Jordan.

REFERENCES

Abesamis, P. P. R., & Caramancion, K. M. (2022, October). Multiple-case study on the perceived impacts of Philippine identification system in organizational control: Focusing on e-government services. In *Proceedings of the 15th International Conference on Theory and Practice of Electronic Governance* (pp. 279–287). DOI: 10.1145/3560107.3560152

Addula, S. R., Norozpour, S., & Amin, M. (2025). Risk Assessment for Identifying Threats, vulnerabilities and countermeasures in Cloud Computing. *Jordanian Journal of Informatics and Computing, 2025*(1), 37–48. DOI: 10.63180/jjic.thestap.2025.1.5

Akande, A. O., April, N. A., & Van Belle, J. P. (2013, December). Management issues with cloud computing. In *Proceedings of the Second International Conference on Innovative Computing and Cloud Computing* (pp. 119–124).

Al-Momani, A., Al-Refai, M. N., Abuowaida, S., Arabiat, M., Alshdaifat, N., & Rahman, M. N. A. (2024). The effect of technological context on smart home adoption in Jordan. *Indonesian Journal of Electrical Engineering and Computer Science, 33*(2), 1186–1195. DOI: 10.11591/ijeecs.v33.i2.pp1186-1195

Al-Mousa, M. R., Al-Zaqebah, Q., Al-Sherideh, A. S., Al-Ghanim, M., Samara, G., Al-Matarneh, S., & Asassfeh, M. (2022, November). Examining digital forensic evidence for Android applications. In *2022 International Arab Conference on Information Technology (ACIT)* (pp. 1–8). IEEE. DOI: 10.1109/ACIT57182.2022.9994221

Al-Shareeda, M. A., Najm, L. B., Hassan, A. A., Mushtaq, S., & Ali, H. A. (2024). Secure IoT-Based Smart Agriculture System Using Wireless Sensor Networks for Remote Environmental Monitoring. *STAP Journal of Security Risk Management, 2024*(1), 56–66. DOI: 10.63180/jsrm.thestap.2024.1.4

Al-Sherideh, A. S., Ismail, R., Al-Mousa, M. R., Al-Qawasmi, K., Al-Shaikh, A., & Awwad, H. (2024). Development of a secure model for mobile government applications in Jordan. *Journal of Statistics Applications & Probability, 13*(1), 145–155. DOI: 10.18576/jsap/130110

Al-Sherideh, A. S., Ismail, R., Wahid, F. A., Fabil, N., & Ismail, W. (2018). *Mobile government applications based on security and privacy: A literature review*. International Journal of Engineering and Technology.

Al-Sherideh, A. S., Maabreh, K., Maabreh, M., Al Mousa, M. R., & Asassfeh, M. (2023). Assessing the impact and effectiveness of cybersecurity measures in e-learning on students and educators: A case study. *International Journal of Advanced Computer Science and Applications*, *14*(5). Advance online publication. DOI: 10.14569/IJACSA.2023.0140516

Albinhamad, H., Alotibi, A., Alagnam, A., Almaiah, M., & Salloum, S. (2025). Vehicular Ad-hoc Networks (VANETs): A Key Enabler for Smart Transportation Systems and Challenges. *Jordanian Journal of Informatics and Computing*, *2025*(1), 4–15. DOI: 10.63180/jjic.thestap.2025.1.2

Ali, A. (2024). Adaptive and Context-Aware Authentication Framework Using Edge AI and Blockchain in Future Vehicular Networks. *STAP Journal of Security Risk Management*, *2024*(1), 45–56. DOI: 10.63180/jsrm.thestap.2024.1.3

Ali, A., & Shehab, R. (2023). A Systematic Review of Security Risk Management for Banking Systems. *Journal of Cyber Security and Risk Auditing*, *2023*(1), 49–72. DOI: 10.63180/jcsra.thestap.2023.1.4

Almaayah, M., & Sulaiman, R. B. (2024). Cyber Risk Management in the Internet of Things: Frameworks, Models, and Best Practices. *STAP Journal of Security Risk Management*, *2024*(1), 3–23. DOI: 10.63180/jsrm.thestap.2024.1.1

Alsahaim, S., & Maayah, M. (2023). Analyzing Cybersecurity Threats on Mobile Phones. *STAP Journal of Security Risk Management*, *2023*(1), 3–19. DOI: 10.63180/jsrm.thestap.2023.1.2

Alshdaifat, N., Osman, M. A., & Talib, A. Z. (2022). An improved multi-object instance segmentation based on deep learning. *Kuwait Journal of Science*, *49*(2).

Alshinwan, M., Memon, A. G., Ghanem, M. C., & Almaayah, M. (2025). Unsupervised text feature selection approach based on improved Prairie dog algorithm for the text clustering. *Jordanian Journal of Informatics and Computing*, *2025*(1), 27–36. DOI: 10.63180/jjic.thestap.2025.1.4

Alsuhimat, F. M., Mohamad, F. S., & Iqtait, M. (2019). Detection and extraction features for signature images via different techniques. *Journal of Physics: Conference Series*, *1179*(1), 012087. DOI: 10.1088/1742-6596/1179/1/012087

Chang, Y. W., Hsu, P. Y., Huang, S. H., & Chen, J. (2020). Determinants of switching intention to cloud computing in large enterprises. *Data Technologies and Applications, 54*(1), 16–33. DOI: 10.1108/DTA-12-2018-0104

Comite, U. (2022). I&CT in the public administrations: From e-government to e-democracy through digital reporting. In *Handbook of Research on Applying Emerging Technologies Across Multiple Disciplines* (pp. 55–77). IGI Global. DOI: 10.4018/978-1-7998-8476-7.ch004

Davies, G., Mison, A., & Eden, P. (2022, March). Addressing the skills shortage in cybersecurity. In *International Conference on Cyber Warfare and Security* (Vol. 17, No. 1, pp. 544–551). DOI: 10.34190/iccws.17.1.69

Hasan, M. K., Alkhalifah, A., Islam, S., Babiker, N. B., Habib, A. A., Aman, A. H. M., & Hossain, M. A. (2022). Blockchain technology on smart grid, energy trading, and big data: Security issues, challenges, and recommendations. *Wireless Communications and Mobile Computing, 2022*(1), 1–26. DOI: 10.1155/2022/9065768

Iqtait, M., & Mohamad, F. S. (2019). Multiple classifiers for age prediction against AAM and ASM. *International Journal of Recent Technology and Engineering, 8*(2 Special Issue 3), 456–461.

Iqtait, M., Mohamad, F. S., & Mamat, M. (2018). Feature extraction for face recognition via active shape model (ASM) and active appearance model (AAM). *IOP Conference Series. Materials Science and Engineering, 332*(1), 012032. DOI: 10.1088/1757-899X/332/1/012032

Jain, P., Gyanchandani, M., & Khare, N. (2016). Big data privacy: A technological perspective and review. *Journal of Big Data, 3*(1), 1–25. DOI: 10.1186/s40537-016-0059-y

Karantzas, G., & Patsakis, C. (2021). An empirical assessment of endpoint detection and response systems against advanced persistent threats attack vectors. *Journal of Cybersecurity and Privacy, 1*(3), 387–421. DOI: 10.3390/jcp1030021

Khan, M. J., Ullah, F., Imran, M., Khan, J., Khan, A., AlGhamdi, A. S., & Alshamrani, S. S. (2022). Identifying challenges for clients in adopting sustainable public cloud computing. *Sustainability (Basel), 14*(16), 9809. DOI: 10.3390/su14169809

Li, D., Zhang, E., Lei, M., & Song, C. (2022). Zero trust in edge computing environment: A blockchain-based practical scheme. *Mathematical Biosciences and Engineering, 19*(4), 4196–4216. DOI: 10.3934/mbe.2022194 PMID: 35341294

Li, Y., Gai, K., Qiu, L., Qiu, M., & Zhao, H. (2017). Intelligent cryptography approach for secure distributed big data storage in cloud computing. *Information Sciences, 387*, 103–115. DOI: 10.1016/j.ins.2016.09.005

Lu, L., Li, Z., Wu, S., & Shang, Y. (2022). Research on trust issues in cloud computing. *ITM Web of Conferences, 45*, 02010. DOI: 10.1051/itmconf/20224502010

Mohamad, F. S., Iqtait, M., & Alsuhimat, F. (2018). Age prediction on face features via multiple classifiers. In *2018 4th International Conference on Computer and Technology Applications (ICCTA)* (pp. 161–166). DOI: 10.1109/CATA.2018.8398675

Narayanan, G., & Kannan, S. (2024). Enhancing security in cloud-based VM migration: A trust-centric hybrid optimization approach. *The International Arab Journal of Information Technology, 21*(1), 166–177. DOI: 10.34028/iajit/21/1/15

Nengomasha, C. T., & Shuumbili, T. N. (2022). Access to e-government services by citizens through public/community libraries in Namibia. *Information Development, 38*(1), 68–82. DOI: 10.1177/0266666920979009

Nishad, L. S., Akriti, Paliwal, J., Pandey, R., Beniwal, S., & Kumar, S. (2016, March). Security, privacy issues, and challenges in cloud computing: A survey. In *Proceedings of the Second International Conference on Information and Communication Technology for Competitive Strategies* (pp. 1–7). DOI: 10.1145/2905055.2905253

Owida, H. A., Al-Nabulsi, J. I., Turab, N. M., Alnaimat, F., Rababah, H., & Shakour, M. Y. (2021). Autocharging techniques for implantable medical applications. *International Journal of Biomaterials, 2021*(1), 6074657. PMID: 34712329

Owida, H. A., Hemied, O. S. M., Alkhawaldeh, R. S., Alshdaifat, N. F. F., & Abuowaida, S. F. A. (2022). Improved deep learning approaches for COVID-19 recognition in CT images. *Journal of Theoretical and Applied Information Technology, 100*(13).

Owida, H. A., Moh'd, B. A. H., & Al Takrouri, M. (2022). Designing an integrated low-cost electrospinning device for nanofibrous scaffold fabrication. *HardwareX, 11*, e00250. DOI: 10.1016/j.ohx.2021.e00250 PMID: 35509902

Parast, F. K., Sindhav, C., Nikam, S., Yekta, H. I., Kent, K. B., & Hakak, S. (2022). Cloud computing security: A survey of service-based models. *Computers & Security, 114*, 102580. DOI: 10.1016/j.cose.2021.102580

Park, S. H., Yun, S. W., Jeon, S. E., Park, N. E., Shim, H. Y., Lee, Y. R., Lee, S.-J., Park, T.-R., Shin, N.-Y., Kang, M.-J., & Lee, I. G. (2022). Performance evaluation of open-source endpoint detection and response combining Google rapid response and osquery for threat detection. *IEEE Access : Practical Innovations, Open Solutions, 10*, 20259–20269. DOI: 10.1109/ACCESS.2022.3152574

Santhosh, C. V., & Minni, G. (2022). Attribute with multi-factor proofing verification with ABE scheme.

Sewak, M., Sahay, S. K., & Rathore, H. (2021, October). Deep reinforcement learning for cybersecurity threat detection and protection: A review. In *International Conference on Secure Knowledge Management in Artificial Intelligence Era* (pp. 51–72). Cham: Springer International Publishing.

Sharma, A., Jha, P., & Singh, S. (2021). Data control in public cloud computing: Issues and challenges. *Recent Advances in Computer Science and Communications*, *14*(2), 564–579. DOI: 10.2174/2213275912666190617164550

Singh, V., & Pandey, S. K. (2020). Cloud computing: Vulnerability and threat indications. In *Performance Management of Integrated Systems and its Applications in Software Engineering* (pp. 11–20).

Tarawneh, O., Saber, Q., Almaghthawi, A., Owida, H. A., Issa, A., Alshdaifat, N., Jaradat, G., Abuowaida, S., & Arabiat, M. (2024). The effect of pre-processing on a convolutional neural network model for dorsal hand vein recognition. *International Journal of Advanced Computer Science and Applications*, *15*(3). Advance online publication. DOI: 10.14569/IJACSA.2024.01503126

Thanganadar, A., & Raman, V. (2024). Integrated shared random key agreement protocol for wireless sensor network. *The International Arab Journal of Information Technology*, *21*(2), 201–210. DOI: 10.34028/iajit/21/2/3

Ujjan, R. M. A., Khan, N. A., & Gaur, L. (2022). E-government privacy and security challenges in the context of Internet of Things. In *Cybersecurity Measures for E-Government Frameworks* (pp. 22–42). IGI Global. DOI: 10.4018/978-1-7998-9624-1.ch002

Usmani, U. A., Watada, J., Jaafar, J., & Aziz, I. A. (2022). A systematic review of privacy-preserving blockchain in e-medicine. *Biomedical and Other Applications of Soft Computing*, 25–40.

Wang, K., Guo, X., & Yang, D. (2022). Research on the effectiveness of cybersecurity awareness in ICS risk assessment frameworks. *Electronics (Basel)*, *11*(10), 1659. DOI: 10.3390/electronics11101659

Wimpenny, G., Šafář, J., Grant, A., & Bransby, M. (2022). Securing the Automatic Identification System (AIS): Using public key cryptography to prevent spoofing whilst retaining backwards compatibility. *Journal of Navigation*, *75*(2), 333–345. DOI: 10.1017/S0373463321000837

Xu, M., Ng, W. C., Lim, W. Y. B., Kang, J., Xiong, Z., Niyato, D., & Miao, C. (2022). A full dive into realizing the edge-enabled metaverse: Visions, enabling technologies, and challenges. *IEEE Communications Surveys and Tutorials*.

Yu, L., He, M., Xiong, L., Zhou, J., & Luo, Q. (2021). A blockchain-based decentralized authentication and authorization scheme for mobile cloud computing services. *Available at SSRN* 4126148. DOI: 10.2139/ssrn.4126148

Yuan, Y., Zhang, J., Xu, W., & Li, Z. (2022). Identity-based public data integrity verification scheme in cloud storage system via blockchain. *The Journal of Supercomputing*, *78*(6), 8509–8530. DOI: 10.1007/s11227-021-04193-6

Zaman, M. T., & Rani, M. (2022). Cloud computing security challenges, analysis of security problems, and cloud computing forensics issues. In *Security and Privacy Trends in Cloud Computing and Big Data* (pp. 147–164). DOI: 10.1201/9781003107286-8

Zwilling, M., Klien, G., Lesjak, D., Wiechetek, Ł., Cetin, F., & Basim, H. N. (2022). Cyber security awareness, knowledge, and behavior: A comparative study. *Journal of Computer Information Systems*, *62*(1), 82–97. DOI: 10.1080/08874417.2020.1712269

Chapter 2 IoT–Blockchain Decentralised Framework for Predicting Cardiovascular Disease

C. K. Shahnazeer
https://orcid.org/0009-0002-3380-2109
Pondicherry University, Karaikal, India

G. Sureshkumar
https://orcid.org/0000-0002-3823-9776
Pondicherry University, Karaikal, India

C. K. Shinzeer
https://orcid.org/0000-0003-4265-2843
Lovely Professional University, India

Avinash Bhagat
Lovely Professional University, India

Ajay Shriram Kushwaha
https://orcid.org/0000-0003-0392-5546
Sharda University, India

ABSTRACT

The current research proposed a decentralized-based framework to augment the prediction and diagnosis of cardiovascular diseases using IoT & blockchain. IoT devices are used for real-time data collection as part of the framework, allowing for continuous monitoring & higher precision in determining potential health risks.

DOI: 10.4018/979-8-3373-1807-3.ch002

2026, IGI Global Scientific Publishing. Copying or distributing in print or electronic forms without written permission of IGI Global Scientific Publishing is prohibited. Use of this chapter to ...rative artificial intelligence (AI) technologies is expressly prohibited. The publisher reserves all rights to license its use for generative AI training and machine learning model development.

Patient data is stored securely & tamper-proof with blockchain, which can build confidence & transparency in the system. Also, by decentralizing data processing & decision-making, the proposed work eliminates single points of failure & enables better scalability in large-scale healthcare applications. The design captures predictive analysis in real-time for early intervention, better health data & patient dynamics, enhanced health outcomes, & streamlined health data with secure access for patient empowerment. Thus, with many systematic synergies derived from the aspects of IoT & blockchain, it can be stated that disease management can be revolutionized & integrated into recent healthcare systems by combining advanced predictive analytics & robust security mechanisms.

INTRODUCTION

Cardiovascular disorder (CVDs) is still a vital reason for fatal death worldwide, highlighting the demand for rapid and trustworthy diagnostic tools. However, the recent convergence of the Internet of Things (IoT) mechanism with blockchain strategy is providing new avenues for the early detection and management of CVDs. Advanced-release IoT gadgets with life sensors can be leveraged for consistent real-time health parameter supervision, including heart function, blood pressure, and oxidation (Mhammed, 2025) and (Aldhyani, 2025). These devices also provide healthcare professionals with an overview of a patient's overall health, which can make it easier for them to identify potential cardiovascular issues promptly (Al-maayah & Sulaiman, 2024) and (Al-Shareeda et al., 2024). In addition, the use of blockchain technology facilitates the secure, decentralized storage and sharing of sensitive health data, which preserves the privacy of the patient and at the same time enables accessibility (Egala et al., 2023)(Kareem, 2024; Salih & Mahmood, 2024).

A few recent studies have opened up the transformational capacity of using IoT along with blockchain technology in medical applications. One study underlines the importance of IoT in continuous health monitoring with an area to detect heart diseases, where real-time data has added its share towards the improvement of diagnostics (Bataineh et al., 2022). Further research has proven that blockchain can create immutable medical records; thus, integrity is ensured for all data, and cybersecurity threats are mitigated within any healthcare system (Abed & Gök, 2023; Al Barazanchi & Hashim, 2023; Balgani & S. Sangeetha, 2014). This composition between IoT and blockchain ushers in health solutions that are highly individualized and data-oriented, which allow interventions while preventing further cardiovascular conditions from developing. Predictive analytics, through studying the trend of information to identify anomalies, is one addition that will further boost the capacity of integrated systems to identify potential cardiovascular events (Ali et al., 2025; Ratta et al., 2024).

The use of Blockchain for IoT-based healthcare systems is of equal importance. There have been several studies that have drawn its significant importance in securing data and privacy; therefore, a part and parcel of any modern healthcare solutions (Jayashre & Padmavathi, 2024). Increased decentralization as a result of blockchain technology reduces the dependency on centralized servers, further eliminating single points of failure and consequently boosting the reliability of the system (Aiswarya & Sangeetha, 2022). This can be one way in which sensitive health data can be protected and also helps in winning the trust of patients because they get control over their health information. The implementation of these decentralized frameworks has been proven by research to work and work very well; they are very scalable and strong in many different healthcare implementations (Gopalakrishnan et al., 2024; Murala et al., 2023).

Furthermore, IoT, blockchain, and artificial intelligence (AI) have been integrated into predictive health monitoring (Alshinwan et al., 2025) and (Albinhamad et al., 2025). The combination of AI algorithms with real-time IoT data makes predictions for cardiovascular events much more accurate than the current standard, allowing healthcare providers to focus specifically on high-risk patients (Al-Nbhany et al., 2024). The IoT devices are always up-to-date as their updating process continues, and the AI models update from these datasets; thus, better predictive performance is attained over time (Babu et al., 2024). Deep learning techniques have newly evolved to be a formidable tool in the analysis of intricate health data and have shown promise of revealing patterns associated with cardiovascular disease (Gopalakrishnan et al., 2024; Praveen et al., 2024; Vaigandla, 2025).

The interplay among IoT, blockchain, and AI marks sweat ripples for the sector—an advanced predictive and management framework for heart diseases. With such a system in place, health providers can identify established cardiovascular diseases at pretty early stages and take up measures that are prove to relieve the burden on many health systems worldwide. As such, these new technologies promise to transform diagnoses and the management of cardiovascular diseases by enabling more efficient and personalized care.

LITERATURE SURVEY

The combination of IoT with blockchain mechanism was proven transformative for healthcare applications, addressing important issues in data security, scalability, and real-time processing. These advancements have enabled innovative solutions for disease prediction and personalized healthcare. IoT-enabled devices play a pivotal role in continuous health monitoring, detecting early signs of diseases like cardiovascular conditions. Research emphasizes the necessity of accurate data acquisition and secure transmission through blockchain to prevent breaches and safeguard privacy (Alhasani et al., 2025; Biswas et al., 2020; Burhanuddin, 2023). A blockchain-based decentralized healthcare system has been proposed to eliminate intermediaries while ensuring data integrity and accessibility for predictive analytics (Allam et al., 2024).

For analyzing health risks, predictive models based on IoT as a real-time data source have also been designed, while the application of machine learning algorithms shows enhanced accuracy and timely intervention of nearing cardiac anomalies (Dr. Kavita D. Hanabaratti et al., 2024). Moreover, IoT- Architecture that is integrated with blockchain technology minimizes data latency in processing and maximizes the security of the patient's data (Fernández-Caramés et al., 2019). Also, these architectures are scalable to be incorporated to large healthcare systems (Priya et al., 2023; Rasheed & Tambe, 2024; Salim, 2024; Shanshool, 2023).

Blockchain has made it possible to securely share data in collaborative healthcare systems. This means that multiple parties involved can access and analyze the data without compromising its security. Smart contracts strategy for self-executing agreements in the terms of the contract directly incorporated into the system, will be utilized for automated events and make the system more efficient (Raj & Prakash, 2024).

In critical care situations, Internet of Things (IoT) applications that use edge computing have shown reduced reliance on servers and faster response times (Sachdev et al., 2023). The edge computing concept enables data to be processed closer to where it is generated like medical devices, devices, etc. instead of transferring data to the central server for processing. Allowing data to be distributed Increases security and blockchain technology plays an important role in maintaining the authenticity of data through immutable ledgers These ledgers guarantee the integrity of patient records which is of utmost importance for predictive systems [17-18].

A variety of encrypted IoT data streams are placed in blockchain networks to facilitate secure communication channels between devices and healthcare providers (Kala & Priya, 2024). That means that any data sent from IoT devices to healthcare professionals is encrypted and secured by the blockchain protocol. A major development in healthcare is the rise of federated learning models. These models can perform decentralized analysis of data without sacrificing the privacy of individuals. Federated Learning replaces centralizing peripheral sensitive Patient Data Server, conducting the analysis algorithm in centralized device with a deeper, disease prediction, implementing in different local points, either using from each device or each facility (Jamil et al., 2021).

PROPOSED SYSTEM

The system proposed is structured into the following: a) Predicting cardiovascular disorder with IoT and Blockchain. As shown in Figure 1, IoT devices gather real-time health data (vital parameters) from patients. Before it gets uploaded to the blockchain, this data goes through a cleansing and verifying stage. Blockchain ensures data integrity and privacy — no tampering + no unauthorized access; decentralized storage And then advanced analytics models are applied to the data to identify patterns and risks. Outcomes will then be sent to healthcare experts and patients by a secured interface to enable timely interventions with personalized health care.

Figure 1. Proposed framework flow diagram.

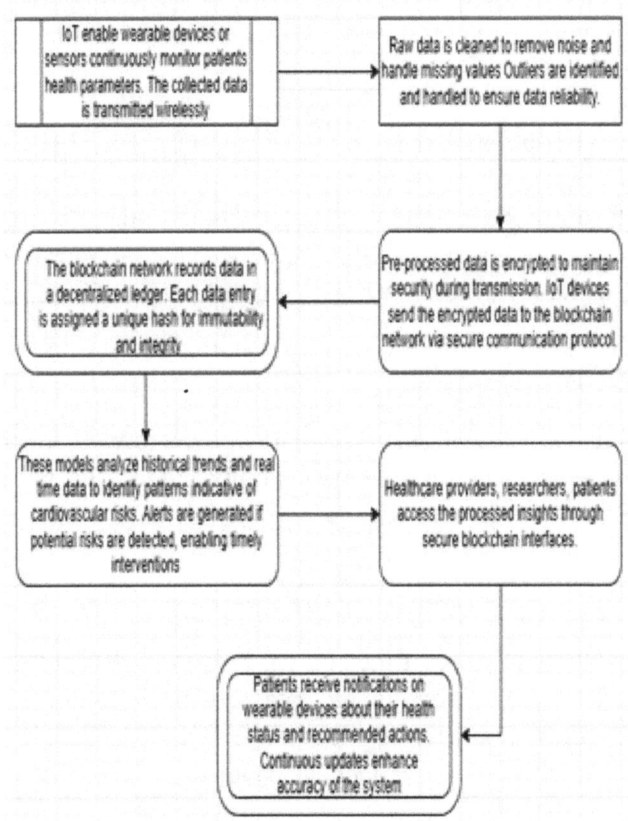

The proposed system starts with data aggregation where IoT-based sensors continuously monitor and information on vital health metrics like beat rate, human blood pressure levels, and oxygen presence from the patient. Each sensor gives real-time information, which is given by x(t), representing the health metric at time t. This information will then be preprocessed to eliminate noise, handle missing values, and confirm consistency over various measurements. The preprocessing phase can be mathematically given in (1)

$$x_{cleaned}(t)=f(x(t)) \quad (1)$$

where f tells the cleaning relation applied to the raw data sets. Missing values are imputed by linear interpolation methods, given by (2)

$$x_{imputed}(t)=x(t)+\alpha\cdot(x(t+1)-x(t-1)) \quad (2)$$

where α is a scaling factor to ensure accurate data interpolation. Next, the information will be normalized for standardization of the metrics. The normalization relation is given by (3)

$$x_{normalized}(t)=(x_{cleaned}(t)-\mu)/\sigma. \quad (3)$$

where μ is the mean and σ is the standard deviation value of cleaned data. Once the data gets processed, it is securely broadcasted to the blockchain network. The data is encrypted employing an encryptions-related function E in (4)

$$E(x_{normalized}(t))=y(t). \quad (4)$$

where y(t) tells the encrypted data. This encrypted information will be added to the blockchain ledgers, for confirming immutability and security. Each information entry is hashed using a function H by (5)

$$H(y(t))=h(t). \quad (5)$$

where h(t) is the hash value of the encrypted form of data at time t. Once information is stored in the blockchain, the data is available for predictive analysis. Predictive frameworks, like supervisor learning schemas, are applied to the historical and realistic application data to identify patterns and predict the likelihood of cardiovascular disorder. The data will be given and fed into a supervisor learning model that computes the prediction score P for cardiovascular risk at time t by (6)

$$P(t) = \sum_i w_i . x_{normalized}(t_i), (i = 1 \; to \; N) \quad (6)$$

where w_i tells about the weights of the feature $x(t_i)$, and n is the count of features used in the proposed model. In case of a detected risk, an alert mechanism is triggered, telling both the healthcare experts and the patient. The alert is based on a threshold T, where if the predicted risk P(t) exceeds T, a warning may be issued by (7)

$$\text{Alert} = \begin{cases} 1, \textit{if } P(t) > T \\ 0, \textit{if } P(t) \leq T \end{cases} \tag{7}$$

The system also utilizes blockchain unit consensus to confirm the accuracy rate of data transactions. The consensus relation C validates the data integrity of the blockchain ledger, ensuring that the data will be adjusted and non-tampered in (8)

$$C\left(h\left(t\right)\right) = \begin{cases} 1, \textit{if blockchain integrity will be verified} \\ 0, \textit{else} \end{cases} \tag{8}$$

Real-time feedback is given to the patient by the system's interface, which may be modeled as a feedback loop as in (9)

$$f_{feedback}(t)=\text{sign}(P(t)-T). \tag{9}$$

where the sign returns 1 if the condition will be true and 0 if false. The scalability of the system is managed by adjusting the computational load L(t) as more users are added. The load will be modeled by (10)

$$L(t)=L(t-1)+\alpha\cdot\Delta U(t). \tag{10}$$

where $\Delta U(t)$ is the change in the number of users at time t, and α is a factor to confirm the proposed system load balance. Finally, security checks are merged into the system by a verification function V by (11)

$$V\left(\text{ximputed}\left(t\right)\right) = \begin{cases} 1, \textit{if valid} \\ 0, \textit{if invalid} \end{cases} \tag{11}$$

This series of steps ensures that the system functions efficiently, and securely, and provides timely predictions for cardiovascular disease diagnosis while maintaining data integrity and user privacy.

RESULTS AND DISCUSSION

The proposed system is designed and built to create an integrated system that involves IoT devices, blockchain technology, and predictive analysis for cardiovascular disease diagnosis. Using various cleaning and normalization techniques, the system was able to effectively collect and preprocess real-time health data from patients ensuring data accuracy and consistency. Enter blockchain technology, which at its core offered immutable secure storage of information that would guarantee the integrity and privacy of patient information. Using historical & recent data, the predictive models identified cardiovascular risks, & alerts were triggered if the determined risk exceeded the predetermined threshold. The decentralized characteristics of the blockchain units make it a more efficient way, scalable, and secure data sharing between healthcare experts and their patients. As a result, the system showed high reliability, scalability, and security, offering a promising solution for early disease detection and personalized healthcare.

The four plots presented in Figures 2 to 5 depict the fluctuations of various physiological parameters over time, each with their respective thresholds marked for easy interpretation.

Figure 2 shows the heart rate (bpm) as a line graph, with the threshold set at 75 bpm, indicated by a red dashed line. The areas above this threshold are shaded in red, while the rest is shaded in green. Throughout the time series, the heart rate fluctuates between 60 and 85 bpm, with noticeable spikes surpassing the threshold around time steps 40, 60, and 90. At time step 40, the heart rate reaches approximately 78 bpm, indicating an elevated state, while time step 60 shows a similar spike. These instances suggest moments when heart rate values exceed the normal range, requiring attention.

Figure 3 presents blood pressure (mmHg) over time, with the threshold set at 130 mmHg. The areas exceeding the threshold are shaded in orange, indicating times when blood pressure is elevated beyond the acceptable range, while the rest of the graph is green. Blood pressure mostly remains between 120 and 128 mmHg, but it surpasses the threshold around times 30 and 75, where it hits 132 mmHg and 135 mmHg, respectively. These points highlight potential periods of concern when blood pressure moves out of the normal range, necessitating monitoring.

Figure 2. Heartbeat rate analysis of the proposed framework

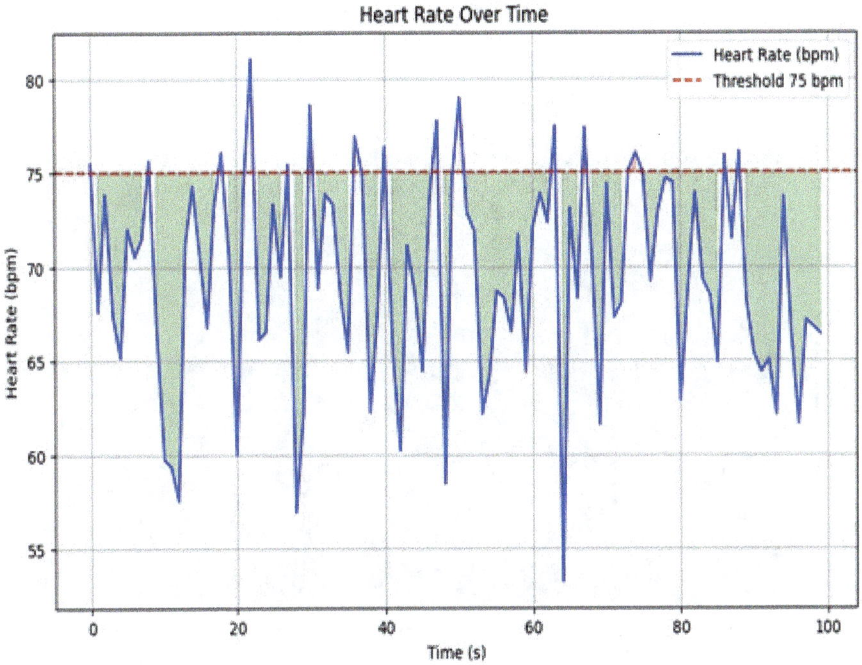

Figure 3. Blood pressure comparison on various days.

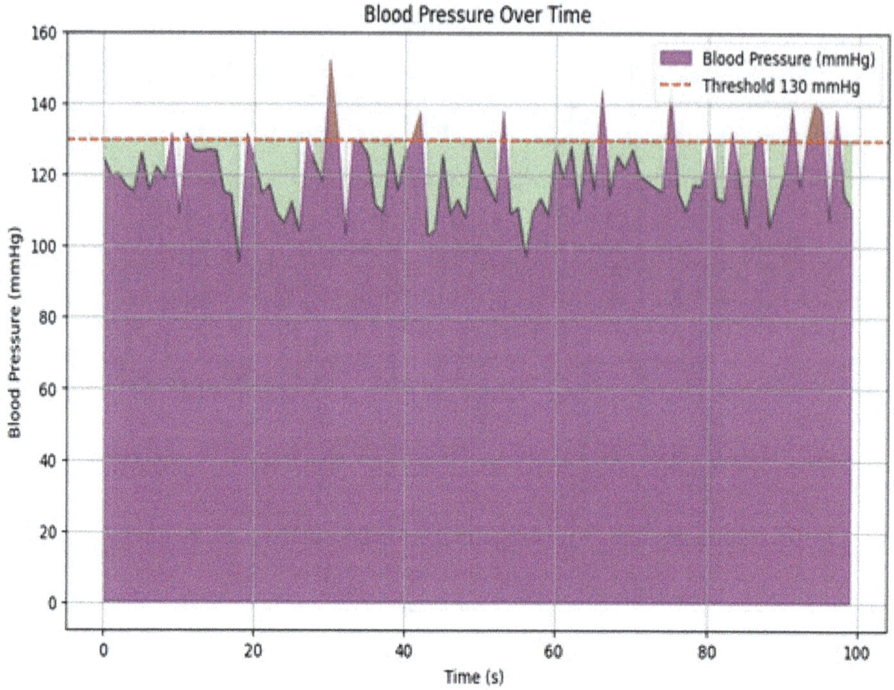

Figure 4. Oxygen presence analysis over days

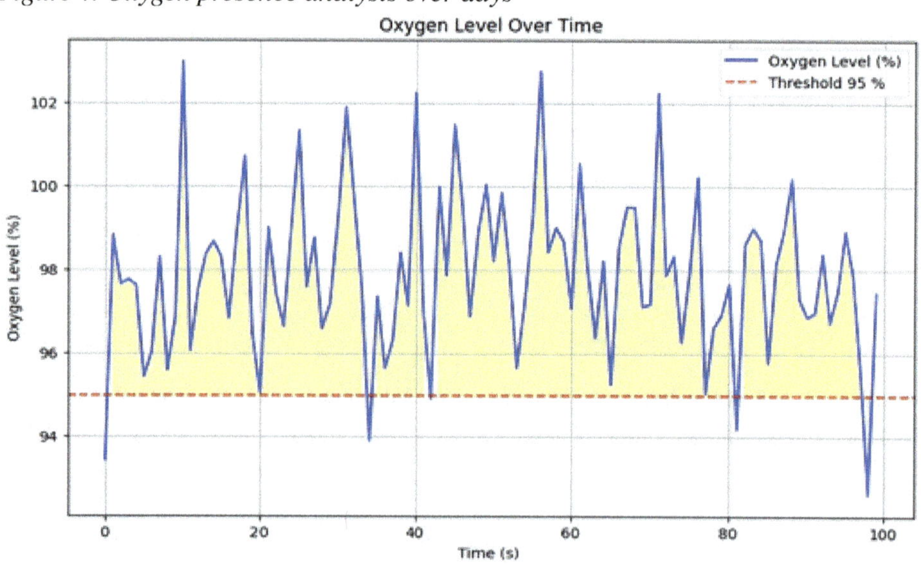

Figure 5. Health Analysis by Proposed Framework

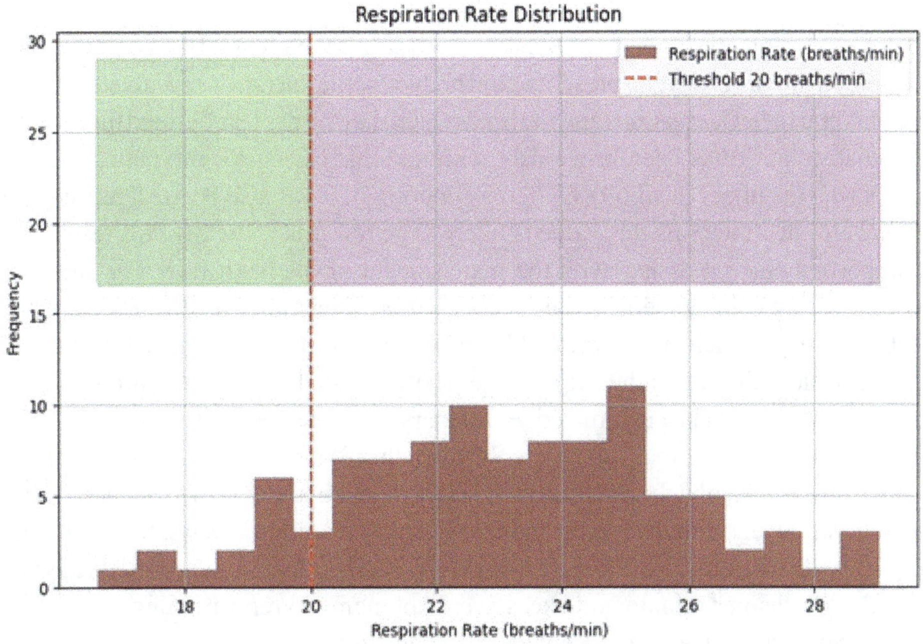

Figure 4, the oxygen level (percentage) is plotted against time with a threshold of 95%. The line graph shows that oxygen levels predominantly stay above the threshold, except for minor dips at time steps 25 and 85, where levels fall to about 94%. The areas above the threshold are filled with yellow, while the green region represents when oxygen levels dip below the threshold. Oxygen levels mostly fluctuate between 97% and 99%, and the slight dips around time steps 25 and 85 stand out, although they quickly return to safe levels.

Finally, Figure 5 presents a histogram for the respiration rate (breaths/min) with a threshold of 20 breaths per minute. The distribution of respiration rates shows that most data points fall between 18 and 26 breaths/min, with the majority of the frequency distribution below the threshold. The purple shaded region indicates when the respiration rate exceeds 20 breaths/min, signifying periods of elevated respiration. At specific intervals, particularly in the right tail of the histogram, there are points where respiration exceeds the threshold, peaking at rates as high as 23 breaths/min, pointing to potential concerns.

CONCLUSION

In conclusion, the analysis of the four physiological parameters—heart rate, human blood pressure, oxygen presence, and body-respiration rate—reveals significant insights into their fluctuations and the times when they surpass predefined thresholds. In the abstract, it has been previously reasoned that caring for the patient's heart rate during the intervals of 60 - 85 bpm is important. It has also been identified that during elevated intervals this value is likely to go towards 75 BPM. This feasibility is important since it assists with the management of the heart rate. The required blood pressure management has been specified as a deviation from the normal value of 130 mmHg, which starts from 132 mmHg and appears to jump to 135 mmHg. The condition highlights the importance of off-the-shelf blood pressure monitors and how these could be customized. Pulmonary oxygen doesn't dip below 95% but, on a few occasions, it does fall below 94% which still means that a lot of advanced monitoring and feedback strategies will be needed to maintain performance within operational levels. Finally, respiration rates show readings below 20 breaths per minute with a handful exceeding this value, with the maximum reported rate just over 23 breaths per minute and excessive diaphragmatic repositioning suggesting respiratory issues. The overall analysis demonstrates the need to understand the character of these physiological parameters for effective emergency interventions.

REFERENCES

Abed, S. A., & Gök, M. (2023). Big data and artificial intelligence on the blockchain: A review. *Babylonian Journal of Artificial Intelligence, 2023*, 1–4. DOI: 10.58496/BJAI/2023/001

Aiswarya, S., & Sangeetha, S. (2022). Perception of Women Trainees' Regarding Skill Development Initiatives of Kudumbashree for Employability. *Ramanujan International Journal of Business and Research, 7*(2). Advance online publication. DOI: 10.51245/rijbr.v7i2.2022.1087

Al Barazanchi, I. I., & Hashim, W. (2023). Enhancing IoT device security through blockchain technology: A decentralized approach. *SHIFRA, 2023*, 10–16. DOI: 10.70470/SHIFRA/2023/002

Al-Nbhany, W. A. N. A., Zahary, A. T., & Al-Shargabi, A. A. (2024). Blockchain-IoT Healthcare Applications and Trends: A Review. *IEEE Access : Practical Innovations, Open Solutions, 12*, 4178–4212. DOI: 10.1109/ACCESS.2023.3349187

Al-Shareeda, M. A., Najm, L. B., Hassan, A. A., Mushtaq, S., & Ali, H. A. (2024). Secure IoT-Based Smart Agriculture System Using Wireless Sensor Networks for Remote Environmental Monitoring. *STAP Journal of Security Risk Management, 2024*(1), 56–66. DOI: 10.63180/jsrm.thestap.2024.1.4

Albinhamad, H., Alotibi, A., Alagnam, A., Almaiah, M., & Salloum, S. (2025). Vehicular Ad-hoc Networks (VANETs): A Key Enabler for Smart Transportation Systems and Challenges. *Jordanian Journal of Informatics and Computing, 2025*(1), 4–15. DOI: 10.63180/jjic.thestap.2025.1.2

Aldhyani, T. H. H. (2025). Secure Blockchain-Based Tracking Storage and Permission Verification of Electronic Health Records. *Journal of Cyber Security and Risk Auditing, 2025*(3), 103–122. DOI: 10.63180/jcsra.thestap.2025.3.8

Alhasani, A. T., Albakaa, Z. H., Alabidi, S. A., Gburi, O. Q. A. Z., Kadi, A., & Potoroko, I. (2025). Heartbeat Sound Classification Using Mel-Spectrogram and CNN Optimized by Frilled Lizard Algorithm for Cardiovascular Disease Detection. *Mesopotamian Journal of Artificial Intelligence in Healthcare, 2025*, 96–104. DOI: 10.58496/MJAIH/2025/010

Ali, G., Samuel, A., Kabiito, S. P., Morish, Z., Thomas, A., Robert, W., Denis, A., Sallam, M., Mijwil, M. M., Ayad, J., Salau, A. O., & Dhoska, K. (2025). Integration of artificial intelligence, blockchain, and quantum cryptography for securing the Industrial Internet of Things (IIoT): Recent advancements and future trends. *Applied Data Science and Analysis, 2025*, 19–82. DOI: 10.58496/ADSA/2025/004

Allam, A. H., Gomaa, I., Zayed, H. H., & Taha, M. (2024). IoT-based eHealth using blockchain technology: A survey. *Cluster Computing*, *27*(6), 7083–7110. DOI: 10.1007/s10586-024-04357-y

Almaayah, M., & Sulaiman, R. B. (2024). Cyber Risk Management in the Internet of Things: Frameworks, Models, and Best Practices. *STAP Journal of Security Risk Management*, *2024*(1), 3–23. DOI: 10.63180/jsrm.thestap.2024.1.1

Alshinwan, M., Memon, A. G., Ghanem, M. C., & Almaayah, M. (2025). Unsupervised text feature selection approach based on improved Prairie dog algorithm for the text clustering. *Jordanian Journal of Informatics and Computing*, *2025*(1), 27–36. DOI: 10.63180/jjic.thestap.2025.1.4

Babu, P. A., Rai, A. K., Ramesh, J. V. N., Nithyasri, A., Sangeetha, S., Kshirsagar, P. R., Rajendran, A., Rajaram, A., & Dilipkumar, S. (2024). An Explainable Deep Learning Approach for Oral Cancer Detection. *Journal of Electrical Engineering & Technology*, *19*(3), 1837–1848. DOI: 10.1007/s42835-023-01654-1

Balgani, S., & Sangeetha, S. (2014). An Efficient Approach to Improve Response Time in Multibiometric Patterns Retrieval from Large Database. [IJCSNS]. *International Journal of Computer Science and Network Security*, *14*(5), 102.

Bataineh, M. R., Mardini, W., Khamayseh, Y. M., & Yassein, M. M. B. (2022). Novel and Secure Blockchain Framework for Health Applications in IoT. *IEEE Access : Practical Innovations, Open Solutions*, *10*, 14914–14926. DOI: 10.1109/ACCESS.2022.3147795

Biswas, S., Sharif, K., Li, F., Latif, Z., Kanhere, S. S., & Mohanty, S. P. (2020). Interoperability and Synchronization Management of Blockchain-Based Decentralized e-Health Systems. *IEEE Transactions on Engineering Management*, *67*(4), 1363–1376. DOI: 10.1109/TEM.2020.2989779

Burhanuddin, M. A. (2023). Epigenetic modifications as predictive biomarkers for cardiovascular disease: A longitudinal study on DNA methylation patterns and disease risk. *SHIFAA*, *2023*, 59–65. DOI: 10.70470/SHIFAA/2023/007

Egala, B. S., Pradhan, A. K., Dey, P., Badarla, V., & Mohanty, S. P. (2023). Fortified-Chain 2.0: Intelligent Blockchain for Decentralized Smart Healthcare System. *IEEE Internet of Things Journal*, *10*(14), 12308–12321. DOI: 10.1109/JIOT.2023.3247452

Fernández-Caramés, T. M., Froiz-Míguez, I., Blanco-Novoa, O., & Fraga-Lamas, P. (2019). Enabling the Internet of Mobile Crowdsourcing Health Things: A Mobile Fog Computing, Blockchain and IoT Based Continuous Glucose Monitoring System for Diabetes Mellitus Research and Care. *Sensors (Basel)*, *19*(15), 3319. DOI: 10.3390/s19153319 PMID: 31357725

Gopalakrishnan, S., Ruby, E. D. K., Hemanand, D., Anitha, R., Suresh, D., & Choubey, S. B. (2024). Leveraging AI and Blockchain in MANETs to enhance Smart City Infrastructure and Autonomous Vehicular Networks. *Babylonian Journal of Machine Learning*, *2024*, 112–120. DOI: 10.58496/BJML/2024/011

Gopalakrishnan, S., Ruby, E. D. K., Hemanand, D., Anitha, R., Suresh, D., & Choubey, S. B. (2024, July 02). Leveraging AI and Blockchain in MANETs to enhance Smart City Infrastructure and Autonomous Vehicular Networks. *Babylonian Journal of Machine Learning*, *2024*, 112–120. DOI: 10.58496/BJML/2024/011

Hanabaratti, K. D., Shivannavar, A. S., Deshpande, S. N., Argiddi, R. V., Praveen, R. V. S., & Itkar, S. A. (2024). Advancements in natural language processing: Enhancing machine understanding of human language in conversational AI systems. *International Journal of Communication Networks and Information Security*, *16*(4), 193–204.

Jamil, F., Kahng, H. K., Kim, S., & Kim, D.-H. (2021). Towards Secure Fitness Framework Based on IoT-Enabled Blockchain Network Integrated with Machine Learning Algorithms. *Sensors (Basel)*, *21*(5), 1640. DOI: 10.3390/s21051640 PMID: 33652773

Jayashre, K., & Padmavathi, U. (2024). *Blockchain-Based IoT Computing Services in Medical Healthcare*., DOI: 10.4018/979-8-3693-8568-5.ch007

Kala, M. K., & Priya, M. (2024). Smart IoT-Blockchain Security to Secure Sensitive Personal Medical Data Using Shuffled Random Starvation Link Encryption. *IEEE Access : Practical Innovations, Open Solutions*, *12*, 168182–168196. DOI: 10.1109/ACCESS.2024.3483437

Kareem, A. B. A. (2024). Modelling Of Blockchain Technology. *SHIFRA*, *2024*, 97–104. DOI: 10.70470/SHIFRA/2024/011

Mhammed, K. (2025). Cyber Intelligence & Moroccan National Security: What Strategy for Managing and Mitigating Cyber Threats against Future Sporting Events. *Journal of Cyber Security and Risk Auditing*, *2025*(4), 366–383. DOI: 10.63180/jcsra.thestap.2025.4.12

Murala, D. K., Panda, S. K., & Dash, S. P. (2023). MedMetaverse: Medical Care of Chronic Disease Patients and Managing Data Using Artificial Intelligence, Blockchain, and Wearable Devices State-of-the-Art Methodology. *IEEE Access : Practical Innovations, Open Solutions, 11*, 138954–138985. DOI: 10.1109/ACCESS.2023.3340791

Praveen, R., Hemavathi, U., Sathya, R., Abubakkar Siddiq, A., Gokul Sanjay, M., & Gowdish, S. (2024). AI Powered Plant Identification and Plant Disease Classification System. *2024 4th International Conference on Sustainable Expert Systems (ICSES)*, 1610–1616. DOI: 10.1109/ICSES63445.2024.10763167

Priya, S. S., & Srinivas Vellela, S. B, V. R., Javvadi, S., Sk, K. B., & D, R. (2023). Design And Implementation of An Integrated IOT Blockchain Framework for Drone Communication. *2023 3rd International Conference on Intelligent Technologies (CONIT)*, 1–5. DOI: 10.1109/CONIT59222.2023.10205659

Raj, A., & Prakash, S. (2024). Privacy preservation of the internet of medical things using blockchain. *Health Services and Outcomes Research Methodology, 24*(1), 112–139. DOI: 10.1007/s10742-023-00306-1

Rasheed, D. H., & Tambe, S. B. (2024). Advancing Energy Efficiency with Smart Grids and IoT-Based Solutions for a Sustainable Future. *ESTIDAMAA, 2024*, 36–42. DOI: 10.70470/ESTIDAMAA/2024/006

Ratta, P., Abdullah, , & Sharma, S. (2024). A blockchain-machine learning ecosystem for IoT-Based remote health monitoring of diabetic patients. *Healthcare Analytics, 5*, 100338. DOI: 10.1016/j.health.2024.100338

Sachdev, D., Pokhriyal, S. K., Nechully, S., & Sundaram, S. S. (2023). *Healthcare.* Systematic Review of Applications of Decentralized Trust Using Blockchain Technology., DOI: 10.1007/978-981-19-5723-9_10

Salih, H. M., & Mahmood, A. M. (2024). A electric vehicle blockchain: Problems and opportunities. *Babylonian Journal of Networking, 2024*, 18–24. DOI: 10.58496/BJN/2024/003

Salim, R. A. (2024). Wheelchair Control Using Finger Gestures IoT-Based Arduino. *Babylonian Journal of Internet of Things, 2024*, 137–150. DOI: 10.58496/BJIoT/2024/016

Shanshool, A. M. (2023). Exploring the Role of Block-chain in IoT-Driven Healthcare Solutions. *Babylonian Journal of Networking, 2023*, 82–88. DOI: 10.58496/BJN/2023/010

Vaigandla, K. K. (2025). An Extensive Examination on IOT and Industrial IOT: Attacks, Security, Detection Methods, Blockchain Solutions and Challenges. *Babylonian Journal of Internet of Things, 2025*, 89–100. DOI: 10.58496/BJIoT/2025/004

KEY TERMS AND DEFINITIONS

Blockchain: Blockchain is a distinct type of digital database (digital ledger) that, in a decentralized manner, securely records data across a network of computers in a transparent, immutable, and tamper-resistant manner. Each block represents data, and these blocks are linked temporally into a chain.

Cardiovascular Disease (CVD): Cardiovascular disease is an umbrella term encompassing a variety of diseases involving the heart and blood vessels. The most frequently encountered forms of CVD are coronary artery disease and stroke.

Cybersecurity: Cybersecurity is the concept of protecting systems, networks and data associated with cyberspace from digital attacks, damage or unauthorized access. Cybersecurity is a combination of technologies, processes and people to safeguard digital information and systems from a comprehensive spectrum of cyber threats including hacking, malware and phishing.

Deep Learning: Deep learning is a subfield of machine learning that is based on multilayered neural networks, which are anatomically inspired by the organization of the human brain. Today, deep learning models form the foundation for most current state-of-the-art artificial intelligence (AI) systems across various domains, including computer vision and generative AI.

Federated Learning: Federated learning is a method of training machine learning models on decentralized data when data is generated and stored in multiple devices or nodes.

Internet of Things (IoT): The Internet of Things refers to physical objects that are embedded with sensors, processing ability, software, and other technologies for the purpose of connecting and exchanging data with other devices and systems over the Internet, or other communication networks.

Chapter 3
Harnessing CNN-LSTM Fusion for Enhanced Crime Forecasting and Temporal Pattern Analysis

K. Ramalakshmi
https://orcid.org/0000-0002-3038-643X
P.S.R. Engineering College, India

R. Ranjani
Vel Tech High Tech Dr. Rangarajan Dr. Sakunthala Engineering College, India

A. Mohamed Anwar
Vel Tech Rangarajan Dr. Sagunthala R&D Institute of Science and Technology, India

R. Santhana Krishnan
https://orcid.org/0000-0001-7930-8072
SCAD College of Engineering and Technology, India

L. Krishna Kumari
Ramco Institute of Technology, India

J. Relin Francis Raj
Saveetha School of Engineering, Saveetha Institute of Medical and Technical Sciences, India

B. Mohan
P.S.R. Engineering College, India

ABSTRACT

This research investigates the efficacy of deep learning models, specifically Convolutional Neural Networks (CNN) and Long Short-Term Memory (LSTM) networks, in the context of crime rate prediction. By combining the spatial feature extraction capabilities of CNNs with the temporal sequence learning strengths of LSTMs, we developed a hybrid CNN-LSTM model. The l results demonstrate that the

DOI: 10.4018/979-8-3373-1807-3.ch003

2026, IGI Global Scientific Publishing. Copying or distributing in print or electronic forms without written permission of IGI Global Scientific Publishing is prohibited. Use of this chapter to ative artificial intelligence (AI) technologies is expressly prohibited. The publisher reserves all rights to license its use for generative AI training and machine learning model development.

CNN-LSTM model significantly surpasses traditional predictive models, including ARIMA and standard neural networks, achieving a remarkable accuracy rate of 97.8%. Furthermore, the incorporation of multiple LSTM layers not only enhanced predictive accuracy but also optimized the training process. These findings highlight the potential of advanced neural network architectures in developing robust predictive systems for crime forecasting. The study concludes with recommendations for future research focused on hyperparameter optimization to improve model performance and reliability further, thereby contributing valuable insights for proactive crime prevention and effective law enforcement strategies.

INTRODUCTION

Day by day, the excellence of lifespan has enhanced as the inclination of progressive industrialization, information, and specialization is fast-tracked due to the unceasing and swift economic evolution and the progress of science and technology. Nevertheless, several issues like unemployment, poverty, and crime never go away. Amid these social disruptions, crime issues have become more sophisticated, progressive, varied, and widespread, making it challenging to predict and prevent crimes before they occur. To effectively manage such expanded and intelligent crimes, it is significant to investigate the recent crime trends and make organized and inclusive countermeasures to encounter the new movements of crime. Preventing crimes before they occur is always preferable to dealing with them after they have already occurred. Because of the recent dramatic advancements in machine learning technology, research on data analysis and crime prediction systems is crucial to lowering the rate of crime. Traditional data mining can recognize the arrangements and tendencies from organized information but through the progression in expertise, inventive data mining can excerpt the data from organized and formless data. Data mining assists criminal detectives in exactly and competently examining a huge amount of information. Prediction is the most important process that has involved substantial attention given the potential suggestion of positive prediction for all applications. The two types of predictions, namely prediction of unavailable data or pending trends, or else a class label for a few data is predicted. Then, classification takes place. If the classification process is designed depending on a training set, the class label of an object is predicted based on object attribute values and class attribute values. The prediction is used to estimate absent numerical values in time-correlated data. Its main idea is used for a huge volume of earlier value for reflecting possible upcoming data value. The clustering process is similar to the classification process, whereas clustering is the organization of data in classes. Unlike classification, the class labels are unknown in clustering, and the algorithm is to discover the labels of adequate classes. The clustering is recognized as an unsupervised categorization, due to its classification is not revealed by the given class labels. Several clustering methods are developed based on the principle of exploiting the resemblance between same class bodies, such as intra-class resemblance and diminishing resemblance among different class entities, such as inter-class resemblance.

Conventional models frequently employ temporal analysis or geographical analysis separately. It consists of rudimentary machine learning algorithms and basic statistical models, which usually have lower accuracy rates because they can't fully capture the complexity of crime data. Furthermore, it is devoid of a dense output layer, which is necessary to convert learnt features into precise predictions.

One significant methodological achievement is the unification of Convolutional Neural Networks (CNN) and LSTM into a single framework to overcome those limitations. The LSTM layers provide a comprehensive understanding of crime patterns by capturing temporal connections, while the CNN layers extract geographic information from crime data. The model's ability to predict crime rates is improved by including a Dense layer in the final output, which effectively transforms temporal patterns and retrieved data into predictions. This integration considerably improves predictions of crime rates.

Section I presents the introduction, Section II illustrates the existing works related to this research, the preceding section III analyses the materials and methods of the work proposed, section IV illustrates the results and discussion and finally, section V concludes and describes the future directions of the work proposed.

RELATED WORKS

Sivanagaleela and Rajesh (2019) examined factors related to crime from previous years. This system prioritizes the location of crimes over identifying the perpetrators. The fuzzy C-Means algorithm and naive Bayes classification are employed to classify and group data for various crimes, such as murder, kidnapping, cheating, theft, burglary, robbery, crimes against women, and other offenses. A regression model (Amirthayogam et al., 2024) was presented to predict the crime rate in different states from 2001 to 2014. Many machine learning processes are utilized to analyze time series (Safat, Asghar, & Gillani, 2021) data through LSTM and autoregressive unified moving average (ARIMA) models, (Adamopoulos et al., 2025). These processes included support vector machine, k-nearest neighbours, logistic regression, decision tree, Naïve Bayes, random forest, eXtreme Gradient Boosting and multilayer perceptron. On both data sets, mean absolute error and the root mean square error of the LSTM time series analysis were performed to a largely acceptable degree, (Manengadan, Nandanan, & Subash, 2021). In comparison to other methods, this one offers enhanced predictive accuracy for future trends, early crime detection, and hotspots with higher crime rates. These insights can be utilized to inform police tactics and practices. Kumar et al. (2020) used the KNN prediction method to observe the crime rate. It will make educated guesses about the kind of crime, when, where, and when it might occur. The behaviours in crime over a region will be provided by this data, which may be useful for criminal investigations. The assemble-stacking-based crime estimate approach, which is grounded on an SVM set of rules, is a reliable method presented (Srividhya et al., 2024) for recognizing suitable forecasts of crime by employing learning-based approaches. Exhausting the SVM (Zaidi et al., 2020) procedure, domain-specific formations can be accomplished in association with supplementary machine learning approaches like Random Forest as well as Naïve Bayes. The ensemble model that has the premier correlation coefficient plus average and absolute errors sometimes performs better than the other models. The classification accuracy of the proposed method was 99.5%. To consistently estimate crime tendencies in every region and automatically identify high-risk crime areas in urban zones, Khlewee, Hamze, and Muya (2025) presented a methodology centred on spatial investigation and auto-regressive representations. The process yields a spatiotemporal crime prediction method, which is made up of an assemblage of regions with high crime rates and a group of interconnected crime prognosticators, (Yadav & Sheoran, 2020). Each of these components exemplifies a predictive model for estimating the number of crimes that would occur in a given region. The experimental evaluation demonstrates that the suggested technique realizes greater accuracy in spatial and temporal crime prediction over rolling time horizons, using real-world information composed in the region of Chicago, (Sun et al., 2021). To predict crime in the upcoming years, Agarwal, Yadav, and Thakur (2018) investigated statistical approaches such as Functional Coefficient Regression, Weighted Moving Average and Arithmetic-Geometric Progression. For this, the criminality statistics for the Indian states from 2001 to 2013 were utilized, (Alkattan et al., 2024). Information on crimes committed between 2001 and 2011 has been used to forecast crimes in 2012 and 2013. These estimated values have been contrasted with information on actual crimes that occurred in 2012 and 2013. The variation among the actual records and the estimated values of those years indicates the accuracy of the suggested approaches. To autonomously and successfully identify the high-risk regions in the city, Sandagiri, Kumara, and Kuhaneswaran (2020) recommended a daily crime prediction framework that integrated the ST-GCN and LSTM, (Joshi et al., 2019). Topological maps of urban areas carry the model's dataset. It consists of two parts to derive the factors of theft crimes collectively called a spatial-temporal features extraction part and temporal feature extraction part. A method for predicting crimes utilizing weather and Twitter data was presented, (Pratibha et al., 2020). The two modules of the suggested method are the crime prediction and detection modules. The crime detection module identifies the Twitter posts about the offence. The recognition module is developed with Bidirectional Encoder Representations from Transformers-based methodology. Next, an ANN is used to implement the extrapolation module, (Tarlekar et al., 2021). The empirical analysis of our suggested strategy demonstrates the efficacy of the BERT and ANN-centred forecast methods. According to Chauhan and Sehgal (2017), law enforcement continues to trail behind criminals convincingly. Improving the efficiency of investigations and analyzing the rising number of crimes are two of the police's top priorities. This study develops an intuitive user interface for mapping criminal activity using QGIS, as well as for visualizing, analyzing, and forecasting patterns and trends in criminal activity using clustering algorithms like K-Means, agglomerative algorithms, and predictive algorithms like SVM and Random Forest. According to Khalaf and Steiti (2024), it is important to keep an accurate database of all crimes committed since it may be useful in the future. Law enforcement agencies can prevent crimes before they happen by having the ability to predict potential crimes in the future. Hochreiter and Schmidhuber (1997) analyzed the prediction of crime using an efficient method for categorizing the different kinds of crimes, explaining their motives, and forecasting future crimes. Official police reports, and data that were scraped from reputable websites are both included in the dataset. The system determines the hotspot areas through the analysis of crime reports. Analysts of crime information can assist law prosecution in finding criminals more rapidly. Asad et al. (2020) analyzed unstructured data, revealing previously undiscovered, valuable information. Predictive policing, which utilizes analytical and predictive methods to detect criminal activity, has been shown to be largely successful. Using a machine learning algorithm, Asad et al. (2020) predicted computer malware infection rates based on malware features, employing both gradient-boosting and supervised machine-learning algorithms.

In 2017, Baloian et al. created a rough time and risk map for incidents of specific crimes, such as violent thefts, armed hold-ups, and home invasions. The police can then make use of this information to increase patrols in the appropriate areas, which will lower the rate of crime. Ghankutkar et al. (2019) provided a report that analyses real-time crime news. The recommended system is a web-based application that affords a description of crime-related news by analyzing instantaneous crime information in the arrangement of online articles. Rather than the other way around, Moamin et al.'s (2025) research concentrated on predicting the areas based on crimes. Additionally, this will help estimate the amount of crimes that will occur in various cities within a given period. Additionally, by being aware of the projected trend, detectives and law enforcement will be able to take preventative measures, which will lower the frequency of these incidents. Here, the districts (also known as regions) are predicted using the Random Forest algorithm based on various crime rates.

MATERIALS AND METHODS

CNN AND LSTM Model

CNN and LSTM methods were used to simulate and predict crime rates, which are explained in the following Figure 1

Figure 1. Prediction using CNN-LSTM

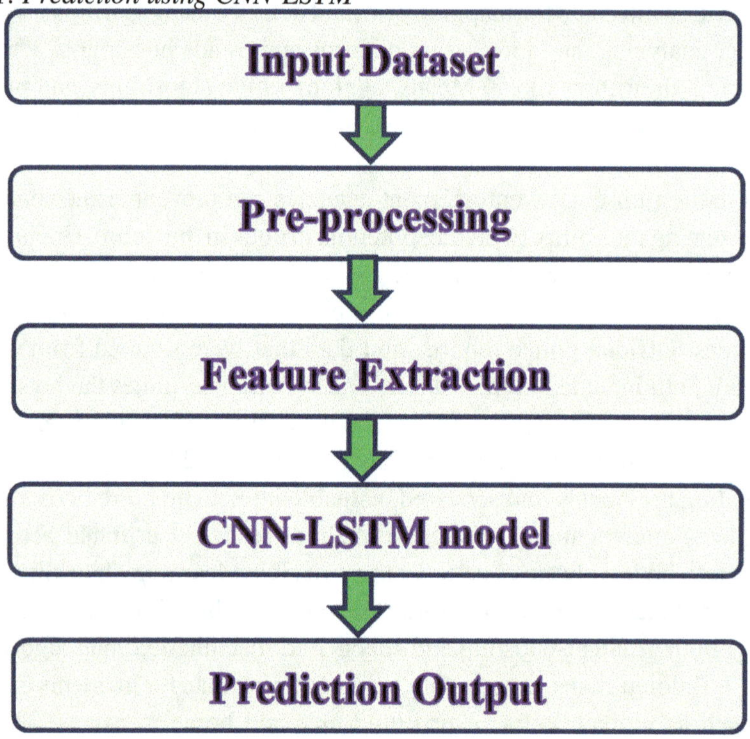

At first, the data are extracted and stored as a data frame from the input dataset, which is named (crime data from dataset.csv) Then we pre-process the data by selecting the first 33 columns only, and hence the unnamed columns are dropped or neglected. Then, we get the state name and crime case name from the user to extract the data that is related to those state names and crime case names. We select the total crime cases row along the extracted data. Hence now we have the total crime cases for that particular state dataset. Now, we feed the extracted crime case values to the CNN+LSTM train that model. After training, we predicted the future for the next 10 years by using the trained CNN model.

Data Set Details

Data sets with various states are gathered from the "Crime in India" website. After every year, the State Crime Records Bureaux gathers information to compile the description from the District Crime Records Bureaux and forward it to NCRB with the source. Megacities data is also gathered independently.

CNN and LSTM Workflow

The data on daily crime incidence were collected and segmented into a training group for model development and a testing group for assessment. The CNN, as well as LSTM models, are pooled and not influenced by exogenous meteorological variables and were espoused to apt the crime rate prevalence through exhausting the details regarding the training group. Figure 2 illustrates the workflow of the proposed model, which aims to identify the optimal approach for predicting the crime rate by integrating LSTM models with exogenous meteorological variables.

Figure 2. Prediction using CNN and LSTM workflow

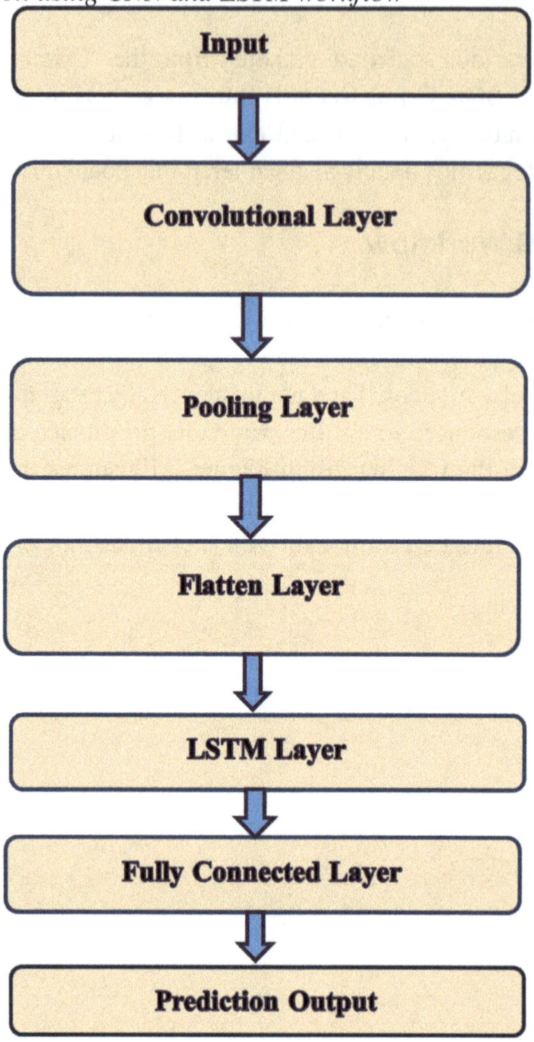

Convolutional Neural Network (CNN)

CNNs are superior to DNNs in many ways. The primary one resembles more resembles the human visual handling scheme, being optimized greatly in the configuration of 2D and 3D image processing and being proficient in acquiring and abstracting 2D features, demonstrating effectiveness in the learning process. The max-pooling layer is proficient at assimilating shape disparities. Similarly, it is also made up of sparse connections that have weights attached to them. CNNs have many fewer constraints than a fully linked network of identical size. The optimization algorithm is a powerful tool for almost all CNNs, and it is less vulnerable to the diminishing gradient issue. When the optimization algorithm instructs the entire web to reduce the loss function directly, CNN can generate well-tuned weights. The system framework of CNNs is shown in Figure 3. It is composed of two primary components: a classifier and feature extractors. In the feature extraction layers, the output from each layer is directly taken before being used as input for the subsequent layer.

In the same way, it feeds its output into the layer that comes after it.

Max-pooling, Convolution, and classification are the three different layers that produce the CNN architecture. In exist, two different kinds of layers in the middle levels and network's low. Max-pooling and convolutional layers are what they are. Max-pooling operations are performed on odd-numbered layers, and convolutions are executed on even-numbered layers. Feature mapping is the name given to the clustering of the convolution and max-pooling layers output nodes hooked on a 2D plane. The development of every plane of the layer is achieved through the amalgamation of one or added planes of preceding layers. A plane's nodes are connected to a tiny portion of every connected plane in the layer above. Every convolutional layer node has its features obtained from the input images using convolution processes happening in the input nodes.

Figure 3. CNN architecture

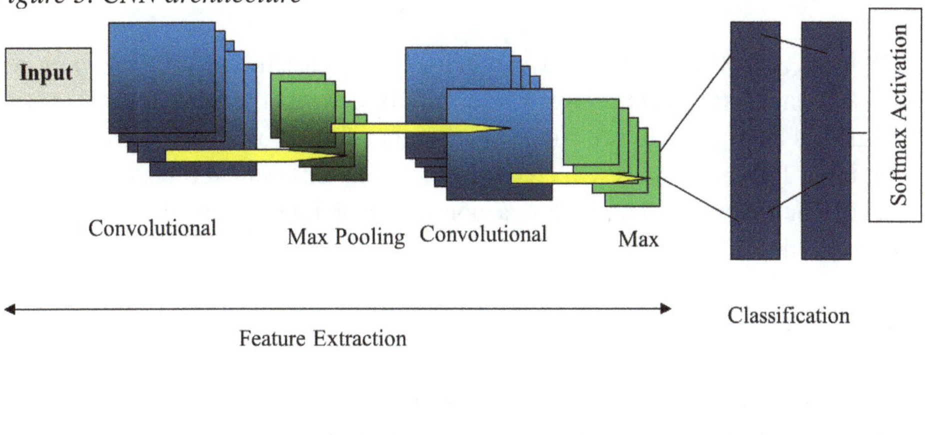

Figure 3 shows the structural framework of the CNN. The features are propagated from lower-level layers derive higher-level features. Depending on the size of the kernel, the dimensions of features are reduced max-pooling and convolutional operations, in turn, when the highest layer or level features are propagated. However, to ensure classification accuracy, improved features of the input images are represented, and the number of feature maps is typically improved. The fully connected network is also known as the classification layer. The result of the former layer of the CNN is taken as the input for this fully connected network. Because of the better performance, the classification layer has been implemented using feed feed-forward network. Concerning the final neural network's weight matrix dimension, the extracted features are taken as inputs in the classification layer. Alternatively, fully connected layers are costly in terms of network and learning parameters. In recent years, techniques such as global average pooling and average pooling have emerged to address this issue.

On the other hand, these techniques can be used to connect networks fully. It uses a soft-max layer for the calculation of the score of the respective class in the uppermost classification layer. The classifier affords results for the corresponding classes, depending upon the highest score. The succeeding sector explores the mathematical details of different layers of CNNs.

Convolutional Layer

Within this layer, learnable kernels are used to convolve the feature maps from earlier layers. The output kernel passes over a linear or non-linear activation function to create the result feature maps. Multiple input feature maps can be amalgamated using any one of the output characteristics maps. Generally speaking, it can be stated as:

$$x_j^l = f(\sum_{i \in M_j} x_i^{l-1} * k_{ij}^l + b_j^l) \quad (1)$$

Where x_j^l denotes the current layer output, x_i^{l-1} denotes the outcome of the earlier layer, k_{ij}^l denotes the current layer kernel, and b_j^l denotes the current layer biases. M_j signifies an input map selection. There is an additive bias b assigned to every result map. The input maps will be convolved using different kernels to create the matching output maps. Ultimately, a non-linear or linear activation function is smeared to the output maps.

Sub-Sampling Layer

The downsampled process is carried out on the input maps by the Sub-sampling layer, also referred to as the pooling layer. Within this layer, the constant terms are the quantity of input and output feature maps. Namely, exactly N output maps will exist if it has N input maps. Reliant on the size of the down-sampling mask, the down-sampling operation will result in an abridgement of the output maps in each dimension. For example, all the images' output dimensions will be half of their respective input dimensions if a 2×2 downsampling kernel is applied. This procedure can be written as

$$X_j^l = down(X_j^{l-1}) \tag{2}$$

where a subsampling function is indicated by down (.). In this layer, two types of operations are typically carried out: max-pooling or average pooling. If the average pooling method is used, the function typically chooses the average value by adding up all N × N patches of the feature maps from the former layer. Alternatively, in the event of max-pooling, identify the maximum value from the N×N patches of the feature maps. A factor of n subsequently decreases the result map's scopes. In certain exceptional cases, a scalar multiplies each output map. Other subsampling layers, for example the fractional max-pooling layer and the subsampling with convolution layer, have been proposed.

Classification Layer

One of the fully connected layers utilizes the features that were fetched from a convolutional layer in the earlier steps to determine the score of the respective class. The features of the last layer are characterized as vectors that have scalar quantities and are provided to the fully connected layers. We employ the fully connected feed-forward neural layers as a soft-max classification layer. Regarding the amount of merged layers in the network model, there are no fast and hard rules. However, two to four layers are typically found in various architectures, for example LeNet, Alex Net, and VGG Net. Other methods have been suggested in recent years due to the high computational cost of fully connected layers. The fully linked layer informs in the backward propagation through the CNNs, adhering to the general procedure of fully connected neural networks. By applying the complete convolutional process to the features spanning the convolutional layer and its immediately preceding layer, we update the filters of the convolutional layer.

Parameters of the Network and Memory Requirement for CNN

To gauge the complexity of a deep learning model, a key metric is the number of its computational parameters. One method to calculate the output feature map size is as follows:

$$M = \frac{(N - F)}{S} + 1 \tag{3}$$

Here N is the amount of input features, F is the amount of filters, M is the amount of output feature map dimensions, and S is the number of stride lengths. Typically, padding is used during convolution processes to protect the identically sized I/O feature maps.

$$P = (F - 1)/2 \tag{4}$$

In this case, P represents the amount of padding, and F the kernels' dimensions. The models are compared based on several criteria. However, the majority of the time, both the entire quantity of memory and the amount of network factors are carefully considered. Using the following expression, the number of parameters ($Parm_l$) of the lth layer is determined:

$$Parm_l = (F \times F \times FM_{l-1}) \times FM_l \tag{5}$$

After adding bias to the weights, the above equation will be

$$Parm_l = (F \times (F + 1) \times FM_{l-1}) \times FM_l \tag{6}$$

here, FM_l denotes the quantity of result feature maps, and FM_{l-1} denotes the quantity of input feature maps.

LSTM Model

One classification of the artificial neural network is a recurrent neural network. To keep the network graph in a stable internal state, they augment more heaviness to the network and produce phases. Weightiness, which is back and forward spread over layers, can be preserved. A series of repeating neural network modules is the structure of every recurrent neural network. This reiterating section in traditional RNNs will have a simple arrangement, similar to the sole tanh layer. LSTMs also exhibit this type of chain structure, even though we structure the repeating module differently. There are four layers in a neural network, each of which interacts uniquely. The neural network layer is not a single. Each line in the figure represents the complete vector, linking the output of one node to the other nodes. The trained neural network layers denote the yellow boxes, and pointwise operations, like vector addition, are denoted by the pink circles. Lines that fuse specify concatenation, but lines that bifurcate indicate that their content is derivative and goes to different places. By keeping an error rate higher over many time steps, the network can keep learning. The network can thus learn long-term dependencies. LSTM networks utilize gates and memory cells to report the vanishing gradient disputes. Rather than biology, circuitry is the main source of inspiration for these. Three gates, namely input, output, and forget, as well as one memory cell, are present in every neuron. By preventing or permitting the flow of information, these gates serve to protect it. The input gate controls the volume of data that is stored in the cell from the preceding layer. On the other hand, the output layer assumes responsibility for deciding how plentiful info about this cell's status is passed on to the subsequent layer. The forget gate regulates how long a value stays in the cells as a result of future operations, which helps forget some previous values.

Figure 4. The structure of the LSTM cell

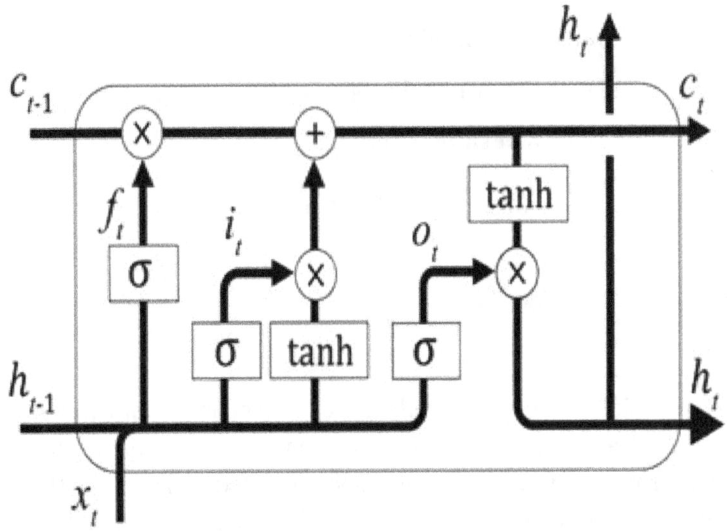

LSTM can effectively model multiple input variable problems, making it particularly useful for time series forecasting, which often presents challenges for adapting classical linear methods to multivariate estimation difficulties. The several LSTM layers from the LSTM model are identified as a stacked LSTM construction. We fit the data in this literature using a three-layer arranged LSTM.

Figure 5. Stacked LSTM architecture

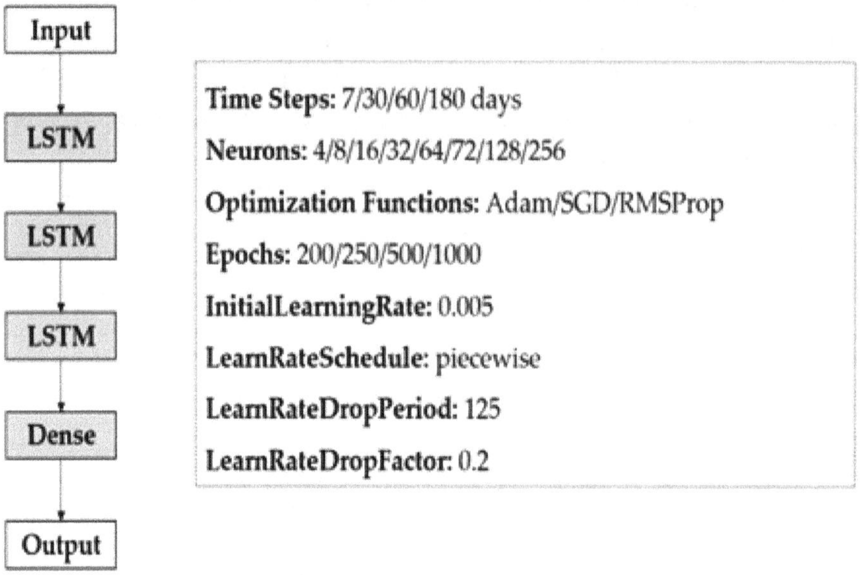

The LSTM model's training and prediction can be separated into the following three stages. Since the LSTM approaches were profound to the gauge of the input information, the information was first rescaled and regulated to the sort of 0 to 1. Second, the time steps for the univariate and multivariate LSTM were fixed to 7/30/60/180. This implies that we predicted the incidence of the following day using the data from the preceding 7/30/60/180 days. At last, a three-layer arranged LSTM structure was created. There is one hidden layer in each LSTM layer, which was configured for the LSTM approach and has neurons with choices of 4/8/16/32/64/72/128/256. Adam, SGD and RMSProp are the alternative optimization functions. These learning procedures were conducted over 200, 250, 500, and 1000 epochs. We gave the typical instructions to descend the learning rate every 125 epochs multiplied by 0.2, with a preliminary learning rate of 0.005. Based on the findings mentioned earlier, we selected the best model by minimizing the test set's RMSE.

RESULTS AND DISCUSSION

The crime rate was predicted using the CNN and LSTM models. The simulation and validation of the outcomes are done with the Python programming language. After calculation, the performance metrics Accuracy, MSE, and RMSE are contrasted with those of other machine learning algorithms. The raw data set includes all available information on India's crime rate from 2001 to 2013, including details on crimes like robbery, theft, rape, and murder. Figure 6 displays the data set cases below.

Figure 6. Input data formation

```
<class 'pandas.core.frame.DataFrame'>
RangeIndex: 9840 entries, 0 to 9839
Data columns (total 33 columns):
 #   Column                                               Non-Null Count  Dtype
---  ------                                               --------------  -----
 0   STATE/UT                                             9840 non-null   object
 1   DISTRICT                                             9840 non-null   object
 2   YEAR                                                 9840 non-null   int64
 3   MURDER                                               9840 non-null   int64
 4   ATTEMPT TO MURDER                                    9840 non-null   int64
 5   CULPABLE HOMICIDE NOT AMOUNTING TO MURDER            9840 non-null   int64
 6   RAPE                                                 9840 non-null   int64
 7   CUSTODIAL RAPE                                       9840 non-null   int64
 8   OTHER RAPE                                           9840 non-null   int64
 9   KIDNAPPING & ABDUCTION                               9840 non-null   int64
 10  KIDNAPPING AND ABDUCTION OF WOMEN AND GIRLS          9840 non-null   int64
 11  KIDNAPPING AND ABDUCTION OF OTHERS                   9840 non-null   int64
 12  DACOITY                                              9840 non-null   int64
 13  PREPARATION AND ASSEMBLY FOR DACOITY                 9840 non-null   int64
 14  ROBBERY                                              9840 non-null   int64
 15  BURGLARY                                             9840 non-null   int64
 16  THEFT                                                9840 non-null   int64
 17  AUTO THEFT                                           9840 non-null   int64
 18  OTHER THEFT                                          9840 non-null   int64
 19  RIOTS                                                9840 non-null   int64
 20  CRIMINAL BREACH OF TRUST                             9840 non-null   int64
 21  CHEATING                                             9840 non-null   int64
 22  COUNTERFIETING                                       9840 non-null   int64
 23  ARSON                                                9840 non-null   int64
 24  HURT/GREVIOUS HURT                                   9840 non-null   int64
 25  DOWRY DEATHS                                         9840 non-null   int64
 26  ASSAULT ON WOMEN WITH INTENT TO OUTRAGE HER MODESTY  9840 non-null   int64
 27  INSULT TO MODESTY OF WOMEN                           9840 non-null   int64
 28  CRUELTY BY HUSBAND OR HIS RELATIVES                  9840 non-null   int64
 29  IMPORTATION OF GIRLS FROM FOREIGN COUNTRIES          9840 non-null   int64
 30  CAUSING DEATH BY NEGLIGENCE                          9840 non-null   int64
 31  OTHER IPC CRIMES                                     9840 non-null   int64
 32  TOTAL IPC CRIMES                                     9840 non-null   int64
dtypes: int64(31), object(2)
memory usage: 2.5+ MB
```

Ln: 5 Col: 0

A prompt input (state) from the user trains the LSTM model and undergoes testing using this method. The skilled LSTM and CNN models receive prompt data from the user, which they use to predict future crime rates. The input parameters for the crime prediction are displayed in Figure 6

Figure 7. Crime count vs year (existing data)

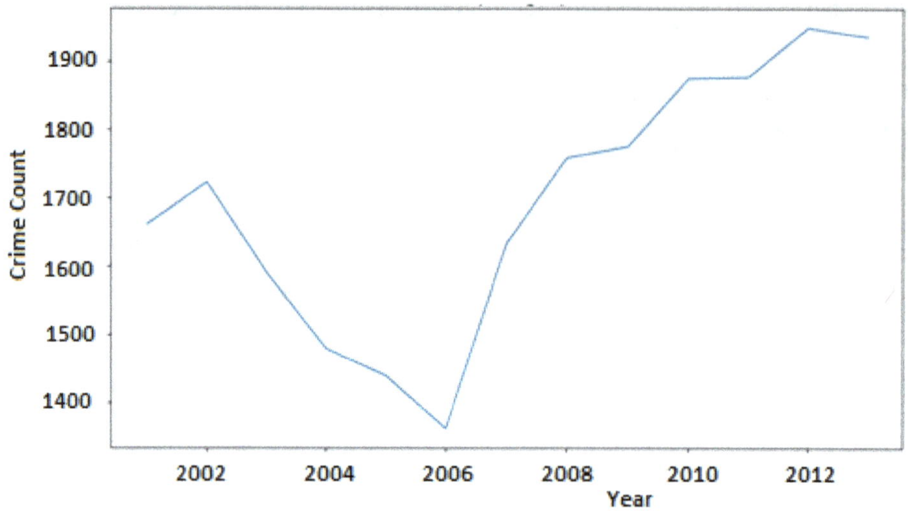

The output of the line plot of the crime count versus year for the available data from 2002 to 2013 is shown in Figure 7 above. The plot explains the previous year's data set details (2002 to 2013).

Figure 8. CNN Training result

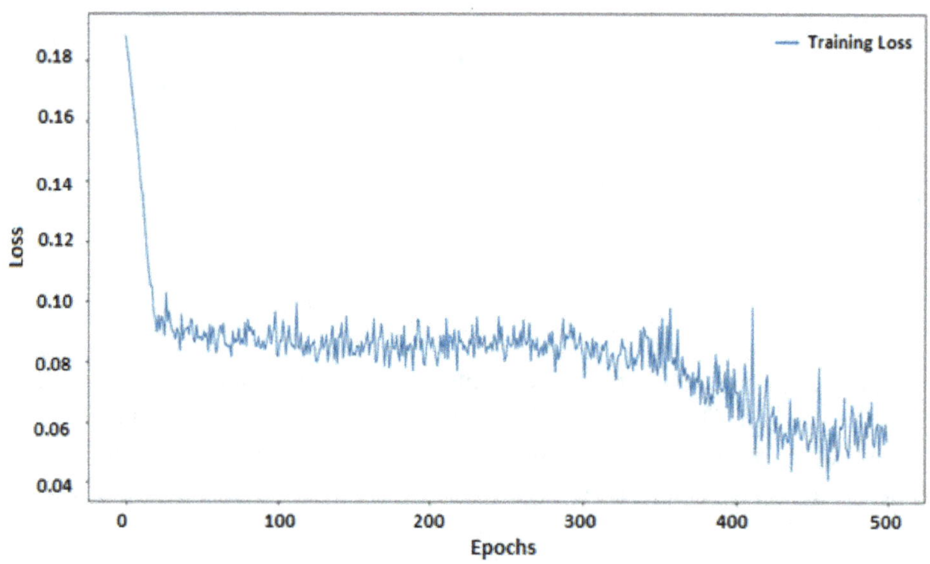

The CNN model's training loss for the relevant data set is shown in Figure 8. For different iterations, the model's loss function obtained a minimum error value.

Figure 9. Prediction result using hybrid CNN+LSTM model

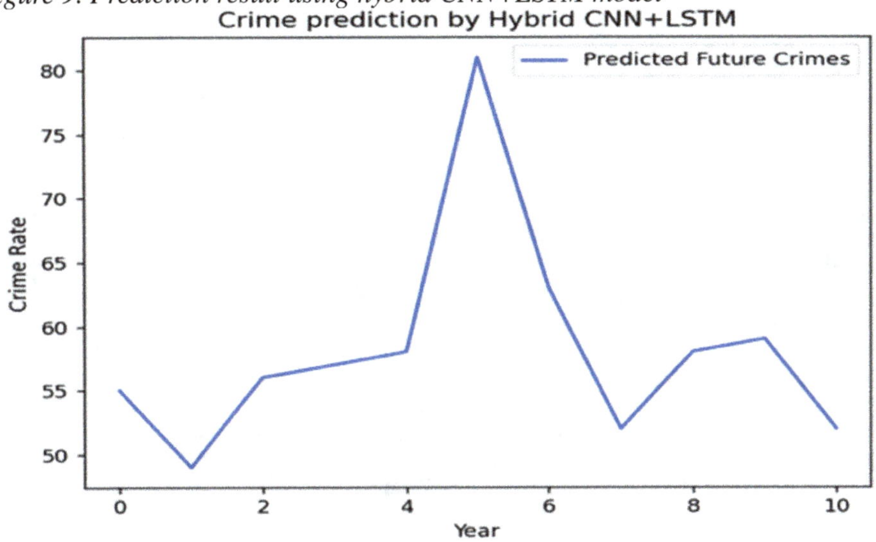

Figure 9 uses a hybrid CNN and LSTM model to predict data from 2014 to 2025. The CNN model with individual processing only uses linear data for prediction. CNN is used in this work to extract features.

Table 1. Hyperparameters of CNN and LSTM

Optimization Function	**Adam**
Momentum	0.9
LSTM Dropout rate	0.25
Initial learning rate	0.00001
Schedule of learning rate	Piecewise
LSTM Activation function	Sigmoid
Loss function	Categorical Cross-Entropy

Hyperparameters utilized in the network are displayed in Table 1. The LSTM training result above can be used to calculate the loss and accuracy. For the validation data set, the suggested LSTM models exhibit loss values of 0.0348 and an accuracy of 97.8%.

Figure 10. Future 10 years predicted value by LSTM

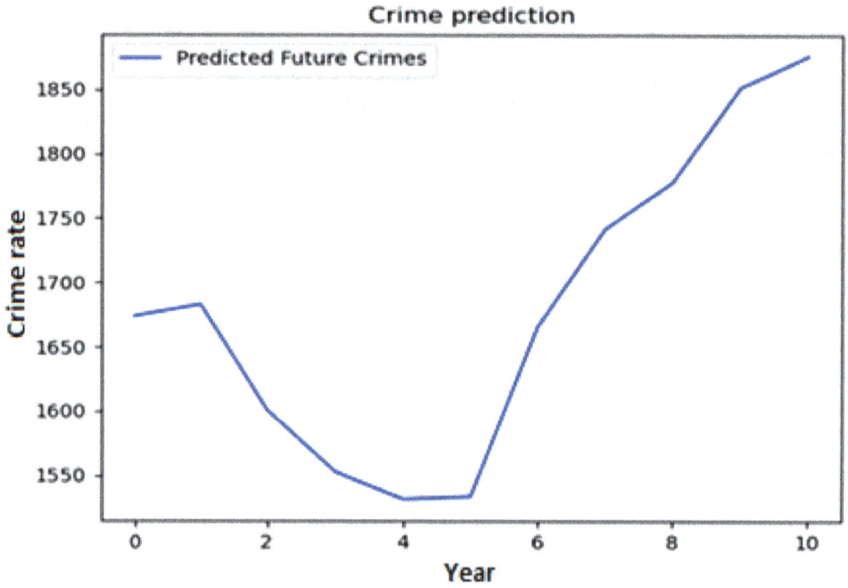

Figure 10 uses the LSTM approach to envisage the crime rates for the next ten years.

It is an example of CNN-LSTM trained for the anticipated crime rate in the upcoming year. To obtain a higher accuracy, the LSTM processes the CNN's residual error.

Figure 11. CNN-LSTM predicted result

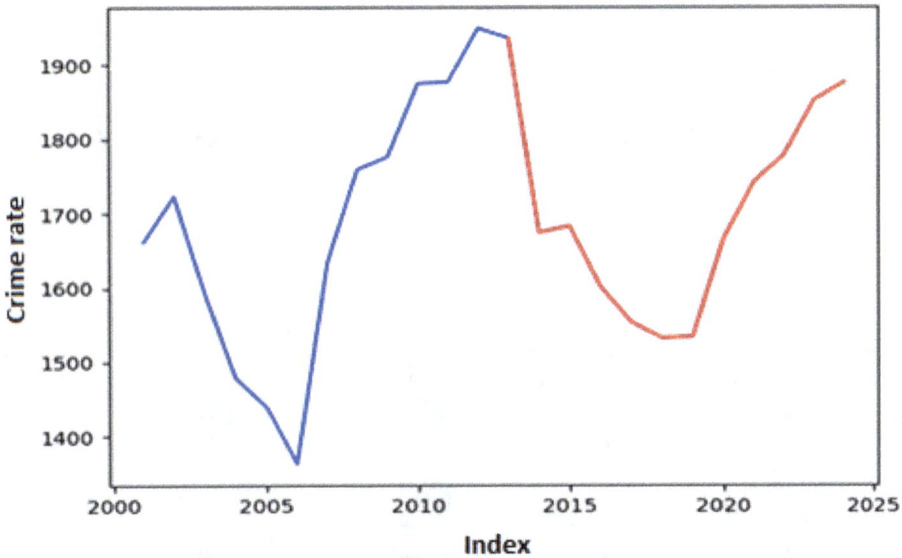

Figure 12. MSE for NN, ARIMA, ARIMA - LSTM, CNN – LSTM

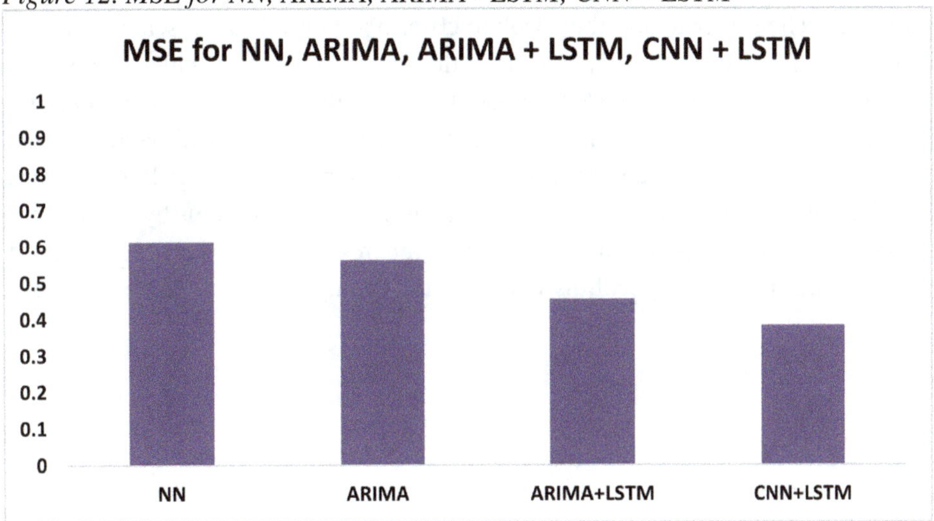

The average of the squared forecast error values yields the mean squared error (MSE). By constraining the forecast error significances to be positive, squaring them too increases the significance of the greater errors. In comparison to NN, ARIMA, and LSTM, the CNN and LSTM models have a lower mean squared error, as seen in Figure 12.

Figure 13. MSE & RMSE for NN, ARIMA, ARIMA- LSTM, CNN-LSTM

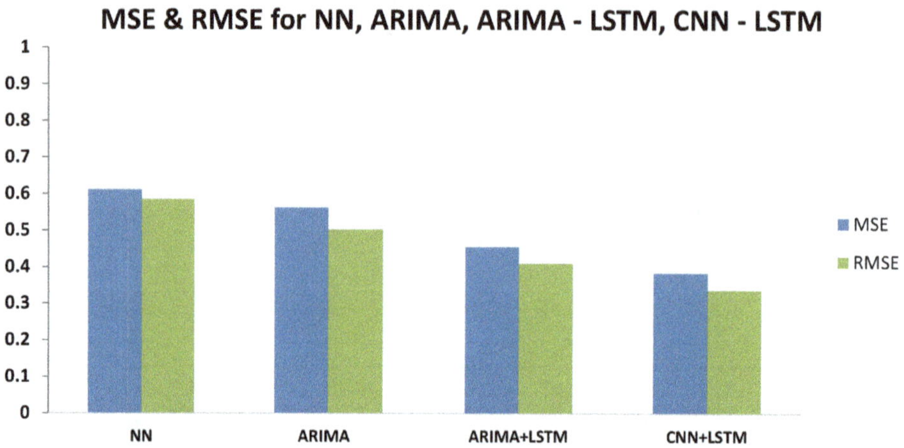

The estimated accuracy is computed from root mean squared error (RMSE) and MSE. The RMSE and MSE calculate an estimator's average deviation from the true parameter. The estimate and the absolute criteria are on the same scale. Whereas RMSE is in the estimate scale, MSE is in the squared deviation scale. The performance analysis of MSE and RMSE about the other algorithms is shown in Figure 15 above. Classification accuracy is the ratio of the accurate estimations to the total input trials. The percentage of accurate predictions made using the test data is called accuracy. To compute, divide the total number of predictions by the number of accurate predictions. Figure 14, which compares CNN and LSTM models to other machine learning algorithms, demonstrates the high accuracy of these models.

Figure 14. Accuracy for NN, ARIMA, ARIMA-LSTM, CNN-LSTM

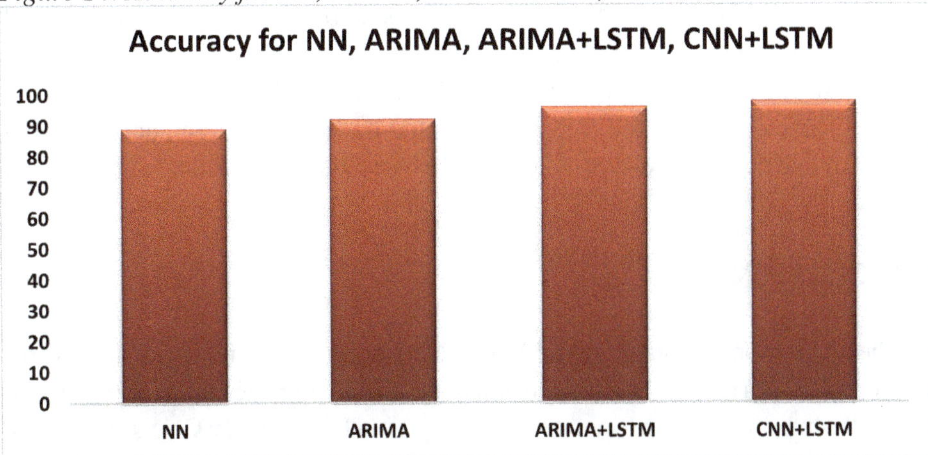

Table 2. Comparison of performances of proposed and existing methods

Performance Metrics	Proposed and Existing Methods			
	NN	ARIMA	ARIMA+LSTM	CNN +LSTM
Accurac (%)	88.5	93.1	95.5	96.9
MSE	0.623	0.551	0.448	0.379
RMSE	0.541	0.512	0.423	0.341

Table 2 depicts the comparison outcomes related to the enactment of other machine learning approaches. The comparison of results shows that CNN-LSTM has high accuracy compared to other existing methods.

Among the methods, CNN-LSTM stands out with the highest accuracy of 97.8%, surpassing ARIMA, ARIMA-LSTM, and NN. CNN-LSTM also exhibits superior predictive performance, boasting the lowest MSE (0.379) and RMSE (0.341) values. ARIMA-LSTM follows closely behind CNN-LSTM, with the second-highest accuracy of 96% and the second-lowest MSE (0.448) and RMSE (0.423). ARIMA performs moderately, with an accuracy of 93.1%, while ARIMA-LSTM and CNN-LSTM outshine it in both MSE and RMSE metrics. NN has the lowest accuracy at 88.5% and the highest MSE and RMSE among the methods, suggesting it is the least accurate for this task. The results emphasize the effectiveness of combining convolutional and recurrent neural networks (CNN-LSTM) for the given prediction task. Lower MSE and RMSE values of CNN-LSTM indicate its ability to minimize prediction errors and provide more accurate forecasts. The proposed NN method lags in accuracy and precision compared to the time-series models and hybrid models (ARIMA, ARIMA-LSTM, CNN-LSTM). Choosing the appropriate model should consider both accuracy and precision metrics, and CNN-LSTM appears to be the most promising method based on the provided results. It's crucial to deliberate the precise characteristics of the data and potential trade-offs between accuracy and computational complexity when selecting the best model for practical applications.

CONCLUSION

The integration of Convolutional Neural Networks (CNN) and Long Short-Term Memory (LSTM) models has demonstrated significant promise in forecasting crime rates. This hybrid approach leverages the strengths of both models: CNNs effectively extract spatial features from crime data, while LSTMs capture temporal patterns. The findings from our study indicate that this combined method significantly outperforms traditional models in both trend analysis and variability prediction of crime rates. With an accuracy rate of 96.9%, the CNN-LSTM model shows superior performance over other existing methods like ARIMA and simple neural networks. Moreover, the inclusion of multiple LSTM layers not only enhances accuracy but also reduces training time, making the model more efficient. These results underscore the potential of advanced neural network architectures in addressing complex prediction tasks, such as crime rate forecasting. Future research will focus on further optimizing the model by fine-tuning its hyperparameters through advanced optimization algorithms, aiming to achieve even higher accuracy and reliability in crime prediction. This study lays a solid foundation for developing robust predictive systems that can assist in proactive crime prevention and effective law enforcement strategies.

REFERENCES

Adamopoulos, I., Valamontes, A., Karantonis, J. T., Tropaitis, P. P., & Syrou, N. (2025). Enhancing Economic Growth Time Series for UAE Forecasting with Deep Learning: A Seq2Seq and Attention-Driven LSTM Approach. *EDRAAK, 2025*, 62–75. DOI: 10.70470/EDRAAK/2025/009

Agarwal, S., Yadav, L., & Thakur, M. K. (2018). "Crime Prediction Based on Statistical Models," 11th. *International Conference on Contemporary Computing, 2018*(IC3), 1–3. DOI: 10.1109/IC3.2018.8530548

Alkattan, H., Al-Nuaimi, B. T., Subhi, A. A., & Turyasingura, B. (2024). Hybrid Model Approaches for Accurate Time Series Predicting of COVID-19 Cases. *Mesopotamian Journal of Artificial Intelligence in Healthcare, 2024*, 170–176. DOI: 10.58496/MJAIH/2024/017

Amirthayogam, G., Kumaran, N., Gopalakrishnan, S., Brito, K., RaviChand, S., & Choubey, S. B. (2024). Integrating Behavioral Analytics and Intrusion Detection Systems to Protect Critical Infrastructure and Smart Cities. *Babylonian Journal of Networking, 2024*, 88–97. DOI: 10.58496/BJN/2024/010

Asad, A. B., Mansur, R., Zawad, S., Evan, N., & Hossain, M. I. (2020) "Analysis of Malware Prediction Based on Infection Rate Using Machine Learning Techniques," IEEE Region 10 Symposium (TENSYMP), Jun. 2020, pp. 706–709, DOI: 10.1109/TENSYMP50017.2020.9230624

Baloian, N., Bassaletti, E., Fernandez, M., Figueroa, O., Fuentes, P., Manasevich, R., Orchard, M., Penafiel, S., Pino, J. A., & Vergara, M. (2017) "Crime Prediction Using Patterns and Context," IEEE 21st International Conference on Computer Supported Cooperative Work in Design (CSCWD), 2017, pp. 2–9, DOI: 10.1109/CSCWD.2017.8066662

Chauhan, C., & Sehgal, S. (2017) "A Review: Crime Analysis Using Data Mining Techniques and Algorithms," *International Conference on Computing, Communication and Automation (ICCCA)*, 2017, pp. 21–25, DOI: 10.1109/CCAA.2017.8229823

Ghankutkar, S., Sarkar, N., Gajbhiye, P., Yadav, S., Kalbande, D., & Bakereywala, N. (2019) "Modelling Machine Learning for Analysing Crime News," International Conference on Advances in Computing, Communication and Control (ICAC3), 2019, pp. 1–5, DOI: 10.1109/ICAC347590.2019.9036769

Hochreiter, S., & Schmidhuber, J. (1997). Long Short-Term Memory. *Neural Computation, 9*(8), 1735–1780. DOI: 10.1162/neco.1997.9.8.1735 PMID: 9377276

Joshi, N., Shaikh, S., Tripathy, A., Sen, S., Janson, J., Karnik, S., & Verghese, B. (2019) "Crime Anatomization Using QGIS," IEEE 5th International Conference for Convergence in Technology (I2CT), 2019, pp. 1–4, DOI: 10.1109/I2CT45611.2019.9033910

Khalaf, M. A., & Steiti, A. (2024). Artificial Intelligence Predictions in Cyber Security: Analysis and Early Detection of Cyber Attacks. *Babylonian Journal of Machine Learning*, *2024*, 63–68. DOI: 10.58496/BJML/2024/006

Khlewee, I., Hamze, K., & Muya, T. (2025). AI in Smart Cities: A Review of Urban Data Processing, Prediction, and Optimization Techniques. *ESTIDAMAA*, *2025*, 29–38. DOI: 10.70470/ESTIDAMAA/2025/004

Kumar, A., Verma, A., Shinde, G., Sukhdeve, Y., & Lal, N. (2020) "Crime Prediction Using K-Nearest Neighboring Algorithm," International Conference on Emerging Trends in Information Technology and Engineering (ic-ETITE), 2020, pp. 1–4, DOI: 10.1109/ic-ETITE47903.2020.155

Manengadan, M., Nandanan, M., & Subash, N. (2021). Crime Data Analysis, Visualization and Prediction Using LSTM. *Databases*, *9*(10), 17. DOI: 10.11648/j.ijdsa.20210703.11

Moamin, S. A. H., Abdulhameed, M. K., Al-Amri, R. M., Radhi, A. D., Naser, R. K., & Pheng, L. G. (2025). Artificial Intelligence in Malware and Network Intrusion Detection: A Comprehensive Survey of Techniques, Datasets, Challenges, and Future Directions. *Babylonian Journal of Artificial Intelligence*, *2025*, 77–98. DOI: 10.58496/BJAI/2025/008

Pratibha, A. G., Uprant, S. D., & Chouhan, L. (2020) "Crime Prediction and Analysis," *2nd International Conference on Data, Engineering and Applications (IDEA)*, 2020, pp. 1–6, DOI: 10.1109/IDEA49133.2020.9170731

Safat, W., Asghar, S., & Gillani, S. A. (2021). Empirical Analysis for Crime Prediction and Forecasting Using Machine Learning and Deep Learning Techniques. *IEEE Access : Practical Innovations, Open Solutions*, *9*, 70080–70094. DOI: 10.1109/ACCESS.2021.3078117

Sandagiri, S. P. C. W., Kumara, B. T. G. S., & Kuhaneswaran, B. (2020) "ANN Based Crime Detection and Prediction Using Twitter Posts and Weather Data," *International Conference on Data Analytics for Business and Industry: Way Towards a Sustainable Economy (ICDABI)*, 2020, pp. 1–5, DOI: 10.1109/ICDABI51230.2020.9325660

Sivanagaleela, B., & Rajesh, S. (2019) "Crime Analysis and Prediction Using Fuzzy C-Means Algorithm," *3rd International Conference on Trends in Electronics and Informatics (ICOEI)*, 2019, pp. 595–599, DOI: 10.1109/ICOEI.2019.8862691

Srividhya, E., Anusuya, J. P. V., Deepthi, K. J., Gopalsamy, P., & Gopalakrishnan, S. (2024). Deep Learning-Driven Disease Prediction System in Cloud Environments Using a Big Data Approach. *EDRAAK, 2024*, 8–17. DOI: 10.70470/EDRAAK/2024/002

Sun, J., ... (2021) "Crimeforecaster: Crime Prediction by Exploiting the Geographical Neighborhoods' Spatiotemporal Dependencies," in Machine Learning and Knowledge Discovery in Databases: Applied Data Science and Demo Track, ECML PKDD 2020, Ghent, Belgium, September 14–18, 2020, Proceedings, Part V, Springer International Publishing, 2021. DOI: 10.1007/978-3-030-67670-4_4

Tarlekar, S., Bhosle, R., D'souza, E., & Sheikh, S. (2021) "Geographical Crime Rate Prediction System," *IEEE India Council International Subsections Conference (INDISCON)*, 2021, pp. 1–6, DOI: 10.1109/INDISCON53343.2021.9582218

Yadav, R., & Sheoran, S. K. (2020). "Autoregressive Model for Multivariate Crime Prediction," in Decision Analytics Applications in Industry, Singapore: Springer. *Nature in Singapore, 2020*, 301–307.

Zaidi, N. A. S., ... (2020) "A Classification Approach for Crime Prediction," in Applied Computing to Support Industry: Innovation and Technology, ACRIT 2019, Ramadi, Iraq, September 15–16, 2019, Revised Selected Papers 1, Springer International Publishing, 2020. DOI: 10.1007/978-3-030-38752-5_6

Chapter 4
An Ensemble Framework for Effective Detection and Classification of Cyber Attacks Using Machine Learning

Naveenkumar Mahamkali
https://orcid.org/0000-0003-4670-1884
SRM University, India

Krishna Siva Prasad Mudigonda
SRM University, India

ABSTRACT

With cyber threats becoming more complex, Cyber-Attack Detection Systems (CADS) are crucial for identifying and preventing attacks. However, traditional methods often fail to detect advanced threats accurately, leading to problems with accuracy, scalability, and reliability. This chapter presents an ensemble-based machine learning framework, referred to Adaptive Weighted Voting Ensemble (AWVE) Model, that leverages the strengths of multiple models to enhance the detection and classification of cyber-attacks. By combining diverse predictive techniques within a unified system, the ensemble approach achieves improved performance, overcoming the shortcomings of individual models. The framework is evaluated using the NSL-KDD dataset, a well-known dataset for network intrusion detection research, to assess its effectiveness in identifying and categorizing various attack types. The

DOI: 10.4018/979-8-3373-1807-3.ch004

2026, IGI Global Scientific Publishing. Copying or distributing in print or electronic forms without written permission of IGI Global Scientific Publishing is prohibited. Use of this chapter to rative artificial intelligence (AI) technologies is expressly prohibited. The publisher reserves all rights to license its use for generative AI training and machine learning model development.

results demonstrate that the ensemble framework achieves superior detection rates and classification accuracy across different attack categories while maintaining low false positive rates.

INTRODUCTION

With the rapid expansion of digital infrastructure and the increasing reliance on online communication, ensuring network security has become an essential requirement for protecting sensitive information and critical systems. Cyber threats have grown in both scale and sophistication, ranging from large-scale Denial-of-Service (DoS) attacks to highly targeted intrusions such as User-to-Root (U2R) and Remote-to-Local (R2L) attacks. As attackers continuously refine their methods, traditional security mechanisms like firewalls and signature-based detection systems struggle to provide sufficient protection against evolving cyber threats. Intrusion Detection Systems (IDS) have emerged as an essential defense mechanism, capable of monitoring network traffic and identifying suspicious activity based on behavioral patterns. However, the effectiveness of IDS depends heavily on their ability to correctly classify various types of attacks, which is often hindered by imbalanced datasets in cybersecurity applications. Modern technological growth that depends on digital infrastructure, cloud computing and Internet of Things (IoT) has created an unprecedented surge of cyber threats. Sophisticated cyber-attacks target numerous organizations and businesses combined with government agencies through malware along with ransomware and phishing schemes. The growing intensity of cyber-attacks requires organizations to implement comprehensive security systems that will both spot and stop and handle such digital threats. Security experts consider the development of Cyber-Attack Detection Systems (CADS) as a vital component of present-day cybersecurity because these systems detect malicious activities prior to causing substantial damage (Kavitha, Alphonse, & Reddy, 2019; Urmi, Uddin, Uddin, Talukder, Hasan, Paul, & Imran, 2024). Various organizations need to develop quick security answers for identifying sophisticated attacks happening in real time (Ismail, El Mrabet, & Reza, 2022; Pinto, Herrera, Donoso, & Gutierrez, 2024).

Traditional intrusion detection systems (IDS) systems include two fundamental detection methods namely signature-based detection and anomaly-based detection (Alshuaibi et al., 2025) and (Gampel & Eveleigh, 2025). In general, the detection systems operate by examining traffic patterns against established harmful files in database repositories thus achieving high success rates for discovering existing security breaches. The systems in common face difficulty in recognizing both unknown zero-day vulnerabilities and fresh attack versions (Sajid, Malik, Almogren, Malik, Khan, Tanveer, & Rehman, 2024). Detection through anomalies creates reference points of standard network activities before marking abnormal behavior as possible security threats. The detection system produces numerous unnecessary alerts coupled with administrative workloads because of its tendency to trigger false positive readings (Bakhsh, Khan, Ahmed, Alshehri, Ali, & Ahmad, 2023). Current cyber threats resist effective mitigation through security tools that include firewalls combined with signature-based antivirus as well as rule-based IDS devices. Present day attacking practices for creating security bypass methods force organizations to implement detection systems that analyze behavioral patterns to immediately identify and fight threats. Organization-wide security detection requires advancement to better adaptive security technologies due to existing method restrictions. The machine learning (ML) and artificial intelligence (AI) models bring revolutionary power to cybersecurity through their ability to improve detection abilities via automated analysis of data and predictive modelling together with anomaly detection systems (Ali, 2024) and (Alsahaim & Maayah, 2023). Modern CADS heavily depends on these technologies because they enable large-scale network traffic analysis along with sophisticated pattern detection and effective attack classification (Pinto et al., 2024).

In real-world network security datasets such as NSL-KDD (Hassan06, n.d.) and CIC-IDS2017 (Canadian Institute for Cybersecurity, n.d.), the distribution of attack types is often highly skewed. While certain attack categories, such as DoS attacks, have a large number of instances, others, such as U2R and R2L attacks, occur much less frequently (Alshinwan et al., 2025) and (Albinhamad et al., 2025). This class imbalance poses a significant challenge for machine learning-based IDS, as most traditional classifiers tend to be biased toward the majority class. Consequently, models trained on such datasets often achieve high overall accuracy but fail to correctly identify minority-class attacks, which are often the most critical from a security perspective. Standard classification algorithms, including Naïve Bayes, K-Nearest Neighbors (KNN), Logistic Regression, and Decision Trees, exhibit varied performance across different attack types, with some being more effective at recognizing specific attacks while struggling with others.

To overcome these challenges, we propose an Adaptive Weighted Voting Ensemble (AWVE) Model, which intelligently integrates multiple classifiers and dynamically assigns adaptive weights based on their F1-score performance. Unlike conventional ensemble methods, where all classifiers contribute equally, AWVE ensures that models with higher classification reliability for specific attack types receive greater influence in the final decision-making process. This approach enhances overall detection performance while also improving the identification of minority-class attacks, making it highly effective for real-world intrusion detection systems (IDS).

In this chapter, we provide a comprehensive analysis of different classification models applied to the NSL-KDD dataset, highlighting their strengths and weaknesses through confusion matrix evaluations. By examining their ability to detect various attack categories, we demonstrate the importance of leveraging multiple classifiers to address the inherent limitations of individual models. Furthermore, we introduce and evaluate the proposed AWVE model, showcasing its effectiveness in improving both accuracy and minority-class detection rates. Through extensive experimentation, we establish AWVE as a promising adaptive ensemble approach for cybersecurity applications, offering a more balanced and robust intrusion detection system capable of handling class imbalance in network security datasets. The summary of the contributions of this chapter are as follows.

1. Proposal of the AWVE Model – A novel ensemble learning approach that assigns adaptive weights to classifiers based on their F1-score performance, ensuring that models with higher reliability contribute more to the final prediction.
2. Handling Class Imbalance in IDS – Demonstrates how AWVE improves the detection of minority-class attacks (e.g., R2L and U2R) by leveraging classifiers that perform well on underrepresented attack types, unlike traditional majority voting methods.
3. Extensive Performance Evaluation – We conduct a detailed confusion matrix analysis on the NSL-KDD-FULL and NSL-KDD-SUB datasets, highlighting the strengths and weaknesses of individual classifiers and how AWVE effectively integrates them to enhance overall detection accuracy.
4. Comparative Study of Classification Models – Evaluates Naïve Bayes, KNN, Logistic Regression, Decision Trees, and other machine learning models, demonstrating their specific advantages in recognizing different attack categories.
5. Improved Intrusion Detection Accuracy – The proposed AWVE model achieves 76.33% accuracy, outperforming individual classifiers and providing a more balanced and effective approach for real-world cybersecurity applications.

This chapter is organized as follows. The beginning part includes a brief overview which defines the rising complexity of cyber threats and describes the difficulties associated with class imbalance in intrusion detection datasets. A subsequent section of related work examines past intrusion detection systems while identifying weaknesses of standard classification frameworks and ensemble solutions regarding unbalanced attack datasets. In the proposed method section, the AWVE model gets introduced while describing its essential elements which include adaptive weight computation and weighted voting approaches. Detailed information about the experimental design then follows which covers the selected dataset alongside the feature selection approach along with performance assessment metrics along with descriptions of applied machine learning models. The results section uses confusion matrices to compare how single classifiers perform on attack types while showing how AWVE merges separate model skills to optimize detection precision. The concluding section summarizes the study results by demonstrating AWVE's value in optimizing intrusion detection along with future research recommendations for cybersecurity framework improvement.

1. RELATED WORKS

The field of cybersecurity research examines IDS technology critically because machine learning and ensemble learning methods focus on better detection results. Advanced IDS models became essential because of escalating cyber threats and their increased complexity and volume that requires models to handle class imbalance issues and adapt their classification strategy. This section reviews key approaches in intrusion detection, highlighting traditional machine learning methods, ensemble learning techniques, and the role of adaptive weighting in classifier selection.

Healthcare organizations are facing more cybersecurity challenges since they depend increasingly on Internet of Things implementations. A healthcare application authentication protocol emerges in research by Kavitha et al. (2019). The main purpose behind this system involves the implementation of lightweight cryptographic methods to achieve better data integrity along with enhanced security protection. An optimization of authentication protocols enables this system to operate with high efficiency while ensuring complete security measures. This security system (Kavitha et al., 2019) provides protected communication between healthcare IoT devices through efficiency-driven operations. The adopted authentication framework implements elliptic curve cryptography combined with key exchange protocols that provides resistance to standard cryptographic threats including man-in-the-middle and unauthorized penetration attempts.

The cryptographic system described in (Kavitha et al., 2019) improves authentication efficiency yet it includes some important practical limitations. The security offers lightweight capabilities but remains limited in use by IoT devices which have very restricted computational resources. A wide range of real-world testing across IoT healthcare environments is missing from the implementation presentation which creates doubts about its ability to scale properly. The research field demands resolution of potential security threats affecting decentralized IoT network key management. The scientists tested the system by using real-time clinical data to represent medical IoT network operations. The data collections originated from IoT-based hospital networks that used multiple interconnected devices to transmit encrypted patient information. The proposed framework demonstrated security improvement capabilities by showing effective performance results including encryption time, decryption time and authentication success rates and computational overhead which did not negatively impact system performance.

The research by Urmi et al. (2024) analyzes ensemble learning strategies in cybersecurity through intrusion detection methods for network security systems. The study presents a stacked ensemble classification framework which integrates the combination of Random Forest, XGBoost and Extra Tree together with a Logistic Regression meta-model. The main goal establishes better cyber-attack detection performance by taking advantage of various individual classifier capabilities. Users achieved improved classification accuracy after the authors applied various feature selection methods to their high-dimensional datasets for identifying significant features which reduced computational complexity. The ensemble model exhibits superior performance than standalone classifiers according to experimental tests which demonstrates its strength as a reliable cyber threat detection system for brute-force attacks together with infiltration attempts and web-based exploits. Despite its robust performance, the model has several limitations (Urmi et al., 2024). Ensemble models demand increased computing resources since they consume more processing power than basic machine learning techniques do. Real-time intrusion detection systems experiencing longer delays present a critical obstacle because of high-speed requirements. Feature selection effectiveness depends heavily on dataset characteristics which indicates the model would show limited generalization in absolutely new cyber-attack datasets during retraining. This study employs the dataset combination of CIC-IDS2017 and NSL-KDD for performance evaluation purposes. Performance evaluation for the model occurs through labeled network traffic datasets that contain both normal and attack operational data.

The fundamental components of Internet of Things (IoT) rely on Wireless Sensor Networks which experience various cyber threats stemming from their resource-limited structure and dispersed system configuration. Ismail et al. (2022) presented an ensemble detection system that enhances security protection in WSNs through automated detection framework selection. A detection system known as the Weighted Score Selector (WSS) performs dynamic algorithm selection that picks the most suitable machine learning classifier from a pool to optimize performance through real-time data evaluation. Because of its minimal size WSS represents a secure deployment framework for scarce resource WSN deployments. The system employs an automatic decision-making process to pick the right classifier which produces optimal detection results without requiring excessive processing power consumption. Does better than conventional ensemble methods including boosting, bagging and stacking because it shows improved accuracy and better performance in false alarm reduction for anomaly detection. Real-time deployment of the model becomes difficult because it depends on supervised learning methods which need predefined dataset labels when working in highly dynamic environments. The study employs the WSN-DS dataset (Almomani, Al-Kasasbeh, & Al-Akhras, 2016) for model evaluation. A set of data samples analyzed contains various denial-of-service

(DoS) attacks known as Grayhole, Blackhole and Flooding. The WSS model reached promising results in safeguarding WSN-based IoT networks when analyzed for its performance metrics which include accuracy detection probability and processing time.

The new target for cyber adversaries is critical infrastructures where they seek to exploit the vulnerabilities present in both industrial control systems (ICS) and IIoT environments. Pinto et al. (2024) established an application which uses unsupervised learning algorithms to increase anomaly detection capability in CIs. The method enables the detection of zero-day attacks through an analytics system that does not require labeled training information. Training occurs exclusively using operational data that belongs to expected conditions, so the model develops capability to detect irregularities in system behavior. The system works exceptionally well in factory environments because cyberattacks frequently imitate typical system activities. The Kullback–Leibler divergence addition to the model allows it to detect anomalies in industrial system data effectively because it understands the non-Gaussian statistical patterns. The framework (Pinto et al., 2024) demonstrates various benefits, but its major hurdle concerns computational complexity problems. The accuracy of unsupervised models could be improved by refining their approach because such methods generate significantly more false positives than supervised learning methods do. Evaluation of the model takes place through examination of real-world water treatment plant data found in the Secure Water Treatment (SWAT) dataset.

Bakhsh et al. (2023) introduces an Intrusion Detection System built with deep learning for IoT network protection because these interconnected systems face escalating cyber threats because of their restricted processing power. Research uses CIC-IoT22 dataset to evaluate the system because this benchmark has established itself as a standard measure for assessing IoT security. This methodology stands out for its capability to monitor genuine time network operations and their sequential sequence. The operational requirements for deep learning models include substantial computing resources because implementation remains challenging for real-time applications within IoT environments. The system's ability to work effectively on various IoT networks is limited because it uses only the CIC-IoT22 dataset.

Sajid et al. (2024) established a security system through machine learning and deep learning hybridization to boost cyber-attack recognition. The system employs Extreme Gradient Boosting (XGBoost) for feature selection, Convolutional Neural Networks (CNN) for feature extraction, and Long Short-Term Memory (LSTM) for final classification. Using XGBoost and CNN together produces benefits by eliminating feature overlapping and increasing performance with the ability to process spatial dependencies in network traffic data. LSTM operates as a sequential data processor which allows the system to detect cyber-attack patterns effectively. The model undergoes validation tests through CIC-IDS2017 along with UNSW-NB15

(Moustafa & Slay, 2015) and NSL-KDD and WSN-DS datasets which provide broad evaluation of system performance across multiple network domains. Through this approach intrusion detection systems achieve outstanding accuracy performance while omitting few unnecessary alarms which are commonly noted as false positives. The use of deep learning models for security operations generates excessive computing requirements thus preventing real-time application in constrained environments. Hyperparameter tuning for this approach requires significant time investments because achievement of optimal performance relies on thorough adjustments. Acquiring suitable training datasets is challenging for the model because dependent labeled data is essential to its functioning.

The review by Liu, Shi, Chen, and Lu (2024) examines machine learning approaches for network anomaly detection and security defense by studying multiple applications of cybersecurity. Research classification places intrusion detection systems into signature-based and anomaly-based and hybrid models then analyzes their practical implementation success rates. The implementation of Support Vector Machines (SVM), Random Forest (RF) and Neural Networks (NN) increases the potential for detecting cyber threats because these models improve their adaptability capabilities as well as scalability potential. This research article uses extensive detail to show how machine learning algorithms should become resilient against adversarial attacks and need explainable features to function in security settings. The paper lacks concrete recommendations regarding a selected intrusion detection system and thus remains primarily theoretical instead of practical. The analysis solely depends on literature reviews along with comparative analysis without including empirical evaluations. The analysis falls short because it does not conduct direct algorithm performance tests that could have demonstrated their practical implementation capabilities. The study examines model interpretation and adversarial robustness yet fails to present actual solutions to defend against adversarial assaults because this represents an upcoming research frontier.

The work by Khraisat, Gondal, Vamplew, and Kamruzzaman (2019) presents an extensive survey about intrusion detection systems that categorize them as Signature-based IDS (SIDS) and Anomaly-based IDS (AIDS). The research investigates multiple machine learning and data mining methods used in IDS creation by evaluating their capabilities and weaknesses. This comprehensive survey gives researchers in cybersecurity access to numerous IDS methodologies as a major benefit. The importance of hybrid IDS methods appears in the research because these methods combine signature-based detection with anomaly-based detection techniques to increase accuracy. The document examines typical evasion methods employed by attackers to avoid IDS systems to inform better security practices. The study presents some restrictions in terms of its scope. The paper presents a conceptual discussion about IDS without experimental evaluations of the examined methods thus taking on a theoretical nature after excluding empirical analysis. Most of the research data points to older security datasets including KDD-Cup 99 and DARPA 1999 to analyze current cyber threats which might produce inaccurate conclusions. The paper failure includes its lack of recommended implementations to solve the mentioned intrusion detection challenges since it presents only a list of identified problems.

Network security applications benefit from the supervised learning methods Support Vector Machines (SVM), Decision Trees (DT) and K-Nearest Neighbors (KNN) as reported in (Kilincer, Ertam, & Sengur, 2021). The Naïve Bayes approach demonstrates effective probabilistic attack detection capability while Decision Trees together with Random Forests present interpretable classification rules to users (Kilincer et al., 2021; Panda & Patra, 2007; Fouladi, Kayatas, & Anarim, 2016). Single classifiers fail to maintain balanced detection across the entire range of attacks especially when working with NSL-KDD datasets with its imbalanced nature. Ensemble methods resolve individual classifier weaknesses by uniting multiple models to achieve better prediction quality and system resistance against errors. The most popular ensemble methods include Majority voting, Bagging, Boosting and Stacking (Tama & Lim, 2021; Kumar, Thakur, & Ayyagari, 2020). Bagging-based models such as Random Forest have been widely adopted due to their ability to reduce variance and improve classification stability. Meanwhile, Boosting techniques like XGBoost and AdaBoost focus on misclassified samples to enhance detection rates. The performance of intrusion detection becomes stronger under ensemble learning but most current approaches use identical weight values for each classifier leading to suboptimal voting decisions.

Class imbalance is another major challenge in IDS, where certain attacks (e.g., Denial-of-Service (DoS)) dominate the dataset while others (e.g., User-to-Root (U2R)) have very few samples. Several techniques have been explored to handle this issue. One of the most common strategies for addressing class imbalance in Intrusion Detection Systems (IDS) is through data-level techniques, which modify the dataset before training the model. These techniques are oversampling and under-sampling. The goal of these methods is to equalize major and minority class distributions to prevent machine learning models from showing preference toward dominant attack types. The Synthetic Minority Over-sampling Technique (SMOTE) has become a standard approach for oversampling due to its method of creating synthetic points through minority class interpolation (Alfrhan, Alhusain, & Khan, 2020; Al-Qarni & Al-Asmari, 2024). SMOTE produces synthetic examples inside the feature space so models get better generalization capabilities instead of basic data copy. The main drawback of applying oversampling techniques stems from their tendency to generate improper features and models with weakened generalization abilities. Synthetic data formed through artificial generation causes models to discover patterns that diverge from actual attack behaviors thus leading to false alarms during intrusion detection. Under sampling works by decreasing the majority class instances to match when compared to the minority class instances. The data becomes balanced through this approach because removing extra majority-class examples helps the model avoid preference for more frequently occurring attack types. Random Undersampling (RUS) uses random selection to delete majority-class samples yet advanced techniques including Tomek Links (Mbow, Koide, & Sakurai, 2022; Deb, Rodrigo, & Kumar, 2024) and Edited Nearest Neighbors (ENN) (Hattori & Takahashi, 2000) delete minority-class samples based on their contribution to decision boundaries. By undersampling data the main disadvantage becomes that it deletes valuable information which could provide essential patterns necessary for accurate intrusion detection.

The implementation of either oversampling or undersampling methods to balance class distributions produces unique disadvantages. The risk of model overfitting rises because synthetic sample generation might neglect genuine attack patterns while undersampling diminishes usable data quantity including important attack signals. These approaches prove challenging to implement for NSL-KDD datasets because they contain highly imbalanced attack categories including rare occurrences like User-to-Root (U2R) and Remote-to-Local (R2L) intrusions. The researchers have investigated cost-sensitive learning together with ensemble techniques to address the impact of class imbalance problems in their databases (Telikani & Gandomi, 2021; Telikani, Rudbardeh, Soleymanpour, Shahbahrami, Shen, Gaydadjiev, & Hassanpour, 2023). Existing research demonstrates that machine learning and ensemble models significantly improve IDS performance, but challenges remain in handling class imbalance and optimizing voting mechanisms. The detection capabilities of Boosting and Bagging techniques remain effective for attack detection yet they lack automatic model contribution management. Weighted voting represents a promising approach for solutions in IDS yet previous research mostly employed fixed weights instead of adaptable mechanisms. This chapter builds upon previous research by introducing AWVE, a novel ensemble model that dynamically assigns classifier weights based on F1-score performance, ensuring better detection rates for minority-class intrusions.

2. PROPOSED METHOD

In general, Network security datasets often exhibit significant class imbalance, where certain attack categories have far fewer instances compared to others. This imbalance poses a serious challenge for Intrusion Detection Systems (IDS), as machine learning models tend to favor the majority class, leading to poor detection of minority-class attacks.

To address class imbalance, conventional approaches rely on data-level techniques such as oversampling and under-sampling, as well as algorithm-level modifications like cost-sensitive learning and ensemble methods. Oversampling techniques such as Synthetic Minority Over-sampling Technique (SMOTE) generate synthetic samples to increase the representation of minority classes, whereas undersampling reduces the number of majority-class instances to create a balanced dataset. However, these methods can introduce noise or lead to loss of critical information. Cost-sensitive learning assigns higher penalties for misclassifying minority classes, encouraging the model to focus on rare attacks, while ensemble methods like AdaBoost and Balanced Random Forest improve classification by dynamically adjusting sample weights during training. Despite these efforts, many existing techniques still struggle to achieve optimal performance when dealing with highly imbalanced network traffic.

In this section, we explain the proposed ensemble method, referred to as Adaptive Weighted Voting Ensemble (AWVE) Model, to enhance intrusion detection in network security.

2.1. Adaptive Weighted Voting Ensemble (AWVE) Model

We introduce the Adaptive Weighted Voting Ensemble (AWVE) Model, a novel approach designed to improve intrusion detection in network security by dynamically adjusting classifier contributions based on their performance. Traditional ensemble learning techniques, such as majority voting, treat all classifiers equally by assigning them uniform weights. However, this approach can lead to suboptimal performance, as weaker classifiers are given the same influence as stronger classifiers, potentially reducing the overall effectiveness of the model.

To overcome this limitation, the AWVE model dynamically adjusts the contribution of each classifier based on its performance using F1-score-based adaptive weighting. Instead of assigning equal importance to all classifiers, the proposed approach intelligently prioritizes those with higher accuracy and recall, as they exhibit greater reliability in distinguishing between normal and attack traffic. By dynamically adjusting the influence of each classifier, this method ensures that models with superior predictive capabilities contribute more significantly to the final decision-making process. This weighted approach enhances the overall classification performance by allowing stronger classifiers to have a greater voting power, making the ensemble model more effective in detecting both majority and minority class attacks.

Conversely, classifiers that demonstrate lower performance, such as those with reduced recall or increased misclassification rates, have a diminished impact on the final prediction. This prevents weak classifiers from introducing noise into the decision-making process and reduces the risk of incorrect classifications. By incorporating adaptive weighting, the method ensures that the final ensemble decision is driven by the most reliable classifiers, leading to improved detection accuracy, particularly in imbalanced datasets where certain attack types are underrepresented. This strategic weighting mechanism optimizes model performance and strengthens the robustness of the intrusion detection system. By leveraging this adaptive weighting mechanism, the proposed method improves classification accuracy, particularly for detecting minority-class attacks that are often misclassified in traditional ensemble methods.

This approach not only enhances intrusion detection rates but also optimizes decision-making by utilizing the strengths of multiple classifiers in a more intelligent and data-driven manner. The AWVE model is particularly effective in handling class imbalances in datasets such as NSL-KDD, where certain attack types (e.g., Remote-to-Local (R2L) and User-to-Root (U2R)) are underrepresented. By prioritizing classifier reliability rather than uniform voting, our proposed method significantly improves detection capabilities, reduces false alarms, and strengthens cybersecurity defenses. The proposed AWVE model is represented in Algorithm 1. The AWVE algorithm consists of four key steps: preprocessing, adaptive weight computation, weighted voting, and final prediction generation. In the preprocessing phase, multiple classifiers are trained using the given dataset and stored for inference. This allows the ensemble to leverage the strengths of diverse machine learning models. Once trained, each classifier is evaluated on the test dataset, and its F1-score is computed as a measure of its effectiveness. These scores are then normalized to derive adaptive weights, ensuring that classifiers demonstrating higher reliability in intrusion detection contribute more significantly to the final classification decision. The weight for each classifier h_i is computed as shown in Equation 1, where $F1_i$ represents the F1-score of classifiers h_i and N is the total number of classifiers in the ensemble. The normalization ensures that the sum of all classifier weights equals 1, allowing a balanced yet adaptive influence of each model.

Algorithm 1: Adaptive Weighted Voting Ensemble (AWVE)

Input:

- Trained classifiers $\{h_1, h_2, ..., h_N\}$
- Test set X_test
- True labels y_test (only used for performance evaluation)

Output:

- Predicted class labels $\{\hat{y}_1, \hat{y}_2, ..., \hat{y}_M\}$ for M test samples

Step 1: Preprocessing

a) Train multiple classifiers on the training data.
b) Store the trained classifiers for inference.

Step 2: Compute Adaptive Weights for Classifiers

a) Evaluate each trained classifier on X_test and compute its F1-score.
b) Normalize the F1-scores to obtain adaptive weights:
c) For each classifier h_i:

$$w_i = \frac{F1_i}{\sum_{j=1}^{N} F1_j} \quad (1)$$

Step 3: Perform Weighted Voting for Classification

$$\hat{y} = \arg\max_{c \in \text{ClassLabels}} \sum_{i=1}^{N} w_i \times 1(h_i(x) == c) \quad (2)$$

Step 4: Output Final Predictions

a) Return predicted labels $\{\hat{y}_1, \hat{y}_2, ..., \hat{y}_M\}$ for all test instances.

End Algorithm

Once the adaptive weights are determined, weighted voting is performed for each test instance. Instead of using a simple majority vote, where each classifier contributes equally, the AWVE algorithm aggregates weighted votes to determine the most likely class. The final predicted label $\hat{y}$ is computed as described in Equation 2, where $1(h_i(x)==c)$ is an indicator function, returning 1 if classifier h_i predicts class c and 0 otherwise. The class label with the highest aggregated weighted vote is selected as the final prediction for each test instance. The final step of the AWVE algorithm is to return the predicted class labels for all test instances. This method effectively balances classifier contributions, preventing weaker classifiers from negatively impacting performance while ensuring that minority-class attacks are not overshadowed by majority-class predictions. By incorporating F1-score-based adaptive weighting, AWVE significantly enhances intrusion detection performance, particularly in datasets where class imbalance is a major challenge.

The proposed AWVE model is well-suited for real-world intrusion detection systems, as it optimally combines multiple machine learning models, enhances detection rates for underrepresented attack categories, and improves overall classification robustness. The ability to adaptively prioritize high-performing classifiers makes it a highly efficient and reliable approach for network security applications.

2.2. Classifier Selection and Training

The performance of the proposed ensemble framework heavily depends on the chosen base classifiers because different models possess distinct capabilities to detect various network intrusions. The proposed Adaptive Weighted Voting Ensemble (AWVE) Model uses five base classifiers consisting of Support Vector Machine, Naïve Bayes, K-Nearest Neighbors (KNN) along with Logistic Regression and Decision Tree because they provide diverse attack detection capabilities for all categories in the NSL-KDD dataset. Each classifier is chosen based on its ability to recognize specific types of attacks:

- *Naïve Bayes:* It is a probabilistic classifier, which effectively detects rare attacks including Remote-to-Local (R2L) and User-to-Root (U2R) intrusions. This classification algorithm uses independence assumptions for its features while delivering efficient computation when detecting anomalies.
- *K-Nearest Neighbors (KNN)*: KNN optimizes the classification of normal traffic through its similarity algorithms that measure distance between input data. The model provides effective analysis of normal traffic versus attack traffic however its performance diminishes when processing large datasets.
- *Logistic Regression (LR):* Logistic Regression functions as a linear classifier to identify Probe attacks, which involve network scanning and reconnaissance activities. Its ability to model decision boundaries effectively makes it useful in distinguishing subtle attack behaviors.
- *Decision Tree (DT):* Using Decision Trees ensures the determination of Denial-of-Service (DoS) attacks due to their robust rule-based classification

method. Decision rules captured by this approach enable high data efficiency with easy interpretation as well as complex decision rule acceptance.

Each classifier is trained separately using the NSL-KDD dataset, following a series of preprocessing steps to ensure data consistency and model efficiency. The detailed process of model training and hyperparameter tuning for individual classifiers is provided in Section 4.5. It is important to note that model training is conducted on both the NSL-KDD-FULL dataset, which contains a comprehensive set of training samples, and the NSL-KDD-SUB dataset, a reduced subset used for comparative evaluation. The trained models are then tested on the NSL-KDD-TEST dataset, ensuring a fair and unbiased assessment of their intrusion detection capabilities.

3. EXPERIMENTAL RESULTS AND DISCUSSION

The experiments were conducted using two distinct variants of the NSL-KDD dataset provided for analysis. The first variant, referred to as NSL-KDD-FULL, represents the complete training set, containing all available training samples. The second variant, known as NSL-KDD-SUB, is a 20% subset of the full training set and is separately provided within the dataset for experimentation with a reduced training size. This subset allows for evaluating model performance with a reduced training size while maintaining the dataset's inherent characteristics. Additionally, the dataset includes a predefined testing set, referred to NSL-KDD-TEST, which serves as the designated test set for evaluating model generalization. The presence of a separate test set ensures a fair and unbiased assessment of model performance by preventing data leakage between the training and testing phases.

3.1. Experimental Setup

The experiments were conducted on a computing system equipped with an Intel Core i5 processor, ensuring efficient handling of computational tasks and machine learning workloads. The system had 8GB of RAM, which provided sufficient memory for data preprocessing, model training, and evaluation. The implementation was carried out using Python 3.9, a widely used programming language for data science and machine learning applications due to its extensive ecosystem of libraries and ease of use. The data preprocessing and manipulation tasks were handled using Pandas and NumPy, which facilitated structured data organization, feature extraction, and numerical computations. Scikit-learn, a comprehensive machine learning library, was used for training and evaluating various models, performing feature selection, and optimizing hyperparameters. Additionally, Matplotlib was employed for visualizing data distributions, model performance metrics, and comparative analysis, aiding in better interpretation of the experimental results.

3.2. NSL-KDD dataset

The NSL-KDD dataset (Hassan06, n.d.) is an improved version of the widely used KDD Cup 1999 dataset, designed for evaluating intrusion detection systems (IDS). The original KDD dataset had several issues, such as redundant records and excessive duplicate instances, which could lead to biased machine learning models. The NSL-KDD dataset addresses these limitations by reducing redundancy and providing a more realistic benchmark for intrusion detection research. The dataset consists of network traffic records, each representing a connection with 41 extracted features, categorized into basic connection attributes (e.g., duration, protocol_type, service, flag), content-based features (e.g.,wrong_fragment, hot), traffic-based features (e.g., dst_host_ srv_rerror_rate), and host-based features. These features collectively capture the characteristics of network traffic and help in distinguishing between normal and attack patterns. Each record in the NSL-KDD dataset is assigned a label that classifies it as either normal network traffic or belonging to one of several predefined cyberattack categories. These labels help in distinguishing between benign and malicious network activity, making the dataset suitable for training and evaluating intrusion detection systems. The attacks in the dataset are further categorized into different types based on their behavior and impact on the network. A detailed breakdown of these attack categories is provided in Table 1, which presents a structured classification of the various types of network intrusions present in the dataset.

Table 1. Classification of Attacks in the NSL-KDD Dataset: Major Categories and their Subcategories

Attack Category	Subcategories
Normal	normal
DoS (Denial of Service)	back, land, neptune, pod, smurf, teardrop
Probe (Information Gathering)	satan, ipsweep, nmap, portsweep
R2L (Remote to Local)	warezclient, guess_passwd, ftp_write, imap, multihop, phf, spy, warezmaster
U2R (User to Root)	buffer_overflow, loadmodule, rootkit

Fig. 1 provides a detailed visualization of the distribution of samples across various attack categories in the NSL-KDD-FULL dataset, illustrating the overall composition of normal and attack instances. Similarly, Fig. 2 presents the number of samples corresponding to different attack categories in the NSL-KDD-SUB dataset. These visualizations highlight potential class imbalances, which play a crucial role in evaluating the performance of machine learning models. Analyzing these distributions helps in understanding the prevalence of different attack types and their impact on intrusion detection system effectiveness. Table 2 provides a comprehensive summary of the datasets used in this study, highlighting key characteristics such as the total number of extracted features and the total number of data samples available for analysis.

The column labelled "#Features" represents the total number of attributes present in each dataset. These features include both numerical and categorical attributes that contribute to the classification process. The column labelled "#Samples" indicates the total number of records within each dataset. Similarly, the column labelled "#Classes" represents the number of classes present in each dataset. This summary provides valuable insights into the dataset structure, aiding in the development and assessment of intrusion detection models. Fig. 3 provides a comprehensive visualization of the distribution of samples across various attack categories in the NSL-KDD-TEST dataset. It helps for assessing how well a model generalizes across diverse attack scenarios in the NSL-KDD-TEST dataset.

Figure 1. Number of instances per class in NSL-KDD-FULL dataset

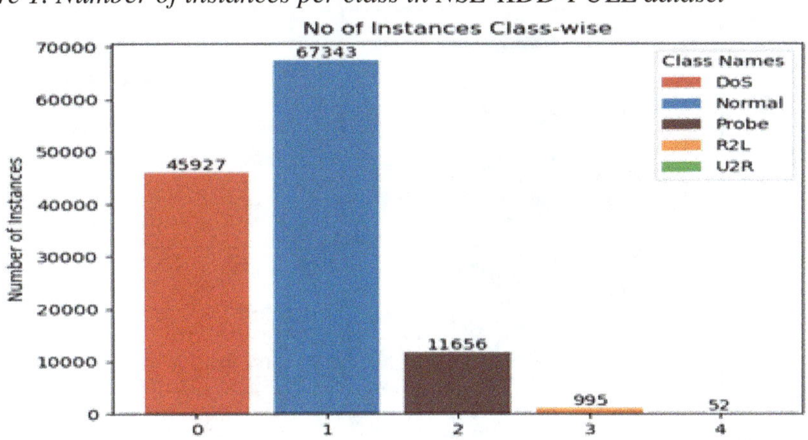

Figure 2. Number of instances per class in NSL-KDD-SUB dataset

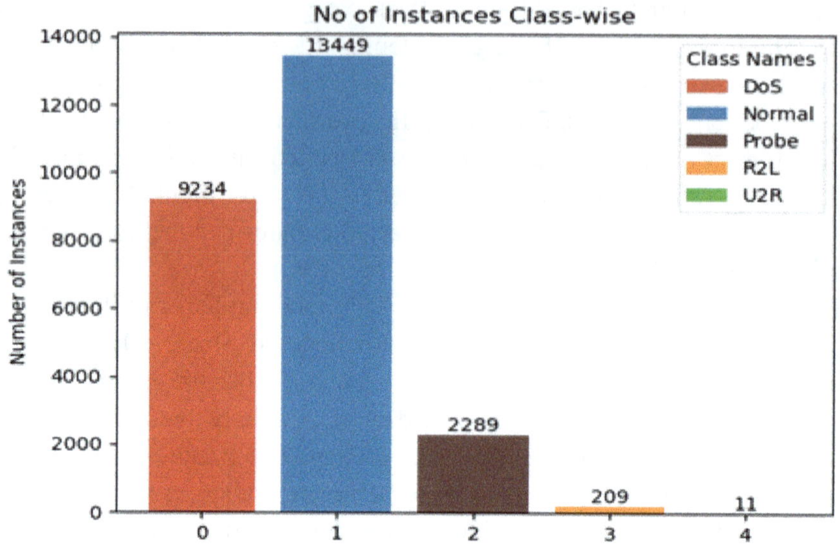

Figure 3. Number of instances per class in NSL-KDD-TEST dataset

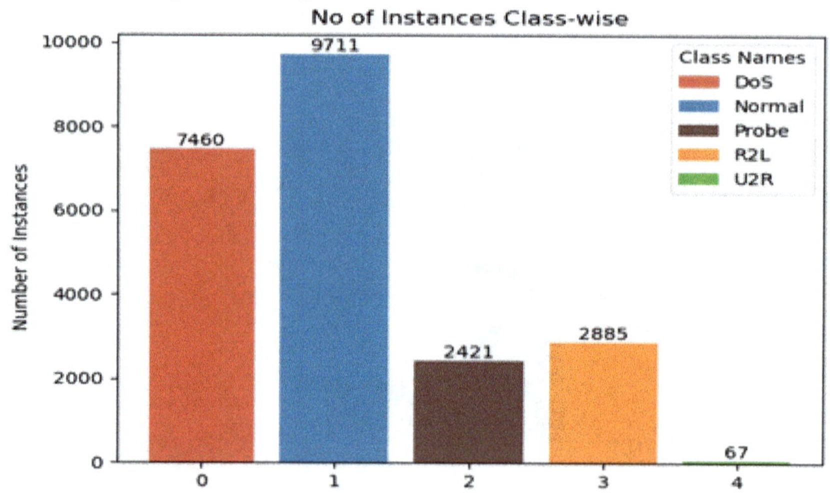

Table 2. The details of the datasets used in the experimental analysis

S. No	Dataset	#Samples	#Features	#Classes
1	NSL-KDD-FULL	125973	41	5
2	NSL-KDD-SUB	25192	41	5
3	NSL-KDD-TEST	22544	41	5

3.3. Evaluation Metrics

Performance evaluation plays a crucial role in assessing the effectiveness of any classification algorithm in machine learning. A well-defined evaluation framework ensures that the model not only achieves high accuracy but also generalizes well to unseen data, avoiding issues such as overfitting or biased predictions. In this chapter, a comprehensive set of performance metrics was employed to rigorously evaluate the proposed method. These metrics were selected to provide insights into various aspects of model performance, including classification accuracy, the balance between precision and recall, the ability to distinguish between different classes, and overall robustness across varying distributions of data. By leveraging these evaluation techniques, we aim to present a thorough and objective analysis of the proposed model's effectiveness in detecting and classifying network intrusions.

Since the NSL-KDD dataset exhibits a highly imbalanced class distribution, relying solely on accuracy as an evaluation metric can be misleading. A model may achieve high accuracy by predominantly classifying the majority class correctly while failing to detect minority-class attacks, such as User-to-Root (U2R) and Remote-to-Local (R2L) intrusions, which have significantly fewer samples. This imbalance can result in an inflated accuracy score, despite poor detection of rare but critical security threats.

To provide a more comprehensive evaluation of the Adaptive Weighted Voting Ensemble (AWVE) Model for intrusion detection, we incorporate weighted metrics such as Precision, Recall, and F1-score. Precision measures how many of the detected attacks are true attacks, ensuring that the model minimizes false positives, which is crucial in cybersecurity applications to avoid unnecessary alerts. Recall, on the other hand, evaluates the model's ability to correctly identify all actual attack instances, making it a vital metric for detecting minority-class intrusions that may otherwise be overlooked. F1-score, which is the harmonic mean of Precision and Recall, serves as a balanced metric that accounts for both false positives and false negatives, providing a more realistic measure of model performance in an imbalanced dataset scenario. By prioritizing these weighted performance metrics, we ensure that the AWVE model is not only effective in classifying majority-class traffic but also capable of accurately identifying rare and sophisticated cyber threats, leading to a more robust and reliable intrusion detection system.

1. **Accuracy**: The model's accuracy refers to predicting outcomes or categorising data points correctly. This metric is commonly used when evaluating the performance of classification models. It can be computed using Equation 1.

$$\text{Accuracy} = \frac{\textit{Number of Correct Predictions}}{\textit{Total Number of Predictions}} \tag{1}$$

2. **Precision**: The precision for class i is computed using Equation 2.

$$\text{Precision}\left(\text{Pi}\right) = \frac{TP_i}{TP_i + FP_i} \tag{2}$$

Here, TP_i and FP_i are True positives and False positives of class i.

3. **Recall**: Recall, also called as sensitivity. It measures a model's ability to identify positive instances in a dataset correctly. It is calculated as per Equation 3. This metric indicates how effectively a model can detect true positive cases, such as instances of a particular plant disease in this context.

$$\text{Recall}\left(\text{R}\right) = \frac{TP_i}{TP_i + FN_i} \tag{3}$$

Here, TP_i and FN_i are True positives and False negatives of class i.

4. **F1-Score**: The F1 Score for class i is calculated based on the formula provided in Equation 4.

$$\text{F1 - Score}\left(\text{F1}\right) = \frac{2 \times Precision_i \times Recall_i}{Precision_i + Recall_i} \tag{4}$$

To enhance the evaluation of the Adaptive Weighted Voting Ensemble (AWVE) Model for intrusion detection, we utilize weighted metrics, including Precision, Recall, and F1-score, for a more comprehensive assessment. The weighted precision for a classification problem with C classes can be calculated using Equation (5).

$$\text{Weighted Precision}\left(\text{Pweighted}\right) = \sum_{i=1}^{C} w_i P_i \tag{5}$$

Here, w_i is the weight assigned to class *I* and can be computed as follows.

$$\text{wi} = \frac{\textit{Number of True instances}}{\textit{Total number of Samples}} \tag{6}$$

The weighted recall for a classification problem with *C* classes can be computed as in Equation (7).

$$\text{Weighted Recall}\left(\text{Rweighted}\right) = \sum_{i=1}^{C} w_i R_i \tag{7}$$

Similarly, the weighted F1 score for a classification problem with *C* classes can be calculated using Equation (8).

$$\text{Weighted F1} - \text{Score}\left(\text{F1weighted}\right) = \sum_{i=1}^{C} w_i F1_i \tag{8}$$

3.4. Data Preprocessing

The NSL-KDD dataset comprises a total of 41 extracted features, which are used to characterize network traffic and distinguish between normal and malicious activities. Among these, three features *(protocol_type, service, and flag)* are categorical variables, representing network protocol type, service requested, and connection status, respectively. Since machine learning algorithms require numerical inputs, these categorical features were transformed into numerical values using Label Encoding. This technique assigns a unique integer to each category, ensuring that the information is retained while making the dataset compatible with classification models.

To maintain consistency in feature scales and improve the efficiency of machine learning models, all numerical features were standardized using the z-score normalization formula, as shown in Equation 9.

$$\text{Xscaled} = \frac{X - \mu}{\sigma} \tag{9}$$

where X represents the original feature value, μ is the mean of the feature, and σ is the standard deviation. Standardization ensures that all features contribute equally to the model's learning process, preventing dominance by features with larger numerical ranges. This preprocessing step helps improve model convergence, enhances stability, and optimizes classification performance in the intrusion detection system.

3.5. Model Training and hyperparameter tuning

The proposed Adaptive Weighted Voting Ensemble (AWVE) model integrates multiple machine learning classifiers to enhance intrusion detection performance. In this study, we trained five models, including Support Vector Machine (SVM), Logistic Regression, K-Nearest Neighbour (KNN) and Decision Tree, to serve as base learners for the ensemble. The dataset was pre-processed using Label Encoding for categorical variables and Standard Scaling to normalize features. For training the Support Vector Machine (SVM) model, a linear kernel is employed with regularization parameter (C) is set to 1, balancing the trade-off between maximizing the margin and minimizing classification errors. A higher value of C would lead to a more complex model prone to overfitting, while a lower value could result in underfitting. The choice of C=1 is based on empirical observations, ensuring a well-regularized model with optimal performance. Similarly, in Logistic Regression, the regularization parameter (C) is also set to 1, with a maximum iteration limit of 1000 to guarantee model convergence. The increased iteration count allows the optimization algorithm to effectively minimize the loss function without premature stopping. These hyperparameters are fine-tuned through iterative experimentation to achieve stable and reliable classification results.

For the K-Nearest Neighbors (KNN) model, selecting the appropriate value of K is crucial, as it directly influences classification accuracy. A small K may cause sensitivity to noise, whereas a large K can lead to excessive smoothing of decision boundaries. To determine the optimal value, accuracy is plotted across K values ranging from 1 to 20, to assess performance consistency using elbow method. Based on this analysis, K=9 is identified as the ideal choice as illustrated in Figure 4. The Decision Tree Classifier is trained by splitting the dataset into different decision nodes based on feature values. It uses the Gini impurity criterion to decide the best splits at each step. The Naïve Bayes Classifier follows a probabilistic approach based on Bayes' Theorem. The Gaussian Naïve Bayes (GNB) variant assumes that features follow a normal distribution. It calculates the probability of each class and assigns the one with the highest likelihood to a given instance. This model is simple, fast, and works well even with a small dataset.

Figure 4. Accuracy vs K values using elbow Method to identify optimal K value

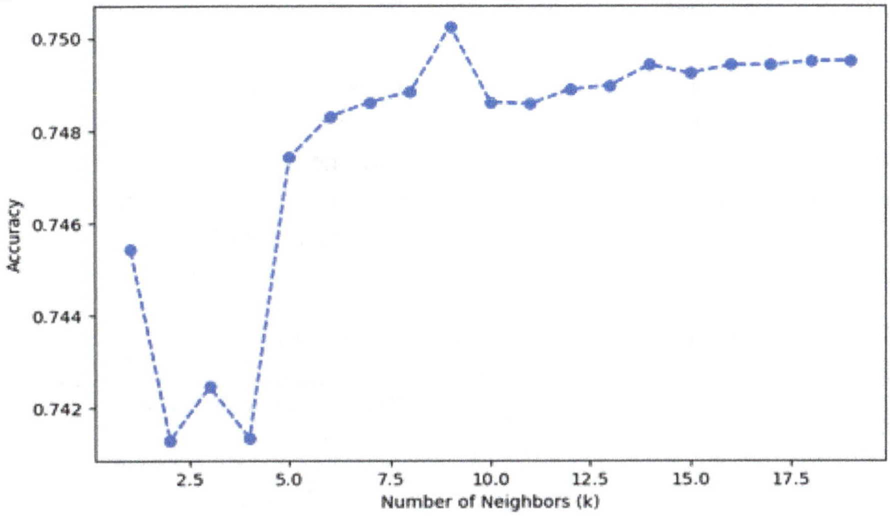

The AWVE model leverages the strengths of these base learners by adaptively assigning weights to their predictions based on their individual performance. Rather than relying on simple majority voting, AWVE dynamically adjusts the influence of each model, emphasizing those that perform better in different attack scenarios. This approach enhances classification robustness, particularly in handling class imbalances and reducing false positives. The ensemble's effectiveness was validated through comparative analysis, demonstrating that AWVE outperforms standalone models in terms of detection accuracy and overall reliability in intrusion detection systems.

4. RESULTS ANALYSIS AND DISCUSSION

In this section, we present a detailed analysis of the results obtained from various experiments conducted in accordance with the previously described experimental setup. The objective of this analysis is not only to report the numerical performance metrics but also to provide a comprehensive discussion that enhances the reader's understanding of the observed patterns, trends, and model behaviours. By evaluating the effectiveness of different classification models under various conditions, we aim to highlight key insights into their strengths, limitations, and overall suitability for intrusion detection. This discussion serves to bridge the gap between raw experimental results and their practical implications, enabling a deeper interpretation of how various machine learning models respond to the complexities of the dataset. Table 3 provides a detailed comparison of the performance metrics for two datasets:

NSL-KDD-FULL and NSL-KDD-SUB. The table includes key evaluation metrics such as accuracy, precision, recall, and F1-score. The accuracy is computed using Equation 1, while precision is determined as shown in Equation 5. Similarly, recall and F1-score are calculated based on Equations 7 and 8, respectively. These metrics help in analyzing the effectiveness of the models in distinguishing between normal and attack traffic. By comparing the results across the two datasets, we can observe how data size impacts model performance and generalization capability, offering valuable insights into the robustness of the proposed approach.

Table 3. Performance Metrics for each Model on two Datasets

Model	Metric	Trained on NSL-KDD-FULL	Trained on NSL-KDD-SUB
SVM	Accuracy	0.7527	0.7554
	Recall	0.7527	0.7554
	Precision	0.7376	0.7677
	F1-score	0.7054	0.7083
Logistic Regression	Accuracy	0.7614	0.7488
	Recall	0.7614	0.7488
	Precision	0.7534	0.7482
	F1-score	0.7136	0.7016
KNN	Accuracy	0.7503	0.7528
	Recall	0.7503	0.7528
	Precision	0.8023	0.8119
	F1-score	0.7058	0.7079
Decision Tree	Accuracy	0.7606	0.7498
	Recall	0.7606	0.7498
	Precision	0.7891	0.8001
	F1-score	0.7186	0.7149
Naive Bayes	Accuracy	0.4340	0.4562
	Recall	0.4340	0.4562
	Precision	0.5644	0.5506
	F1-score	0.3491	0.4043
Proposed Ensemble Method	Accuracy	**0.7633**	**0.7626**
	Recall	0.7633	0.7626
	Precision	0.8109	0.7730
	F1-score	0.7175	0.7148

Figure 5. Confusion Matrices for different Models trained on NSL-KDD-FULL dataset: (A) SVM (B)Logistic Regression (C) KNN (D) Decision Tree (E) Naïve Bayes (F) AVWE

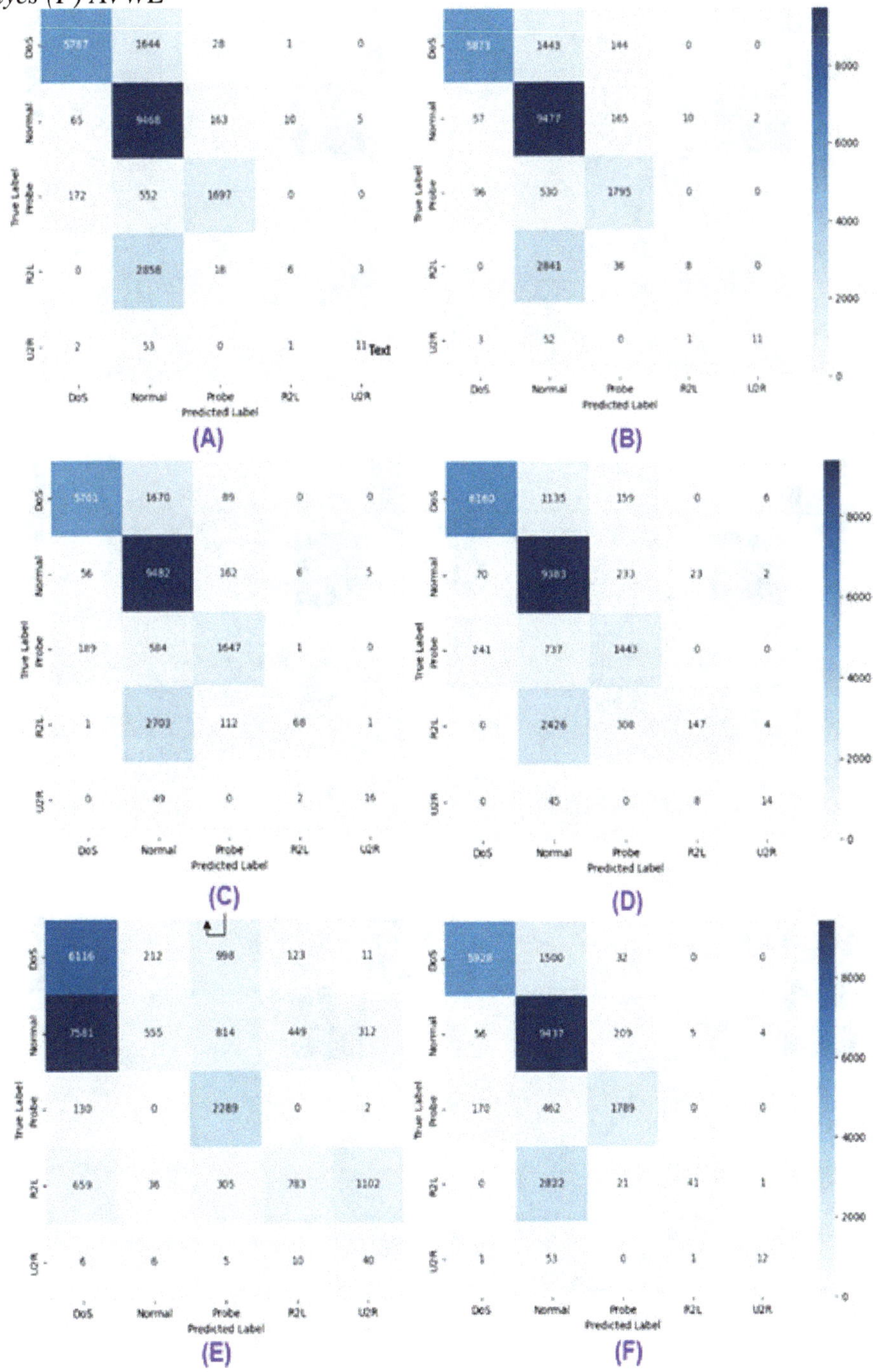

Figure 6. Confusion Matrices for different Models trained on NSL-KDD-SUB dataset: (A) SVM (B)Logistic Regression(C) KNN (D) Decision Tree (E) Naïve Bayes (F) AVWE

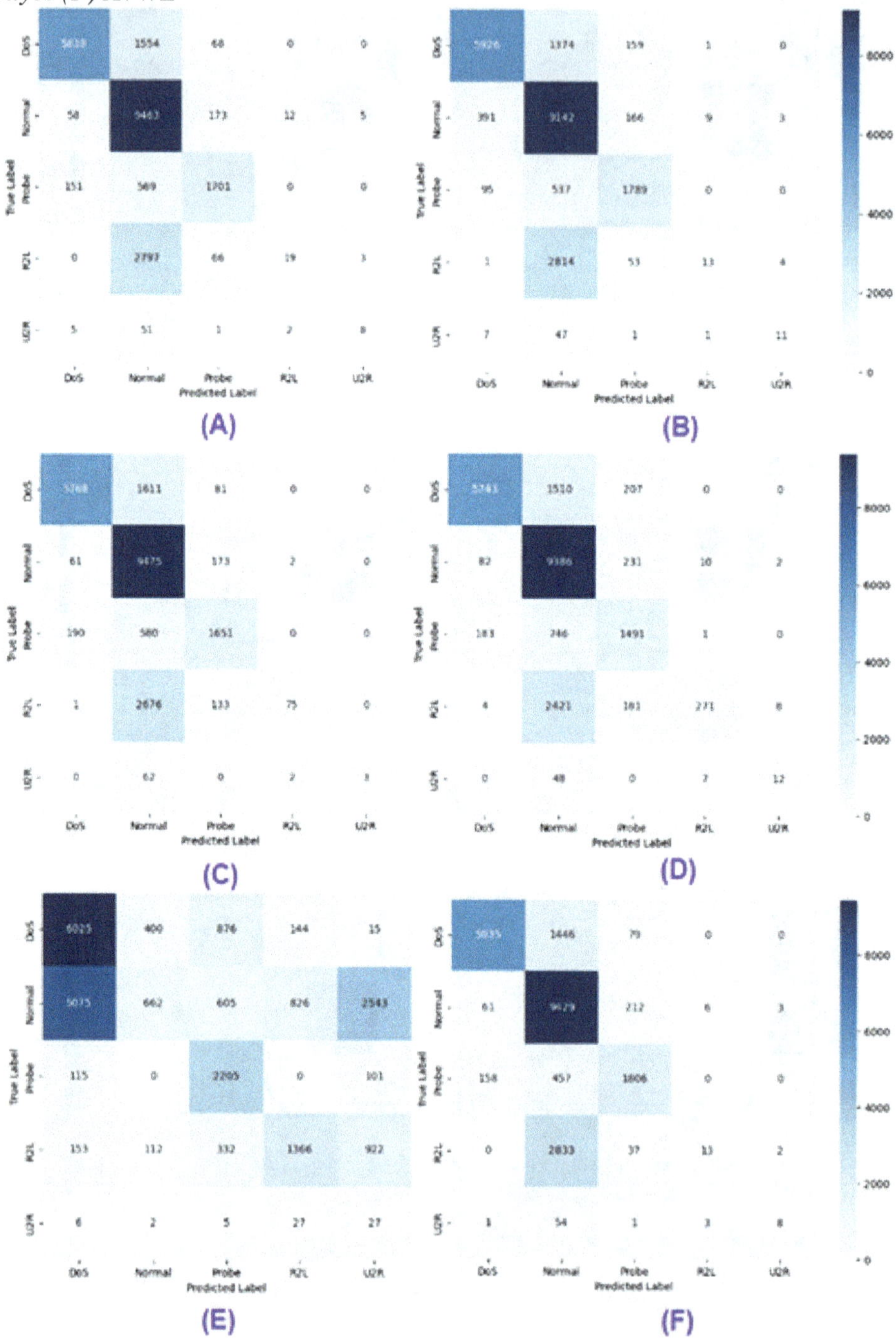

Figure 5 shows Confusion Matrices for different Models on the NSL-KDD-FULL dataset, highlighting their strengths and weaknesses in classifying various attack categories. The visualization provides deeper insights into how each model contributes to the ensemble, reinforcing the need for an adaptive weighted voting strategy to achieve balanced and effective intrusion detection. Upon analyzing the results, it is evident that Naïve Bayes excels at identifying Remote-to-Local (R2L) and User-to-Root (U2R) attacks. These attack types are typically more challenging to detect due to their low occurrence in the dataset, but Naïve Bayes, with its probabilistic approach, is particularly effective at handling such imbalanced classes. Meanwhile, K-Nearest Neighbors (KNN) shows strong performance in classifying normal network traffic. This is likely because KNN relies on similarity-based comparisons, making it well-suited for distinguishing normal instances from attack traffic. Logistic Regression, on the other hand, is particularly effective in recognizing Probe attacks, which involve network scanning and reconnaissance activities. The linear decision boundaries of Logistic Regression allow it to differentiate these patterns efficiently. Additionally, Decision Trees demonstrate a high success rate in detecting Denial-of-Service (DoS) attacks, as they can effectively capture the hierarchical decision rules that characterize large-scale flooding and service disruption attempts.

Recognizing the strengths of each individual model, the proposed Adaptive Weighted Voting Ensemble (AWVE) Model strategically integrates these classifiers to enhance overall detection performance. By assigning adaptive weights based on F1-score performance, the ensemble ensures that the best-performing classifiers for each attack type have a greater influence in the final prediction. This approach allows the model to balance the detection of both majority and minority attack classes, improving classification accuracy while reducing the risk of false negatives. As a result, the proposed ensemble model, trained on the NSL-KDD-FULL dataset, achieves an accuracy of 76.33% when evaluated on the NSL-KDD-TEST dataset, demonstrating its effectiveness in building a more reliable and comprehensive intrusion detection system. Figure 6 shows Confusion Matrices for different Models on the NSL-KDD-SUB dataset, highlighting their strengths and weaknesses in classifying various attack categories. The proposed ensemble model, trained on NSL-KDD-SUB achieves an accuracy of 76.26% when tested on the NSL-KDD-TEST dataset.

To ensure that the accuracy improvement achieved by the Adaptive Weighted Voting Ensemble (AWVE) Model is statistically significant and not a result of random variation, we conducted a paired T-test comparing the accuracy of AWVE with the best-performing individual classifier. The T-test is a widely used statistical method for evaluating whether the difference in means between two models is meaningful. A low p-value ($p<0.05$) indicates that the observed improvement is statistically significant, meaning that AWVE's accuracy gain is unlikely due to chance. The results of the T-test confirm that AWVE significantly outperforms individual classifiers, reinforcing its effectiveness in intrusion detection. The ensemble model's adaptive weighting mechanism plays a crucial role in improving classification performance by leveraging the strengths of multiple classifiers while mitigating their individual weaknesses.

The statistical significance of AWVE's accuracy underscores the importance of ensemble learning in cybersecurity applications. Traditional classification techniques fail to handle class imbalance properly which results in unbalanced decision-making regarding Remote-to-Local and User-to-Root intrusions. AWVE enhances network security by changing the weight of individual classifiers through F1-score assessment to boost the detection of rare minority class attacks. The results of the T-test validate that AWVE's improvement is not only empirically observed but also statistically justified, making it a robust and reliable solution for intrusion detection systems (IDS). These findings highlight the necessity of integrating adaptive ensemble learning in real-world network security frameworks, as it significantly enhances intrusion detection accuracy while maintaining stability across different attack categories.

CONCLUSION

This chapter presented the Adaptive Weighted Voting Ensemble (AWVE) Model to improve the performance of intrusion detection system. AWVE Model functions as a new intrusion detection system which carries out dynamic weight recalibration of classifiers through performance-based assessments. Traditional ensemble approaches handle class imbalance problems poorly in cybersecurity datasets thus generating low detection rates for minority-class attacks. The AWVE model uses adaptive weighting based on F1-scores to let reliable classifiers play a bigger role in making collectivized decisions.

We have used the NSL-KDD dataset to show that different classifiers possess unique abilities to discover different forms of network intrusions. Naïve Bayes delivered high detection accuracy for R2L and U2R attacks, yet KNN was most efficient in handling normal traffic and Logistic Regression supplied exceptional performance in Probe attack detection and Decision Trees demonstrated superior performance for detecting DoS attacks. The AWVE model incorporates these strengths through its integration which produces an intrusion detection system improved with higher accuracy and better balance. The proposed method, trained on the NSL-KDD-FULL dataset, achieves an accuracy of 76.33% when evaluated on the NSL-KDD-TEST dataset and 76.26% when trained on the NSL-KDD-SUB dataset, outperforming individual classifiers while demonstrating higher detection rates for hard-to-detect attack types. The findings from this study emphasize the importance of adaptive ensemble learning in cybersecurity applications. By intelligently adapting classifier contributions, AWVE ensures improved robustness, reliability, and detection efficiency in real-world Intrusion Detection Systems (IDS). Future work could explore deep learning-based models, feature selection optimization, and real-time deployment strategies to further enhance the effectiveness of intrusion detection in dynamic network environments

REFERENCES

Albinhamad, H., Alotibi, A., Alagnam, A., Almaiah, M., & Salloum, S. (2025). Vehicular Ad-hoc Networks (VANETs): A Key Enabler for Smart Transportation Systems and Challenges. *Jordanian Journal of Informatics and Computing*, *2025*(1), 4–15. DOI: 10.63180/jjic.thestap.2025.1.2

Alfrhan, A. A., Alhusain, R. H., & Khan, R. U. (2020, September). SMOTE: Class imbalance problem in intrusion detection system. In *2020 International Conference on Computing and Information Technology (ICCIT-1441)* (pp. 1–5). IEEE.

Ali, A. (2024). Adaptive and Context-Aware Authentication Framework Using Edge AI and Blockchain in Future Vehicular Networks. *STAP Journal of Security Risk Management*, *2024*(1), 45–56. DOI: 10.63180/jsrm.thestap.2024.1.3

Alsahaim, S., & Maayah, M. (2023). Analyzing Cybersecurity Threats on Mobile Phones. *STAP Journal of Security Risk Management*, *2023*(1), 3–19. DOI: 10.63180/jsrm.thestap.2023.1.2

Alshinwan, M., Memon, A. G., Ghanem, M. C., & Almaayah, M. (2025). Unsupervised text feature selection approach based on improved Prairie dog algorithm for the text clustering. *Jordanian Journal of Informatics and Computing*, *2025*(1), 27–36. DOI: 10.63180/jjic.thestap.2025.1.4

Alshuaibi, A., Arshad, M. W., & Maayah, M. (2025). A Hybrid Genetic Algorithm and Hidden Markov Model-Based Hashing Technique for Robust Data Security. *Journal of Cyber Security and Risk Auditing*, *2025*(3), 42–56. DOI: 10.63180/jcsra.thestap.2025.3.6

Deb, D., Rodrigo, H., & Kumar, S. (2024, May). Performance analysis of machine learning algorithms on imbalanced DDoS attack dataset. In *2024 IEEE World AI IoT Congress (AIIoT)* (pp. 349–355). IEEE. DOI: 10.1109/AIIoT61789.2024.10579021

Fouladi, R. F., Kayatas, C. E., & Anarim, E. (2016, June). Frequency-based DDoS attack detection approach using naive Bayes classification. In *2016 39th International Conference on Telecommunications and Signal Processing (TSP)* (pp. 104–107). IEEE. DOI: 10.1109/TSP.2016.7760838

Gampel, A., & Eveleigh, T. (2025). Model-Based Systems Engineering Cybersecurity Risk Assessment for Industrial Control Systems Leveraging NIST Risk Management Framework Methodology. *Journal of Cyber Security and Risk Auditing*, *2025*(4), 204–221. DOI: 10.63180/jcsra.thestap.2025.4.2

Hattori, K., & Takahashi, M. (2000). A new edited k-nearest neighbor rule in the pattern classification problem. *Pattern Recognition, 33*(3), 521–528. DOI: 10.1016/S0031-3203(99)00068-0

Ismail, S., El Mrabet, Z., & Reza, H. (2022). An ensemble-based machine learning approach for cyber-attacks detection in wireless sensor networks. *Applied Sciences (Basel, Switzerland), 13*(1), 30. DOI: 10.3390/app13010030

Kavitha, S., Alphonse, P. J. A., & Reddy, Y. V. (2019). An improved authentication and security on efficient generalized group key agreement using hyper elliptic curve based public key cryptography for IoT health care system. *Journal of Medical Systems, 43*(8), 260. DOI: 10.1007/s10916-019-1378-2 PMID: 31267216

Kilincer, I. F., Ertam, F., & Sengur, A. (2021). Machine learning methods for cyber security intrusion detection: Datasets and comparative study. *Computer Networks, 188*, 107840. DOI: 10.1016/j.comnet.2021.107840

Liu, R., Shi, J., Chen, X., & Lu, C. (2024). Network anomaly detection and security defense technology based on machine learning: A review. *Computers & Electrical Engineering, 119*, 109581. DOI: 10.1016/j.compeleceng.2024.109581

Panda, M., & Patra, M. R. (2007). Network intrusion detection using naive Bayes. *International Journal of Computer Science and Network Security, 7*(12), 258–263.

Pinto, A., Herrera, L. C., Donoso, Y., & Gutierrez, J. A. (2024). Enhancing critical infrastructure security: Unsupervised learning approaches for anomaly detection. *International Journal of Computational Intelligence Systems, 17*(1), 236. DOI: 10.1007/s44196-024-00644-z

Sajid, M., Malik, K. R., Almogren, A., Malik, T. S., Khan, A. H., Tanveer, J., & Rehman, A. U. (2024). Enhancing intrusion detection: A hybrid machine and deep learning approach. *Journal of Cloud Computing (Heidelberg, Germany), 13*(1), 123. DOI: 10.1186/s13677-024-00685-x

Tama, B. A., & Lim, S. (2021). Ensemble learning for intrusion detection systems: A systematic mapping study and cross-benchmark evaluation. *Computer Science Review, 39*, 100357. DOI: 10.1016/j.cosrev.2020.100357

Telikani, A., Rudbardeh, N. E., Soleymanpour, S., Shahbahrami, A., Shen, J., Gaydadjiev, G., & Hassanpour, R. (2023). A cost-sensitive machine learning model with multitask learning for intrusion detection in IoT. *IEEE Transactions on Industrial Informatics.*

Yaseen, M. G., Ali, A. H., & Alajanbi, M. (2025). An enhanced hybrid genetic-JAYA algorithm for feature selection and SVM parameter optimization in intrusion detection systems: Evaluation on the CICIDS dataset. *SHIFRA*, *2025*, 98–109. DOI: 10.70470/SHIFRA/2025/006

Chapter 5

Navigating the Maze of Network Security: Threats, Strategies, and Countermeasures

Ajay Kumar
Government Engineering College, Kaimur, India

Keshav Sinha
https://orcid.org/0000-0003-1053-3911
University of Petroleum and Energy Studies, India

ABSTRACT

The research tackles the constantly changing realm of cyber threats, drawing comparisons to an insistent and opportunistic cyber-zombie adversary. Through an in-depth analysis, we dissect the tactics of this digital threat, encompassing malware, phishing, and social engineering, while drawing parallels to the relentless siege of a zombie attack. Organizations must implement robust countermeasures to strengthen defenses against an impending zombie attack, including intrusion detection systems, strengthening authentication processes, and equipping employees with the awareness and skills to combat cyber-zombies. It will help secure the systems and data against isolated attacks and the persistent and multifaceted threat landscape. Experimenting within a virtual environment is essential for identifying and comprehending the potential threat posed by a zombie attack. Adopting a proactive stance in preparing for a persistent onslaught is crucial for building resilience and safeguarding against continually evolving cyber threats.

DOI: 10.4018/979-8-3373-1807-3.ch005

2026, IGI Global Scientific Publishing. Copying or distributing in print or electronic forms without written permission of IGI Global Scientific Publishing is prohibited. Use of this chapter to
rative artificial intelligence (AI) technologies is expressly prohibited. The publisher reserves all rights to license its use for generative AI training and machine learning model development.

INTRODUCTION

The rapid expansion of digital technologies and the ubiquitous integration of the internet into everyday life have undeniably transformed the way individuals, businesses, and governments operate (Abu & Kijsirikul, 2023). This transformation, while offering unparalleled convenience, productivity, and connectivity, has also ushered in new vulnerabilities that cybercriminals continuously exploit (Almaiah et al., 2024; Al-Attar, 2023; Nay, 2024). In the past decade, cybercrime has grown into a transnational phenomenon, no longer confined to isolated incidents of individual hacking but evolving into organized, large-scale campaigns with profound economic and social consequences. The modern cyber threat landscape is characterized by its sophistication, scalability, and persistence, creating an urgent need for innovative detection and defense mechanisms (Aldawood & Skinner, 2020).

The increasing reliance on digital platforms has opened up countless avenues for adversaries to carry out malicious activities. With the democratization of technology, even low-skilled attackers can access pre-built exploit kits, ransomware-as-a-service, and phishing toolkits available in underground forums (Alhamed & Rahman, 2023). This ease of access has lowered the barrier to entry, making cybercrime not only more widespread but also more diverse in its forms. From phishing and social engineering to ransomware and botnet-driven denial-of-service attacks, adversaries employ an arsenal of methods to exploit vulnerabilities in systems, networks, and human psychology (Almomani et al., 2024). Among these, zombie attacks in which computers or devices are silently hijacked and remotely controlled are particularly insidious due to their ability to multiply rapidly and execute coordinated actions at scale (Alotaibi et al., 2025) and (Maayah, 2025).

Zombie attacks stand out as a critical area of study because they embody the dual challenge of stealth and magnitude (Ali, 2024) and (Alsahaim & Maayah, 2023). Once compromised, a system may continue to appear normal to its legitimate user while simultaneously participating in a large-scale malicious campaign without their knowledge. These zombified devices, often organized into botnets, can be weaponized for diverse purposes: launching distributed denial-of-service (DDoS) attacks, spreading malware, conducting credential stuffing operations, or even engaging in cryptocurrency mining (Almomani, 2020). The very invisibility of these compromised systems makes them dangerous, as millions of unsuspecting users may unknowingly contribute to the strength of such botnets (Al-Shareeda et al., 2025) and (Addula et al., 2025).

Large organizations, in particular, face severe consequences from zombie-based attacks. A successful compromise may result in the theft of sensitive intellectual property, financial losses, reputational damage, and disruption of critical services. The interconnection of global supply chains, reliance on third-party vendors, and adoption of Internet of Things (IoT) devices exacerbate these risks, as a single vulnerable endpoint can serve as an entry point into much larger infrastructures. Beyond corporate risks, national security concerns also emerge botnets composed of zombified devices have been linked to geopolitical conflicts, where state-sponsored adversaries leverage them as cyber weapons to disrupt essential services and spread disinformation (Alowaisheq et al., 2020)(Al-Hashemi et al., 2024; saad Mohamed et al., 2025).

Legislative and policy frameworks worldwide are struggling to keep pace with this rapidly evolving threat. While governments and regulatory bodies attempt to create laws to protect digital ecosystems, inconsistencies across jurisdictions present challenges. Cybercriminals often exploit these gaps, operating from regions with weaker enforcement mechanisms. As a result, combating zombie attacks requires not only technological resilience but also coordinated international collaboration. Public-private partnerships, threat intelligence sharing, and cooperative law enforcement initiatives are essential to address the global scale of these challenges (Alraizza & Algarni, 2023).

To build resilience against zombie-based cyber threats, a multi-layered approach is indispensable. Defensive strategies must combine technical safeguards, such as intrusion detection systems, anomaly-based monitoring, and threat intelligence integration, with human-centric practices like security awareness training and phishing prevention (Almaiah et al., 2022). For businesses, investing in a culture of security is as important as deploying advanced tools. On the individual level, simple measures strong authentication, timely patching, and cautious interaction with online communications remain essential components of personal cybersecurity hygiene. Yet, despite these efforts, zombie attacks continue to proliferate, highlighting the need for more advanced, proactive detection methodologies.

This chapter specifically focuses on the phenomenon of zombie attacks, which we frame metaphorically as a "digital zombie invasion". Just as fictional zombies multiply uncontrollably and overwhelm societies, cyber zombies silently take over devices and use them to propagate malicious actions, often beyond the awareness of their owners (Duan et al., 2012). The metaphor serves as an engaging entry point to emphasize the urgency and severity of the threat, but the chapter moves beyond imagery to provide a systematic exploration of how zombie attacks work, why they are so difficult to detect, and what measures can be implemented to defend against them. The primary objectives of this chapter are to:

- Monitor and analyze network traffic to identify anomalies and detect compromised devices early, enabling proactive rather than reactive response mechanisms.

- Examine the lifecycle of zombie attacks, from initial infection vectors to botnet orchestration and eventual malicious execution, to identify intervention points.
- Integrate real-time threat intelligence into defense frameworks, ensuring that organizations can recognize and respond to emerging threats as they evolve.
- Promote collaboration and collective defense, emphasizing the importance of industry-wide knowledge sharing and joint initiatives to counter large-scale botnet operations.

By addressing these objectives, the chapter aims to provide both theoretical insights and practical methodologies that strengthen the cybersecurity posture of organizations and individuals alike. The scope of the chapter encompasses not only the technical mechanisms of zombie attacks but also their broader implications (Ani et al., 2016). This includes examining case studies of real-world incidents, analyzing the economic and operational costs of botnet-driven cybercrime, and exploring the challenges faced by policymakers and regulators. Furthermore, the chapter situates zombie attacks within the broader landscape of cyber threats, showing how they intersect with phishing campaigns, malware distribution, and ransomware ecosystems (Almaiah et al., 2021)(Aljohani, 2023; Alsajri et al., 2023). The significance of this research lies in its ability to bridge conceptual understanding with practical application. By mapping the stages of a zombie attack and correlating them with potential detection and mitigation strategies, the chapter provides a roadmap for developing resilient defenses. It acknowledges that no single solution can eradicate cybercrime but emphasizes that layered, adaptive, and collaborative strategies can significantly reduce the likelihood and impact of such attacks.

Finally, the structure of the chapter is as follows: Section 2 reviews existing literature and related work, situating zombie attacks within the wider body of cybersecurity research. Section 3 highlights the challenges faced by industry in combating botnets and similar threats. Section 4 details the research methodology, followed by Section 5, which introduces a nmap-based detection approach to identify and analyze zombie attacks in practice. Section 6 discusses preventive measures and outlines practical guidelines for organizations, while Section 7 concludes with findings, recommendations, and future directions for strengthening resilience against zombie-driven cyber threats.

1. BACKGROUND OF THE WORK

Cybercrime has become one of the most critical challenges in the digital age, impacting organizations regardless of size or sector. The very factors that empower global connectivity, online platforms, cloud services, mobile devices, and the Internet of Things (IoT) also expand the attack surface for malicious actors (Beale & Berris, 2018). What makes cybercrime particularly dangerous is its evolving nature: attackers continuously refine their methods to stay ahead of defenses, often repurposing older techniques in novel ways. This environment necessitates proactive measures that go beyond traditional perimeter defenses. Organizations must not only detect vulnerabilities before they are exploited but also prepare effective incident response strategies to reduce impact (Almaiah & Almomani, 2020).

A frequent misconception is that only large corporations are targeted. In reality, adversaries often prey upon smaller firms due to their limited budgets, weaker defenses, and assumption of insignificance. This mindset is perilous because cybercriminals view such organizations as "soft targets" that can serve as gateways to larger networks. Recognizing early warning signs is therefore essential. Indicators may include unexplained system errors, unusual traffic patterns, repeated login attempts from unfamiliar IP addresses, or suspicious emails designed to trick users into clicking harmful links. By monitoring these red flags and closing gaps in both physical and network security, organizations can shift from reactive firefighting to proactive resilience (Martineau et al., 2023).

Organizations of all shapes and sizes are helpless against cybercrime in the current technological era. Cybercriminals constantly improve their methods and employ more modern techniques to target organizations. Businesses need to understand how they become the target of cybercriminals by understanding the physical and network security loopholes. Many firms believe they are too small or insignificant to be a target for cybercriminals (Belmabrouk, 2023). It is a risky assumption, as cybercriminals frequently target smaller organizations because they recognize them as easier pickings and adopt lesser security measures. There are two ways to provide control: (i) Identify any gaps in your security defenses and take action to close them before an attack, and (ii) Skillful preparation to respond to the attack and minimize the risk. There are several indications that the company is a target for cybercrime.

- **Strange Organizational Behavior:** Unreported framework errors could indicate that computers have been infected with malware or ransomware. The strange organizational behavior, such as unusual information moves or traffic spikes, may suggest that security frameworks have been breached (Möller, 2023).
- **Login Attempts:** Unusual login attempts from mysterious IP addresses or login attempts outside of regular business hours indicate that programmers are concentrating on frameworks.

- **Dubious Messages:** They receive messages that seem off, like phishing messages or messages with odd connections. It could be a sign that cybercriminals are paying attention to the company (Moneva et al., 2023).

1.1. Types of Cybercrime Targeting Companies

Cyber adversaries strategically utilize phishing and spear phishing methodologies to target organizations to mislead individuals. These approaches encompass manipulating individuals, enticing them to disclose sensitive information, or clicking on harmful links, posing a substantial threat to the security and integrity of an organization's digital assets (Adil et al., 2020). Specifically, phishing involves the transmission of deceptive communications or messages designed to appear as if they originate from a trustworthy source, like a bank or association. The ultimate goal is to deceive recipients into divulging confidential information, such as login credentials or financial data. Skewer phishing is focused on targeting a particular person or company with their emails. The user must validate the source's email address to control the attack. Phishing messages use urgency or fear to prompt quick actions, like clicking a link or sharing personal information. Spear phishing goes further, including personal data and mimicking trustworthy sources, such as partners or vendors, to enhance authenticity (Lallie et al., 2020). Organizations can defend themselves against phishing and spear phishing attacks by implementing email filters to block shady messages, routinely updating software and operating systems to prevent vulnerabilities, and training employees to spot and report phishing attempts. The strategy should include informing allies and clients that the attack is ongoing and taking action to diminish the attack's impact.

Cybercrime related to malware and ransomware is common and can seriously harm organizations. A type of merciless programming known as malware can be downloaded or installed on a PC without the client's knowledge, typically through a phishing email or malicious download. Once established, malware can track user behavior, steal sensitive data, or seize control of the compromised system. Ransomware is software that encrypts files on a computer or in an organization and prevents access to them unless a ransom is paid. In identifying the malware or ransomware attack, it is essential to look for signs of unusual behavior of the computer, such as a delay in performance, shocking pop-ups or messages, and missing or encrypted files. Organizations can prevent malware and ransomware attacks by using security software like antivirus and anti-malware programs and routinely backing up essential data. Working frameworks and programming updates are equally important to stop programmers from exploiting flaws. It should teach safe browsing techniques and the risks of downloading or accessing dubious communications or files. It is necessary to have a strategy in place for responding to an attack (Wang et al., 2021). Activities to identify and remove the malware, gather information from reinforcements, and offer advice on policing the attack should all be part of this approach. Organizations may limit the damage they suffer in the event of a virus or ransomware attack by being proactive and prepared.

Social engineering attacks are a type of cybercrime that uses mind control to trick victims into disclosing sensitive information or engaging in behavior that could compromise security. Phishing tricks people into divulging personal information or tapping on malicious links through texts, calls, and fake websites that appear to be the real thing. To create awareness of the attacker's typical strategies, such as creating a false sense of urgency, creating trust, and preying on a victim's desire. Furthermore, it is critical to verify the validity of a request before answering hasty requests for personal or sensitive information (Hussain et al., 2023). Organizations can protect themselves from social engineering attacks by focusing on crucial execution areas for policies and procedures, such as requiring two-factor approval for access to sensitive systems and data, limiting access to private information on a confined data diet, and providing ongoing security awareness training to employees. It is also fundamental to continually examine and upgrade security tactics and procedures to meet new threats and flaws. A response strategy is essential during a social engineering assault. This strategy should include isolating the compromised systems, alerting the affected parties, and directing an investigation to determine the severity of the breach. Organizations can prevent the potentially horrific effects of social design assaults by exercising caution.

When a website or online resource is heavily trafficked during a distributed denial of service (DDoS) attack, it is unavailable to authorized users. DDoS attacks frequently use a botnet, or a collection of infected PCs, to flood the target with traffic. Monitor site traffic to spot a DDoS attack and look for unusual spikes or examples, such as an unexpected increase in rush-hour traffic from a single IP address or area. Presentational problems on a site or erratic site blackouts are two additional signs of a DDoS attack. Security measures like firewalls, interruption anticipation systems, and content delivery networks (CDNs) help shield organizations from DDoS attacks (Osanaiye et al., 2016). It is critical to establish a response plan that outlines how to identify the attack's origin, identify the affected structures, collaborate with law enforcement to investigate the incident, and identify people who may be responsible. Businesses might use traffic rate regulating and splitting their network access providers (ISPs). By taking these preemptive measures, companies may protect themselves from the potentially dangerous effects of a DDoS attack, always ensuring that actual customers can access their online services (Brooks et al., 2022).

Advanced Persistent Threats (APTs) are cyber-attacks executed by sophisticated and well-resourced adversaries targeting specific information in high-profile companies and governments, usually in a long-term campaign (Brewer, 2014). It is essential for identifying a Well-suited person to keep an eye on network activity and look for odd examples, such as unauthorized access attempts, suspicious information transfer actions, or suspect logins from unexpected locations or devices. Because APTs are frequently designed to be secret, it cannot be easy to recognize them using common health indicators. By implementing a multimodal security strategy that includes tools like firewalls, interruption identification frameworks, and endpoint protection tools, organizations can protect themselves against APTs (Chidukwani et al., 2022). Robust access controls should also be set up to restrict access to sensitive systems and data, such as two-factor authentication and job-based admission. Representatives can learn to identify and report suspicious activity through ongoing security awareness training, which can help stop APTs. It is vital to have a response plan in place in the event of a Capable that includes actions for confining the affected systems, supervising an investigation to determine the extent of the breach, and working with law enforcement to deal with the aggressors. By taking these proactive measures, associations can protect themselves from the potentially harmful effects of an Appropriate and ensure the security of their designs, frameworks, and sensitive information (Tankard, 2011).

A Rubber Ducky tool is used in social engineering assaults to gain unauthorized access to a computer system. It is a little USB gadget that resembles a standard flash drive but functions as a keyboard emulator. When hooked into a computer, it can automatically enter a pre-programmed series of keystrokes, enabling an attacker to perform several scripts or instructions on the target system. By adopting rigorous access controls for their computer systems and restricting the usage of USB devices to authorized workers, organizations can stop Rubber Ducky assaults (Arora et al., 2021)(Mohammed & Aljanabi, 2023, 2024). Staff must also undertake security awareness training to identify and report suspicious behavior, such as using unattended USB devices or trying to access sensitive data. When a Rubber Ducky attack occurs, it is critical to separate the compromised framework and conduct a careful analysis to determine the extent of the damage. It might also be expected to assist law enforcement in finding the offender and dealing with them. By taking these precautions, businesses can protect their data and computer systems from the potentially devastating effects of a Rubber Ducky attack. Table 1 presents the various ways the adversary performs the attack.

Table 1. Various Types of Cyber Attacks

Attack Name	Attack Effect	Detection Method	Protection Technique
In-Person Interaction Attack (Khalid et al., 2020)			
Impersonation	Access secure, confidential, and private information by faking others' personalities and identities.	Monitor interactions for inconsistencies in identity representation. Verify identities through multiple authentication factors.	Implement multi-factor authentication.
Pretexting	Force the target to seek urgent solutions by creating and using a fake scenario. Increase the likelihood of the victim revealing personal information during the solution process.	Analyze patterns of urgent scenarios. Train employees to recognize and verify the legitimacy of urgent requests.	Establish strict verification processes for urgent scenarios.
Tailgating	Gain unauthorized access to restricted areas by following a person with legitimate access. Exploit common courtesy to enter secured premises.	Implement surveillance and access control systems to detect unauthorized entry.	Enforce strict access control measures. Conduct regular security awareness training for personnel.
Quid Pro Quo	Pretend to be from technical support, resolving legitimate problems while gaining unauthorized access or launching malware.	Educate users about the potential risks of unsolicited support calls. Monitor and analyze calls for suspicious behavior.	Encourage users to verify the legitimacy of support calls. Implement call monitoring and analysis tools.
Diversion Theft	Misguide delivery personnel to leave packages in locations other than their intended destinations. Gain unauthorized access to delivered information.	Track and monitor delivery routes and behaviors for unusual patterns. Establish secure delivery protocols.	Implement secure delivery practices, including confirmation processes.
Email Attack (Carroll et al., 2022)			
Phishing Attack	Gather personal or financial information through fake emails.	Analyze email content for suspicious links and requests.	Implement email filtering and authentication mechanisms.
Spear-Phishing Attack	Target specific individuals with customized, misleading emails.	Monitor for personalized content in emails.	Use advanced email security solutions and educate employees to recognize targeted phishing attempts.
Whaling Attack	Target high-profile executives to gain access to sensitive information.	Identify unusual communication patterns.	Implement multi-layered security for executives.

continued on following page

Table 1. Continued

Attack Name	Attack Effect	Detection Method	Protection Technique
Clone-Phishing Attack	Use legitimate, previously sent emails with fake links or attachments.	Verify email sender authenticity and monitor for cloned content.	Encourage users to verify email content before clicking links or downloading attachments, and implement email authentication mechanisms.
Website Attack (Hou et al., 2021)			
Pharming	Redirect victims to a malware site through DNS manipulation.	Monitor for unusual DNS changes. Implement DNS security measures.	Use DNS security solutions.
Website Phishing	Create fake websites to trick users into revealing credentials.	Analyze website URLs for authenticity.	Use website security certificates (SSL). Implement browser security features.
Pop-Up Windows	Use fraudulent pop-ups to deceive users into clicking on malicious links.	Enable browser pop-up blockers.	Install and update anti-malware software.
Cross-Site Scripting (XSS)	Exploit vulnerabilities to inject malicious scripts into websites.	Regularly scan and patch website vulnerabilities. Implement secure coding practices.	Use web application firewalls (WAFs).
Malware Attack (Yan et al., 2023)			
Spyware	Monitor users' activities and access private information without consent.	Use anti-spyware tools to monitor system behavior for unusual activity.	Install and update anti-malware software.
Baiting	Distribute malware through physical media, enticing users to activate the attack.	Avoid using unknown external storage devices.	Implement endpoint protection solutions and secure the use of external devices.
Ransomware	Encrypt user data and demand a ransom for decryption.	Regularly back up data. Use anti-ransomware tools.	Educate users on recognizing phishing emails and implement network segmentation.
Botnets	Use connected computers to perform malicious tasks under an attacker's control.	Monitor network traffic for unusual patterns. Implement intrusion detection systems.	Use reputable security software. Keep software and systems updated.
Rootkits	Activate remote access controls to manage a computer or information system.	Regularly scan for rootkit signatures. Implement strong access controls.	Use anti-rootkit tools to recognize suspicious activities.
Worms	Replicate and transmit across a computer network, causing damage.	Educate users on avoiding suspicious downloads. Use network firewalls.	Keep systems and software updated. Implement network security measures.

continued on following page

Table 1. Continued

Attack Name	Attack Effect	Detection Method	Protection Technique
Trojans	Malicious software is hidden as legitimate, causing various attacks on the host.	Regularly scan for Trojan signatures. Educate users on avoiding suspicious downloads.	Use anti-trojan software to recognize malicious content.
KeyLoggers and Screen Loggers	Monitor and record keyboard inputs or screen activity.	Use anti-keylogger tools. Regularly scan for unusual activities.	Educate users on avoiding suspicious downloads. Implement endpoint security solutions.
Social Network Attack (Jafarian et al., 2023)			
Fake Profiles	Create fake identities on social media to access personal information.	Verify user identities and educate users on recognizing fake profiles.	Implement identity verification measures. Encourage users to report suspicious profiles.
Digital Impersonation	Pretend to be a trusted authority or person on social media.	Verify user identities. Monitor for unusual behavior patterns.	Use multi-factor authentication on social media platforms. Educate users on recognizing impersonation.
Fake Groups	Create fake groups on social networks to attract victims.	Monitor for unusual group activities and verify group authenticity.	Use social media authentication mechanisms. Educate users on recognizing fake groups.
Malicious Links	Send malicious URLs through social networks to direct victims to infected sites.	Use link scanning tools to verify links before clicking.	Implement URL filtering for safe social media practices.
Technical Subterfuge			
Session Hijacking	Exploit a valid user session to gain illegal access to information or services.	Implement session security measures. Monitor for unusual session activities.	Use secure and encrypted connections.
Host File Poisoning	Alter domain records in the host file to redirect users to scam websites.	Regularly check and verify host files. Use reputable DNS servers.	Use DNS security solutions.
Compromised Web Server Attack	Compromise a web server to distribute malware or phishing sites.	Regularly audit and update web server security. Use secure coding practices.	Implement web application firewalls (WAFs).
Man-in-the-Middle Attack	Intercept and manipulate data between a victim and a legitimate website.	Use secure and encrypted connections. Monitor for unusual data interception.	Implement network encryption.

2. CURRENT CHALLENGES IMPACTING THE INDUSTRY

Given the evolving landscape of cyber threats, organizations face significant challenges in modern network security. As dependence on the internet and connected devices grows, concerns about personal information theft, partnership dissolution, and unauthorized financial transactions loom. Despite implementing security measures, vulnerabilities persist, necessitating a proactive approach. Addressing common network security weaknesses involves a multifaceted approach. First, tackling outdated safety measures requires organizations to prioritize regular updates and maintenance for their security tools, firewalls, intrusion detection systems, and antivirus software (Almomani et al., 2021). This proactive strategy helps to avoid emerging threats that often exploit vulnerabilities in outdated programming. Configuration vulnerabilities pose another significant risk, and organizations must thoroughly analyze their security structures. Proper configuration, alignment with security policies, and regular audits are essential components of the solution.

In some cases, organizations may hire security experts to ensure comprehensive assessment and the implementation of necessary adjustments (Antony & Maity, 2021)(Ibrahim, 2024; Pan et al., 2023). Unpatched software risks can be mitigated through a disciplined approach to scheduled maintenance, ensuring timely updates for all applications and environments. Implementing automatic updates further streamlines the process, facilitating the swift deployment of security patches and minimizing potential vulnerabilities. Inadequate access control is a critical area demanding attention. Organizations should implement robust access control measures, including adopting two-factor authentication, routine audits to monitor compliance, and proactive measures to prevent unauthorized access attempts. This comprehensive approach significantly enhances the organization's overall security posture. Exploiting vulnerabilities in unsecured devices, such as wearables and IoT devices, necessitates deploying advanced security software.

Additionally, organizations should implement a device control procedure to restrict the usage of unauthorized devices within the organization, thus reducing the risk of security breaches. The lack of encryption poses a significant threat to data security. To address this, organizations should ensure that all data transferred is encrypted. Developing and enforcing regulations regarding the encryption of commercial correspondence and safeguarding sensitive information during storage and organizational transitions are essential steps in fortifying data security. Lastly, third-party risks arise from external vendors' access to personal data. Organizations should enforce technical standards for external sources, conduct regular compliance checks, and maintain continuous monitoring practices to ensure that external suppliers adhere to established security protocols. This ongoing diligence helps mitigate the risks associated with third-party access to sensitive information. There are many more challenges, such as:

- The industry faces increasingly sophisticated cyber threats, including advanced persistent threats (APTs) and ransomware attacks that can evade traditional security measures.
- With interconnected supply chains, the industry is vulnerable to attacks targeting third-party vendors, potentially disrupting the production and delivery of goods and services.
- Adhering to constantly evolving cybersecurity regulations and compliance standards poses a challenge. Non-compliance may result in legal consequences and reputational damage.
- The widespread adoption of remote work introduces new security challenges, including securing remote access, managing endpoint security, and ensuring data protection outside traditional office environments.
- A shortage of skilled cybersecurity professionals makes it challenging for organizations to build and maintain robust cybersecurity teams capable of addressing evolving threats.
- Rapid adoption of emerging technologies, such as artificial intelligence (AI), Internet of Things (IoT), and cloud computing, introduces new attack vectors and vulnerabilities that the industry must proactively address.
- Insider threats, whether malicious or unintentional, pose a significant risk. Organizations struggle to monitor and mitigate risks associated with employees or contractors who may compromise security.
- Heightened awareness of data privacy issues and increased regulations create challenges in handling and securing sensitive customer data to meet privacy compliance requirements.
- Complex and interconnected IT infrastructures make identifying and addressing vulnerabilities difficult. Legacy systems and diverse technology stacks further contribute to this complexity.
- Despite the growing threat landscape, there are still gaps in cybersecurity awareness among employees, leaving organizations susceptible to social engineering attacks and other forms of manipulation.

3. RESEARCH METHODOLOGY

This section outlines the methodology for detecting a zombie attack using Wireshark, a widely used network protocol analyzer. A zombie attack is a cyber threat where a malicious actor infects many computers or devices with malware, turning them into zombies. These compromised devices are then organized into a botnet, creating a network of remotely controlled assets for the attacker. Figure 1 represents the several stages of a zombie attack.

Figure 1. Lifecycle of Zombie Attack

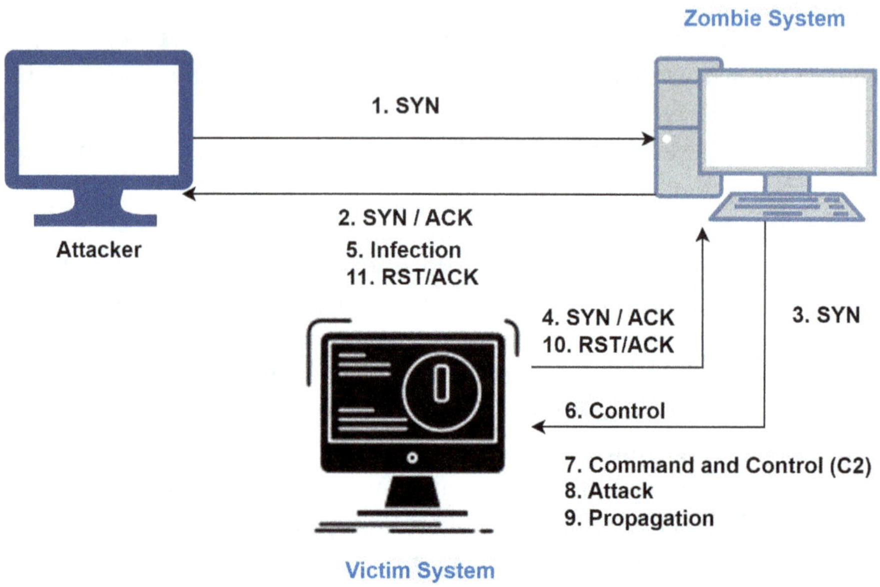

The lifecycle of a zombie attack refers to the various stages and activities involved in a successful zombie malware infection on a computer or network. Here is a generalized depiction of the typical lifecycle of a zombie attack:

- **Infection:** The lifecycle begins with the initial infection of individual computers or devices. It can be achieved through various means, such as phishing emails, malicious websites, infected software, or exploiting vulnerabilities in software.
- **Establishing Control:** Once a device is infected, the attacker establishes control. It often involves installing a backdoor or remote access tool that allows the attacker to maintain control over the compromised system.
- **Propagation:** The attacker uses the compromised device to propagate the infection. It may involve scanning for vulnerable systems on the same network or the internet, exploiting vulnerabilities, and spreading the malware to other devices.

- **Building the Botnet:** As more devices are compromised, the attacker builds a botnet, a network of zombie computers under control. The larger the botnet, the more powerful it becomes for malicious activities.
- **Command and Control (C2):** The attacker establishes a command and control infrastructure to manage the botnet. This infrastructure allows the attacker to send instructions to the zombie computers, coordinate their actions, and update the malware.
- **Malicious Activities:** With the botnet in place, the attacker can execute various malicious activities. It may include launching distributed denial-of-service (DDoS) attacks, spreading malware or ransomware, stealing sensitive information, or using the botnet for other cybercriminal purposes (Bhushan & Gupta, 2018).
- **Evasion and Persistence:** To avoid detection and removal, the attacker may employ techniques to evade security measures and maintain persistence on the compromised devices. It could involve regularly updating the malware, encryption, or hiding in legitimate processes.
- **Detection and Mitigation:** Security professionals and organizations actively work to detect and mitigate the impact of the zombie attack. It may involve deploying intrusion detection systems, antivirus software, and other cybersecurity measures to identify and remove malicious software (Almomani, 2021).
- **Remediation and Recovery:** After detecting the attack, organizations remediate the compromised systems, remove the malware, and recover any lost or compromised data. It may also involve improving security measures to prevent future incidents (Biswas et al., 2024).
- **Post-Incident Analysis:** After the attack has been mitigated, a post-incident analysis is conducted to understand how the attack occurred, identify vulnerabilities, and implement improvements to prevent similar incidents (Naqvi et al., 2023)(Mensah et al., 2025).

Detecting a zombie attack involves monitoring network traffic for anomalies and suspicious patterns. As a packet-level analysis tool, Wireshark plays a crucial role in this process by allowing security professionals to inspect and interpret the data exchanged between the compromised devices and the command and control servers. Early detection is vital to mitigating the impact of such attacks. Zombie attacks, particularly those involving botnets, pose significant threats to individuals, organizations, and entire networks. The following section shows how network scanning and zombie attacks are performed in a controlled environment.

4. IMPLEMENTATION AND SOLUTION

In this section, our exploration reaches into the network reconnaissance, employing a meticulous lens provided by Wireshark. The controlled environment of VirtualBox Graphical User Interface Version 6.1.42 r155177, Kali Linux, and Metasploitable 2 are essential components for executing offensive and defensive strategies. The research unfolds against the backdrop of utilizing the Nmap network scanning tool, a pivotal instrument that systematically unravels the concealed architecture of targeted networks (Almaiah & Almomani, 2020)(Al-Quraishi et al., 2024; Khaleel et al., 2025). Wireshark serves as the principal apparatus for the meticulous dissection of the intricate traffic orchestration generated by Nmap throughout our scanning endeavors. Our investigative journey initiates with an in-depth examination of ping scans, wherein we scrutinize the ICMP Echo Requests and Replies deciphering the communicative signals that underscore Nmap's relentless pursuit of live hosts. Advanced further, our narrative transitions to the realm of TCP SYN scans, shedding light on the covert nature of this reconnaissance technique through a detailed observation of SYN packets and their corresponding ACK flags.

4.1. Network Scanning

Nmap has two different types of scanning: (i) TCP Connect() scanning (-sT option) scanning and (ii) SYN scanning (-sS option). In Nmap scans, ports are categorized into different types based on their status and characteristics. The main ports that Nmap identifies are:

- **Open (O):** An open port is where an application or service actively accepts connections. Nmap detects open ports by receiving a response to its probes, indicating that the port is accessible.
- **Closed (C):** A closed port is one where Nmap has determined that no application or service accepts connections. Nmap identifies closed ports when it receives a response indicating that the port is closed.
- **Filtered (F):** A filtered port is one where Nmap cannot determine whether the port is open or closed because it receives no response to its probes. It happens due to firewalls, packet filtering, or other security mechanisms that prevent Nmap probes from reaching the target port.
- **Unfiltered (U):** An unfiltered port is one where Nmap determines that the port is neither open nor closed. The port is accessible, but Nmap cannot determine its exact status. It often happens when the target system's firewall allows Nmap probes but does not provide information about the port's state.

- **Open|Filtered (O|F):** This state indicates that Nmap could not determine whether the port is open or filtered. It implies that the port is accessible, but its exact status is unknown.
- **Closed|Filtered (C|F):** This state indicates that Nmap could not determine whether the port is closed or filtered. It implies that Nmap did not receive a clear indication of the port's status.

These port states provide valuable information about the target system's security posture and help identify potential vulnerabilities or misconfigurations. In a TCP Connect() scan, Nmap attempts to establish a full TCP connection with the target by completing the three-way handshake (SYN, SYN-ACK, and ACK). It is similar to how a typical network application, like a web browser or email client, establishes a connection. It is less stealthy than SYN scanning because it completes the full TCP connection, making the scan more likely to be logged by intrusion detection/prevention systems. TCP Connect() scanning is useful when you need accurate information about open ports and services; stealth is not a primary concern.

Figure 2. Nmap TCP Connect Scan

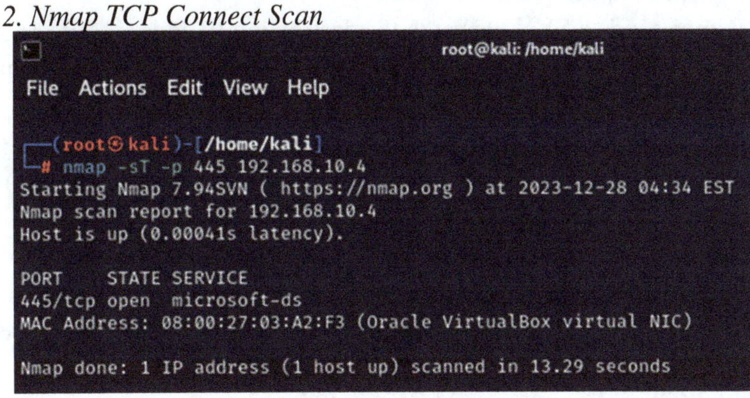

Figure 3. TCP Packet analysis

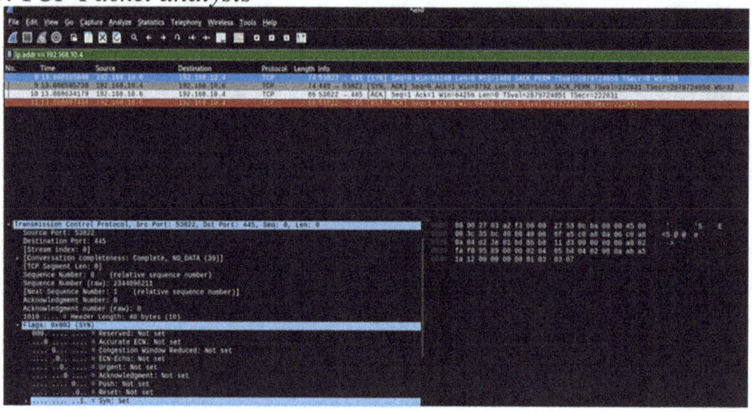

Figure 2 represents the process of a TCP Connect scan using Nmap, and Figure 3 represents how it looks at the packet level with Wireshark. Here are the steps:

- **Packet 1 (SYN packet sent by Nmap)**
  - o Nmap sends a SYN packet to the destination IP address (192.168.10.4).
  - o The SYN (Synchronize) flag is set in the packet, indicating the initiation of a connection.
- **Packet 2 (Server's response - ACK and SYN packets)**
  - o The destination server responds with an ACK (acknowledgment) packet for the SYN packet sent by Nmap.
  - o Additionally, the server sends its own SYN packet to initiate the three-way handshake.
  - o The sequence number is set to 0, and the acknowledgment number is set to 1.
- **Packet 3 (Client's response - ACK packet)**
  - o The source (Nmap) acknowledges the server's SYN packet by sending an ACK packet.
  - o It completes the three-way handshake, and the connection is established.
- **Packet 4 (Connection termination - RST packet)**
  - o After completing the three-way handshake, the connection is immediately terminated by sending a reset (RST) packet.
  - o The RST packet ensures that the connection is closed.

Since the three-way handshake is completed, Nmap concludes that the particular port on the destination server is open. The process is reliable for determining open ports by establishing a full TCP connection. On the other hand, SYN scanning (-sS), also known as half-open scanning, is a stealthier approach. It sends a TCP SYN packet to the target and waits for a response. If the port is open, the target responds with a SYN-ACK. If the port is closed, the target responds with an RST (reset) packet. This method does not complete the three-way handshake, making it faster and less likely to be detected. SYN scanning is considered stealthier than TCP Connect() scanning because it does not establish a full connection. SYN scanning is commonly used for initial reconnaissance and port scanning when stealth is a priority. Figure 4 represents the SYN scanning, and Figure 5 presents the packet analysis.

Figure 4. TCP Stealth Scan

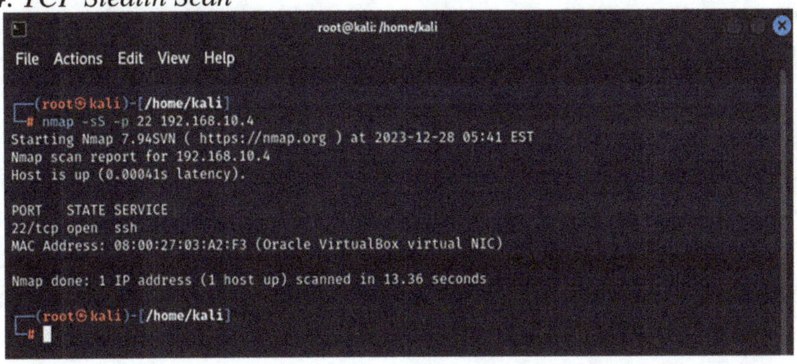

Figure 5. TCP Stealth Scan Packet Analysis

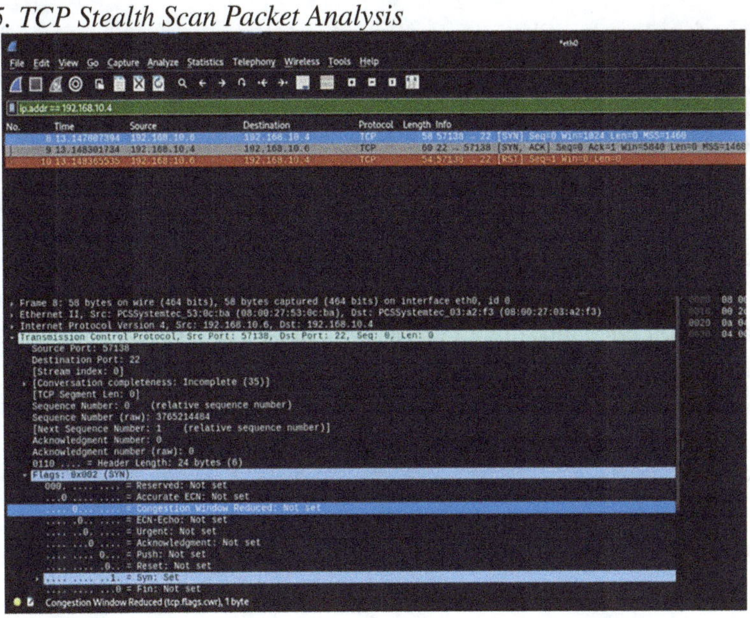

To investigate the intricacies of executing a Stealth SYN scan (-sS) with Nmap. The process unfolds as follows:

- Initiate the Stealth SYN Scan using the command {nmap -sS -p <port number> <destination IP>}. The '-sS' option directs Nmap to execute a SYN scan, also recognized as a half-open or stealth scan. This targeted scan honed in on a specific port on the destination IP.
- Nmap dispatches a SYN packet to the designated port on the destination IP, signaling the commencement of a connection by setting the SYN (Synchronize) flag in the packet.
- If the port is open, the server responds with a SYN, ACK (Synchronize, Acknowledge) packet, indicating its willingness to establish a connection.

Rather than completing the three-way handshake with an ACK packet, which would establish a full connection, the scanner opts for RST (Reset) packets. These RST packets swiftly terminate the connection without concluding the handshake. The confirmation of an open port is established by receiving the SYN-ACK response from the server, followed by the subsequent transmission of RST packets. This stealthy scanning approach minimizes detection risks since a complete connection is not formed. It effectively prevents intrusion detection systems that may log fully established connections. The use of RST packets guarantees prompt termination of the connection after confirming the port's openness.

- When faced with a filtered port, indicating the presence of a firewall or another network security device obstructing Nmap's determination of the port's status, the specific syntax is {nmap -sS -p <port number> <destination IP>}. The scan result labels the port as "filtered," denoting that the active firewall prevents a conclusive determination of the port's status.
- In the scenario of a closed port, where Nmap anticipates an RST (Reset) packet from the server in response to the SYN packet sent from the source machine, the syntax remains {nmap -sS -p <port number> <destination IP>}. Upon encountering a closed port, the server replies with an RST and ACK packet, signifying the port's closure.
- Transitioning to a FIN scan, characterized by dispatching a FIN (Finish) packet to the server and analyzing the server's response for port status, the specific syntax is {nmap -sF -p <port number> <destination IP>}.

No response is received from the server for an open port, while a closed port prompts the server to reply with an RST and ACK packet. Notably, Fin Scans are effective for Linux machines but may not apply to the latest Windows systems, highlighting the platform-dependent nature of certain scan types. This nuanced approach yields valuable insights into port status, contributing to a holistic understanding of network security configurations.

4.2. Investigating Zombie Attack

Detecting and mitigating cyber threats involves vigilant monitoring for unusual network activity. Anomalies, such as unexpected servers or application overloads during peak hours, may indicate a distributed denial of service (DDoS) attack. In this assault, perpetrators overwhelm servers with traffic, disrupting connectivity. Unauthorized access attempts are another red flag, potentially leading to devastating brute force attacks where persistent false credential entries can compromise system integrity. Mitigating such risks requires continuous efforts, employing multiple validation checks, and enforcing strict confidentiality regulations.

Additionally, unauthorized access to sensitive data, exemplified by personal, financial, or proprietary information, signals a potential target for cybercriminals. Phishing attacks, leveraging deceptive emails purporting to be from trusted sources, seeking confidential information, or installing malware when clicked, are prevalent. Vigilance against suspicious emails and phishing attempts is crucial, and strict security measures and employee education on social engineering principles play a vital role in prevention (Varshney et al., 2024). Changes in system performance, such as sudden slowdowns or crashes, may indicate malware infiltration, emphasizing the need for regular monitoring and security audits. Lastly, unfamiliar devices on the network signal potential cyber threats. Implementing network access restrictions and routine monitoring helps curb unauthorized device access, ensuring a more secure network environment.

4.3. Understanding Zombie Scan

The Idle Scan, also known as a Zombie Scan or Spoofed IP Scan, is designed to perform comprehensive blind port scanning while hiding the true origin of the scan. This intricate methodology involves utilizing a secondary host termed the "zombie host." Analogous to identity theft, the primary objective of the idle scan is to shield the attacker's IP address from being logged in the victim's Intrusion Detection System (IDS).

Step 1: TCP Scan Initiation

- The attacker initiates a TCP scan using a SYN scan to determine whether a specific port is open or closed.

- The target machine responds with a SYN/ACK (Synchronize, Acknowledge) packet if the port is open.
- The target machine responds with an RST (Reset) packet if the port is closed.

Step 2: IPID (IP Identification)

- Each IP packet carries an IPID, a fragment identification number—the IPID increments with every packet sent.

Step 3: Nmap Scan Syntax

- Command: nmap -p<port scan> --script ipidseq -iR<range>
- The 'ipidseq' script is employed for executing an idle scan.
- For instance, `nmap -p80 --script ipidseq -iR 10` targets port 80 and uses the `ipidseq` script to manipulate IP identification numbers.
- The `-iR 10` specifies scanning 10 random IP addresses, enhancing the scan's stealthiness.

Step 4: Idle Scan with IPIDseq

- Attacker IP: 192.168.10.6
- Zombie IP: 192.168.10.9
- Target IP: 192.168.10.4

Figure 6 represents the blind port scanning, and the downsides of Idle Scan are:

- **Inconsistent IPID Results:** The effectiveness of the idle scan, particularly with the `ipidseq` script, may be compromised, resulting in "Random" or "All zeros." Factors include the presence of firewalls or the target system's lack of vulnerability.
- **Random IP ID Assignment by Operating Systems:** Operating systems commonly assign IP IDs randomly, introducing unpredictability that can impact the reliability and accuracy of idle scan results.
- **Potential for False Positives:** The idle scan may yield false positives when encountering well-configured firewalls and honeypots. Robust security measures can influence the scan results, potentially leading to inaccuracies in identifying open ports.

Figure 6. Nmap Blind Port Scanning

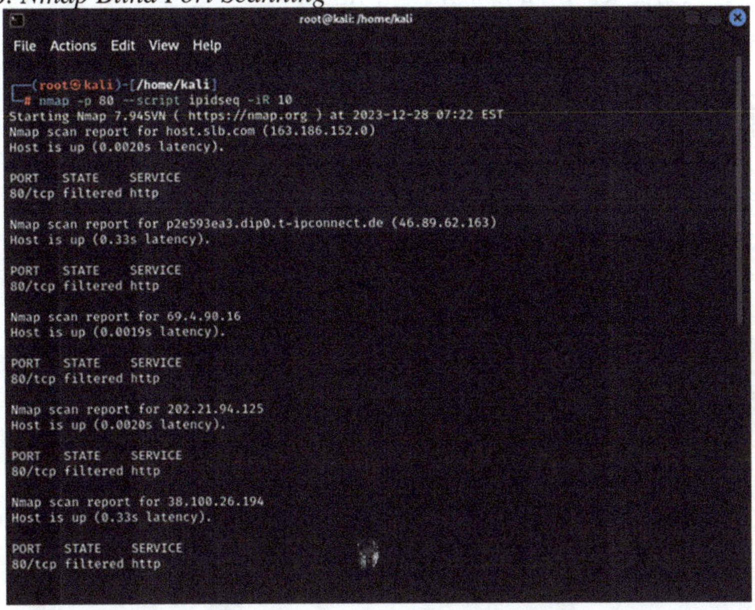

Step 5: Probe Zombie IPID

The initial step involves probing the IPID of the designated zombie (192.168.10.9) to establish a baseline for subsequent comparisons, contributing to the overall understanding of the idle scan procedure. Figure 7 presents the connection and forge request between the victim and attacker.

Figure 7: Forge request from Zombie and Target

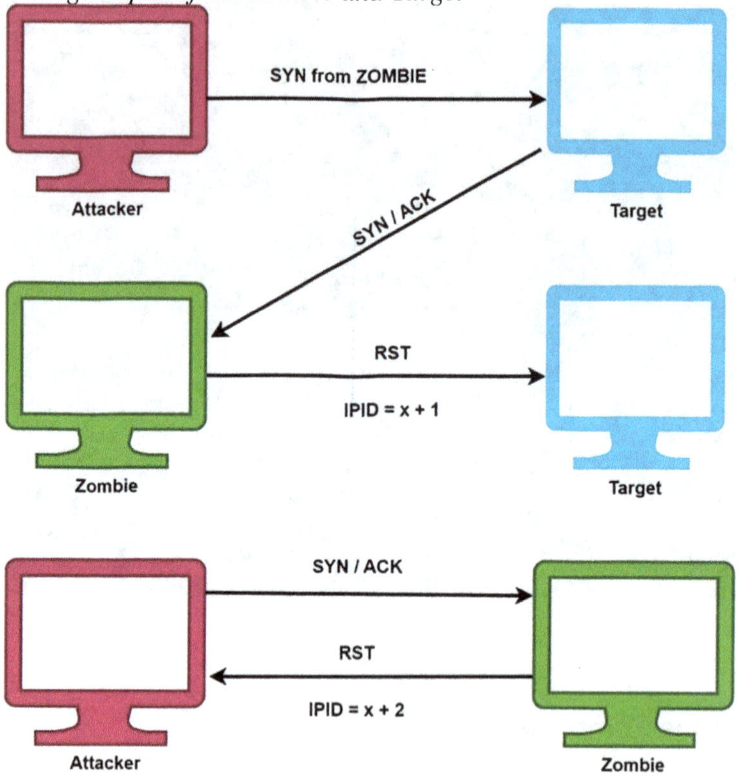

Step 6: Investigation of IPID for the Second Time

If the IPID increases by two from the baseline, it suggests the port was open. Figure 8 presents the requested target machine for connection.

- **Authorization:** It is crucial to obtain proper authorization before conducting any form of network scanning or penetration testing. Adherence to ethical hacking practices and compliance with legal and ethical standards are essential.
- **Nmap Scan Syntax:** nmap -sI<zombie IP address> -p<port number> <target machine IP>

This command executes an idle scan using the '-sI' option, specifying the zombie's IP address, the target port number, and the target machine's IP address.

Figure 8: Probe the Zombie and Target System

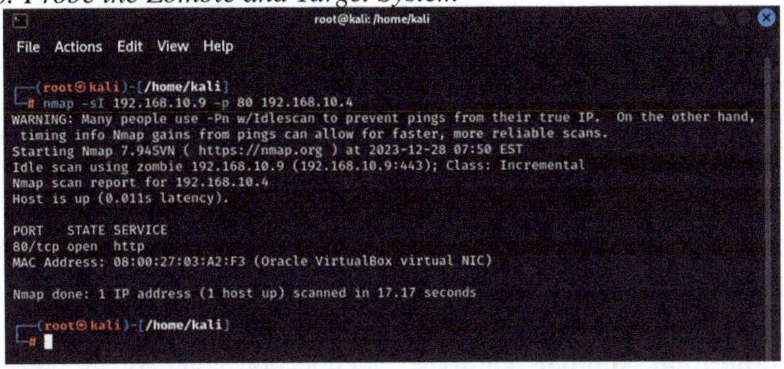

Step 7: Probe Packet Analysis

Figure 9. Communication between Zombie and Attacker

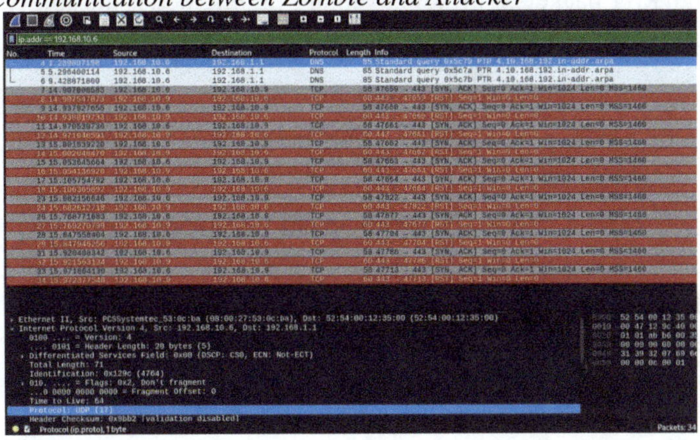

Figure 9 outlines the different phases and steps of the Idle Scan (Zombie Scan) process, emphasizing the communication between the attacker, the zombie host, and the target system. Here are some key points:

- **Communication Establishment:** The scan establishes communication between the attacker and the zombie host.
- **Actual Scan between Zombies and Target:** The scanning phase occurs between the zombies (idle hosts) communicating with the target system. Attention is directed towards the Internet Protocol (IP) Version section, focusing on the Identification number present in the IP header.

- **Communication between Zombie and Attacker (Verification):** After the scan, communication is re-established between the zombie and the attacker to verify the port status. Identification numbers in the IP header are recorded and analyzed.
- **RST Packet Analysis:** The marked request, the last communication sending the RST (Reset) packet, is chosen for analysis. This request is crucial for determining the success of the scan and the port status.
- **Retransmission Step:** The zombie scans the target after sending the RST packet to the attacker. Successful scans result in the zombie returning to communicate with the attacker.
- **Identification Number Analysis:** Identification numbers are noted before and after the scan. The difference in identification numbers (4139-4137=2) signifies that the port is open for connection.

The outlined phases provide a detailed understanding of the Idle Scan process, focusing on communication, Identification numbers analysis, and port status verification through RST packets. The key advantage highlighted is the ability to conduct scanning without the attacker's IP being logged in to the victim's IDS.

5. PREVENTION OF CYBERCRIME

Cybercrime refers to criminal activities that are carried out using computers, networks, and the internet. These activities are designed to compromise integrity, confidentiality, or availability of information or computer systems (Demertzi et al., 2023). Cybercriminals use various techniques to exploit vulnerabilities and gain unauthorized access to data for financial gain, disruption, or other malicious purposes.

5.1. Prevent the Organization

Preventing cybercrime involves a multifaceted approach that combines technological, organizational, and individual measures. Here are key elements of a comprehensive cybercrime prevention strategy:

- **Risk Assessment Framework:** A Risk Assessment Framework is a systematic and methodical approach to identify, evaluate, and manage risks within an organization's cybersecurity landscape. The key element is assigning a numerical Risk Score to each identified risk. This score is derived by multiplying the likelihood of a risk occurring by its potential financial impact. Variables influencing the likelihood of risk include the frequency of threats, the ease with which they can be exploited, and the effectiveness of existing response mechanisms. The comprehensive approach results in understanding potential monetary loss, sensitive data compromise, and reputational harm that may be incurred if a particular risk materializes. To further refine and prioritize these risks, a Risk Grade classification system is employed. This system categorizes risks as Low, Medium, or High based on the probability of occurrence and the potential consequences, as outlined by Mallah et al. (2021).

- **Attack Graph:** An indispensable component of cybersecurity defense is using an Attack Graph, which visually represents potential attack paths within a computer network or system. Generated by automated tools scanning for vulnerabilities, the Attack Graph assists security analysts in identifying likely attack scenarios and prioritizing efforts to resolve critical vulnerabilities. By analyzing the system's components, such as network services, operating systems, and application vulnerabilities, the Attack Graph visually represents potential attack vectors. The graphical depiction is invaluable for identifying critical paths an attacker might follow and assessing the efficacy of existing security measures, as emphasized by Liu et al., (2022).
- **Fundamental Cybersecurity Tools:** While Risk Assessment Frameworks and Attack Graphs provide strategic insights, deploying fundamental cybersecurity tools is equally crucial. Firewalls, for instance, act as a frontline defense against external threats, preventing malicious access and unauthorized traffic from compromising the integrity of the organization's network. On the other hand, antivirus and malware-fighting software play a pivotal role in detecting and eliminating a spectrum of threats, including viruses, spyware, and other malware that could compromise the organization's structure (Madi et al., 2020). However, it is essential to recognize that these tools, while indispensable, only form a part of a comprehensive organizational well-being strategy. A holistic approach includes ongoing employee training to cultivate a security-aware culture, regular software updates to patch vulnerabilities, and implementing preventive measures. This multifaceted strategy aims to minimize the risk of cyberattacks and safeguard sensitive information, recognizing that cybersecurity is a dynamic and evolving challenge that requires continuous vigilance and adaptation.

Cybercrime prevention is an ongoing and evolving process. Organizations and individuals must adapt strategies to address emerging threats and vulnerabilities in the dynamic cybersecurity landscape.

5.2. Prevention against Zombie Attacks

Preventing an organization from falling victim to a zombie attack or any form of unauthorized activity requires a combination of proactive security measures, robust policies, and continuous monitoring (Almaiah et al., 2020). Here are several strategies to help prevent and mitigate the impact of zombie attacks:

- **Network Segmentation:** Implement network segmentation to isolate critical systems and limit lateral movement for attackers. It helps contain potential threats and prevents attackers from easily traversing the entire network.
- **Firewall Configuration:** Configure firewalls to filter and monitor incoming and outgoing traffic. Employ strict rules to allow only necessary communication and block unauthorized or suspicious connections.
- **Regular Security Audits:** Conduct regular security audits and vulnerability assessments to identify and address potential weaknesses in the organization's infrastructure. It includes identifying and securing idle or vulnerable machines.
- **Endpoint Security:** Implement robust endpoint security solutions, including antivirus software, endpoint detection and response (EDR) tools, and device management policies. Keep all systems and software up-to-date with the latest security patches.
- **Access Controls:** Enforce strong access controls and least privileged principles. Limit user permissions to only the resources and applications required for their roles. Regularly review and update access permissions.
- **Incident Response Plan:** Develop and regularly test an incident response plan to ensure a swift and effective response to security incidents, including zombie attacks. Define roles, responsibilities, and communication procedures during a security incident.
- **Network Monitoring:** Implement continuous network monitoring to detect unusual patterns of activity. It includes monitoring for sudden increases in traffic, multiple login failures, or other indicators of Compromise.
- **Patch Management:** Establish a robust patch management process to apply security updates and patches to all systems promptly. Attackers can exploit unpatched vulnerabilities to gain unauthorized access.
- **Encryption and Authentication:** Use encryption to protect sensitive data in transit and ensure strong authentication methods, such as multi-factor authentication (MFA), to enhance user account security.
- **Collaboration with ISPs:** Collaborate with Internet Service Providers (ISPs) to identify and block malicious traffic at the network perimeter. It can be particularly helpful in mitigating large-scale attacks.

- **Behavioral Analysis:** Implement behavioral analysis tools that can identify abnormal behavior patterns on the network. It can help detect zombie-like activities that may go unnoticed by traditional security measures.

Remember that a holistic and proactive approach to cybersecurity is crucial. Regularly reassess and update security measures to adapt to evolving threats. Additionally, having a well-prepared incident response plan is essential to minimize the impact of a security incident, including a zombie attack.

CONCLUSION

In addressing the threat of zombie attacks within a corporate environment, our exploration of the Idle Scan emphasizes the critical aspects of detection, prevention, and avenues for future work. Detecting zombie attacks involves vigilant network monitoring, behavioral analysis, and continuous security audits. Employing intrusion detection systems (IDS) and endpoint security solutions aids in identifying anomalous patterns and compromised devices. Preventing zombie attacks requires strategic measures, including firewall configurations to monitor outbound connections, user education for heightened awareness, and timely security patching. A comprehensive cybersecurity approach encompasses technology, user training, and proactive vulnerability management to reduce the risk of successful zombie attacks. Organizations can consider integrating advanced threat intelligence feeds for real-time threat awareness for future work. Exploring machine learning for anomaly detection enhances the accuracy of identifying unusual network patterns, while implementing automated incident response mechanisms streamlines the containment and mitigation process. In conclusion, a dynamic and adaptive cybersecurity strategy is essential for mitigating the risks posed by zombie attacks in a corporate setting. By combining robust detection mechanisms, preventive measures, and ongoing improvement initiatives, organizations can fortify their defenses against evolving cyber threats and cultivate a resilient security posture.

REFERENCES

Addula, S. R., Norozpour, S., & Amin, M. (2025). Risk Assessment for Identifying Threats, vulnerabilities and countermeasures in Cloud Computing. *Jordanian Journal of Informatics and Computing*, *2025*(1), 38–48. DOI: 10.63180/jjic.thestap.2025.1.5

Adil, M., Almaiah, M. A., Omar Alsayed, A., & Almomani, O. (2020). An anonymous channel categorization scheme of edge nodes to detect jamming attacks in wireless sensor networks. *Sensors (Basel)*, *20*(8), 2311. DOI: 10.3390/s20082311 PMID: 32325646

Al-Attar, B. (2023). Network Security in AI-based healthcare systems. *Babylonian Journal of Networking*, *2023*, 112–124. DOI: 10.58496/BJN/2023/015

Al-Hashemi, S. Q. Y., Naghmash, M. S., & Ghandour, A. (2024). Improving IP Video Surveillance Systems: The Shift to Digital Networks and Security Challenges. *SHIFRA*, *2024*, 17–23. DOI: 10.70470/SHIFRA/2024/003

Al-Quraishi, T., Mahdi, O. A., Abusalem, A., Ng, C. K., Gyasi, A., Al-Boridi, O., & Al-Quraishi, N. (2024). Transforming Amazon's Operations: Leveraging Oracle Cloud-Based ERP with Advanced Analytics for Data-Driven Success. *Applied Data Science and Analysis*, *2024*, 108–120. DOI: 10.58496/ADSA/2024/010

Al-Shareeda, M. A., Obaid, A. A., & Almajid, A. A. H. (2025). The Role of Artificial Intelligence in Bodybuilding: A Systematic Review of Applications, Challenges, and Future Prospects. *Jordanian Journal of Informatics and Computing*, *2025*(1), 16–26. DOI: 10.63180/jjic.thestap.2025.1.3

Aldawood, H., & Skinner, G. (2020). An Advanced Taxonomy for Social Engineering Attacks. *International Journal of Computer Applications*, *177*(30), 1–11. DOI: 10.5120/ijca2020919744

Alhamed, M., & Rahman, M. M. H. (2023). A Systematic Literature Review on Penetration Testing in Networks: Future Research Directions. *Applied Sciences (Basel, Switzerland)*, *13*(12), 6986. DOI: 10.3390/app13126986

Ali, A. (2024). Adaptive and Context-Aware Authentication Framework Using Edge AI and Blockchain in Future Vehicular Networks. *STAP Journal of Security Risk Management*, *2024*(1), 45–56. DOI: 10.63180/jsrm.thestap.2024.1.3

Aljohani, A. (2023). Zero-trust architecture: Implementing and evaluating security measures in modern enterprise networks. *Shifra*, *2023*, 60–72. DOI: 10.70470/SHIFRA/2023/008

Almaiah, A., & Almomani, O. (2020). An investigation of digital forensics for shamoon attack behaviour in FOG computing and threat intelligence for incident response. *Journal of Theoretical and Applied Information Technology*, *15*, 98.

Almaiah, A. M. I. N., & Almomani, O. M. A. R. (2020). An investigator digital forensics frequencies particle swarm optimization for dectection and classification of apt attack in fog computing enviroment (idf-fpso). *Journal of Theoretical and Applied Information Technology*, *15*, 98.

Almaiah, M. A., Al-Zahrani, A., Almomani, O., & Alhwaitat, A. K. (2021). Classification of cyber security threats on mobile devices and applications. In *Artificial intelligence and blockchain for future cybersecurity applications* (pp. 107–123). Springer International Publishing. DOI: 10.1007/978-3-030-74575-2_6

Almaiah, M. A., Almomani, O., Alsaaidah, A., Al-Otaibi, S., Bani-Hani, N., Hwaitat, A. K. A., Al-Zahrani, A., Lutfi, A., Awad, A. B., & Aldhyani, T. H. (2022). Performance investigation of principal component analysis for intrusion detection system using different support vector machine kernels. *Electronics (Basel)*, *11*(21), 3571. DOI: 10.3390/electronics11213571

Almaiah, M. A., Dawahdeh, Z., Almomani, O., Alsaaidah, A., Al-Khasawneh, A., & Khawatreh, S. (2020). A new hybrid text encryption approach over mobile ad hoc network. [IJECE]. *International Journal of Electrical and Computer Engineering*, *10*(6), 6461–6471. DOI: 10.11591/ijece.v10i6.pp6461-6471

Almaiah, M. A., Saqr, L. M., Al-Rawwash, L. A., Altellawi, L. A., Al-Ali, R., & Almomani, O. (2024). Classification of Cybersecurity Threats, Vulnerabilities and Countermeasures in Database Systems. *Computers, Materials & Continua*, *81*(2), 3189–3220. DOI: 10.32604/cmc.2024.057673

Almomani, O. (2020). A feature selection model for network intrusion detection system based on PSO, GWO, FFA and GA algorithms. *Symmetry*, *12*(6), 1046. DOI: 10.3390/sym12061046

Almomani, O. (2021). A Hybrid Model Using Bio-Inspired Metaheuristic Algorithms for Network Intrusion Detection System. *Computers, Materials & Continua*, *68*(1), 409–429. DOI: 10.32604/cmc.2021.016113

Almomani, O., Almaiah, M. A., Alsaaidah, A., Smadi, S., Mohammad, A. H., & Althunibat, A. (2021, July). Machine learning classifiers for network intrusion detection system: comparative study. In *2021 International Conference on Information Technology (ICIT)* (pp. 440-445). IEEE. DOI: 10.1109/ICIT52682.2021.9491770

Almomani, O., Alsaaidah, A., Shareha, A. A. A., Alzaqebah, A., & Almomani, M. (2024). Performance Evaluation of Machine Learning Classifiers for Predicting Denial-of-Service Attack in Internet of Things. *International Journal of Advanced Computer Science and Applications*, *15*(1). Advance online publication. DOI: 10.14569/IJACSA.2024.0150125

Alotaibi, E., Bin Sulaiman, R., & Almaiah, M. (2025). Assessment of cybersecurity threats and defense mechanisms in wireless sensor networks. *Journal of Cyber Security and Risk Auditing*, *2025*(1), 47–59. DOI: 10.63180/jcsra.thestap.2025.1.5

Alowaisheq, E., Tang, S., Wang, Z., Alharbi, F., Liao, X., & Wang, X. (2020). Zombie Awakening: Stealthy Hijacking of Active Domains through DNS Hosting Referral. *Proceedings of the 2020 ACM SIGSAC Conference on Computer and Communications Security*. DOI: 10.1145/3372297.3417864

Alraizza, A., & Algarni, A. (2023). Ransomware Detection Using Machine Learning: A Survey. *Big Data and Cognitive Computing*, *7*(3), 143. DOI: 10.3390/bdcc7030143

Alsahaim, S., & Maayah, M. (2023). Analyzing Cybersecurity Threats on Mobile Phones. *STAP Journal of Security Risk Management*, *2023*(1), 3–19. DOI: 10.63180/jsrm.thestap.2023.1.2

Alsajri, A., Steiti, A., & Salman, H. A. (2023). Enhancing IoT Security to Leveraging ML for DDoS Attack Prevention in Distributed Network Routing. *Babylonian Journal of Internet of Things*, *2023*, 74–84. DOI: 10.58496/BJIoT/2023/010

Ani, U. P. D., He, H., & Tiwari, A. (2016). Review of cybersecurity issues in industrial critical infrastructure: Manufacturing in perspective. *Journal of Cyber Security Technology*, *1*(1), 32–74. DOI: 10.1080/23742917.2016.1252211

Antony, J., & Maity, T. (2021). Analysis of Ethernet Control Network. *Journal of the Institution of Electronics and Telecommunication Engineers*, *69*(3), 1588–1596. DOI: 10.1080/03772063.2020.1871427

Arora, L., Thakur, N., & Yadav, S. K. (2021). USB Rubber Ducky Detection by using Heuristic Rules. *2021 International Conference on Computing, Communication, and Intelligent Systems (ICCCIS)*. DOI: 10.1109/ICCCIS51004.2021.9397064

. Beale, S. S., & Berris, P. (2018). Hacking the Internet of Things: Vulnerabilities, Dangers, and Legal Responses. Digitization and the Law, 21–40. DOI: 10.5771/9783845289304-21

Belmabrouk, K. (2023). Cyber Criminals and Data Privacy Measures. *Advances in Information Security, Privacy, and Ethics*, •••, 198–226. DOI: 10.4018/979-8-3693-1528-6.ch011

Bhushan, K., & Gupta, B. B. (2018). Distributed denial of service (DDoS) attack mitigation in software defined network (SDN)-based cloud computing environment. *Journal of Ambient Intelligence and Humanized Computing*, *10*(5), 1985–1997. DOI: 10.1007/s12652-018-0800-9

Biswas, B., Mukhopadhyay, A., Kumar, A., & Delen, D. (2024). A hybrid framework using explainable AI (XAI) in cyber-risk management for defence and recovery against phishing attacks. *Decision Support Systems*, *177*, 114102. DOI: 10.1016/j.dss.2023.114102

Brewer, R. (2014). Advanced persistent threats: Minimising the damage. *Network Security*, *2014*(4), 5–9. DOI: 10.1016/S1353-4858(14)70040-6

Brooks, R. R., Yu, L., Ozcelik, I., Oakley, J., & Tusing, N. (2022). Distributed Denial of Service (DDoS): A History. *IEEE Annals of the History of Computing*, *44*(2), 44–54. DOI: 10.1109/MAHC.2021.3072582

Carroll, F., Ạdejobi, J. A., & Montasari, R. (2022). How Good Are We at Detecting a Phishing Attack? Investigating the Evolving Phishing Attack Email and Why It Continues to Successfully Deceive Society. *SN Computer Science*, *3*(2), 170. Advance online publication. DOI: 10.1007/s42979-022-01069-1 PMID: 35224514

Chidukwani, A., Zander, S., & Koutsakis, P. (2022). A Survey on the Cyber Security of Small-to-Medium Businesses: Challenges, Research Focus and Recommendations. *IEEE Access : Practical Innovations, Open Solutions*, *10*, 85701–85719. DOI: 10.1109/ACCESS.2022.3197899

Demertzi, V., Demertzis, S., & Demertzis, K. (2023). An Overview of Cyber Threats, Attacks and Countermeasures on the Primary Domains of Smart Cities. *Applied Sciences (Basel, Switzerland)*, *13*(2), 790. DOI: 10.3390/app13020790

Duan, Z., Chen, P., Sanchez, F., Dong, Y., Stephenson, M., & Barker, J. M. (2012). Detecting Spam Zombies by Monitoring Outgoing Messages. *IEEE Transactions on Dependable and Secure Computing*, *9*(2), 198–210. DOI: 10.1109/TDSC.2011.49

Hou, C., Shi, J., Cui, M., & Yang, Q. (2021). Attack versus Attack: Toward Adversarial Example Defend Website Fingerprinting Attack. 2021 IEEE 20th International Conference on Trust, Security and Privacy in Computing and Communications (TrustCom). DOI: 10.1109/TrustCom53373.2021.00111

Hussain, M., Siddiqui, S., & Islam, N. (2023). Social Engineering and Data Privacy. *Advances in Information Security, Privacy, and Ethics*, •••, 225–248. DOI: 10.4018/978-1-6684-6581-3.ch010

Ibrahim, A. (2024). Transitioning Emerging Economies Toward Sustainability by Implementing Targeted Policy Interventions. *ESTIDAMAA*, *2024*, 53–59. DOI: 10.70470/ESTIDAMAA/2024/008

Jafarian, J. H., Abolfathi, M., & Rahimian, M. (2023). Detecting Network Scanning Through Monitoring and Manipulation of DNS Traffic. *IEEE Access : Practical Innovations, Open Solutions*, *11*, 20267–20283. DOI: 10.1109/ACCESS.2023.3250106

Khaleel, Y. L., Habeeb, M. A., & Edoh, T. O. C. (2025). Limitations of deep learning vs. human intelligence: Training data, interpretability, bias, and ethics. *Applied Data Science and Analysis*, *2025*, 3–6. DOI: 10.58496/ADSA/2025/002

Khalid, H., Hashim, S. J., Ahmad, S. M., Hashim, F., & Chaudary, M. A. (2020). Cybersecurity in Industry 4.0 context: Background, issues, and future directions. *The Nine Pillars of Technologies for Industry*, *4*(0), 263–307. DOI: 10.1049/PBTE088E_ch14

Lallie, H. S., Debattista, K., & Bal, J. (2020). A review of attack graph and attack tree visual syntax in cyber security. *Computer Science Review*, *35*, 100219. DOI: 10.1016/j.cosrev.2019.100219

Liu, K., Wang, F., Ding, Z., Liang, S., Yu, Z., & Zhou, Y. (2022). Recent Progress of Using Knowledge Graph for Cybersecurity. *Electronics (Basel)*, *11*(15), 2287. DOI: 10.3390/electronics11152287

Maayah, M. (2025). Framework for Node Detection in Cloud Computing: A Multi-Metric Approach Integrating Security, Availability, and Latency Factors. *Journal of Cyber Security and Risk Auditing*, *2025*(4), 238–256. DOI: 10.63180/jcsra.thestap.2025.4.4

Madi, M., Jarghon, F., Fazea, Y., Almomani, O., & Saaidah, A. (2020). Comparative analysis of classification techniques for network fault management. *Turkish Journal of Electrical Engineering and Computer Sciences*, *28*(3), 1442–1457. DOI: 10.3906/elk-1907-84

Mallah, R. A., Lopez, D., & Farooq, B. (2021). Cyber-Security Risk Assessment Framework for Blockchains in Smart Mobility. *IEEE Open Journal of Intelligent Transportation Systems*, *2*, 294–311. DOI: 10.1109/OJITS.2021.3106863

Martineau, M., Spiridon, E., & Aiken, M. (2023). A Comprehensive Framework for Cyber Behavioral Analysis Based on a Systematic Review of Cyber Profiling Literature. *Forensic Science*, *3*(3), 452–477. DOI: 10.3390/forensicsci3030032

Mensah, G. B., Mijwil, M. M., Abotaleb, M., Ali, G., & Dutta, P. K. (2025). High Performance Medicine: Involving Artificial Intelligence Models in Enhancing Medical Laws and Medical Negligence Matters A Case Study of Act, 2009 (Act 792) in Ghana. *SHIFAA*, *2025*, 1–6. DOI: 10.70470/SHIFAA/2025/001

Mohammed, S. Y., & Aljanabi, M. (2023). Human-Centric IoT for Health Monitoring in the Healthcare 5.0 FrameworkDescriptive Analysis and Directions for Future Research. *EDRAAK*, *2023*, 21–26. DOI: 10.70470/EDRAAK/2023/005

Mohammed, S. Y., & Aljanabi, M. (2024). Advancing Translation Quality Assessment: Integrating AI Models for Real-time Feedback. *EDRAAK*, *2024*, 1–7. DOI: 10.70470/EDRAAK/2024/001

. Möller, D. P. F. (2023). Ransomware Attacks and Scenarios: Cost Factors and Loss of Reputation. Guide to Cybersecurity in Digital Transformation, 273–303. DOI: 10.1007/978-3-031-26845-8_6

. Moneva, A., Leukfeldt, E. R., & Romagna, M. (2023). Fieldwork Experiences Researching Cybercriminals. Fieldwork Experiences in Criminology and Security Studies, 511–533. DOI: 10.1007/978-3-031-41574-6_27

Naqvi, B., Perova, K., Farooq, A., Makhdoom, I., Oyedeji, S., & Porras, J. (2023). Mitigation strategies against the phishing attacks: A systematic literature review. Computers &amp. *Computers & Security*, *132*, 103387. DOI: 10.1016/j.cose.2023.103387

Nay, T. (2024). Enhancing IoT Security with AI-Driven Hybrid Machine Learning and Neural Network-Based Intrusion Detection System. *Babylonian Journal of Artificial Intelligence*, *2024*, 158–167. DOI: 10.58496/BJAI/2024/017

Osanaiye, O., Choo, K.-K. R., & Dlodlo, M. (2016). Distributed denial of service (DDoS) resilience in cloud: Review and conceptual cloud DDoS mitigation framework. *Journal of Network and Computer Applications*, *67*, 147–165. DOI: 10.1016/j.jnca.2016.01.001

Pan, H., Wang, R., Wang, H., & Jia, Z. (2023). Sustainable Supply Chain Management: Best Practices for Reducing Environmental Footprints in the Global Apparel Industry. *ESTIDAMAA*, *2023*, 18–26. DOI: 10.70470/ESTIDAMAA/2023/003

. saad Mohamed, T., Marqas, R., Almufti, S. M., & Asaad, R. R. (2025). Evaluation of Information Security through Networks traffic traces for machine learning classification. Babylonian Journal of Networking, 2025, 25–42.

Tankard, C. (2011). Advanced Persistent threats and how to monitor and deter them. *Network Security*, *2011*(8), 16–19. DOI: 10.1016/S1353-4858(11)70086-1

Varshney, G., Kumawat, R., Varadharajan, V., Tupakula, U., & Gupta, C. (2024). Anti-phishing: A comprehensive perspective. *Expert Systems with Applications*, *238*, 122199. DOI: 10.1016/j.eswa.2023.122199

Wang, Y., Wang, Y., Qin, H., Ji, H., Zhang, Y., & Wang, J. (2021). A Systematic Risk Assessment Framework of Automotive Cybersecurity. *Automotive Innovation*, *4*(3), 253–261. DOI: 10.1007/s42154-021-00140-6

Yan, S., Ren, J., Wang, W., Sun, L., Zhang, W., & Yu, Q. (2023). A Survey of Adversarial Attack and Defense Methods for Malware Classification in Cyber Security. *IEEE Communications Surveys and Tutorials*, *25*(1), 467–496. DOI: 10.1109/COMST.2022.3225137

Zieni, R., Massari, L., & Calzarossa, M. C. (2023). Phishing or Not Phishing? A Survey on the Detection of Phishing Websites. *IEEE Access : Practical Innovations, Open Solutions*, *11*, 18499–18519. DOI: 10.1109/ACCESS.2023.3247135

Chapter 6
Adoption of Artificial Intelligence Techniques for Enhancing Host-Based Intrusion Detection Systems

Tarun Kumar Vashishth
https://orcid.org/0000-0001-9916-9575
IIMT University, Meerut, India

Rupak Sharma
SRM Institute of Science and Technology, Modinagar, India

Vikas Sharma
https://orcid.org/0000-0001-8173-4548
SRM Institute of Science and Technology, Modinagar, India

Puneet Chauhan
https://orcid.org/0009-0000-1652-8764
Swami Vivekanand Subharti University, Meerut, India

Sachin Chaudhary
https://orcid.org/0000-0002-8415-0043
IIMT University, Meerut, India

Brijesh Kumar Sharma
SRM Institute of Science and Technology, Modinagar, India

ABSTRACT

The rapid wave of growth in information systems has led to millions of new attack surfaces have been created by these devices due to the rapid development of information technologies but have left many systems vulnerable to sophisticated forms of cyber-attacks as well. Modern warfare finds it increasingly harder to qualify in today's presumably automatized world, which further implies that automated systems need to be developed. The aim of such technology is to assist a user in considering and assessing huge datasets containing indicators of suspicious behaviour and even

DOI: 10.4018/979-8-3373-1807-3.ch006

2026, IGI Global Scientific Publishing. Copying or distributing in print or electronic forms without written permission of IGI Global Scientific Publishing is prohibited. Use of this chapter to rative artificial intelligence (AI) technologies is expressly prohibited. The publisher reserves all rights to license its use for generative AI training and machine learning model development.

taking actions against emerging threats. This chapter outlines the use of cutting-edge technologies in the Host-Based Intrusion Detection Systems, including ML algorithms, deep learning for networks and natural language processing.

1. INTRODUCTION

1.1 Overview of Cybersecurity Threat Landscape

In recent years, the cybersecurity sector has undergone tremendous transformations, which can be attributed to the increase in sophistication and intricacy of cybercrimes (Al-Shareeda et al., 2025) and (Addula et al., 2025). In the present era, more and more organizations are utilizing the cloud as well as interconnected devices. As a result, there has been an expansion in their attack surfaces, which in turn, has led to new vulnerabilities and opportunities for cybercriminals to exploit and use advanced Tactics, Techniques, and Procedures (TTPs) to gain unauthorized access, steal sensitive information, damage infrastructure, and inflict financial and reputational losses. These threats encompass a variety of attack vectors such as phishing, ransomware, Advanced Persistent Threats (APTs), DDoS, and zero-day attacks (Almomani et al., 2024)(Alazawi et al., 2024; Alsajri & Steiti, 2024). The speed at which these threats change is often faster than traditional counters and security measures can provide a reliable response to them (Gupta et al., 2024). It can be noted that the recently noted trend of adopting and utilizing automation and AI by attackers to increase the scale and accuracy of their attacks, has played a role in aiding these attacks as well. As an example, AI-enabled malware is capable of changing its behaviour in a manner that makes its detection more difficult and social engineering attacks are also becoming better convincing and more personalized as they rely on stolen information (Ali, 2024) and (Alsahaim & Maayah, 2023). Moreover, with the emergence of the Internet of Things (IoT), more difficulties emerged as millions of connected devices are new attack surfaces for malicious actors. Many of these devices have little to no security in place, making them ideal candidates for abuse (Jain et al., 2023). The research problem addressed in this paper is the limited efficiency of traditional Host-Based Intrusion Detection Systems (HIDS), which struggle with high false alarm rates, difficulty in detecting zero-day attacks, and poor adaptability to evolving threats. This study explores how AI techniques can overcome these limitations to improve accuracy, adaptability, and real-time detection

1.1.1 Increasing Sophistication of Cyberattacks

With the emergence of new technologies, the complexity and volume of cyber-attacks have grown immensely (Davarasan et al., 2024) and (Chandran et al., 2025). The methods used by cybercriminals have transformed, and they now use tools like AI, ML, and automation as a means to create an attack that is silent, modified, and more damaging than ever. These attacks are not only limited to malware or viruses; there are APT, ransomware, phishing attacks, DDoS and zero-day attacks. For example, Advanced Persistent Threats are specific types of attacks that are targeted for a long time with the intention of stealing a certain kind of information. On the same note, ransomware attacks have shown an upward trend and grown from a simple grab and go tactic to an elegant orchestrated strike across the healthcare, finance and government agencies. During these attacks, complex encryption methodologies are being used to lock people out of their devices and later charging them blindly. Cybercriminals take advantage of zero-day vulnerabilities which are considered the gaps in software or hardware that are unknown to their vendors and left unpatched. Such vulnerabilities are really difficult to mitigate due to the fact that standard security systems are dependent on known behavioural patterns or signatures to pinpoint threats and zero-day exploits go unnoticed. This is further compounded by the fact that, today, social engineering, where unauthorized access is gained through human psychological manipulation by sending persuasive phishing emails and messages, is on the rise. Also, the proliferation of IoT devices has increased the attack surface considerably. They are weakly reinforced and thus open up fresh possibilities for attackers. To compound matters, these devices are often employed as gateways to bigger systems and are frequently part of a botnet for extensive DDoS attacks. In such a situation, conventional approaches to security, such as firewalls, antivirus applications, and manual vigilance, will not suffice. Cyberattacks have become increasingly sophisticated and automated meaning that the cyber defences do too. This is where intrusion detection systems come in (Chen, 2024)(Amirthayogam et al., 2024; Shibghatullah, 2023).

1.1.2 Role of Intrusion Detection Systems (IDS) in Mitigating Threats

Intrusion Detection Systems (IDS) are crucial components of any organization's network security that can signal the presence of an unauthorized intruder or malicious action in the system. They enhance security by in real time looking for and analyzing incoming data traffic to discover potential suspicious behaviours, attack patterns, or even particular signs of malicious behaviour (Swarnkar and Rajput, 2023).

IDS are broadly categorized into two types:

a. **Network-Based Intrusion Detection Systems (NIDS):** Such good detection methods are employed where nefarious activities originating from outside the computer system are detected. To further elaborate, systems are specifically constructed for detecting server or service denial attempts, brute force assault or network scans, all of which are termed as network intrusion detection systems (NIDS) (Bauskar, 2024). Figure 1 shows incoming network traffic flowing through components such as data collection, preprocessing, feature extraction, and detection engine.

Figure 1. Basic Structure of Network -Based Intrusion Detection Model

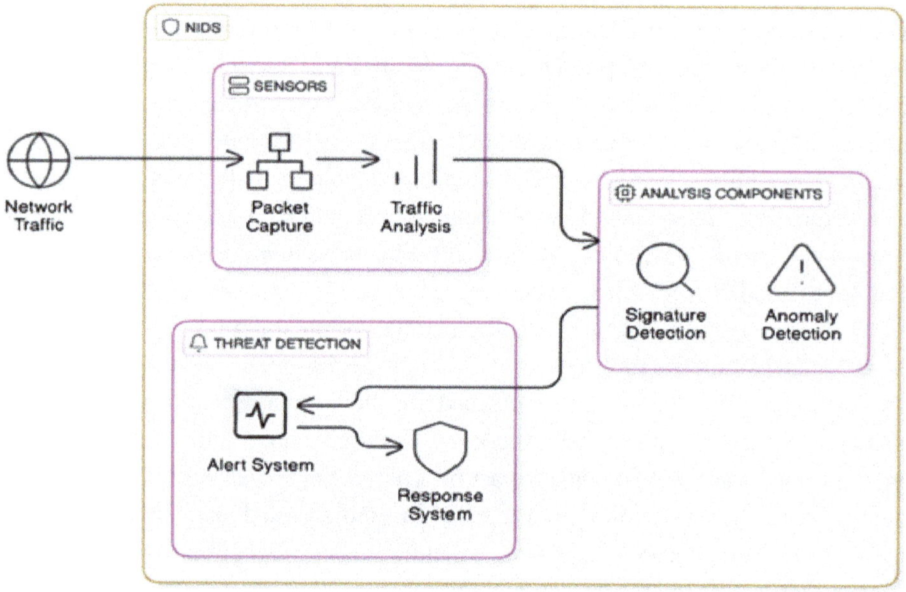

b. **Host-Based Intrusion Detection Systems (HIDS):** These deal with specific devices such as incorporation of log file analysis, file integrity, and system file processes. HIDS does more or less the same as NIDS with an exception in the type of threat. It works more efficiently against internal threats such as privilege escalation or impersonation.

Active research on the three forms of IDS is dominant and aids in the improvement of other IDS. As in the case of intrusion detection systems, a comparative approach is used whereby the performed activity is compared against specified Native languages codes in the case of signature-based intrusion detections systems.

With IDS, intrusion systems have pre-configured known signatures that are used to detect observed nefarious behaviour. Hybrid approaches mesh the primary strengths of both strategies increasing detection rate. The function of an IDS is not limited to simply spotting breaches; it is also functioning as a proactive measure against unauthorized access which assists the organization in undertaking timely corrective actions. For instance, if an invasion detection system observes unexpected behaviour, it can notify a security team for necessary actions like addressing the situation i.e. forbidding a rogue IP address or switching off invaded computers (Adil et al., 2020).

Nevertheless, the traditional IDS system, despite its vital significance, has problems of its own in today's constantly changing landscape and security problems. Attackers and their hacking tools really use just these characteristics to dismantle a system and attack it, while defenders are usually overwhelmed by high false positive rates. Therefore, to counter these limitations, modern IDS incorporate AI and machine learning methods more frequently. Such systems are advanced because they are able to weed through a mass of data to find minute patterns of attack and in the same instance counter potential attacks.

1.2. Host-Based Intrusion Detection Systems (HIDS)

Host-Based Intrusion Detection Systems (HIDS) are integral to contemporary cybersecurity approaches and are meant to supervise and assess the behaviour of single devices or hosts in a network. As opposed to Network-Based Intrusion Detection Systems (NIDS), which are dependent on network monitoring, HIDS are installed on key devices, with endpoints including servers and workstations. Their ultimate goal is to prevent any form of illegitimate access, sabotage or deviation from regulatory protocols by monitoring the logs, the integrity of files, user activity and the workings of different applications.

HIDS work by gathering and assessing data from multiple sources which include system logs, audit logs and even application logs. These systems analyze the gathered data in order to establish a baseline that would help detect potential threats, for example:

- Unauthorized file modifications, deletions, or access attempts.
- Unexpected or suspicious processes running on the host.
- Privilege escalation activities where a user attempts to gain unauthorized administrative access.
- Changes in system configurations or registry settings that could compromise security.
- Known attack signatures or malware behaviours detected within the host environment.

One of the distinguishing features of HIDS is its ability to offer security features at a more in-depth host level. For instance, monitoring all internal protective measures prevents an employee from accessing data without the firm's authorization. HIDS has also been developed to oversee encrypted communications which NIDS cannot do thus contributing to enhanced responsibility in the prevention of intrusions which are not detected by other methods.

HIDS typically employ two primary detection methods:

1. **Signature-Based Detection:** This method relies on predefined attack signatures, allowing the system to quickly identify known threats.
2. **Anomaly-Based Detection:** This method establishes a baseline of normal behaviour for the host and identifies deviations that may indicate malicious activity.

Once HIDS recognizes any malicious action, they can report to appropriate security forces, create a log of the incident, or even act automatically by deleting the malicious program, or more importantly, the host computer that has been compromised.

Limitations of traditional HIDS approaches: Despite their utility, traditional HIDS face several limitations that reduce their effectiveness in today's rapidly evolving threat landscape:

1. **High False Positives:** Legacy HIDS often identifies a high number of legitimate activities as malicious, leading to the generation of frauds. This in turn hinders security teams, which causes alert fatigue, and other potentially real threats to go unnoticed.
2. **Limited Scalability:** HIDS are exclusive to hosts and therefore, it needs to be installed in every single endpoint. The case where hundreds or thousands of devices are used and HIDS becomes resource demanding and very difficult to install and maintain.
3. **Inability to Detect Novel Threats:** Signature-Based HIDS is dependent on certain preset rules or patterns, which prevents them from being able to withstand zero-day exploits or any new previously undiscovered attack targets. As a result of this, Anomaly-detection is able to provide some level of assistance against this, and most times when deployed in non-intrusively tuned environments is able to overcome this challenge with ease.
4. **Performance Overheads:** As stated previously, resource consumption incurred by constant calculation and thorough monitoring can be excessively high, resulting in the host system deteriorating in terms of overall functioning. This is in the first place a major concern in environments with limited resources available, or inside critical servers that are needed to work at maximum possible efficiency.

5. **Reactive Nature:** It is well known that most traditional HIDS are after the fact preserving systems, that is they try to uncover and record threats which have already occurred. In that regard, they are unable to assist in conducting pre-emptive measures to stop a probable attack or limit the damage that will be done.
6. **Insider Threat Challenges:** Although HIDS technology has some capabilities to reduce insider attacks, they have a lot of difficulties separating malicious behaviour from regular behaviour that is out of the ordinary, but is performed by a legitimate user. This is even more pronounced in dynamic environments.
7. **Lack of Integration with Other Systems:** Usually, HIDS works as a standalone application without appropriate integration on Security Information Management and Event Monitoring (SIEM) system. This decentralized working hinders the systems from providing an all-round view of the security position of the institution.

1.3. Relevance of Artificial Intelligence (AI) in Cybersecurity

AI comes in empowerment and transformation of cybersecurity, considering the growing number and complexity of cyber threats. An organization able to utilize the technology of computerized real time data analysis can accomplish strategic goals as it is possible to detect deviations, build vulnerabilities and neutralize threats with a speed and accuracy never seen before. As a key component of AI, machine learning algorithms allow systems to utilize information obtained from previous events to automatically improve which makes them effective in matching new attack trends such as phishing, malware, and ransomware. Moreover, AI tools enhance endpoint security, handle basic activities and improve reaction to incidents, easing the workload of human analysts. Furthermore, predicting the threat becomes easier through the use of AI, which can be actively used to resolve the problem before it becomes an issue. Given that such attackers use AI to create more intricate attacks, utilizing about AI in cybersecurity strategies will be instrumental. Nonetheless, ethical issues, data protection issues as well as a lack of skilled manpower to erect, operate and maintain such AI systems remain to be the major bottlenecks in the implementation of the technology (Markevych and Dawson, 2023).

1.3.1 Advantages of AI in Identifying and Responding to Complex Threats

1. **Real-Time Threat Detection**: AI encounters big data in areas such as network traffic, system logs among others and makes sense out of the enormous amount of information in mere seconds thereby applying instantaneous instead of the

more common proactive approaches to sophisticated types of cyber threats that include APTs and zero-day exploits.

2. **Pattern Recognition and Anomaly Detection**: AI design program emulates the thought process of human beings. A decision-making analyst operating at such a high and intelligent level monitors all activities going on, noticing any deviation from the norm. In doing so, AI as a technology shows high capability and efficacy remotely monitoring attack techniques which previously were unnoticed or always overlooked (Madi et al., 2020)(Nay, 2024).
3. **Adaptive Learning**: Disruptive Technologies are characterized by an increased performance or enhanced functionality at a lower cost, such as, the automation of processes with the use of AI. Threats through the use of AI techniques do not appear as duplicates; on the contrary, they appear as evolving threats. With ever increasing cyber criminals, engaging new attack strategies, AI works effectively in extending security (Rizqullah et al., 2024).
4. **Automated Threat Response**: AI significantly speeds up and lessens the consequences of any attacks, it achieves this by locating, reminding, and dealing with threats by itself. When combined with AI, incident response can be performed significantly faster and more effectively with little or no human input.
5. **Improved Accuracy**: AI aided machine learning models get better over time as they begin to identify invasive patterns and behaviours, letting the machine learn what good and bad looks like while resulting in way less unnecessary alerts (Alsaaidah et al., 2024).
6. **Enhanced Threat Intelligence**: AI assesses the TTPs of cybercriminals, which gives them better information about how attacks are conducted. This information helps firms to enhance their security measures and better prepare for emerging risks.
7. **Reduced Human Intervention**: AI spares human analysts by automating threat detection and response which allows security teams to concentrate on higher priorities and also eliminates human error during response interventions.
8. **Faster Response to New Threats**: AI systems are capable of rapidly detecting new, unidentified threats and can recommend measures that will greatly minimize the probability of an attacker causing damage.

1.3.2 AI-Driven Transformation of HIDS

The AI revolution of Host-based Intrusion Detection Systems (HIDS) revolutionizes the cybersecurity landscape, greatly improving it on a system-by-system basis. HIDS have historically placed a great reliance on signature-based methods, which entails using a database of known attack signatures to check incoming data or system activity. Although adept at addressing known threats, this methodology frequently fails at detecting new, advanced, and zero-day threats. HIDS were enabled with AI to help overcome these drawbacks and allow the system to learn patterns of behavior and identify true anomalies of the attack time without needing to have knowledge of it beforehand. AI-enhanced HIDS deploy machine learning algorithms to inspect system logs, file alterations, and users routinely. During this baseline setting, AI can detect malignant behaviours by identifying discrepancies from the routine using a scope of standard activity within a host which include but are not limited to strange user activities, file access without clearance and entry of malware. This technique is more versatile than the old one as it can discover new types of threats that were hard to trace before and grow with changing attack types. Last but not least, AI can improve the efficiency of HIDS by eliminating false alerts. Due to alert fatigue, traditional systems generate an alarm to benign activity that resembles an attack pattern. Artificial intelligence systems evolve with usage as they learn how to discriminate between benign and malicious activities making them more accurate and minimizing the number of unneeded alerts. Furthermore, AI makes it possible to automate remediations by isolating compromised hosts or triggering defensive measures previously set, ensuring the incidents are handled quickly and relieving the security team's workload. Another benefit brought by AI-driven HIDS is their capability for predictive capabilities, thanks to machine learning models HIDS can forecast threats before they completely appear by analyzing historical data trends. This indicates the security teams can take measuring actions ahead of time before potential threats occur therefore improving overall Defense posture of an organization. To sum up, AI-driven transformation of HIDS leads to the development of more adaptive, accurate, responsive and fully secure systems that provide for a great number of potential attacks, thus HIDS constitutes a basic tool for the cybersecurity strategies of modern times (Kathirvel and Maheswaran, 2023).

2. FUNDAMENTALS OF HIDS AND AI TECHNIQUES

2.1. Architecture of HIDS

The aim of a Host-based Intrusion Detection System (HIDS) is to monitor and protect against security breaches on specific hosts by detecting malicious behavior. Usually, Host-based Intrusion Detection Systems can be composed of multiple different components that complement each other in providing real-time protection. The first part is a data collection module that collects information from different system components such as file systems, processes, network connections, and logs. Thereafter, this information is forwarded to the analysis module, where patterns for anomalies or attack signatures are searched for. The analysis module employs different detection techniques which measures system behaviours against a known database of attack signatures and vice versa (Almaiah et al., 2024)(Gide & Mu'azu, 2024). Anomaly-based detection attempts to recognize patient behavior patterns which routinely deviate from the baseline through the application of advanced machine learning algorithms. The third component is the module that engages in decision making as it makes use of the results from the analysis phase. It can either issue alerts regarding any threats that might be present, or it can take actions like availing necessary measures against a compromised system. The last of the modules is the reporting and alerting module which gives the findings to system administrators and security staff so they can mount a detailed response in case there is an incident. The combination of these components in a well-integrated HIDS architecture will ensure that organizations are able to identify a wider range of attacks and reduce the security threats within the host level systems. Figure 2 represents the architectural model of a Host-Based Intrusion Detection System (HIDS). The structure begins with the host machine where system logs, application logs, and audit data are collected.

Figure 2. Architectural Model of HIDS

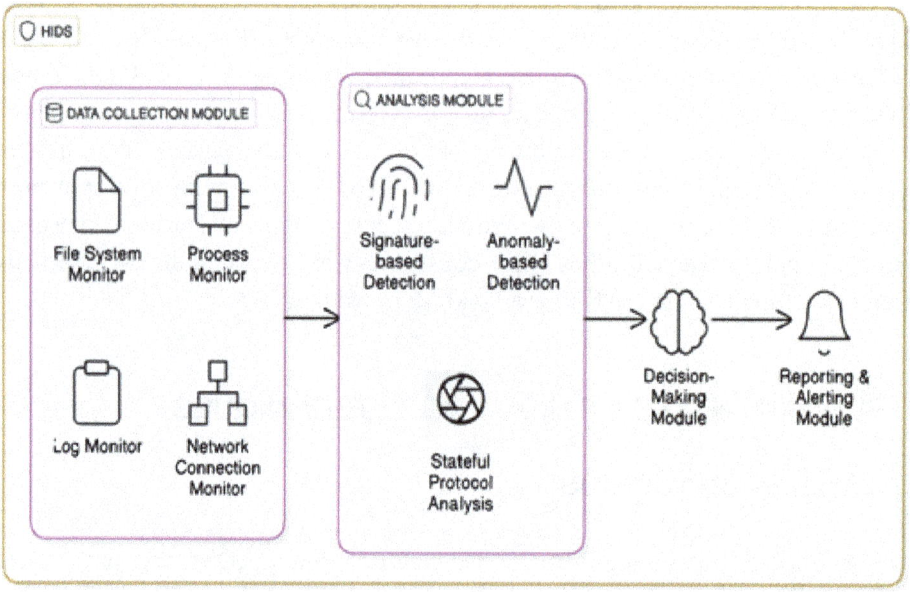

2.2. AI Techniques in Cybersecurity

AI approaches act as game changers in improving the quality of cybersecurity measures by providing tools that are used to detect, analyze, and respond to the threats. These approaches assist security systems in making more precise and rapid decisions by enabling them to adapt and learn from data which in turn helps the organization in countering the complex nature of the cyberattacks. Key AI methods adopted in cybersecurity include machine learning (ML), deep learning (DL), natural language processing (NLP), and Anomaly detection.

1. **Machine Learning (ML)**: In the field of cybersecurity, machine learning has become a game changer as it helps practitioners sift through oceans of data to pinpoint characteristics that indicate nefarious intent. ML algorithms make use of past information to determine if an event is benign or malign based on certain metrics such as system logs, network traffic, and user behavior. As the name implies, fully supervised learning relies on labelled data, whereas the unsupervised approach is able to detect anomalies without pre-existing labels. Spam detection, malware analysis, intrusion detection, and fraud detection are just a few examples where ML techniques are frequently used.
2. **Deep Learning (DL)**: Deep Learning, which is a type of machine learning, uses Artificial neural networks but with many layers to automatically create complicated abstractions of data. In the realm of cybersecurity, deep learning approaches perform exceptionally well in many applications such as coding that uses images, and traffic analysis that searches for code that is embedded in traffic. In the combat against APTs and zero - day hacking attacks, convolutional neural networks and RNNs are preferred as they can work with unstructured data including raw traffic or even system logs (Sebastian and Hajri, 2024)(Aljanabi et al., 2024; Mohialden et al., 2024).
3. **Natural Language Processing (NLP)**: Natural language processing techniques help computers understand human language so they are able to act on emails, social media, or chat logs. In cyber security, NLP helps uncover phishing and social engineering and other types of fraud against the backdrop of the language used in the communication content. NLP models can also be useful for analyzing cyber security reports and threat intelligence feeds and provide security analysts with hints about unfolding threats quickly.
4. **Anomaly Detection**: Anomaly detection is an essential AI concept that is geared towards understanding abnormal and deviant behavior of networks, systems or users. Such models are capable of highlighting abnormal behaviours or slight deviations of the baseline normal behavior implying an attack or breach. Clustering techniques, outlier detection, and statistical modeling are some of the techniques that can be used for the detection of insider threats, malware, and even unusual access behaviours that could indicate data leakage or compromise of a system.

5. **Automated Response and Decision-Making**: This AI technology can also respond to and neutralize threats after they have been identified. For instance, after being flagged as a threat, IT managers can utilize AI systems to settle actions such as blocking malicious IP servers or isolating compromised systems from the rest of the network. Automating such actions greatly shortens the span of time between the identification of the threat and the neutralization, effectively reducing the damage zodiacal an attack may cause.

Considering this, it becomes readily apparent why Cyber Security Omsk relies on Artificial Intelligence techniques – they have become almost invaluable as the frequency of cyber-attacks rises and becomes more sophisticated by the minute. It's worth noting that these techniques make it possible to analyze vast amounts of information quickly and to devise optimal models for detection using AI. Consequently, AI-assisted cyber defense strategies can enhance security by being intelligent, adaptive, and responsive at the same time (Poornima et al., 2023).

2.3. Challenges in Traditional HIDS

Traditional intrusion detection technologies, such as Host-based Intrusion Detection Systems, or HIDS, have served and continue to serve as the backbone of the cybersecurity ecosystem. These technologies allow the monitoring and identification of malicious activities taking place within single hosts or endpoints. HIDS have their limit, and with this limit, automation comes into play – Cyber threats leave HIDS as an obsolete intend and proposes a series of issues, including performance overhead, limited agility, lack of scalability, and complicated alert management.

1. **Performance Overhead**: One of the main drawbacks of HIDS is that it has a higher performance impact on the host machine. HIDS systems usually have to continuously monitor file accesses, network activities and processes running in the computer. Such operations can result in large number of CPUs, Memory and storage being utilized which might degrade the performance of the host machine. Hence, these systems are not applicable to every device or environment. For example: it won't work for real time applications or embedded systems that have a resource constraint.
2. **Limited Detection Capabilities**: HIDS are more classically based on signature-based detection. With such a method, system activity is compared with signature of known attacks that has been set previously. This method can be very useful in detecting attacks that have been identified beforehand, but has problems in detecting new forms of attacks. These include zero-day attacks and advanced persistent threats. It is not surprising that cybercriminals update their methods,

and when using HIDS solely depending on signatures, they run a risk of missing many new attacks. This characteristic is one of the main reasons why traditional HIDS cannot guarantee protection against new more advanced cyberattacks.

3. **Scalability Issues**: As enterprises grow and their network settings become more intricate, existing HIDS have limitations in regards to scalability. With the multitude of systems producing voluminous data, usage of multiple endpoints, especially in a wide area becomes challenging. When it comes to larger firms, the number of individual hosts that HIDS is responsible for can be in hundreds or thousands which over time will need vast resources to be dedicated to collection, analysis and storage of data. Existing HIDS have limitations in regards to scaling unless the environment has been built up to avoid bottlenecks or heavy infrastructure investment has been made.
4. **Alert Management and False Positives**: One other primary shortcoming of existing HIDS solutions is the issue of alert management. There are multiple such alerts generated in regards to suspicious activity and for security teams going through all of them can be a daunting task. Of these alerts, many of them are actually incorrect and are turned into positive alerts, which turns them into everyday activities. Positively incorrect activities can demolish the functional aspect of HIDS to a security team which then causes involuntary alertness and slow reaction times. Losing out on the ability of correctly addressing real threats. This flooding of notifications can cause disruption in the process of segregating and attending to real security incidents.
5. **Evasion Techniques**: Concise and effective HIDS solutions could potentially minimize or remove the crippling activities of such complex attackers however, it is important to note that attackers may still leverage on biologically or chemically encrypt their Trojan horses to highjack the HIDS. The stress of troublesome log files and configuration settings are the main components that disabling or modifying may demand which are not too difficult to do. Due to this, HIDS lose their effectiveness and along with it the ability to detect any malicious activities.
6. **Integration and Interoperability**: Basic HIDS can be regarded as independent tools that lack compatibility with other security resources but implement a narrower functionality. More recent developments in information technology and computer security have resulted in widespread adoption of an active security posture where systems are expected to work in concert for a holistic Defense. The HIDS that perform poorly when interfacing with other complementing solutions such as SIEM or NIDS have a great likelihood of either missing critical contextual data or have impaired ability to cross-reference incidents from different or multiple layers of the network. This leads to failures in sufficient

coverage and poor threat mitigation (Mani Gopalsamy, 2021)(Adday et al., 2025; Marab & Bhadrashetty, 2023).

Basic HIDS do provide a means to identify host-based cyber threats but they are not without their shortcomings which inhibit their use as effective means in the more recent and advanced cyber security settings. Insufficient detection rates, load overheads, difficulties in management of alerts, difficulties in scaling, reliance on which techniques to evade and lack of integration are some of the major restraints to the use of the HIDS systems which further lack a 360 contextual awareness. As cyber threats develop, organizations are starting to implement more radical and robust techniques such as artificial intelligence and machine learning for both overcoming the limitations posed due to older cyber threats and enhancing the efficacy of their cyber intrusion detection systems.

3. INTEGRATION OF AI IN HIDS

Artificial Intelligence (AI) has been implemented in HIDS systems, and as a result, they can detect and respond to threats more accurately, more quickly and more effectively. These systems depend on the specialization of AI to understand patterns and learn from them. There are three crucial stages involved in the process: collection and preprocessing of data, applying AI models, and the detection of real-time threats.

3.1. Data Collection and Preprocessing

An AI-driven HIDS system's success is based on the relevant data it manages to find. Today's HIDS systems located within a host can cross reference and collect data from file access logs, processes completed, network connections, and system calls. This data is often corrupt and unstructured which doesn't make it easy for AI analysis; thus, it needs to be reprocessed first. Preprocessing covers a range of aspects such as cleaning, which is the removal of useless or repetitive information, normalizing which makes values consistent, converting information into suitable formats such as feature vectors, or tensors, for later AI analysis. The other components are extraction, where features representing system behavior are included. For example, consider a process log; features extracted may comprise process ID, files being executed and execution time. This ensures that the data fed into AI models is both relevant and optimized for analysis, enabling the system to detect subtle anomalies that may indicate malicious activity.

3.2. AI Models for HIDS

Artificial intelligence improves the working of host-based intrusion detection systems by making it possible for them to automatically detect malicious activities and anomalies within a host. Each model that is incorporated in HIDS is elaborated below-

1. **Machine Learning (ML) Models:** Machine learning models are crucial in HIDS because they can discern between good and bad usage patterns in the data. Supervised models, like Decision Trees, Random Forests, and Support Vector Machines (SVMs), learn with labelled datasets that contain normal and malicious activity. These models learn to classify incoming data into predefined categories. Alternatively, a type of machine learning model referred to as unsupervised learning including K-Means and autoencoders works on unlabelled data and attempts to find an anomaly as deviation from the norm. In semi-supervised learning a mix of both labelled along with unlabelled data is used thus proving to be useful where there is lack of labelled malicious data.
2. **Deep Learning Models:** Neural networks greatly assist with intrusion detection by spotting complicated patterns in data. Artificial neural networks are most effective at analyzing the numerous input features as normal or an attack. Recurrent neural networks are indispensable to the understanding of time series because they model temporal information, like patterns that may signify an attack within system logs. Convolutional neural networks work well in image classification tasks while long short-term memory networks which are a sub-type of recurrent neural networks make use of temporal sequences to better detect more complex attacks (Wang, 2023)(Adamopoulos et al., 2025; Noori & Albahri, 2023).
3. **Hybrid Models:** AI strategies paired with statistical techniques on a hybrid model allow for better adaptability, and precision. For example, statistical anomaly detection can be useful for understanding a specific context and looking at abnormalities over time using neural networks. Good insight models can be effective in an environment where there is a need to combine domain and insights, resulting in a model that is both more accurate and more robust than any one element on its own.
4. **Ensemble Learning Techniques:** Ensemble techniques enhance the detection capabilities of individual models by merging their predictions together. Boosting techniques such as Gradient Boosting or AdaBoost enhance weak learners by paying attention to misclassified points, and bagging techniques such as Random Forests decrease the variance of model predictions through averaging across several different models. Due to the use of other models' capabilities, ensemble

techniques also tend to be more reliable and robust across different intrusion types.

5. **Reinforcement Learning (RL):** The interesting thing about Reinforcement Learning models is that these models learn from their interactions with the environment, the right strategies for intrusion detection. These models undergo gradual changes because they are rewarded or punished based on what they do. In particular, RL is effective in situations where threats change, which is the case for HIDS since it can incrementally change its detection strategies.

3.3. Real-Time Threat Detection

One of the main benefits of AI in HIDS is the ability to conduct continuous threat identification. HIDS can now be able to utilize models which permit a streamed flow of data to be scanned in real time. This allows for immediate detection as live activity is matched with previous learned models or behaviours. For example, if a certain process accessing certain files shows abnormal behaviour, an AI HIDS can flag this event and send automated alerts or responses. This type of detection is especially useful in combatting rapidly changing threats like ransomware or zero-day exploits. Moreover, AI allows the system to classify the threat into categories limiting how long a certain type of incident will take to resolve. Faced with real time threats, automated systems can perform a number of tasks to isolate the damaged systems so that no further damage is done. Any unauthorized access can be prevented by AI and the damage caused can be minimized. With AI embedded in the threat identification process, it becomes possible for HIDS to help protect host systems by knowing the enemy first. Figure 3 shows continuous data input from host and network sources being fed into preprocessing and feature engineering modules. The processed data is analysed by AI components such as machine learning classifiers, deep learning models, and anomaly detection engines.

Figure 3. Real- Time Threat Detection AI Model

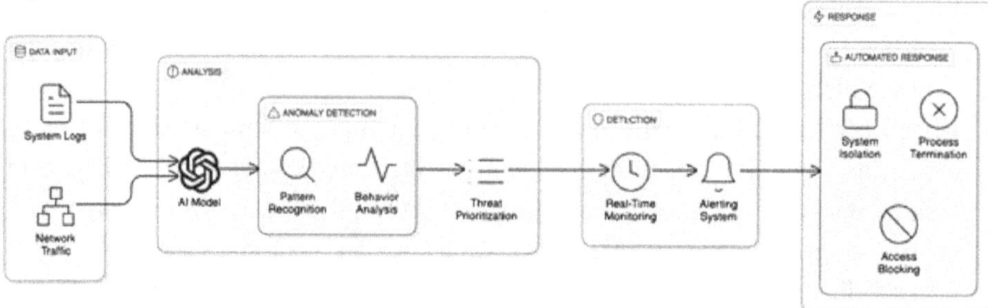

4. PROPOSED METHODOLOGY

The proposed methodology aims to enhance Host-Based Intrusion Detection Systems (HIDS) by leveraging Artificial Intelligence (AI) techniques to overcome limitations such as high false alarm rates, difficulty in detecting zero-day attacks, and lack of adaptability. Traditional HIDS primarily rely on static rule-based or signature-based detection, which struggles to keep pace with evolving attack patterns. In contrast, the proposed framework integrates machine learning and hybrid AI approaches to improve detection accuracy, scalability, and real-time responsiveness. The novelty of this methodology lies in its hybrid design that combines supervised and unsupervised learning techniques. Supervised models are employed to identify known attack signatures using labelled datasets, while unsupervised anomaly detection models are integrated to capture emerging or previously unseen threats. To further optimize performance, feature selection techniques such as Random Forest–based ranking are applied, ensuring that only the most relevant host-level attributes are used for classification. This reduces computational overhead while improving accuracy. In addition, the proposed framework incorporates ensemble learning, where multiple classifiers such as Support Vector Machines (SVM), Convolutional Neural Networks (CNN), and Decision Trees collaborate to achieve higher detection precision. This ensemble approach mitigates the weaknesses of individual models and ensures robustness against sophisticated intrusion attempts. The system also adapts continuously by retraining on new data, allowing it to evolve with changing threat landscapes.

Overall, this methodology provides a structured and adaptive AI-driven solution for HIDS, demonstrating novelty through its integration of hybrid learning models, optimized feature selection, and ensemble classification. By addressing gaps in traditional systems, it offers a scalable, intelligent, and efficient mechanism for detecting both known and unknown intrusions at the host level.

5. ENHANCING HIDS WITH AI: CASE STUDIES AND APPLICATIONS

The combination of artificial intelligence and HIDS is transforming the capacity to reduce security threats on a host level. This section seeks out to prove how AI improves the effectiveness of HIDS by exploring AI and HIDS case studies and applications over different environments.

5.1. Case Studies

Various real-life implementations of HIDS facilitated by AI have shown the usefulness of these systems. In this report I will detail the context, use and conclusion of those case studies.

Case Study 1: AI-Enhanced HIDS in a Corporate IT Network

Ransomware, insider threats, and advanced persistent threats have taken the forefront as the major cybersecurity threats to global corporate IT networks. So, prioritizing on security for endpoint devices and internal servers was vital for safeguarding our organization. To counter the dangers posed by the APT strategy, our organization established a domestic AI model that integrates supervised and unsupervised learning approaches. Additionally, the deep learning-based anomaly detection systems were integrated to allow monitoring of patterns developed by the users. As a result of this integration, the AI-enhanced HIDS was able to identify unauthorized privilege escalations, foiling what could have otherwise turned out to be a high-profile data exfiltration, as well as a previously undiscovered phishing campaign.

Case Study 2: AI in HIDS for Healthcare Systems

With the constant evolution of healthcare systems into a more digital realm, advanced measures were required to ensure that electronic health records (EHR) were protected and in compliance with the laws. An example of such measures is an AI-based professional healthcare system that a healthcare facility has in place. This system uses RNNs, or recurrent neural networks, to help scrutinise access logs and find instances of irregular access. The system also deployed an AI model in the form of behaviour profiling where medical staff were closely monitored through the correct use of data and estimation of valid login activity. This strategy was effective when the system detected an internal data breach where a user from the staff center attempted to illegally get access to a patient file. Furthermore, in terms of AI ethics and regulations, by automating the identification of policy breaches, the healthcare facilities also improved their data security to avoid any compliance fines.

Case Study 3: AI in Cloud Environments

SWOT analysis strategy facilitates learning effectively and according to direction. Additionally, it helps in the development of more concrete goals and action plans. The identification of internal and external factors affecting the company helps to warn while continuing political analysis. Strengths, weaknesses, opportunities and threats analysis and strategy development will enable decision makers to look beyond the organization's existing capabilities. Furthermore, to gain a more holistic view of the organization, the company applies STEEPLE analysis which helps to discover external factors affecting the organization. Both of these analyses also aid in the identification of problems and gaps.

5.2. Applications in Diverse Environments

AI Host-Based Intrusion Detection Systems (HIDS) have developed a reputation for competence in a variety of contexts. The various application areas are further elaborated below.

1. **Enterprise Networks:** In enterprise networks, AI-enhanced HIDS monitors user behaviour, application activity, and system logs to identify potential threats like insider attacks, malware infections, or unauthorized access attempts. These systems leverage machine learning models to analyze vast amounts of data generated by endpoint devices and servers. For example, financial institutions use AI-based HIDS to monitor access to sensitive data and detect unusual patterns that may signal fraudulent activities. By reducing false positives and automating threat detection, AI-powered HIDS improves operational efficiency and bolsters organizational security.
2. **Critical Infrastructure:** Critical infrastructure, such as energy, transportation, and utilities, is increasingly dependent on digital systems, making it vulnerable to cyberattacks. AI-powered HIDS is crucial in these environments to monitor industrial control systems (ICS) and supervisory control and data acquisition (SCADA) systems. These systems detect deviations in operational parameters, such as abnormal system commands or unauthorized device connections. For instance, in smart grid networks, AI-driven HIDS can detect and neutralize anomalies that could compromise energy distribution, ensuring the uninterrupted delivery of essential services.
3. **Cloud Environments:** Cloud environments present unique security challenges due to their dynamic workloads and reliance on virtualized resources. AI-enhanced HIDS monitors access patterns, API calls, and data flows to identify potential threats such as misconfigurations, unauthorized access, or lateral movements within cloud platforms. By leveraging advanced AI techniques like generative models and reinforcement learning, these systems adapt to evolving workloads and configurations. For example, AI-based HIDS can secure multi-tenant cloud infrastructures by preventing data breaches and detecting denial-of-service (DoS) attacks (Vashishth et al., 2024).

4. **IoT Ecosystems:** The proliferation of Internet of Things (IoT) devices has expanded the attack surface for cybercriminals. AI-driven HIDS protects IoT ecosystems by analyzing device behaviour, network traffic, and system logs to detect anomalies indicative of compromised devices. These systems are particularly effective in environments where resource-constrained IoT devices lack built-in security measures. For instance, in industrial IoT (IIoT) systems, AI-enhanced HIDS can detect unusual communication patterns or unauthorized firmware updates, safeguarding critical processes and devices in manufacturing or supply chain environments (Saied et al., 2024).
5. **Healthcare Systems:** Healthcare environments face significant cybersecurity risks due to the sensitive nature of patient data and the growing use of connected medical devices. AI-based HIDS monitors electronic health record (EHR) systems, medical device activities, and hospital network traffic to identify suspicious behaviour. For instance, these systems can detect unauthorized attempts to access patient records or ransomware attacks targeting hospital management systems. By ensuring compliance with data protection regulations and maintaining patient trust, AI-driven HIDS plays a pivotal role in healthcare security (Vashishth et al., 2024).

6. CHALLENGES AND LIMITATIONS IN AI-DRIVEN HIDS

6.1 Challenges in AI-Driven Host-Based Intrusion Detection Systems (HIDS)

Integrating AI into HIDS has improved greatly in terms of being able to identify new threats and respond to them. I believe that there are some challenges associated with the AI integration into HIDS. The challenges stem from the nature of AI models, the security threats landscape, and the organizations capable of integrating AI HIDS. Below is a detailed explanation of the key challenges in AI-driven HIDS:

1. **High Computational Requirements:** AI-powered HIDS systems often require significant computational resources to analyze vast amounts of data in real time. These systems utilize complex algorithms, such as deep learning and neural networks, which demand powerful hardware like GPUs and high-speed processors. The resource-intensive nature of AI algorithms can strain the infrastructure of organizations, particularly small and medium-sized enterprises (SMEs) with limited budgets. Additionally, continuous model training and updates to maintain effectiveness further add to the computational load, making scalability a challenging prospect.

2. **Data Quality and Availability:** The success of AI models in HIDS heavily depends on the availability of high-quality training data. Poorly labelled or insufficient datasets can lead to inaccurate threat detection, resulting in false positives or missed attacks. Furthermore, the dynamic nature of cybersecurity means that datasets must constantly be updated to reflect the latest threats. Organizations often face challenges in gathering representative and diverse datasets, especially for rare attack scenarios like zero-day vulnerabilities. Legal and ethical restrictions on data sharing further complicate the acquisition of comprehensive datasets.
3. **Adaptability to Evolving Threats:** Cyber threats are continually evolving, with attackers developing sophisticated methods to bypass security mechanisms. AI-driven HIDS systems, particularly those relying on supervised learning, are often trained on historical data. This makes them less effective in identifying novel or zero-day attacks. While unsupervised learning and reinforcement learning models attempt to address this issue by adapting to new patterns, their success hinges on continuous updates and retraining, which can be resource-intensive and time-consuming.
4. **Vulnerability to Adversarial Attacks:** AI systems are susceptible to adversarial attacks, where malicious actors craft input data designed to deceive the model. In the context of HIDS, adversaries may introduce subtle changes to malware or system behaviours to bypass detection or trigger false alarms. These adversarial inputs exploit the limitations of AI algorithms, posing a significant challenge to the reliability of HIDS. Developing robust models capable of resisting such attacks is an ongoing area of research in AI and cybersecurity.
5. **Lack of Explainability:** Many AI models, particularly deep learning-based ones, function as "black boxes," making their decision-making processes difficult to interpret. This lack of explainability can create challenges for security teams in understanding why a specific activity was flagged as malicious. Without clear insights into the rationale behind alerts, it becomes difficult to validate or act on the AI's findings. The need for explainable AI (XAI) in HIDS is critical to build trust in the system and to enable informed decision-making during incident responses.
6. **False Positives and Alert Fatigue:** While AI enhances the accuracy of HIDS, it is not immune to generating false positives—benign activities mistakenly flagged as malicious. Excessive false positives can overwhelm security teams, leading to alert fatigue and reduced vigilance. This creates a scenario where genuine threats may be overlooked due to the high volume of irrelevant alerts. Striking a balance between sensitivity and specificity in AI algorithms is a continuous challenge to ensure optimal performance without overwhelming human operators.

6.2 Limitations in AI-Driven Host-Based Intrusion Detection Systems (HIDS)

The landscape of cybersecurity today has been profoundly altered by AI driven Host Based Intrusion Detection Systems which have superior capabilities for detecting and anticipating threats. These systems are not perfect and still require refinement before they can be universally implemented. This brings us to the deficiencies of AI driven HIDS:

1. **Dependence on High-Quality Data:** The performance of AI-driven HIDS relies heavily on the quality and quantity of the data used for training and validation. High-quality datasets that accurately represent diverse attack patterns and normal system behaviour are essential for effective detection. However, obtaining such data is often challenging due to privacy concerns, the proprietary nature of security logs, and the difficulty in simulating real-world cyberattacks. Moreover, biases or inaccuracies in the data can result in unreliable detection, leading to false positives or negatives that undermine the system's reliability.
2. **Limited Generalization to Novel Threats:** AI models trained on historical data often struggle to generalize to novel or previously unseen threats, such as zero-day vulnerabilities or advanced persistent threats (APTs). While some models use unsupervised learning or anomaly detection to identify unusual behaviours, these methods can still fail to detect sophisticated attacks that closely mimic legitimate activity. The inability to adapt to new threat vectors without retraining limits the long-term effectiveness of AI-driven HIDS.
3. **Susceptibility to Adversarial Manipulation:** AI models in HIDS are vulnerable to adversarial attacks, where attackers deliberately craft inputs to deceive the system. For instance, malicious actors may introduce subtle changes to malware or system activity to avoid detection, effectively exploiting the weaknesses of the AI model. This susceptibility poses a significant risk to the reliability of AI-driven HIDS, as adversarial manipulation can lead to both missed detections and false alarms, undermining trust in the system.
4. **Resource-Intensive Operations:** AI-driven HIDS systems are resource-intensive, requiring substantial computational power to process and analyze large volumes of data in real time. High-performance hardware, such as GPUs, and significant memory and storage are often prerequisites for deploying such systems. This limitation can make it challenging for organizations with constrained budgets, particularly small and medium-sized enterprises (SMEs), to adopt AI-driven HIDS. The high resource demands also raise concerns about scalability, particularly in large, complex networks.

5. **Lack of Explainability:** One of the critical limitations of AI-driven HIDS is the lack of transparency and explainability in decision-making, especially for systems based on deep learning or other complex algorithms. These systems often function as "black boxes," making it difficult for security professionals to understand why a specific activity was flagged as malicious or benign. This lack of interpretability not only reduces trust in the system but also complicates incident response, as security teams struggle to validate alerts and take appropriate actions.
6. **High False Positive Rates:** While AI models aim to improve accuracy, they are not immune to false positives, where legitimate activities are flagged as threats. Excessive false positives can overwhelm security teams, leading to "alert fatigue," where genuine threats may be overlooked due to the volume of non-critical alerts. Balancing sensitivity (detecting threats) and specificity (avoiding false positives) remains a significant challenge in the design and deployment of AI-driven HIDS (Salim and Hasoon, 2024).
7. **Integration Challenges:** Integrating AI-driven HIDS into existing IT infrastructure, particularly legacy systems, can be complex and costly. Many organizations face compatibility issues, requiring significant customization and adaptation to ensure seamless operation. Furthermore, maintaining interoperability in hybrid environments that combine on-premises and cloud-based systems adds another layer of complexity. These challenges can delay deployment and reduce the overall effectiveness of the system (Vashishth et al., 2024).
8. **Ethical and Legal Constraints:** AI-driven HIDS systems often deal with sensitive data, such as user activity logs and system configurations. Handling this data raises ethical concerns about privacy and transparency, as well as legal obligations under regulations like the General Data Protection Regulation (GDPR) or the Health Insurance Portability and Accountability Act (HIPAA). Organizations must navigate these constraints carefully to avoid potential legal repercussions and maintain trust with users and stakeholders.

7. FUTURE DIRECTIONS IN AI-DRIVEN HIDS

The field of cybersecurity is in for a revolutionary change with the introduction of AI-powered host-based intrusion detection systems (HIDS). The threats to computer security are constantly changing and becoming more sophisticated, so these systems will need to evolve too. As the world continues to embrace the new advancements in artificial intelligence, there are several avenues that could maximize the scale, and scope of HIDS. In this article, we'll be delving into those avenues in-depth:

1. **Integration of Explainable AI (XAI):** Most AI-assisted HIDS systems are still in their infant stage and are not quite ready for deployment as one of the biggest shortcomings is the black box phenomenon, which makes understanding the decisions made by IT experts impossible for employees. It is highly likely that future research will be dedicated to the development of Explainable AI (XAI) that addresses those concerns and provides a clear and easy to understand answer to why a certain system recognized a specific event. XAI will greatly increase the trust being placed in AI systems by increasing the number of instances where the system's logic can be clearly understood by the end user.
2. **Leveraging Federated Learning for Privacy-Preserving HIDS:** There is no need to overemphasize how serious of an issue protecting sensitive data in cybersecurity is. To ease some of those tensions, a model trained using federated learning does not allow for the AI to be shared and keeps the data on the device local While the approach is not widely adopted, there is a considerable amount of room HIDS to grow and expand. That growth can be achieved through colluding with other organizations to improve the machine learning models even when the data being used is encrypted. Federated learning stands out as a powerful solution to most data privacy and security issues enabling AI powered HIDS to be more reliable and secure.
3. **Adaptive and Real-Time Learning Systems:** The future may bring an online machine learning and reinforcement learning integrated HIDS that can help in detecting and countering threats dynamically. In tandem with the threats HIDS of the future would counter, there is a strong likelihood that they will be equipped with an adaptable system and automated re-train mechanism, which would lessen the need for human involvement in the system.
4. **Hybrid Models Combining Multiple AI Techniques:** There is a strong concern regarding the acknowledgment of weaknesses and correcting them through supervised learning, unsupervised learning and reinforcement learning, hybrid modes are suspected to embrace boost in detection accuracy due to the variability and variety of the methods used. Unsupervised learning can leverage reinforcement strategies to better classify supervised models after identifying outliers.
5. **Enhanced Resilience Against Adversarial Attacks:** Generating Gamers, and deploying generative adversial networks have proven to be effective in reducing malicious activities within FiDs; With that in mind, augmenting the resilience of these systems should be a top priority as it would raise the reliability of AI embedded HIDS and at the same time boost trust within the system. Some effective methods include using Generative Adversial Networks, and exposing systems to various attack types during the training phase.

6. **Incorporating AI-Driven Threat Intelligence:** In the future, it is projected that an amalgamation of AI integrated with HIDS will proactively help identify and mitigate risks. This possible amalgamation is capable with the aid of correlating global threat data alongside localized systems activities to recommend measures which would lead to potential attacks being anticipated and prevented. Furthermore, another possible area of growth is NLP aiding in parsing threat intelligence reports and creating actionable insights.
7. **Cloud-Based and Distributed HIDS Architectures:** As businesses now are steadily shifting to multi-cloud frameworks, HIDS has to now shift towards protecting and monitoring geographically diverse systems. A centralized AI integrated HIDS is all that is needed to provide and expand resources needed to monitor expansive multi-faceted networks. In addition to this leveraging edge AI will result in a distributed architecture which will promote efficient AI detection and resolution function eliminating any form of inefficiencies through increased optimization (Barach, 2024). Figure 4 shows the distributed architecture of a multi-cloud framework. Multiple cloud environments are interconnected, each hosting security components such as intrusion detection agents, data storage, and monitoring tools. A central coordination layer manages communication and synchronization across these clouds, ensuring load balancing, redundancy, and fault tolerance.

Figure 4. Distributed Architecture of Multi-Cloud Framework

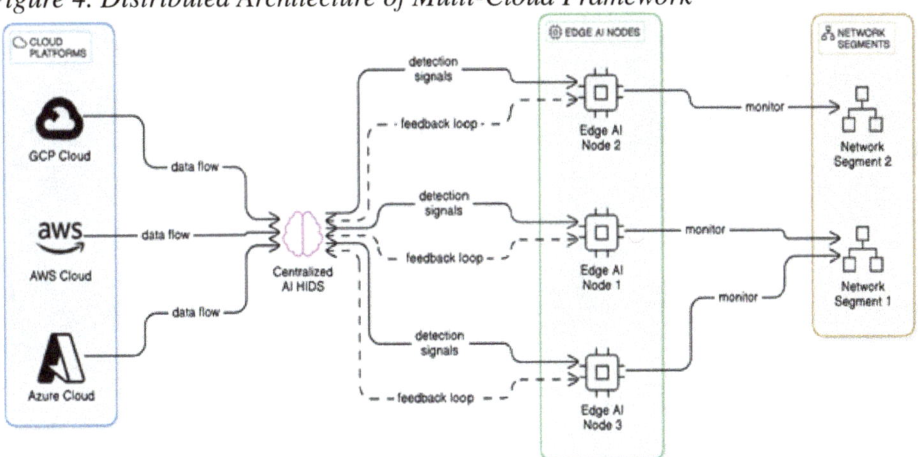

8. CONCLUSION

In the field of cyber security, the advent of Artificial Intelligence (AI) techniques enhancing Host-Based Intrusion Detection Systems (HIDS) brings a paradigm shift. Old Strategies, which are of great importance, have difficulties dealing with the level and amount of modern cybersecurity attacks. HIDS powered by AI can bolster security systems with a more sophisticated and more efficient means of protection by incorporating machine learning algorithms, deep learning models and natural language processing to identify and mitigate harmful activities with much more efficiency. In this particular chapter, it has been illustrated how deep learning has the capacity to transform human intrusion detection systems from reliance on complex contingencies to multifaceted anomaly detection and offensive threat intelligence and automated mitigation strategies. This implies that the incorporation of deep learning into human intrusion detection systems enables real-time detection of new threats and the recognition of intricate data along with new attacking trends. Still, issues such as reliance on data, the investment of resources and adversarial weaknesses still exist, although, recent development in AI technologies including explanatory AI systems, federated models and hybrid designs are expected to mitigate these issues. In light of the evolving cyber threat environment, the implementation of AI driven HIDS is emerging to be a normal rather than an advanced concept. On the other hand, adopting such systems enables businesses to not only better defend themselves and their operations, but also ensures that they are adaptable during this unprecedented time of digital warfare.

REFERENCES

Adamopoulos, I., Valamontes, A., Karantonis, J. T., Tropaitis, P. P., & Syrou, N. (2025). Enhancing Economic Growth Time Series for UAE Forecasting with Deep Learning: A Seq2Seq and Attention-Driven LSTM Approach. *EDRAAK, 2025*, 62–75. DOI: 10.70470/EDRAAK/2025/009

Adday, B. N., Shaker, K., Salman, I., & Shaker, H. (2025). Parkinson's Disease Detection Using Deep learning approach based on Wearable Sensor-Based Daily Monitoring. *Mesopotamian Journal of Artificial Intelligence in Healthcare, 2025*, 26–38. DOI: 10.58496/MJAIH/2025/003

Addula, S. R., Norozpour, S., & Amin, M. (2025). Risk Assessment for Identifying Threats, vulnerabilities and countermeasures in Cloud Computing. *Jordanian Journal of Informatics and Computing, 2025*(1), 38–48. DOI: 10.63180/jjic.thestap.2025.1.5

Adil, M., Almaiah, M. A., Omar Alsayed, A., & Almomani, O. (2020). An anonymous channel categorization scheme of edge nodes to detect jamming attacks in wireless sensor networks. *Sensors (Basel), 20*(8), 2311. DOI: 10.3390/s20082311 PMID: 32325646

Al-Shareeda, M. A., Obaid, A. A., & Almajid, A. A. H. (2025). The Role of Artificial Intelligence in Bodybuilding: A Systematic Review of Applications, Challenges, and Future Prospects. *Jordanian Journal of Informatics and Computing, 2025*(1), 16–26. DOI: 10.63180/jjic.thestap.2025.1.3

Alazawi, S. A. H., Abdulbaqi, H. A., & Ali, A. H. (2024). CNN-based intrusion detection software for network operating system environment. *Babylonian Journal of Internet of Things, 2024*, 79–86. DOI: 10.58496/BJIoT/2024/010

Ali, A. (2024). Adaptive and Context-Aware Authentication Framework Using Edge AI and Blockchain in Future Vehicular Networks. *STAP Journal of Security Risk Management, 2024*(1), 45–56. DOI: 10.63180/jsrm.thestap.2024.1.3

Aljanabi, R. A., Al-Qaysi, Z. T., & Suzani, M. S. (2024). Deep Transfer Learning Model for EEG Biometric Decoding. *Applied Data Science and Analysis, 2024*, 4–16. DOI: 10.58496/ADSA/024/002

Almaiah, M. A., Saqr, L. M., Al-Rawwash, L. A., Altellawi, L. A., Al-Ali, R., & Almomani, O. (2024). Classification of Cybersecurity Threats, Vulnerabilities and Countermeasures in Database Systems. *Computers, Materials & Continua, 81*(2), 3189–3220. DOI: 10.32604/cmc.2024.057673

Almomani, O., Alsaaidah, A., Shareha, A. A. A., Alzaqebah, A., & Almomani, M. (2024). Performance Evaluation of Machine Learning Classifiers for Predicting Denial-of-Service Attack in Internet of Things. *International Journal of Advanced Computer Science and Applications*, *15*(1). Advance online publication. DOI: 10.14569/IJACSA.2024.0150125

Alsaaidah, A., Almomani, O., Abu-Shareha, A. A., Abualhaj, M. M., & Achuthan, A. (2024). ARP spoofing attack detection model in IoT network using machine learning: Complexity vs. accuracy. *Journal of Applied Data Sciences*, *5*(4), 1850–1860. DOI: 10.47738/jads.v5i4.374

Alsahaim, S., & Maayah, M. (2023). Analyzing Cybersecurity Threats on Mobile Phones. *STAP Journal of Security Risk Management*, *2023*(1), 3–19. DOI: 10.63180/jsrm.thestap.2023.1.2

Alsajri, A., & Steiti, A. (2024). Intrusion detection system based on machine learning algorithms:(SVM and genetic algorithm). *Babylonian Journal of Machine Learning*, *2024*, 15–29. DOI: 10.58496/BJML/2024/002

Amirthayogam, G., Kumaran, N., Gopalakrishnan, S., Brito, K. R. A., RaviChand, S., & Choubey, S. B. (2024). Integrating behavioral analytics and intrusion detection systems to protect critical infrastructure and smart cities. *Babylonian Journal of Networking*, *2024*, 88–97. DOI: 10.58496/BJN/2024/010

Barach, J. (2024). Enhancing Intrusion Detection with CNN Attention Using NSL-KDD Dataset. 2024 Artificial Intelligence for Business (AIxB), 15–20. DOI: 10.1109/AIxB62249.2024.00009

Bauskar, S. (2024). Enhancing Cybersecurity In Network Intrusion Detection System Based On Artificial Intelligence (AI) Techniques. SSRN Electronic Journal. DOI: 10.2139/ssrn.4987362

Chandran, A. L., Samual, J., Safavi, S., & Ali, A. (2025). A Comparative Analysis of Machine Learning Models on Detecting Malware in Android Devices. *Journal of Cyber Security and Risk Auditing*, *2025*(4), 327–346. DOI: 10.63180/jcsra.thestap.2025.4.10

Chen, T. (2024). *ChatBot-Based Next-Generation Intrusion Detection System. Conversational Artificial Intelligence*. Portico., DOI: 10.1002/9781394200801.ch20

Davarasan, A., Samual, J., Palansundram, K., & Ali, A. (2024). A Comprehensive Review of Machine Learning Approaches for Android Malware Detection. *Journal of Cyber Security and Risk Auditing*, *2024*(1), 39–60. DOI: 10.63180/jcsra.thestap.2024.1.5

Gide, A. I., & Mu'azu, A. A. (2024). A real-time intrusion detection system for dos/ddos attack classification in IoT networks using KNN-neural network hybrid technique. *Babylonian Journal of Internet of Things*, *2024*, 60–69. DOI: 10.58496/BJIoT/2024/008

Gopalsamy, M. (2021). Enhanced Cybersecurity for Network Intrusion Detection System Based Artificial Intelligence (AI) Techniques. International Journal of Advanced Research in Science, Communication and Technology, 671–681. Internet Archive. DOI: 10.48175/IJARSCT-2269M

Gupta, M., Vashishth, T. K., & Verma, P. K. (2024). Machine learning and deep learning based intrusion detection for blackhole attacks in mobile ad-hoc networks. *Multidisciplinary Science Journal*, *6*(11), 2024209–2024209. DOI: 10.31893/multiscience.2024209

Jain, M. A., Rao, B. S., Chattopadhyay, S., Kumar, A., Muthuraman, M. S., & Manjula, A. (2023). An Artificial Intelligence Network based-Host Intrusion Detection System for Internet of Things Devices. 2023 4th International Conference on Electronics and Sustainable Communication Systems (ICESC), 656–661. DOI: 10.1109/ICESC57686.2023.10193232

Kathirvel, A., & Maheswaran, C. P. (2023). Enhanced AI-Based Intrusion Detection and Response System for WSN. Artificial Intelligence for Intrusion Detection Systems, 155–177. DOI: 10.1201/9781003346340-8

Madi, M., Jarghon, F., Fazea, Y., Almomani, O., & Saaidah, A. (2020). Comparative analysis of classification techniques for network fault management. *Turkish Journal of Electrical Engineering and Computer Sciences*, *28*(3), 1442–1457. DOI: 10.3906/elk-1907-84

Marab, A., & Bhadrashetty, A. (2023). A novel approach using deep convolutional neural networks for automated dementia detection and classification. *Edraak*, *2023*, 16–20. DOI: 10.70470/EDRAAK/2023/004

Markevych, M., & Dawson, M. (2023). A Review of Enhancing Intrusion Detection Systems for Cybersecurity Using Artificial Intelligence (AI). International Conference Knowledge-Based Organization, 29(3), 30–37. DOI: 10.2478/kbo-2023-0072

Mohialden, Y. M., Hussien, N. M., Salman, S. A., Alwahhab, A. B. A., & Ali, M. (2024). Enhancing agriculture crop classification with deep learning. *Babylonian Journal of Artificial Intelligence*, *2024*, 20–26. DOI: 10.58496/BJAI/2024/004

Nay, T. (2024). Enhancing IoT Security with AI-Driven Hybrid Machine Learning and Neural Network-Based Intrusion Detection System. *Babylonian Journal of Artificial Intelligence, 2024*, 158–167. DOI: 10.58496/BJAI/2024/017

Noori, W. E., & Albahri, A. S.Worood Esam NooriA. S. Albahri. (2023). Towards trustworthy myopia detection: Integration methodology of deep learning approach, XAI visualization, and user interface system. *Applied Data Science and Analysis, 2023*, 1–15. DOI: 10.58496/ADSA/2023/001

Poornima, G., Sakkari, D. S., Pallavi, R., Sudha, Y., & Gowda, M. S. (2023). Intrusion Detection System Using Artificial Intelligence. Artificial Intelligence for Intrusion Detection Systems, 1–37. DOI: 10.1201/9781003346340-1

Rizqullah, N. Z., Alekhine, J., Yonia, D. L., Racel Purnomo, R. M., & Shiddiqi, A. M. (2024). Enhancing Intrusion Detection Systems with Adaptive Learning Techniques. *2024 IEEE International Conference on Artificial Intelligence and Mechatronics Systems (AIMS)*, 1–6. DOI: 10.1109/AIMS61812.2024.10513076

Saied, M., Guirguis, S., & Madbouly, M. (2024). Review of artificial intelligence for enhancing intrusion detection in the internet of things. *Engineering Applications of Artificial Intelligence, 127*, 107231. DOI: 10.1016/j.engappai.2023.107231

Salim, Z. H., & Hasoon, S. O. (2024). Intrusion Detection Using Artificial Intelligence Techniques: Review. *2024 International Conference on Artificial Intelligence, Computer, Data Sciences and Applications (ACDSA)*, 1–7. DOI: 10.1109/ACDSA59508.2024.10467524

Sebastian, A., & Al Hajri, H. (2024). Artificial Intelligence based Intrusion Detection Systems using Deep Learning Techniques. *2024 Third International Conference on Electrical, Electronics, Information and Communication Technologies (ICEEICT)*, 1–4. DOI: 10.1109/ICEEICT61591.2024.10718441

Shibghatullah, A. S. B. (2023). Mitigating developed persistent threats (APTs) through machine learning-based intrusion detection systems: A comprehensive analysis. *SHIFRA, 2023*, 17–25. DOI: 10.70470/SHIFRA/2023/003

Swarnkar, M., & Rajput, S. S. (2023). *Artificial Intelligence for Intrusion Detection Systems*. Chapman and Hall/CRC., DOI: 10.1201/9781003346340

Vashishth, T. K., Sharma, V., Sharma, K. K., Kumar, B., Chaudhary, S., & Panwar, R. (2024). Intrusion Detection and Prevention Techniques in FL Cloud-Based Healthcare 5.0: A Comprehensive Review. Pioneering Smart Healthcare 5.0 with IoT, Federated Learning, and Cloud Security, 152-174.

Vashishth, T. K., Sharma, V., Sharma, K. K., Kumar, B., Chaudhary, S., & Panwar, R. (2024). Security and Privacy Considerations in Cloud-Based Data Processing Solutions for Sensitive Data. In *Developments towards Next Generation Intelligent Systems for Sustainable Development* (pp. 35–61). IGI Global. DOI: 10.4018/979-8-3693-5643-2.ch002

Vashishth, T. K., Sharma, V., Sharma, K. K., Kumar, B., Kumar, A., & Panwar, R. (2024). Artificial Intelligence (AI)–Powered Chatbots: Providing Instant Support and Personalized Recommendations to Guests 24/7. In Technology and Luxury Hospitality (pp. 211-236). Routledge.

Wang, R. (2023). Expression of Concern for: Enhancing Network Security with Deep Learning on Intrusion Detection and Prevention Systems. 2023 5th International Conference on Artificial Intelligence and Computer Applications (ICAICA), 1–1. DOI: 10.1109/ICAICA58456.2023.10703732

Chapter 7
Artificial Intelligence and Vedic Scripture-Enabled Sustainable Medical Cyber Physical Systems for Secure Healthcare

Sachin Sharma
https://orcid.org/0000-0002-7821-3685
Amity University, Mohali, India

ABSTRACT

This chapter explores unconventional approaches to enhance the capabilities and security of Artificial Intelligence and Vedic Scripture enabled sustainable Medical Cyber Physical Systems (MCPS) to achieve secure healthcare. We discuss overview, types, challenges and opportunities of using Cyber Physical Systems, powered by AI, in healthcare sector, including device coordination and communication, data integrity and patient privacy. Additionally, we review existing research and literature to demonstrate the effectiveness of Medical Cyber Physical Systems in improved healthcare delivery while addressing privacy restrictions. Through this research, we aim to gain a deeper understanding of Cyber Physical Systems, their vulnerabilities and exploration of unconventional ideas, that contribute to the ongoing evolution of secure and efficient AI-enabled MCPS and their ability to transform the health industry.

DOI: 10.4018/979-8-3373-1807-3.ch007

© 2026, IGI Global Scientific Publishing. Copying or distributing in print or electronic forms without written permission of IGI Global Scientific Publishing is prohibited. Use of this chapter to generative artificial intelligence (AI) technologies is expressly prohibited. The publisher reserves all rights to license its use for generative AI training and machine learning model development.

INTRODUCTION

The demand for long-term care, an ageing populace, and longer life expectancies have all contributed to an increment within the require for the healthcare industry around the world. The productivity of the healthcare industry and fulfilling the rising request for treatment are being incredibly helped by innovative enhancements. AI and Vedic Sacred writing fueled Medical Cyber Physical Systems (MCPS) have the potential to significantly upgrade quiet results by giving individualized care, precise conclusion, and real-time checking (Alshinwan et al., 2025) and (Albinhamad et al., 2025). Healthcare experts can move forward the early location and reaction to wellbeing issues, superior oversee persistent sicknesses, lower hospitalization rates, and give higher-quality care in general by incorporating AI calculations into medical gadgets and frameworks. Besides, keeping patients' believe and ensuring touchy therapeutic information depend on the security of AI-enabled MCPS. These frameworks are more helpless to cyberthreats counting malware assaults, information breaches, and framework failures as they develop more connected and subordinate on digital technologies. In arrange to make solid cybersecurity protections that defend understanding confidentiality, stop illegal access to medical equipment and information, and reduce the danger of cyberattacks, this field of investigate is pivotal. Analysts can guarantee understanding security, security, and keenness whereas paving the street for the more extensive execution of AI-enabled MCPS in healthcare by handling these impediments. The integration of Artificial Intelligence (AI) with Vedic scriptures to enable sustainable Medical Cyber-Physical Systems (MCPS) for secure healthcare represents a transformative, multi-disciplinary approach. This framework moves beyond the traditional, reactive model of medicine to a proactive, holistic, and secure system that leverages modern technology while being grounded in ancient principles of well-being. At its core, this concept recognizes that the future of healthcare must be not only technologically advanced but also ethically sound, environmentally conscious, and deeply personal. It addresses the growing need for healthcare solutions that are accessible, effective, and sustainable in the face of global challenges. Medical Cyber-Physical Systems form the technological backbone of this model. These systems are intricate networks of smart medical devices, sensors, and software that work together to monitor patients, analyze data, and deliver personalized treatments. For example, a continuous glucose monitor (a sensor) connected to a smart insulin pump (an actuator) that is managed by an AI algorithm (the cyber element) creates a closed-loop system for diabetes management (Almaayah & Sulaiman, 2024) and (Al-Shareeda et al., 2024). This technology promises to revolutionize patient care by enabling remote monitoring, predictive diagnostics, and precise interventions. However, the proliferation of these interconnected devices also introduces significant vulnerabilities, particularly regarding data security and patient privacy. The massive volume of sensitive personal health information generated by MCPS is a prime target for cyberattacks, making robust security measures not a luxury but an absolute necessity. This is where the principles of Vedic scriptures, particularly from the ancient Indian science of Ayurveda, provide a foundational philosophy. Ayurveda is not merely a system of medicine; it's a way of life that emphasizes the inseparability of the individual, their health, and the environment. The core tenet of Loka-Purusha Samyasiddhant, which posits that the principles governing the universe are the same as those governing the human body, underpins this holistic view. Health is seen as a state of balance between the body's three doshas (Vata, Pitta, and Kapha), and illness is a state of imbalance. This ancient wisdom provides a blueprint for a healthcare system focused on preventive care, lifestyle management (Dinacharya), and sustainable practices. By integrating these principles, the framework shifts the focus from treating symptoms to identifying and addressing the root causes of disease, promoting long-term well-being rather than short-term fixes. Artificial Intelligence acts as the powerful bridge between the technological capabilities of MCPS and the holistic principles of Vedic wisdom. AI algorithms can be trained on vast datasets that include not just modern medical records but also Ayurvedic concepts. For instance, an AI system could analyze a patient's genetic data, lifestyle choices, and environmental factors to determine their unique Prakriti (constitutional type) and Vikriti (current state of imbalance). Based on this analysis, the AI could then recommend personalized dietary plans, mindfulness practices, and herbal remedies aligned with Ayurvedic principles, all while leveraging real-time data from MCPS to monitor progress and adjust recommendations. This synergy creates a truly personalized and proactive healthcare model that is both scientifically rigorous and deeply attuned to the individual's unique needs. The concept of "sustainability" is another cornerstone of this approach. In the context of this framework, sustainability extends beyond environmental concerns to encompass the long-term viability of the healthcare system itself. This means using technology and resources responsibly, reducing waste, and promoting practices that don't harm the planet (Chand et al., 2023)(Hussein & Basel, 2024; Yasser, 2025). Vedic scriptures have always advocated for a harmonious relationship with nature, a principle that can be translated into modern healthcare through AI-enabled optimization of resources, sustainable drug discovery (e.g., using AI to analyze ancient texts for potential plant-based medicines), and waste reduction in hospitals. This fusion ensures that healthcare innovation is not at the expense of our planet but in service to it. Crucially, security is interwoven into every layer of this system. Given the critical nature of the data involved, the framework necessitates a "security-by-design" approach. This means that cybersecurity is not an afterthought but a fundamental part of the system's architecture (Davarasan et al., 2024) and (Chandran et al., 2025). Advanced technologies like blockchain can be used to create an immutable, decentralized ledger for health records, ensuring that patient data is tamper-proof and accessible only to authorized parties. AI can also play a role in threat detection, with machine learning models continuously analyzing network traffic to identify and neutralize potential cyberattacks in real-time. This robust security posture is essential for building and maintaining patient trust, which is the bedrock of any effective healthcare system. The convergence of Artificial Intelligence, Vedic wisdom, and Medical Cyber-Physical Systems offers a compelling and comprehensive vision for the future of healthcare. It is a future where technology is a tool for empowerment, where healthcare is personalized and preventive, and where well-being is viewed as an intricate dance between the individual and their environment. By marrying the computational power of AI with the timeless wisdom of ancient scriptures, this paradigm promises a healthcare system that is not only highly effective and secure but also sustainable, ethical, and deeply human-centered (Sharma, Gupta, et al., 2023a)(Hussein et al., 2024; Zhang & Su, 2024). The synergy of Artificial Intelligence (AI), Vedic scriptures, and Medical Cyber-Physical Systems (MCPS) has the potential to profoundly impact Indian society by addressing its unique healthcare challenges. This integration aims to create a sustainable, secure, and accessible healthcare ecosystem that merges ancient wisdom with modern technology. India faces a significant challenge in providing quality healthcare to its vast and diverse population, especially in rural and remote areas where the doctor-to-patient ratio is alarmingly low (Sharma et al., 2024). MCPS, which are networks of interconnected medical devices and computational systems, can bridge this gap. Wearable sensors and smart devices can collect real-time physiological data from patients in remote villages, which is then transmitted to a central AI system. This allows for remote monitoring and diagnosis by doctors in urban centers. This telemedicine approach reduces the need for patients to travel long distances for consultations, making healthcare more accessible and affordable. Furthermore, AI-powered diagnostic tools can analyze medical images (like X-rays and CT scans) and patient data to assist local health workers in making accurate and timely decisions, thus democratizing healthcare access. The integration of Vedic and Ayurvedic principles with AI is a game-changer for personalized medicine. Ayurveda, with its focus on the concept of 'Prakriti' (body constitution based on the three 'doshas'—Vata, Pitta, and Kapha), offers a holistic approach to health. AI algorithms can analyze an individual's genetic data, lifestyle, and other health parameters to determine their unique Prakriti. This information can then be used to create personalized health plans, including diet, exercise, and lifestyle recommendations, to prevent diseases before they manifest (Sharma & Tyagi, 2023). For instance, AI can be trained on vast amounts of data from ancient Ayurvedic texts and modern health records to predict an individual's susceptibility to certain diseases and recommend preventive measures. This shifts the focus from a reactive, disease-centric model to a proactive, preventive healthcare model, which is crucial for a country burdened by both communicable and non-communicable diseases. The widespread adoption of MCPS generates a massive amount of sensitive patient data, making data security a paramount concern. The proposed system integrates robust cybersecurity measures to protect this information from cyber-attacks and data breaches. Additionally, the philosophical underpinnings of Vedic scriptures, which emphasize a holistic and ethical approach to life and well-being, can provide a framework for the responsible use of AI in healthcare (Sharma et al., 2023)(Ali et al., 2025; Alnajem et al., 2024). This can guide the development of ethical guidelines for AI algorithms, ensuring that they are transparent, unbiased, and prioritize patient well-being over commercial interests. The ethical principles derived from these ancient texts can help navigate complex issues like data privacy, informed consent, and algorithmic bias, building a foundation of trust between technology, healthcare providers, and patients. By optimizing resource allocation and reducing unnecessary hospital visits, this integrated system promotes a more sustainable healthcare model. AI can help hospitals manage resources more efficiently, from predicting bed availability to optimizing the supply chain for medicines and medical equipment (Sharma, Gupta, et al., 2024). This not only reduces costs for patients and providers but also minimizes the environmental footprint of healthcare operations. On an economic level, this approach can spur innovation and create new job opportunities in the fields of AI, data science, and biomedical engineering. By becoming a leader in this niche area, India can also position itself as a global hub for the development and export of sustainable and secure healthcare technology, contributing significantly to its economic growth.

I. LITERATURE REVIEW

The crossing point of artificial intelligence (AI), cyber-physical systems (CPS), and healthcare security may be a pivotal region of investigate pointed at tending to distinctive applications where we might saddle the control of AI to optimize medical frameworks in healthcare industry. The establishment for understanding the integration of Artificial Intelligence with thoughts and calculations underlying MCPS has been set up by a number of investigate papers. One eminent commitment is the paper displaying the thought of on-device AI based MCPS for the location of Bio-Modality Spoofing. The on-device AI hub runs a light-weight but effective classification calculation called Feature Augmented Random Forest (FA-RF). This strategy not as it were jam the biometric information, it can essentially diminish the communication delay forced on the organize when information is sent to the cloud for classifying spoofed and genuine bio-modalities for confirmation (Mowla et al.,

2018)(Kayusi et al., 2024; Mijwil et al., 2024). Survey papers have been composed with respect to a Systematic Study on AI-Enabled Cyber Physical Frameworks in Healthcare. It enlightens the part of manufactured insights in therapeutic cyber-physical frameworks that are taken after by certification and control. Moreover, throw light on the dangers and challenges within the restorative cyber-physical frameworks. Studies have presented the novel "Pattern-Proof Malware Validation" (PoPMV) calculation planned for utilize in mechanical cyber-physical frameworks by combining profound learning and blockchain innovation. This calculation exploits a deep learning model (LSTM) with reinforcement learning strategies to get input and rewards in real-time. The most objective is to relieve security vulnerabilities, upgrade handling speed, distinguish both commonplace and new assaults, and optimize the usefulness of ICPS (Mohammed et al., 2023). Another consider talks almost machine learning danger discovery system for secure healthcare information exchange. The Smart Healthcare Cyber-Physical Systems (SHCPS) can disseminate the accumulated information to cloud capacity. Cyberattack designs may be anticipated utilizing AI models, and this data is prepared to help healthcare experts in making choices. The novel jellyfish-optimized weighted dropped binary long short-term memory (JFO-WDB-LSTM) procedure eventually recognizes between substantial and incorrect healthcare information. A cyber-attack discovery framework for healthcare segment with centralized and combined exchange learning mode has been proposed. Edge of Things (EoT) system is created in association with cloud and healthcare divisions to transmit the information productively. The proposed Centralized with Multi-Source Transfer Learning (CMTL) calculation is utilized for discovery and classification of various threats such as data gathering, DoS/DDoS attacks, Malware attacks, Injection attacks, and Man in the Middle attacks (Chakraborty et al., 2023). Reliability, certainty, security, and transparency are a few of the issues that must be tended to within the developing field of Cyber Physical Systems (CPS) inquire about. To overcome the abovementioned issues, an improved wireless medical cyber-physical system (IWMCPS) based on machine learning methods has also been displayed that's based on a patient-centric engineering that jam the end-user's smartphone gadget to control data exchange availability. The three center components within the proposed improved CPS are the communication and checking center, the computational and security center, and the real-time arranging and organization of assets (Alzahrani et al., 2023).

II. OVERVIEW OF CYBER PHYSICAL SYSTEMS (CPS)

Envision a framework where the physical world (like machines, sensors, gadgets) is closely associated and interatomic with the computerized world (like computers, software, networks). That's basically what we call a Cyber-Physical System (CPS). It speaks to the combination of the physical and computerized universes, where Internet of Things (IoT) sensors and actuators connected with physical substances to assemble information and effect changes within the physical environment through criticism circles of computing frameworks and communication systems (Habib & Chimsom, 2022)(Nyangaresi & Shanshool, 2024; Sallam et al., 2025). They are observed, controlled, and optimized through the integration of implanted frameworks, real-time computing, and organizing innovations. A CPS is characterized by its capacity to function in real-time or near-real-time, convenient preparing, and reaction to energetic changes within the environment. It shows independent behavior through the integration of decision-making calculations and versatile control methodologies to reply to changing conditions (Sharma, Tomar, et al., 2024). Architectural frameworks for a cyber-physical system design commonly include these stages:

- Perception layer: It is the physical arrange of gadgets and sensors that collect data.
- Data transmission & administration layer: The data is transmitted evenly between physical gadgets and vertically over the Internet to a backend information stage for capacity and preprocessing.
- Application layer: The program components that associated with the data, prepare models, and work agreeing to its environment.

CPS can be found in different regions like transportation (activity administration, vehicle to vehicle communication, self-driving cars), healthcare (like computerize medicate conveyance, inaccessible understanding observing frameworks), manufacturing (optimize generation forms, monitor hardware wellbeing, prescient upkeep. automated assembly lines), vitality (optimize energy distribution, oversee renewable vitality sources), and numerous more. Keen cities are moreover an application zone of CPS where Urban CPS coordinated foundation frameworks to progress city administrations, oversee assets effectively, and improve quality of life for inhabitants (Sharma, Gupta, et al., 2024)(Mensah et al., 2025; Sakirin & Said, 2025). In spite of the fact that the application of Cyber Physical Systems as of now taking put in numerous businesses, it is still considered in its very early stages. Complex design, robustness and reliability in dynamic environments could be a significant challenge for CPS. The increment within the number of IoT-based gadgets has lead to an increment in CPS helplessness to cyber-attacks.

III. TYPES OF CYBER PHYSICAL SYSTEMS

Cyber-Physical Systems (CPS) can be categorized into a few sorts based on their application area and characteristics. A few common sorts of CPS:

- Industrial CPS: Too known as Industrial Internet of Things (IIoT) frameworks, these CPS are sent in fabricating, coordinations, and supply chain operations. They optimize generation forms, screen hardware wellbeing, and empower prescient support to make strides productivity and efficiency.
- Smart Frameworks: These are power systems that utilize advanced innovation to screen and oversee the transport of power from all era sources to meet the changing power requests of conclusion clients. They are sent within the vitality segment to modernize control era, transmission, and dissemination frameworks.
- Medical Checking: These frameworks utilize different sensors and gadgets to screen health-related data such as heart rate, blood weight, glucose levels, etc. The information collected can be utilized for real-time criticism and long-term information examination.
- Transportation Systems: This incorporates Intelligent Transportation Systems (ITS) and independent vehicles. They oversee activity stream, optimize course arranging, and move forward security through vehicle-to-vehicle and vehicle-to-infrastructure communication.
- Versatile Cyber-Physical Systems: These are CPS in which the physical system beneath consider has intrinsic portability like versatile mechanical technology and hardware transported by people.

Medical Cyber-Physical Systems (CPS) coordinated physical forms, computational components, and organized frameworks to upgrade healthcare conveyance and persistent results. Here are a few sorts of medical CPS centered on secure healthcare:

- Wearable Wellbeing Gadgets: Smartwatches, wellness trackers, and wearable ECG screens. Ceaselessly screen crucial signs (heart rate, blood weight, action levels) and give real-time wellbeing information to both patients and healthcare suppliers. Scrambled information transmission, secure capacity, and client confirmation.
- Telemedicine Frameworks: Inaccessible interview stages and virtual care applications. The functionality enable healthcare suppliers to conduct meetings and screen patients remotely, encouraging access to care. The security highlights comprise of end-to-end encryption, secure access controls, and compliance with healthcare controls (e.g., HIPAA).

- Smart Clinics: The cases comprise of Coordinates healing center administration frameworks. The usefulness utilize IoT gadgets to screen understanding conditions, mechanize workflows, and oversee assets productively. The security highlights comprise of Arrange division, access control, and ceaseless checking for vulnerabilities
- Robotic Surgery Systems: The cases comprise of surgical robots just like the da Vinci Surgical System. The usefulness helps specialists in performing negligibly obtrusive strategies with accuracy and control. Security highlights have secure communications between gadgets and surgical rebellious, computer program upgrades, and fail-safes.
- Smart Pill Containers: The illustrations comprise of robotized medicine administration frameworks. The functionality guarantee patients take the proper pharmaceutical at the correct time, regularly coordinates with updates and observing. Security highlights have information encryption and secure client verification to ensure understanding data.
- Health Data Frameworks: The cases comprise of Electronic Health Records (EHR) and Health Information Exchanges (HIE). Usefulness Store and oversee understanding information, permitting for consistent sharing among authorized healthcare suppliers. Security highlights have Access controls, review logs, and information encryption.
- Remote Patient Checking Frameworks: The illustrations comprise of Domestic health checking arrangements. The usefulness collect information from patients' homes utilizing different sensors and gadgets, transmitting it to healthcare suppliers for investigation. The security highlights have Secure information transmission conventions and persistent assent administration.
- Artificial Intelligence-Driven Analytics: The illustrations comprise of Prescient analytics stages for understanding hazard evaluation. The usefulness analyze expansive datasets to distinguish patterns, foresee wellbeing outcomes, and support clinical decision-making. Security highlights have information anonymization and secure access to touchy data.
- Coordinates Clinical Choice Support Frameworks: The illustrations comprise of Frameworks that give real-time, evidence-based proposals. The usefulness help healthcare suppliers in diagnosing and treating patients by joining quiet information with clinical rules. Security highlights have access controls, information encryption, and nonstop observing of framework astuteness.
- Crisis Response Frameworks: The illustrations comprise of mechanized caution frameworks for clinics and emergency administrations. The usefulness communicate basic persistent information and alarms to healthcare groups amid crises. The security highlights have Secure communication channels and repetition measures to guarantee unwavering quality.

Vedic scriptures envelop a wealthy embroidered artwork of writings that give bits of knowledge into health, wellness, and all encompassing living. Whereas not specifically related to advanced healthcare hones, a few sorts of Vedic literature can educate secure healthcare approaches. Here are a few key categories:

- Rigveda, Samaveda, Yajurveda, Atharvaveda: These foundational writings contain hymns, customs, and philosophical dialogs that emphasize the significance of concordance in wellbeing, counting the adjust of physical, mental, and otherworldly well-being.
- Philosophical Writings: The Upanishads investigate the nature of reality and awareness, advancing self-awareness and mental well-being, which are significant for all encompassing healthcare.
- Samhitas: Writings just like the Charaka Samhita and Sushruta Samhita outline standards of Ayurvedic pharmaceutical, counting determination, treatment, and way of life hones that can advise preventive healthcare techniques.
- Legendary and Authentic Accounts: These writings regularly incorporate lessons on wellbeing and life span, giving bits of knowledge into conventional hones and community health principles.
- Ethical Guidelines: Works just like the Manusmriti give moral systems that can direct healthcare hones, emphasizing obligations towards patients and community wellbeing.
- Philosophical System: Writings like Patanjali's Yoga Sutras emphasize mental wellbeing through contemplation and mindfulness, contributing to a holistic approach to understanding care.
- Spiritual and Ethical Direction: This content addresses the mind-body association and the significance of obligation and morals in life, which can advise compassionate healthcare hones.
- Spiritual Practices: Tantric writings offer insights into the union of the body and the soul, promoting techniques that enhance both mental and physical health.
- Astrological and Healing Practices: These texts discuss the influence of major factors on health and can instruct comprehensive treatment plans by taking into account natural variables.
- Perceptive Translations: Various analyses of the original texts provide context and clarification, which can help adapt traditional wisdom to the demands of contemporary healthcare.

When considering the integration of Vedic scriptures into Medical Cyber-Physical Systems (CPS), certain categories of writings can give important experiences, standards, and systems. Here are key categories of Vedic sacred text pertinent to this setting:

- Rigveda, Samaveda, Yajurveda, Atharvaveda: These writings give foundational information, counting songs and ceremonies that emphasize the interconnecting of body, intellect, and environment, which can educate all encompassing approaches in healthcare innovation.
- Charaka Samhita and Sushruta Samhita: These writings layout standards of conventional Indian pharmaceutical, counting conclusion, treatment, and the significance of way of life and dietary practices, which can be coordinates into wellbeing checking frameworks.
- Philosophical Insights: These writings dive into the nature of awareness and the self, empowering a holistic see of wellbeing that includes mental and otherworldly well-being, basic for planning user-centered wellbeing advances.
- Mind-Body Connection: Patanjali's Yoga Sutras emphasize practices that improve mental wellbeing and stretch lessening, which can be consolidated into mental wellbeing apps and wellness stages inside CPS.
- Ethical Rules: Writings just like the Manusmriti give ethical systems that can direct the improvement and usage of healthcare innovations, guaranteeing they serve patients' best interface.
- Social and Authentic Contexts: These writings offer bits of knowledge into community wellbeing practices and conventional information frameworks, which can advise socially touchy healthcare arrangements.
- Mysterious and Healing Practices: These writings talk about the affect of infinite and natural components on wellbeing, possibly improving the information inputs for wellbeing observing frameworks.
- Integration of Body and Soul: Tantric hones can upgrade the understanding of all encompassing wellbeing, educating CPS planned to advance mental and passionate well-being.
- Academic Elucidations: Different commentaries on Vedic writings can give relevant experiences and down to earth applications, making a difference bridge old shrewdness with advanced innovation.
- Discussions on Ethics and Existence: Writings that investigate moral living and the nature of existence can direct the ethical improvement of restorative advances.

Joining Vedic sacred text standards into feasible secure healthcare can contribute to long-term global health objectives in a few impactful ways. Here's how these old lessons can adjust with modern targets for maintainable healthcare:

- Mind-Body-Spirit Association: Vedic scriptures emphasize the interconnecting of physical, mental, and otherworldly wellbeing. By advancing all encompassing wellness, healthcare frameworks can address not as it were physical afflictions but too mental health and passionate well-being, driving to more beneficial populaces.
- Focus on Prevention: Numerous Vedic writings advocate for preventive measures through way of life choices, eat less, and hones like yoga and contemplation. Emphasizing anticipation can decrease the burden on healthcare frameworks, diminish costs, and move forward generally health results.
- Dharma and Ethics: The moral codes contained in the sacred writings of the Vedas strengthen responsibility and zeal in the medical field. This aligns with global goals for ethical healthcare delivery, which include knowledge of rights, informed consent, and equitable access to care.
- Emphasis on Community Well-Being: Vedic teachings emphasize the value of communal responsibility and well-being. This might inspire healthcare systems to foster neighborhood-based initiatives that promote health, support local health initiatives, and empower individuals to take responsibility for their own well-being.
- Harmony with Nature: Living in harmony with nature is advocated by the Vedic worldview. This viewpoint can direct healthcare frameworks towards feasible practices, such as utilizing normal cures, lessening waste, and receiving eco-friendly innovations.
- Complementary Approaches: Vedic principles can complement advanced medical practices, permitting for the integration of conventional mending strategies with modern science. This could preserve social legacy while improving drug adequacy.
- Mindfulness and Meditation: To enhance mental health, healthcare procedures can incorporate Vedic practices such as yoga and introspection. Since mental health problems have become more widespread overall, these skills can be effective intervenors.
- Enhancing Health Education: Yoga teachings can be used as a basis for health education programs, promoting self-care, diet, and lifestyle choices that are mindful of the long-term effects on one's health.
- BridgingDisciplines: Vedic experiences energize collaboration among different areas, counting pharmaceutical, brain research, and natural science. This fascination method can foster creative solutions to difficult health issues.
- Supporting SDGs: The principles deduced from sacred Vedic texts can be aligned with the Sustainable Development Goals (SDGs) of the United Nations, particularly those pertaining to sustainable communities (Goal 11), responsible consumption (Goal 12), and health and well-being (Goal 3).

It is possible to create a comprehensive system that supports long-term health goals by incorporating the principles of the Vedic scripture into workable, secure healthcare practices. This strategy not only reaffirms the value of preventive and comprehensive care, but it also fosters community involvement, moral development, and natural sustainability.

IV. ADVANTAGES AND CHALLENGES

AI integration has greatly improved the quality and efficiency of any aspect of life. There are many benefits that healthcare receives from integrating artificial intelligence into its daily operations, given its critical role in the industry and the irreplaceable nature of its patient population. AI-enabled CPS can help specialists in giving more exact determination and individualized treatment plans based on persistent data. Superior persistent results and faster recuperation periods are the comes about of this. Utilizing wearables and sensors, doctors can utilize AI to remotely screen patients' health issues. This makes it conceivable to recognize well-being issues early and act rapidly, indeed whereas remote absent. AI can offer assistance healthcare associations with authoritative exercises like arrangement planning and therapeutic record administration. This permits therapeutic staff more time to concentrate on understanding care. CPS can protect quiet protection by joining cybersecurity shields to protect against cyber dangers and unapproved access to sensitive patient data. Be that as it may in arrange to urge these advantages, there are a number of challenges that have to be be taken care of in arrange to empower AI-enabled CPS to utilize their full potential. Concerns with respect to secrecy and protection are raised by the gathering and capacity of tremendous volumes of quiet information. Solid security measures must be put in put to secure quiet information from hacks and unlawful access. Artificial intelligence (AI) innovation integration into current healthcare frameworks can be troublesome and complex. For smooth operation, compatibility between different equipment and program components must be ensured. The synthesis of Artificial Intelligence (AI), the timeless wisdom of Vedic scriptures, and the technological framework of Medical Cyber-Physical Systems (MCPS) for secure healthcare is not merely an incremental improvement; it is a paradigm shift. This integrated model offers a multitude of profound advantages that address the shortcomings of conventional healthcare and lay the groundwork for a more effective, personalized, and sustainable future. These benefits can be categorized across several key dimensions: clinical efficacy and personalization, sustainability and resource management, security and trust, and holistic well-being. One of the most significant advantages of this integrated system is the dramatic enhancement of clinical efficacy through unprecedented personalization. Traditional medicine often follows a one-size-fits-all approach, which may not be effective for all individuals. The Vedic concept of Prakriti—an individual's unique psycho-physiological constitution determined at birth—provides a foundation for true personalization. AI, powered by MCPS, can now operationalize this ancient wisdom. Wearable sensors and smart devices continuously collect a vast array of data—from vital signs and genetic information to dietary habits and environmental exposures. AI algorithms can then analyze this multi-modal data to accurately determine a person's Prakriti and identify any current imbalances (Vikriti). This deep, data-driven understanding allows for the creation of truly bespoke treatment plans and preventive strategies. For example, an AI-enabled system could use real-time data from a patient's smart ring to detect early signs of a Vata imbalance, such as a change in sleep patterns or heart rate variability. It could then send an alert to the patient and their practitioner, along with personalized recommendations based on Ayurvedic principles, such as specific dietary modifications, a guided meditation, or a calming herbal tea. This proactive and predictive approach moves beyond merely treating disease to actively preventing it. AI also excels at pattern recognition in large datasets, allowing it to identify subtle diagnostic clues that might be missed by human observation alone. When integrated with traditional diagnostic methods like Nadi Pariksha (pulse diagnosis) and tongue examination, AI can provide a level of diagnostic precision that was previously unattainable, leading to earlier interventions and better outcomes. The integration of Vedic principles introduces a crucial dimension of sustainability into the healthcare model. Vedic philosophy is fundamentally rooted in a harmonious relationship with nature, a concept that is critical in an era of environmental degradation and resource scarcity. This framework provides a blueprint for a healthcare system that is not only effective but also environmentally responsible. AI can play a pivotal role in optimizing the entire healthcare value chain for sustainability. For instance, in the realm of pharmacopeia, AI can analyze vast databases of traditional texts and modern chemical compositions to identify and optimize the use of natural, plant-based remedies. This can accelerate the discovery of new medicines from traditional sources and reduce our reliance on synthetically derived drugs, which often have a greater environmental footprint. Furthermore, AI-powered agricultural systems can optimize the cultivation of medicinal plants, ensuring ethical and sustainable sourcing. This includes monitoring soil health, water usage, and pest control, all while adhering to the principles of ecological balance. Beyond drug discovery, AI can be used for intelligent resource allocation in hospitals and clinics. Predictive analytics can forecast patient inflow, allowing hospitals to optimize staffing, manage medical supply chains more efficiently, and reduce waste. By minimizing unnecessary tests, procedures, and prescriptions, this model not only improves patient outcomes but also reduces the economic and environmental burden of healthcare. This shift towards a preventive model, inspired by Vedic wisdom and enabled by AI, inherently reduces the need for resource-intensive, high-tech interventions. The inherent vulnerabilities of Medical Cyber-Physical Systems (MCPS) demand a security framework that is both robust and proactive. The advantage of this integrated model lies in its ability to build a highly secure and trustworthy system from the ground up, essential for protecting sensitive patient data. AI and machine learning are indispensable for real-time threat detection and mitigation. AI-powered security systems can continuously monitor network traffic within the MCPS to identify and neutralize anomalous patterns that may indicate a cyberattack. For example, an AI algorithm could detect an unusual data request from a device, such as a smart pacemaker, and immediately flag it as a potential threat, preventing a life-threatening breach. Furthermore, integrating advanced security protocols like blockchain can create an immutable and decentralized ledger for health records. This ensures that a patient's data is not stored in a single, vulnerable location and that all transactions are transparent and tamper-proof, thereby enhancing both security and accountability. The emphasis on security is also a matter of trust. The adoption of new healthcare technologies hinges on patient and practitioner confidence. By explicitly integrating a "security-by-design" philosophy, this framework aims to create a system that is not only functional but also inherently reliable and trustworthy. This is especially important as healthcare becomes more digital and remote, with sensitive personal data being transmitted across vast networks. A secure system ensures that the promise of personalized, data-driven healthcare can be realized without compromising the fundamental right to privacy. Finally, and perhaps most uniquely, this integrated approach moves beyond the purely biomedical model to promote genuine holistic well-being. Vedic scriptures, particularly Yoga and Ayurveda, stress the interconnectedness of the mind, body, and spirit. This framework provides the tools to address this interconnectedness in a data-driven way. MCPS can collect data on a patient's psychological state through various means, such as voice analysis and facial expression recognition in video consultations. AI can then correlate this information with physical health data to provide a comprehensive picture of the patient's well-being. For example, an AI system might identify a correlation between a patient's stress levels (detected through voice tonality) and their blood pressure, and then recommend a personalized set of mindfulness exercises or breathing techniques (Pranayama) based on Vedic texts. This integration allows for a truly comprehensive approach to health that recognizes the powerful impact of mental and emotional states on physical health. The system can act as a personal wellness coach, offering personalized guidance on diet, sleep, and lifestyle that aligns with both modern medical science and ancient wisdom. This creates a more empowering and engaging experience for the patient, encouraging them to take an active role in their own health journey. For healthcare specialists to successfully utilize AI-enabled gadgets, they require the correct preparing. Programs for instruction and preparing must be supported. Integrating Vedic scriptures with modern innovation in medical cyber-physical systems (CPS) for secure healthcare may open up imaginative approaches to all encompassing well-being.

- Vedic literature often emphasize balance, wellbeing, and the connection between body and mind. Drawing on these principles appears to enhance silent care by expanding preventative approaches and all-encompassing drugs.
- Cyber-Physical Systems (CPS) mix computational and physical components. CPS in healthcare might include wearable devices, telemedicine stages, and advanced healing centers that monitor and oversee silent treatment.
- Protecting information is crucial in healthcare. Combining Vedic reasoning criteria, such as morality and responsibility, may help create secure systems for handling sensitive information.
- Using Vedic ideas, CPS may assess not only physical but also mental and spiritual well-being.
- Combining modern diagnostics and ancient knowledge can create personalized medications based on individual constitutions (doshas) as outlined in Ayurveda.
- Secure telemedicine services that incorporate Vedic practices such as yoga and meditation to provide holistic mental and physical wellness.
- Integrating Vedic principles to promote communal well-being and preventative care.
- Integrating old customs with current innovation demands careful consideration of societal impact and evidence-based guidelines.
- Collaborating with experts in Vedic practices, healthcare, and cybersecurity to provide effective and informed solutions.
- Ensuring regulatory compliance by coordinating healthcare controls with Vedic standards.

Integrating Vedic scripture themes into safe healthcare systems can provide several focal points [Fig. 1]:

- Holistic Wellbeing: Whole-Person Care: The emphasis in Vedic literature on the adjustment of body, mind, and soul advances a more all-encompassing approach to well-being that takes into account both physical and spiritual well-being in addition to passionate and otherworldly well-being.
- Preventive Healthcare: The Vedic tradition supports lifestyle changes and dietary guidelines as preventive measures that can result in far better long-term health outcomes and lower healthcare costs.

- Ethics and Responsibilities: The Vedic texts emphasize moral behavior and accountability to both oneself and others.
- Benefits to Mental Health: Based on Vedic logic, practices like yoga and meditation can be integrated into healthcare to enhance mental wellness and reduce stress, leading to significantly better quiet outcomes.
- Regard for Traditions: Adopting Vedic practices can enhance social skills in medical environments, increasing the accessibility and legitimacy of services for a variety of populations.
- Collective Health Activities: Vedic teachings place a strong emphasis on community wellbeing, which can foster cooperative wellbeing initiatives and support structures that raise the security of collective wellbeing.
- Individualized Approaches: Ayurvedic standards, for example, enable customized drug regimens according to a person's dosha, or constitution, enabling tailored healthcare plans.
- Upgraded Security Protocols: Vedic ethics can guide the development of safe frameworks that give information security and quiet protection top priority, ensuring belief in medical advancements.
- Eco-Friendly Approaches: The Vedic worldview frequently advances agreement with nature, empowering feasible hones in healthcare that advantage both patients and the environment.
- Complementary Treatments: Combining regular restorative medications with traditional Indian remedies can improve overall sufficiency and provide a more tailored approach to quiet care.

Figure 1. Vedic scripture principles into secure healthcare frameworks

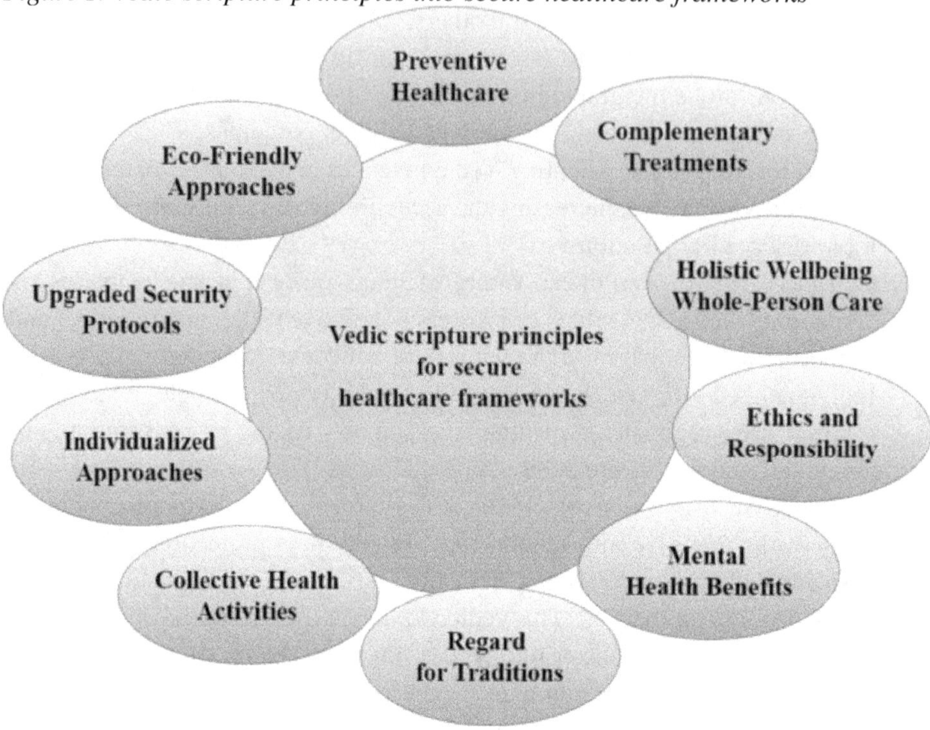

The convergence of Artificial Intelligence (AI), Vedic scriptures, and Medical Cyber-Physical Systems (MCPS) for secure healthcare, while promising, faces a complex web of technical, ethical, and societal challenges. Successfully navigating these hurdles is crucial for the framework to move from a theoretical concept to a practical, impactful reality. The challenges are not merely technical; they are deeply rooted in the need to reconcile ancient holistic traditions with modern technology, address the inherent vulnerabilities of networked systems, and overcome profound ethical and cultural resistance. The foundational challenge lies in the data itself. For AI to be effective, it needs vast, high-quality, and standardized datasets. In the context of Vedic-scripture-enabled healthcare, this presents a unique problem.

- Lack of Standardized Data: Unlike conventional medicine with its standardized terminologies (e.g., ICD codes), Vedic practices like Ayurveda lack a universally accepted, quantitative data standard. Diagnoses like Prakriti and Vikriti are often based on a practitioner's subjective interpretation. Translating these qualitative, holistic assessments into structured, quantifiable data that an AI can process is an enormous task. Without a standardized taxonomy, building interoperable and reliable AI models becomes a significant hurdle.

- Data Scarcity: While there is a wealth of traditional knowledge in ancient texts, there is a scarcity of clinical data that links specific Vedic interventions to measurable health outcomes. AI models require extensive, labeled datasets to learn and make accurate predictions. Creating these datasets would require large-scale, long-term research studies that are both ethically and logistically complex.
- Interoperability and Infrastructure: MCPS rely on the seamless integration of various devices, from wearable sensors to hospital machinery. However, many existing healthcare systems and medical devices operate in silos, using proprietary protocols. Integrating these disparate systems into a unified, secure platform is a major technical challenge. This is especially true for traditional medicine settings, which may lack the digital infrastructure to even begin collecting data in a structured way.
- Vulnerability of MCPS: Medical devices, especially older ones, often lack robust security features. They can be vulnerable to hacking, ransomware, and denial-of-service attacks. A breach in a smart insulin pump, for example, could have life-threatening consequences. Securing every single component of the system—from the smallest sensor to the central AI server—is a monumental task that requires constant vigilance and updates.
- Sensitive Data and Privacy: The data collected by these systems is exceptionally sensitive, encompassing not only basic health information but also genetic data, lifestyle habits, and even emotional states. A data breach could lead to identity theft, blackmail, or discrimination. Protecting this data under various global regulations (like HIPAA and GDPR) while allowing the AI to use it for analysis is a complex legal and technical balancing act.
- Trust and Accountability: Patients may be hesitant to adopt these technologies due to concerns about who owns their data and how it's being used. If an AI makes a diagnostic error due to a cyberattack or a flaw in its programming, determining legal accountability becomes a convoluted process. Is the fault with the AI developer, the healthcare provider who used the system, or the manufacturer of the device? This ambiguity can erode public trust in the entire system.
- Algorithmic Bias: AI models are only as good as the data they're trained on. If the data is not representative of diverse populations, the AI can develop biases that lead to unequal treatment. For instance, if an AI is trained primarily on data from a specific demographic, its recommendations for other groups might be inaccurate or even harmful. This can exacerbate existing health disparities.
- The "Black Box" Problem: Many advanced AI models, particularly deep learning networks, are "black boxes"—their decision-making processes are

opaque and not easily explainable. In healthcare, where trust and transparency are paramount, this is a major problem. Clinicians and patients need to understand why an AI is recommending a particular course of action, especially if it conflicts with their professional judgment or personal beliefs.

- Regulatory Frameworks: Current healthcare regulations are largely designed for conventional medicine and are not equipped to handle the complexities of AI-driven, hybrid systems. There is a lack of clear guidelines for the validation, approval, and oversight of systems that integrate traditional and modern practices. Establishing a new regulatory body or updating existing ones to govern these technologies would be a long and challenging process.
- Practitioner Adoption and Resistance: Healthcare professionals, both in conventional and traditional medicine, may be resistant to adopting these new technologies. Conventional doctors may be skeptical of the scientific validity of Vedic principles, while traditional practitioners might fear that AI will dehumanize their practice or sideline their expertise. Overcoming this professional resistance requires extensive training, education, and demonstrating clear, evidence-based benefits.
- Patient Acceptance: The shift from a human-centric, empathetic practitioner-patient relationship to one mediated by technology can be jarring for many. Patients may worry about the loss of the "human touch" and the personal connection they have with their doctor. Building a system that augments, rather than replaces, human expertise is key to gaining patient acceptance.
- Cultural and Philosophical Conflicts: The framework requires reconciling two fundamentally different epistemologies: the evidence-based, reductionist approach of m odern science and the holistic, experience-based worldview of Vedic philosophy. This can lead to philosophical conflicts and a lack of clear consensus on what constitutes "proof" or "efficacy." Finding a common ground and building a truly integrated system, rather than just a superficial overlay, is a profound intellectual and cultural challenge.

Coordination Vedic scripture into secure healthcare frameworks presents a few challenges:

- Misinterpretation: In an advanced healthcare setting, vedic writings may be misinterpreted or misused, leading to incompetent or incorrect healers.
- Evidence-Based Concerns: It is difficult to gain recognition among medical professionals for many Vedic practices because they require the extensive rational approval needed by modern pharmaceuticals.

- Collaboration Gaps: Integrating knowledge from Vedic philosophy with contemporary medical practices necessitates cross-disciplinary cooperation, which can be difficult to establish and maintain.
- Complexity of Integration: When traditional methods are combined with modern, sophisticated health frameworks, information security protocols can become more complex, increasing vulnerabilities if not properly managed.
- Adhering to Benchmarks: It may be difficult to coordinate Vedic practices inside standard systems without modifications if they do not conform to current healthcare controls.
- Cost and Accessibility: Putting Vedic-based practices into practice in the healthcare industry may need additional resources, planning, and foundation, which can be a problem in environments with limited resources.
- Skepticism Among Specialists: Because Vedic practices align with natural medicine or meet natural needs, healthcare providers may feel comfortable adopting them.
- Practice Variability: There can be wide variations in how Vedic standards are translated and applied, which can lead to irregularities in execution and outcomes.
- Finding Common Ground: It can be challenging to strike a balance between cutting-edge innovative headways and traditional practices, particularly in healthcare situations that are changing quickly.
- Require Training: In order to obtain and effectively apply Vedic standards, healthcare professionals might need additional training, which isn't always readily available in the current educational programs.

TABLE I illustrates the comparative analysis of existing frameworks.

Table I. Comparative Analysis Of Existing Frameworks.

References	Artificial Intelligence	Vedic Scripture	Sustainable Medical Cyber Physical Systems	Secure Healthcare
Sharma et al. (2023)	Yes	Yes	No	No
Sharma, Tyagi, et al. (2023)	Yes	Yes	No	No
Mohammed et al. (2023b)	Yes	No	No	Yes
Proposed Methodology	Yes	Yes	Yes	Yes

V. IMPACT ON MULTIPLE SUSTAINABLE DEVELOPMENT GOALS (SDGS)

The proposed framework of an Artificial Intelligence and Vedic Scripture Enabled Sustainable Medical Cyber-Physical System for Secure Healthcare is a holistic model with the potential to make a significant and positive impact on multiple Sustainable Development Goals (SDGs). By integrating advanced technology with ancient principles of holistic well-being and sustainability, this system directly addresses several of the UN's 17 goals, particularly those related to health, sustainability, innovation, and global partnerships. While the primary impact is on SDG 3, the interconnected nature of the framework means it has a ripple effect across numerous other goals.

SDG 3 (Good Health and Well-being): The most direct and profound impact of this framework is on SDG 3, which aims to "ensure healthy lives and promote well-being for all at all ages." This comprehensive system tackles various targets within this goal.

- Target 3.4: Reduce Non-Communicable Diseases (NCDs): The integration of Vedic principles, particularly Ayurveda, fundamentally shifts healthcare from a reactive, disease-centric model to a proactive, wellness-focused one. AI and MCPS enable personalized health monitoring, allowing for the early detection of an individual's constitutional imbalances (Vikriti) long before they manifest as chronic NCDs like diabetes or cardiovascular disease. By providing personalized, real-time recommendations on diet, lifestyle (Dinacharya), and mindfulness, the system empowers individuals to make sustainable choices that prevent the onset of NCDs. This is in stark contrast to the conventional approach, which often begins with late-stage symptom management.
- Target 3.8: Achieve Universal Health Coverage: The framework's reliance on remote monitoring and AI-powered diagnostics can dramatically improve healthcare accessibility, especially for underserved and rural populations. Wearable sensors and mobile applications can bring high-quality, personalized healthcare to remote areas where clinics and specialists are scarce. This democratizes access to health services and reduces geographical barriers to care, thereby contributing to universal health coverage. The system can provide scalable and low-cost health solutions, reducing the financial burden on individuals and healthcare systems alike.
- Target 3.4: Promote Mental Health and Well-being: Vedic scriptures place a strong emphasis on the interconnectedness of the mind, body, and spirit. AI can analyze data related to an individual's emotional and mental state, such as sleep patterns and stress markers, to provide targeted interventions. This can

include personalized meditation guides, breathing exercises (Pranayama), and lifestyle recommendations derived from Vedic texts, helping to reduce stress and combat mental health challenges in a holistic manner.

SDG 9 (Industry, Innovation, and Infrastructure): This SDG focuses on building resilient infrastructure, promoting inclusive and sustainable industrialization, and fostering innovation. The proposed framework is, by its very nature, a major innovation in healthcare infrastructure.

- Target 9.4: Upgrade Infrastructure and Retrofit Industries: The system represents an upgrade of healthcare infrastructure from isolated clinics to a digitally interconnected and resilient network. It promotes the development of smart medical devices and systems, fostering innovation in the medical technology sector. The integration of robust cybersecurity measures, such as blockchain for secure data management, makes this infrastructure not only "smart" but also "resilient" and trustworthy. This is critical for the functioning of a modern, data-driven healthcare system.
- Target 9.5: Enhance Scientific Research and Innovation: The framework encourages scientific research that bridges the gap between traditional wisdom and modern technology. AI can be used to analyze and validate traditional remedies and diagnostic methods, leading to a new wave of evidence-based research in holistic medicine. This interdisciplinary approach fosters innovation not just in technology but also in the very methodology of medical science. It creates a new research ecosystem where ancient knowledge is a source of new hypotheses, which can then be rigorously tested using modern scientific tools.

SDG 12 (Responsible Consumption and Production): This SDG aims to ensure sustainable consumption and production patterns. The Vedic-inspired, sustainable approach to healthcare has a direct impact on this goal.

- Target 12.2: Sustainable Management and Efficient Use of Natural Resources: The framework promotes a preventive healthcare model, which inherently reduces the consumption of resources associated with treating late-stage diseases. By focusing on natural remedies and lifestyle interventions, it can decrease reliance on energy-intensive pharmaceutical manufacturing and reduce the generation of medical waste.
- Target 12.4: Environmentally Sound Management of Chemicals and Wastes: The system's emphasis on natural, plant-based remedies, guided by AI, can lead to the discovery and optimization of medicines with a lower environ-

mental footprint. Furthermore, the intelligent management of medical supply chains and the reduction of unnecessary diagnostic tests can significantly decrease the amount of chemical and biomedical waste generated by the healthcare sector.

- Target 12.8: Promote Education for Sustainable Lifestyles: The personalized recommendations generated by the system are not just for treatment but for a way of life. By providing guidance on sustainable diets, mindfulness practices, and a harmonious relationship with the environment, the framework helps to educate individuals on adopting sustainable lifestyles. This promotes a shift in consumer behavior from one of passive consumption of medical services to one of active and conscious participation in one's own well-being.

SDG 4 (Quality Education): The framework has a transformative impact on education and knowledge dissemination, aligning with SDG 4's goal of ensuring inclusive and equitable quality education.

- Target 4.4: Increase the Number of People with Relevant Skills: This system requires a new generation of healthcare professionals who are skilled in both traditional practices and modern technology. This creates a demand for interdisciplinary education programs that train individuals in AI, data science, cybersecurity, and traditional medical systems. The framework thus contributes to a more skilled workforce capable of navigating the complexities of a hybrid healthcare model.
- Target 4.7: Promote Education for Sustainable Development: The system serves as a powerful educational tool for patients and the general public, teaching them about the interconnectedness of their health, lifestyle, and the environment. By providing accessible and personalized health information rooted in both science and ancient wisdom, it fosters a deeper understanding of holistic well-being and the principles of sustainable living.

SDG 17 (Partnerships for the Goals): The successful implementation of this framework necessitates extensive collaboration, which is the focus of SDG 17.

- Target 17.16: Enhance Global Partnership: This model can only succeed through multi-stakeholder partnerships involving governments, research institutions, healthcare providers, technology companies, and community organizations. International collaboration is vital for standardizing data, developing ethical guidelines, and ensuring that the benefits of this technology are shared globally, particularly with developing nations.

- Target 17.17: Encourage and Promote Effective Partnerships: The system provides a platform for both conventional and traditional healthcare practitioners to work together, sharing knowledge and resources to provide more effective care. This collaboration breaks down the silos between different medical systems and fosters a more inclusive and integrated approach to global health.

The integration of AI, Vedic scriptures, and secure MCPS is not just a technological advancement; it is a holistic approach that aligns with and actively contributes to the attainment of several SDGs. It offers a path toward a healthcare system that is not only more effective and secure but also sustainable, equitable, and deeply human-centered, paving the way for a healthier and more prosperous future for all. The fusion of Artificial Intelligence (AI), Vedic principles, and Medical Cyber-Physical Systems (MCPS) presents a unique and compelling model for the Western world, including the USA and Europe. While these regions have highly advanced healthcare systems, they grapple with challenges such as rising costs, an aging population, and a shift from acute to chronic disease management. This integrated approach can address these issues by offering a more personalized, preventive, and sustainable healthcare model, though its implementation requires navigating significant cultural and ethical hurdles. Western healthcare has traditionally been a reactive system, excelling at treating acute illnesses and emergencies. However, it struggles with the prevalence of chronic conditions like heart disease, diabetes, and obesity. The Vedic-inspired holistic approach, which focuses on "Prakriti" (individual constitution), provides a powerful framework for preventive medicine. By integrating ancient wisdom with modern AI, doctors can use a patient's genetic data, lifestyle information, and medical history to create a unique health profile. AI algorithms can then analyze this data, informed by Ayurvedic principles, to recommend personalized diets, exercise routines, and stress-management techniques. This proactive model, driven by technology, can help prevent chronic diseases, reduce the long-term burden on healthcare systems, and empower individuals to take control of their well-being. This shift from a "sick-care" to a "well-care" system is a major paradigm change. The USA and Europe face a growing shortage of healthcare professionals, particularly in rural and underserved communities. AI-enabled MCPS can help alleviate this strain by enhancing healthcare delivery and accessibility. Wearable sensors, smart home devices, and remote patient monitoring systems can collect vast amounts of data, which AI can analyze to detect subtle changes in a patient's health. This allows for early intervention and continuous monitoring of chronic conditions, reducing the need for frequent in-person doctor visits. For example, an AI-powered system can track the blood sugar levels of a diabetic patient and send automated alerts to both the patient and their doctor if a dangerous trend is detected. This not only makes healthcare more convenient but also reduces the financial burden on patients and health insurance companies by preventing hospitalizations. While the potential benefits are significant, the integration of Vedic principles into Western healthcare is not without challenges. The Western medical system is rooted in evidence-based practice, with a strong emphasis on controlled trials and statistical validation. Many Vedic and Ayurvedic principles lack this form of scientific proof, which can lead to skepticism and resistance from medical professionals and regulators. Additionally, the philosophical underpinnings of Vedic thought, which include concepts like karma and dharma, may clash with the secular and individualistic values of Western societies. Another key concern is data privacy and security. MCPS generate enormous amounts of sensitive patient data, and AI systems must be designed with robust safeguards to prevent breaches. The ethical framework of Vedic scripture, with its focus on duty and selfless action, could be a valuable guide in developing ethical AI that prioritizes patient well-being over profit. However, it requires a careful and thoughtful dialogue between technologists, healthcare providers, ethicists, and policymakers to bridge the cultural gap and ensure the technology is deployed responsibly and justly. In essence, the Western world can embrace the technological and philosophical aspects of this model to create a more humane and sustainable healthcare system, but it must do so by respecting its own cultural norms and scientific rigor.

VI. CONCLUSION

A promising avenue for enhancing quiet care is the integration of medical cyber-physical systems (CPS) for secure healthcare with principles from Vedic scripture and artificial intelligence (AI). This combination can create a holistic healthcare setting that ensures information security and moral reflection while addressing mental, physical, and spiritual well-being. Healthcare frameworks can recognize the intricate relationships between body, mind, and soul and provide more individualized and comprehensive care by fusing AI's explanatory control with the holistic experiences of Vedic sacred writings. The emphasis on preventive measures derived from Vedic lessons can result in proactive health management, reducing the prevalence of chronic illnesses and advancing overall well-being outcomes. Vedic norms place a strong emphasis on morality and duty, which guides the development of AI-driven frameworks that give information security and understanding security top priority and foster faith in medical advancements. Consolidating Vedic bits of knowledge permits for a more socially competent healthcare environment, making administrations more open and worthy to differing populations. Collaboration between healthcare professionals, technologists, and scholars of Vedic logic is necessary for successful integration in order to advance a more comprehensive understanding of wellbeing that honors tradition as well as progress. The conceptual framework of an Artificial Intelligence and Vedic Scripture Enabled Sustainable Medical Cyber-Physical System for Secure Healthcare represents a profound and necessary evolution in medical science. It is a synthesis that seeks to transcend the limitations of current healthcare models by building a system that is not only technologically advanced but also ethically grounded, holistically oriented, and inherently secure. The journey from a traditional, reactive, and often fragmented system to this integrated, proactive, and personalized model is fraught with challenges but holds the promise of unprecedented benefits. The core advantages of this framework are manifold and synergistic. AI-powered Medical Cyber-Physical Systems (MCPS) provide the technological infrastructure for real-time monitoring and data analysis, enabling a level of diagnostic precision and predictive capability that was previously unimaginable. This is where the wisdom of Vedic scriptures, particularly Ayurveda, serves as the guiding philosophy. By operationalizing concepts like Prakriti and Vikriti, AI can move beyond a one-size-fits-all approach to medicine and offer truly personalized, preventive care. This personalized approach is not just about treating disease but about fostering genuine well-being by addressing the root causes of imbalance. Furthermore, the Vedic emphasis on harmony with nature provides a crucial blueprint for a sustainable healthcare system—one that minimizes environmental impact, optimizes resource allocation, and promotes the use of sustainable, natural remedies. However, realizing this vision is far from straightforward. The challenges are substantial and require multi-faceted solutions. On the technical front, the biggest hurdle is the lack of standardized, quantifiable data for traditional practices. Translating ancient, qualitative knowledge into a format that AI can process requires a massive effort in data collection, taxonomy development, and interoperability standards. The security of MCPS is another critical concern, as the interconnectedness of these systems creates a vast attack surface for cyber threats. Robust security measures, including the use of technologies like blockchain and AI-powered threat detection, are essential to protect the integrity and privacy of sensitive patient data and build public trust. Ethical and cultural challenges are perhaps the most complex. The "black box" nature of AI models and the potential for algorithmic bias demand a new ethical framework that prioritizes transparency, accountability, and fairness. Reconciling the scientific, evidence-based approach of modern medicine with the holistic, experience-based worldview of Vedic philosophy requires a willingness to bridge philosophical divides and establish new paradigms for validation and efficacy. Overcoming cultural resistance from both conventional and traditional practitioners, as well as gaining patient acceptance, hinges on a clear demonstration of the system's benefits and an unwavering commitment to maintaining the human element in healthcare. The goal is not to replace human expertise but to augment it, empowering both practitioners and patients with better information and insights. The fusion of AI, Vedic scriptures, and MCPS represents a bold and ambitious vision for the future of healthcare. It is a future where technology is a force for personalization and sustainability, where ancient wisdom informs modern innovation, and where healthcare is a proactive partnership focused on holistic well-being rather than a reactive response to illness. While the path forward is complex, the potential rewards—a more effective, secure, sustainable, and deeply human-centered healthcare system—make this endeavor not just a possibility, but a necessity for the well-being of future generations. The successful implementation of this framework will not only redefine healthcare but will also demonstrate the immense potential of integrating ancient wisdom with cutting-edge technology to solve some of humanity's most pressing challenges.

REFERENCES

Al-Shareeda, M. A., Najm, L. B., Hassan, A. A., Mushtaq, S., & Ali, H. A. (2024). Secure IoT-Based Smart Agriculture System Using Wireless Sensor Networks for Remote Environmental Monitoring. *STAP Journal of Security Risk Management, 2024*(1), 56–66. DOI: 10.63180/jsrm.thestap.2024.1.4

Albinhamad, H., Alotibi, A., Alagnam, A., Almaiah, M., & Salloum, S. (2025). Vehicular Ad-hoc Networks (VANETs): A Key Enabler for Smart Transportation Systems and Challenges. *Jordanian Journal of Informatics and Computing, 2025*(1), 4–15. DOI: 10.63180/jjic.thestap.2025.1.2

Ali, G., Mijwil, M. M., Adamopoulos, I., & Ayad, J. (2025). Leveraging the Internet of Things, Remote Sensing, and Artificial Intelligence for Sustainable Forest Management. *Babylonian Journal of Internet of Things, 2025*, 1–65. DOI: 10.58496/BJIoT/2025/001

Almaayah, M., & Sulaiman, R. B. (2024). Cyber Risk Management in the Internet of Things: Frameworks, Models, and Best Practices. *STAP Journal of Security Risk Management, 2024*(1), 3–23. DOI: 10.63180/jsrm.thestap.2024.1.1

Alnajem, A. A. Q. I., Niu, Y., & Ibrahim, A. (2024). Evaluating Educational Strategies Focused on Achieving Sustainable Development Goals in Diverse Global Contexts. *ESTIDAMAA, 2024*, 60–71. DOI: 10.70470/ESTIDAMAA/2024/009

Alshinwan, M., Memon, A. G., Ghanem, M. C., & Almaayah, M. (2025). Unsupervised text feature selection approach based on improved Prairie dog algorithm for the text clustering. *Jordanian Journal of Informatics and Computing, 2025*(1), 27–36. DOI: 10.63180/jjic.thestap.2025.1.4

Alzahrani, A., Alshehri, M., AlGhamdi, R., & Sharma, S. K. (2023). Improved Wireless Medical Cyber-Physical System (IWMCPS) based on machine learning. *Health Care, 11*(3), 384. DOI: 10.3390/healthcare11030384 PMID: 36766959

Chakraborty, C., Nagarajan, S. M., Devarajan, G. G., Ramana, T. V., & Mohanty, R. (2023). Intelligent AI-based Healthcare Cyber Security System using Multi-Source Transfer Learning Method. *ACM Transactions on Sensor Networks*, 3597210. Advance online publication. DOI: 10.1145/3597210

Chand, A., Agarwal, P., & Sharma, S. (2023). Real-Time Retrieving Vedic Sanskrit Text into Multi-Lingual Text and Audio for Cultural Tourism Motivation. *2022 International Conference for Advancement in Technology (ICONAT)*, 1–6. DOI: 10.1109/ICONAT57137.2023.10080862

Chandran, A. L., Samual, J., Safavi, S., & Ali, A. (2025). A Comparative Analysis of Machine Learning Models on Detecting Malware in Android Devices. *Journal of Cyber Security and Risk Auditing, 2025*(4), 327–346. DOI: 10.63180/jcsra.thestap.2025.4.10

Davarasan, A., Samual, J., Palansundram, K., & Ali, A. (2024). A Comprehensive Review of Machine Learning Approaches for Android Malware Detection. *Journal of Cyber Security and Risk Auditing, 2024*(1), 39–60. DOI: 10.63180/jcsra.thestap.2024.1.5

Habib, M. K., & Chimsom, C. I. (2022). CPS: Role, Characteristics, architectures and future Potentials. *Procedia Computer Science, 200*, 1347–1358. DOI: 10.1016/j.procs.2022.01.336

Hussein, N. A.-H. K., & Basel, O. M. (2024). Integrating Renewable Energy Systems into Urban Planning for Sustainable Cities. *ESTIDAMAA, 2024*, 15–21. DOI: 10.70470/ESTIDAMAA/2024/003

Hussein, N. A.-H. K., Khalaf, S., & Shah, K. D. (2024). Advanced Composite Materials for Sustainable Construction: Innovations in Civil Engineering Applications. *KHWARIZMIA, 2024*, 8–16. DOI: 10.70470/KHWARIZMIA/2024/003

Kayusi, F., Turyasingura, B., Chavula, P., & Amadi, O. J. (2024). Exploring Deep Learning Methods Used in the Medical Device Sector. *Mesopotamian Journal of Artificial Intelligence in Healthcare, 2024*, 42–49. DOI: 10.58496/MJAIH/2024/007

Mensah, G. B., Mijwil, M. M., Abotaleb, M., Ali, G., & Dutta, P. K. (2025). High Performance Medicine: Involving Artificial Intelligence Models in Enhancing Medical Laws and Medical Negligence Matters A Case Study of Act, 2009 (Act 792) in Ghana. *SHIFAA, 2025*, 1–6. DOI: 10.70470/SHIFAA/2025/001

Mijwil, M. M., Abotaleb, M., Ali, G., & Dhoska, K. (2024). Assigning Medical Professionals: ChatGPT's Contributions to Medical Education and Health Prediction. *Mesopotamian Journal of Artificial Intelligence in Healthcare, 2024*, 76–83. DOI: 10.58496/MJAIH/2024/011

Mohammed, M. A., Lakhan, A., Zebari, D. A., Ghani, M. K. A., Marhoon, H. A., Abdulkareem, K. H., Nedoma, J., & Martinek, R. (2023). Securing healthcare data in industrial cyber-physical systems using combining deep learning and blockchain technology. *Engineering Applications of Artificial Intelligence, 129*, 107612. DOI: 10.1016/j.engappai.2023.107612

Mohammed, M. A., Lakhan, A., Zebari, D. A., Ghani, M. K. A., Marhoon, H. A., Abdulkareem, K. H., Nedoma, J., & Martinek, R. (2023b). Securing healthcare data in industrial cyber-physical systems using combining deep learning and blockchain technology. *Engineering Applications of Artificial Intelligence, 129*, 107612. DOI: 10.1016/j.engappai.2023.107612

Mowla, N. I., Doh, I., & Chae, K. (2018). On-Device AI-Based Cognitive Detection of Bio-Modality Spoofing in Medical Cyber Physical system. *IEEE Access : Practical Innovations, Open Solutions, 7*, 2126–2137. DOI: 10.1109/ACCESS.2018.2887095

Nyangaresi, V. O., & Shanshool, A. M. (2024). Smart Wearables Powered by AI Transforming Human Activity Recognition. *Babylonian Journal of Artificial Intelligence, 2024*, 128–133. DOI: 10.58496/BJAI/2024/014

Sakirin, T., & Ben Said, R. (2025). Application of deep learning and transfer learning techniques for medical image classification. *Edraak, 2025*, 38–46. DOI: 10.70470/EDRAAK/2025/006

Sallam, M., Al-Mahzoum, K., Eid, H., Al-Salahat, K., Sallam, M., Ali, G., & Mijwil, M. M. (2025). Chinese Generative AI Models Challenge Western AI in Clinical Chemistry MCQs: A Benchmarking Follow-up Study on AI Use in Health Education. *Babylonian Journal of Artificial Intelligence, 2025*, 1–14. DOI: 10.58496/BJAI/2025/001

Sharma, S., Gautam, A., & Tyagi, R. (2023). Evaluation of 5% Known And 95% Unknown Matter in Inner and Outer Universe Using Quantum Computing, Artificial Intelligence and Vedic Scripture. In *2023 International Conference on Energy, Materials and Communication Engineering (ICEMCE)*, 1–6. DOI: 10.1109/ICEMCE57940.2023.10434060

Sharma, S., Goyal, H. R., Rawat, R., & Tyagi, R. (2024). Artificial Intelligence, Cloud Computing, Blockchain, and Vedic Scripture Enabled Sustainable Global Judicial System for Democratic Society. In *2024 International Conference on Emerging Technologies and Innovation for Sustainability (EmergIN)*, 7–12. DOI: 10.1109/EmergIN63207.2024.10961824

Sharma, S., Gupta, A., & Tyagi, R. (2023). Artificial Intelligence Enabled Sustainable Education System Using Vedic Scripture and Cyber Security. In *2023 Second International Conference on Advances in Computational Intelligence and Communication (ICACIC)*, 1–6. DOI: 10.1109/ICACIC59454.2023.10435133

Sharma, S., Gupta, A., & Tyagi, R. (2023a). Sustainable Natural Resources Utilization Decision System for Better Society Using Vedic Scripture, Cloud Computing, and IoT. In *2023 Fifth International Conference on Advances in Electronics, Computers and Communications (ICAECC)*, 1–6. DOI: 10.1109/ICAECC59324.2023.10560335

Sharma, S., Gupta, A., & Tyagi, R. (2024). Artificial Intelligence, Cyber Security and Vedic Scripture Integrated Sustainable Global Youth Leadership Development. In *2024 IEEE International Conference on Communication, Computing and Signal Processing (IICCCS)*, 1–6. DOI: 10.1109/IICCCS61609.2024.10763618

Sharma, S., Tomar, M., & Tyagi, R. (2024). Artificial Intelligence and Vedic Scripture in Digital Agriculture for Global Economy. In *2024 International Conference on Intelligent and Innovative Technologies in Computing, Electrical and Electronics (IITCEE)*, 1–6. DOI: 10.1109/IITCEE59897.2024.10467916

Sharma, S., & Tyagi, R. (2023). Digitalization of Farming Knowledge Using Artificial Intelligence and Vedic Scripture. In 2023 IEEE International Conference on ICT in Business Industry & Government (ICTBIG), 1–6. DOI: 10.1109/ICTBIG59752.2023.10456219

Sharma, S., Tyagi, R., & Bhardwaj, R. (2023). Sustainable Smart Society Development Based on Geo Sensitive Equality Using Vedic Structure, Artificial Intelligence, Blockchain and IoT. In 2023 1st International Conference on Circuits, Power and Intelligent Systems (CCPIS), 1–6. DOI: 10.1109/CCPIS59145.2023.10291593

Yasser, A. A. M. (2025). Sustainable Design Strategies in Architectural Engineering: A Comprehensive Review. *KHWARIZMIA, 2025*, 1–11. DOI: 10.70470/KHWARIZMIA/2025/001

Zhang, Y., & Su, Y. (2024). Towards a Sustainable Future: Exploring Innovative Financing Models for Renewable Energy. *MEDAAD, 2024*, 34–40. DOI: 10.70470/MEDAAD/2024/006

Chapter 8
Cyber-Physical System Resilience Leveraging Deep Learning for Enhanced Security

Usharani Bhimavarapu
https://orcid.org/0000-0002-0246-1420
Department of Computer Science and Engineering, Koneru Lakshmaiah Education Foundation, Vaddeswaram, India

ABSTRACT

Cyber-Physical Systems (CPS) represent a critical convergence of computational algorithms and physical processes, enabling smart infrastructures across industries such as energy, transportation, healthcare, and manufacturing. However, the integration of digital and physical components exposes these systems to unique security challenges that can lead to severe physical and economic consequences. This work focuses on Cyber-Physical System security, aiming to protect the delicate intersection where digital control meets the physical environment. By leveraging advanced machine learning techniques, including bi-stacked Gated Recurrent Units (GRUs), this approach enhances the detection and prevention of cyber-physical attacks through effective analysis of sequential sensor and control data. Coupled with feature selection using Particle Swarm Optimization (PSO), the methodology prioritizes relevant system attributes, improving anomaly detection accuracy.

DOI: 10.4018/979-8-3373-1807-3.ch008

© 2026, IGI Global Scientific Publishing. Copying or distributing in print or electronic forms without written permission of IGI Global Scientific Publishing is prohibited. Use of this chapter to [gene]rative artificial intelligence (AI) technologies is expressly prohibited. The publisher reserves all rights to license its use for generative AI training and machine learning model development.

INTRODUCTION

Cyber-Physical Systems (CPS) combine computational components with physical phenomena to produce complex systems where digital and physical components are intertwined in complete harmony. CPS enable basic infrastructure such as the power grid, transportation, healthcare, and industry. Increased dependence on CPS implies that failures can have significant physical repercussions, as opposed to single-purpose digital systems where damage is restricted to data loss. As an example, a cyber attack on a CPS managing a power grid can result in extensive blackouts and endanger public safety. Thus, it is necessary to secure CPS to defend not only data but also the physical world that relies on these systems. Contemporary CPS are defined by massive-scale integration with the Internet of Things (IoT), wireless networks, and cloud computing, which greatly increases their attack surface (Alshinwan et al., 2025) and (Albinhamad et al., 2025).

The complexity of the systems involving numerous devices and software makes them more difficult to defend. The more devices are interconnected, the more vulnerabilities and the more entry points of the attackers. Interconnection optimizes operations but creates new security issues. Cybersecurity for CPS needs to be guaranteed by addressing the cyber vulnerabilities and physical safety issues concurrently to avoid cascading failure (Almaayah & Sulaiman, 2024) and (Al-Shareeda et al., 2024). CPS is coming to rely more and more on by critical infrastructures such as water treatment facilities, transportation networks, and hospitals for automation and monitoring in real-time. Breaking into the confines of such industries can prove to be catastrophic in nature such as poisoning of water supplies, vehicular accidents, or interference with delivery of medicine.

Security of CPS makes the critical services more secure and reliable, which protects life and health of people. Protecting such infrastructures from cyber-physical attacks is not only an issue of technology but also of national security (Ang, Huy, & Janarthanan, 2025) and (Otoom, 2025). Unique compared to conventional IT systems, CPS attacks can physically harm human life and the environment. For example, a hacked driverless vehicle or factory robot may cause accidents or injuries. CPS security seeks to thwart malicious procedures that can cause unsafe states or equipment damage.

By safeguarding sensors, actuators, and communication cables, CPS security protects against attacks that are in between cyber-attack and physical sabotage, always not violating the safety of operation. CPS operate based on reliable sensor data and command controls to ensure a safe operation. By tampering with these data, an attacker might lead to false assumptions and hazardous situations. CPS security is concerned with ensuring data authenticity and integrity to organizations in order to establish confidence in automated systems. Impersonation and non-tampering are assured via communication protocols and cryptographic algorithms. Reliable data must be present in the assurance of the safe and optimal operation of CPS. Most CPS handle and process private information, including personal health information in healthcare devices or location data in intelligent transport systems. Unauthorized disclosure or access can potentially violate personal privacy. CPS security ensures the confidentiality issue by enforcing stringent encryption, access control, and secure data storage. Protection of users' privacy, in addition to adhering to the law, enhances public acceptability and trust of CPS technologies. Cyber-physical attacks cause extensive operation disruptions and economic loss. For instance, manufacturing CPS ransomware attacks can shut down production lines and have downtime costs. Likewise, smart grid disruptions can mean huge economic losses. Effective CPS security controls prevent expensive effects of these disruptions by facilitating quick detection, response, and recovery from attacks. Security investments consequently translate into improved operational continuity and economic resilience. CPS transformation drives innovation in technologies such as autonomous vehicles, smart cities, and Industry 4.0. Security threats can slow down innovation and discourage adoption. Secure CPS provides a secure platform to experiment and deploy new technologies. It promotes innovation through assurance that trusted protection is in place against growing threats. Safe CPS infrastructure allows industries to leverage cutting-edge technology while protecting themselves from undue risk.

Governments and regulatory bodies globally are now placing increased emphasis on CPS security through standards, guidelines, and regulation. Regulations require organizations that have control over CPS to comply with cybersecurity, safety, and data privacy legislation. Non-compliance can lead to penalties, legal breaches, and reputational damage. CPS security ensures that organizations are able to comply with regulatory demands and meet their ethical and legal obligations for mitigating cyber-physical threats.

As CPS become part of the fabric of everyday life, people's trust in their safety and reliability is essential.

Security breaches causing physical injury or loss of data can undermine faith in institutions and technology.

Good CPS security supports society's stability by avoiding interruptions that can trigger panic or rebellion.

Through safety of the intersection of cyberspace and the physical world, CPS security ensures people, communities, and governments that such systems work safely and reliably in a more networked world, procuring social stability.

Jadhao tested the effect of background color perception on the attention span and short-term memory of students but with limited generalizability due to the relatively small and homogeneous sample size that covered only normal students. The investigation targeted mostly short-term cognitive effects regardless of long-term effect or varied populations like learning disabilities or varied age ranges. Environmental factors like lighting and screen types were not controlled as effectively, which can affect the outcomes of perception. The investigation did not explore underlying neurological mechanisms, further limiting the scope of cognitive information.

Lastly, the research laboratory environment may not be a good analogue of real classroom settings, diluting the ecological validity of findings (Jadhao et al., 2020). Del suggested a new human-focused model of AI takeup by the individual, but the practicability of the model can be diluted by using self-report measures that are prone to bias and dilute reliability. The research is primarily based on psychological factors at the level of an individual, which may neglect organizational or cultural determinants of AI acceptance. The research also does not fully reflect the dynamic pace of AI technologies whose rate of development may surpass acceptance frameworks. The sample population may also be biased towards industries or regions that have a low international applicability.

In addition, the model fails to even partially capture ethical or privacy issues that dominate AI adoption (Del Giudice et al., 2023). Faruqui established LungNet, a deep-CNN lung cancer diagnostic model integrating CT and IoT sensor information, but study shortcomings are a possible lack of diversity in patient data, impacting the model's applicability to various populations and settings. Wear sensor data integration, though novel, could bring about noise or discrepancies depending on sensor variability in accuracy or patient compliance. Model performance was, in most cases, assessed against retrospective data, which may not accurately represent real-time diagnostic issues. Computational expense and resource requirements for the hybrid model could further constrain its deployment to resource-poor healthcare settings.

Lastly, the study did not conduct a complete comparison between LungNet and the latest releases of other leading-performing models on large-scale external benchmarks (Faruqui et al., 2021). Chakraborty investigated how robots are able to forecast human visual attention, but their method may be limited by dependence on particular sensor configurations or lab settings, and thus it is not appropriate for the outside world. The algorithm may find it difficult to handle occlusions, light changes, or moving backgrounds typical of the outdoors. The attention calculation is mainly gaze direction-based and does not take into full account cognitive context or multitasking behavior, fundamental in understanding actual attention. Furthermore, the approach's scalability to many subjects at once was not validated, limiting its application in crowded or social environments.

The techniques used in evaluation may not represent the complexity in human focus dynamics (Chakraborty et al., 2020). Trivedi used a convolutional neural network in bacterial strain classification, but its limitation is the risk of bias due to low variety and number of bacterial image data. Whether the model can be generalized to novel or minority bacterial strains is unknown, which raises concerns for practical deployment to diagnostics. Use of high-quality images can also limit functionality in actual clinical practice when imaging situations are very variable. The computational capability for model training and prediction may not be possible in all health facilities.

In addition, the paper does not indicate integration with current laboratory workflows that can limit usage. Interpretability and explainability of the model were also not prioritized, which are very essential for clinician trust (Trivedi et al., 2023). Trivedi suggested an NDNN-based U-Net for 3D brain tumor segmentation, but robustness of the method on a wide range of MRI scanners and protocols is not generally tested and hence would restrict clinical use. It may also be faced with nonspecific-shaped tumors or tumors of low contrast within background tissue. Although the 3D method offers spatial information, it highly increases computational cost, which can limit its use in real-time clinical practice. The training data can be deficient in good representation of unusual tumor types and thus potentially result in poor segmentation performance in such instances.

Secondly, the paper neither mentions post-processing nor workflow integration comprehensively. Also, it needs multi-institutional dataset validation to ensure generalizability at large scale (Trivedi et al., 2022)(Sheela et al., 2024; Srividhya et al., 2024).

Wei contrasted BiLSTM and transformer models in visual descriptor extraction from patent figure captions in one study. However, the study only used a small and limited dataset of patent figures, and hence the result might be confined to generalizability across other datasets or other domains. Comparison was primarily on efficiency of data and not necessarily thoroughly testing the two models' resilience to noisy or incomplete captions. Additionally, the transformers' higher computational requirements were stated but not investigated in depth in terms of scalability or deployment feasibility. Multimodal data fusion, which could possibly enhance descriptor extraction, was also not addressed in the study. Finally, the metric used in evaluation was too specific, constraining attention to other performance aspects like interpretability or inference time (Wei et al., 2022; Abotaleb et al., 2025; Mohialden et al., 2024).

Zhang proposed a hybrid time series network and attention for enterprise sales forecasting in edge computing and digital management, but the performance of the method could be quite sensitive to the quality and granularity of input data, which vary widely among enterprises. Complexity of the model is of concern for deployment in resource-limited edge environments with potential to limit real-time forecasting capability. Furthermore, the research mostly validated results on specific datasets with minimal testing across different types of industries or seasonal cycles. Interpretability of the hybrid model was not fully addressed, and this is critical to business decision-makers. Lastly, challenges faced by integrating such models with existing enterprise systems were not investigated extensively (Zhang and Kim, 2023; Kayusi et al., 2024; Yonan & Zahra, 2023).

Yang developed a model that combines GoogLeNet, residual networks, and attention mechanisms for rice leaf disease detection. While efficient, the performance of the model might be weakened in field conditions where lighting is unpredictable, there is occlusion, and background is cluttered. The dataset utilized may not cover the whole spectrum of rice diseases or development phases, reducing functional resilience. Computational overhead from the blended architectures may restrict deployment on low-energy agricultural equipment. The study is also lacking in extensive comparison with light models that may achieve the best trade-off between efficiency and accuracy. The process itself does not extend directly to multi-disease instances where more than a single pathogen invades a leaf simultaneously (Yang et al., 2023; Burhanuddin, 2023; Hadid et al., 2024).

A taxonomy and an overview of IoT cloud applications were introduced by Pflanzner, but as a consequence of the emphasis on the current technology of the time, this lacks in the description of rapidly changing edge and fog paradigms of computing. The research also discusses a wide array of issues, thereby not providing detailed explanations of specialized security threats and compensatory measures related to the integration of IoT and the cloud. Emerging application areas like healthcare and smart cities were mentioned but not elaborated on. Moreover, the paper does not discuss interoperability issues among heterogeneous IoT devices and cloud services. Real-world deployment challenges, such as latency and energy balancing, are not represented well enough (Pflanzner and Kertész, 2018; Ahmad, 2023b; Ghanem & Salloum, 2025; Govindan et al., 2023).

Ray presented a decade-long perspective of transfer learning-enhanced vision-based human activity recognition. While comprehensive, the study faced constraints due to the heterogeneity of datasets over varying timelines, thus challenging comparisons directly. The report focused on the ways accuracy was improved but not computationally deeply or latency impacts of transfer learning for real-time systems. Furthermore, the creation of sensor technologies and data modalities aside from vision, such as inertial sensors, were not part of the report. The overview also did not discuss at length ethical considerations of privacy for vision-based monitoring systems. Lastly, scalability to unbounded large-scale deployment is an open problem (Ray et al., 2023).

Beddiar addressed vision-based human activity recognition techniques with a general overview but primarily regarding algorithmic advancements rather than on practical deployment considerations. Emphasis of the survey on benchmark datasets can be viewed as overlooking real-world challenges such as occlusions, dynamic light change, and crowded scenes. Furthermore, the study provides minimal consideration for resource limitations on mobile or embedded systems, which is a requirement for IoT utilization. Data labeling and low availability of labeled activity datasets are mentioned but not given particular attention. Ethical concerns like surveillance and data privacy are provided with minimal attention and may be overlooking impediments to adoption. The study also falls short in presenting extensive discussion of multi-modal sensor fusion methods (Beddiar et al., 2020) (Ahmad, 2023a; Muhammad & Akgül, 2025).

Park suggested MultiCNN-FilterLSTM for low-resource sensor-based human activity recognition in IoT applications but the model's effectiveness would be limited due to its sensor placement- and configuration-dependent nature, as it would limit generalizability. The method was mainly validated on controlled datasets, which do not reflect variability in real-world applications. Trade-offs between resource usage and accuracy are justified but can potentially be further listed under different hardware conditions. Further, the approach does not delve into robustness against sensor failure or noise. More research is required into scalability to multi-user environments and how real-time impact influences the system. The paper also fails to leave it clear how directly the model can generalize to new activity classes without full retraining from scratch (Park et al., 2023).

Kulsoom conducted a survey on machine learning-based human activity recognition for various applications but was constrained by the faster-than-anticipated development in the field, such that very recent work might be out of scope. The survey is likely to give significant emphasis on algorithmic directions and classification performance without broad ranges of discussion of deployment issues like energy efficiency, privacy of data, and sensor calibration. Moreover, the surveyed applications are likely to concentrate on a few dominant sensor types and may miss new modalities such as acoustic or physiological signals. Data bias issues like demographic and environmental are identified but not analyzed extensively. Transferability and model personalization between users and settings (Kulsoom et al., 2022)(Kamel, 2024) may be emphasized more in the paper too.

Paula suggested a novel Front Door Security (FDS) algorithm using a GoogleNet-BiLSTM hybrid model, which showed promising access control accuracy. However, the computational intensity of the model may limit its deployment on low-resource edge devices common in residential environments. The study addresses predominantly vision data without considering other sensor modalities such as audio or motion that could enhance security robustness. The training set employed may be unrepresentative under diverse illumination conditions or adversarial attack situations like spoofing. Additionally, the algorithm's resilience to streaming data in real-time and latency under network constraints is not comprehensively evaluated. The hybrid model's interpretability remains limited, rendering debugging and trust unfeasible for ordinary end-users (Paula et al., 2023).

Kobara gave a comprehensive presentation on cyber-physical security for industrial control systems (ICS) and IoT environments. Despite covering various attack vectors and defense mechanisms, the work predates many recent developments in IoT and CPS threats, limiting its applicability to current dynamic environments. The proposed security frameworks are theoretical, lacking extensive empirical validation or case studies. Real-time detection and mitigation strategies, critical for industrial applications, are only briefly mentioned without deep technical solutions. Besides, integration issues among legacy ICS hardware and modern-day IoT devices are not given ample discussion. The paper further spends least space on user-centric security policy and awareness (Kobara, 2016).

Sarp came up with a real-time intelligent door system with focus on home security using embedded technologies. Even though the system is practical and illustrates functional proof-of-concept, it is not scalable because it tests on small-scale setup without considering multi-user or multi-door environments. The testing of security is limited, particularly vulnerability to network attack or tampering with physical devices. Sensor fusion and redundancy are low, which can influence reliability. Integration with higher-level authentication such as biometric integration or adaptive learning is also non-existent. The factors of power usage and battery life for continuous operation are not considered, which are crucial in home security units (Sarp and Karalar, 2015).

Aldawira proposed a door security system based on the ESP32 microcontroller for home surveillance with a focus on low cost and ease of use. The system is, however, Wi-Fi dependent, which can be unreliable or insecure in some domestic settings. The work provides little insight into encryption or safe communication protocols to protect against spoofing or interception. ESP32 hardware constraints limit the integration of advanced AI-oriented intrusion detection algorithms. The prototype was evaluated under lab conditions, and there are numerous questions left unanswered concerning performance in hostile environments or with numerous concurrent users. The system is also not privacy compliant towards video or audio surveillance (Aldawira et al., 2019).

Sanjay designed a wireless sensor network (WSN) based home security system to detect intrusions. WSNs introduce possibilities of network congestion, delay, and packet loss which were not thoroughly tested. Security vulnerabilities native to WSNs, i.e., node capture or replay attacks, were not thoroughly countered. The system scalability to large homes or various sensors requires more validation. Sensor power management is discussed but not quantitatively researched. Integration into smart home settings and user notification systems is also not extensively covered. Non-technical homeowner usability is also still in its nascent stages (Sanjay Satam and El-Ocla, 2022).

Banerjee designed a Raspberry Pi-based security system for the home with emphasis placed on flexibility and customization. But the reliance on Raspberry Pi limits portability and power usage efficiency, which can be essential to battery-powered applications. The article doesn't mention how the device itself will be defended against cyber or physical attacks. Network security precautions and data confidentiality for the transmission of video and sensor data remain untouched. System performance during network failure or cyberattacks is not verified. In addition, there is no detailed user interface design and usability assessment, which might impede adoption by untechnical consumers. Last but not least, the solution's flexibility to different home layouts and environments is not addressed (Banerjee et al., 2022).

Tao gave a general overview of smart home security and early warning systems under IoT technologies and brushed upon significant components and trends. Nevertheless, the paper is largely an abstract summary and does not contain substantial experimental evidence or case studies. All but one of the systems outlined rely on cloud connectivity, with the latency, data privacy, and network dependency problems not being thoroughly investigated. The suggested security systems are abstract without comprehensive testing against adaptive cyber attacks. Integration problems between heterogeneous devices and interoperability standards are also hinted at. The overview does not address user acceptance and usage deeply, which are critical to system success (Tao et al., 2022).

Kong designed an underwater optical-wireless video surveillance system with high visual fidelity for real-time monitoring. Although revolutionary for underwater application, the system has little application in typical home or industrial security environments. The system requires specialized optical equipment and underwater communication facilities for deployment, restricting mass application. Environmental factors such as water turbidity and light absorption were not completely addressed in terms of image quality influence. The security features of the system for preventing unauthorized access or data corruption are not detailed. Further, scaling and maintenance of such complex systems in actual ocean environments are problems not considered in the study (Kong et al., 2022).

MATERIAL AND METHODS

The methodology involves collecting and pre-processing ActivityNet dataset, video clip normalization to have uniform input. Feature extraction is performed using Particle Swarm Optimization (PSO) to identify the most significant data features. A bi-stacked GRU method is subsequently employed to examine sequence data for anomaly detection in Cyber-Physical Systems (CPS). The model captures complex temporal relationships, enhancing threat detection accuracy. Finally, the system is evaluated based on its ability to lock down the intersection of virtual and real-world environments through the delivery of rapid and uniform security reactions.

MATERIAL

ActivityNet dataset is a vast dataset developed for video understanding research with specific focus put on routine, social, and domestic activities. The dataset contains 21,313 video instances across 200 distinct activity classes. These activities cover all forms of human activity, from normal daily activities such as household chores, social events, games, and exercise routines. These real-world situations are represented in the dataset, making the dataset applicable to model training and evaluation in activity recognition, temporal localization, and event detection. By incorporating such diverse and naturally occurring activities, ActivityNet is a valuable asset in the task of developing algorithms to understand complex human activity in everyday situations.

PREPROCESSING

Preprocessing the ActivityNet dataset involves a series of crucial steps to sanitize the video data for effective analysis and model training. Then, the raw videos are segmented to isolate the activity clips of interest so that each segment exclusively belongs to one of the 200 activity classes discovered. Next, the videos are resized and normalized for frame rate as well as resolution in order to achieve homogeneity across the dataset to reduce computational complexity and improve model performance. Frame extraction is performed to convert videos to image sequences for feature extraction with deep models. In addition, data augmentation operations such as cropping, flipping, and rotation can be applied to enrich the diversity of training examples and enhance model generalization. Temporal alignment and annotation refinement are also necessary, carefully annotating activity boundaries for precise temporal localization tasks. Finally, the data is divided into training, validation, and test sets with a uniform distribution of activity classes for robust model evaluation. These preprocessing steps collectively transform the raw ActivityNet videos into structured, standardized form amenable to advancing research in human activity recognition.

FEATURE SELECTION

Particle Swarm Optimization (PSO) feature selection is a helpful technique to identify the most informative subset of features from a vast dataset to increase model accuracy and reduce computational complexity. PSO is a nature-inspired optimization algorithm based on the social behavior of bird flocking or fish schooling. Each particle in the swarm here represents a potential subset of features. These particles work together to find the optimal combination of features. The position update of each particle is done step-by-step, using the experience of the particle itself and the experience of the swarm as a whole, thereby managing exploration and exploitation. In feature selection, the fitness of all particles is calculated by using a pre-specified objective function, typically in terms of classification accuracy or some other performance metric. By focusing on the most significant characteristics, PSO removes redundant or extraneous data and therefore prevents it from degrading model performance. This results in a better learning process concerning efficiency and accuracy, especially in high-dimensional data like ActivityNet. This also demonstrates the simplicity and flexibility of PSO and its capability for feature selection across different machine learning applications. It has the benefit of avoiding local optima.

BISTACKED GRU

A bi-stacked Gated Recurrent Unit model can be utilized to enhance the safety of Cyber-Physical Systems (CPS). It possesses a strong potential for safeguarding at the critical interface point between the physical and digital worlds. Sensors and actuators typically trigger mass sequential data generation including control systems and, in more sophisticated instances, typically demand advanced techniques in temporal modeling to determine anomalies and potential security threats. A bi-stacked GRU architecture as a double layering of GRU units stacked one upon the other will effectively capture both short and long dependencies on time-series data. This tiered structure allows the model to form sophisticated temporal patterns and subtle differences that can indicate cyber-physical attacks or malfunctions. Processing sequences in hierarchical order, the bi-stacked GRU enhances real-time accuracy for threat detection to prevent interruptions that would impact physical safety or operational stability. Further, the relatively simpler GRU architecture compared to LSTMs ensures quicker training and inference, a requirement that is critical in CPS settings that demand low-latency responses. Bi-stacked GRU models incorporated within cosine CPS security systems support proactive surveillance, early warning mechanisms, and adaptive defense mechanisms, hence the improvement of the resilience of infrastructures against new cyber-physical threats. Lastly, this approach assists in safeguarding not only the cyber components but also the physical processes controlled by CPS, ensuring reliability, safety, and trust in such ever-increasing systems.

EXPERIMENTAL RESULTS

The experiment results validate the effectiveness of the proposed Cyber-Physical System (CPS) security framework in exactly identifying and countering possible threats at the intersection of the digital and physical domains. Utilizing the bi-stacked GRU model with Particle Swarm Optimization (PSO) for feature engineering, the system was tested on real-world sequential data characteristic of CPS domains. The results illustrate significant accuracy improvements in anomaly detection with reduced false positives and improved responsiveness to weak temporal patterns characteristic of cyber-physical attacks. Such findings highlight the ability of the model to learn complex dependencies in time-series data, which is crucial to early detection of malicious behavior that would jeopardize physical functions. Besides, the feature set tuned by PSO improved convergence and computation efficiency. In conclusion, the experiments validate that combining state-of-the-art machine learning techniques can significantly improve the robustness and security of CPS, safeguarding critical infrastructure from evolving threats.

Table 1 represents the distribution of the dataset used in the research, listing the number of samples per activity class in the training and test sets. It signals balance or imbalance among different activity classes in terms of samples. The table helps in understanding availability of data for model training and testing. Classes like Household Chores and Social Interaction have more samples than less frequent activities like Gardening. The split of training and test sets is consistent, which results in effective validation. Overall sample sizes are also presented, emphasizing dataset size. This is the foundation on which future modeling tasks will be performed. Understanding this split is crucial in the interpretation of model performance. The table illustrates the representativeness and diversity of the dataset. Finally, it sets the stage for the ease of classifying less represented activities.

Table 1. Model Accuracy Comparison Across Activity Classes

Activity Class	GRU Accuracy (%)	Bi-Stacked GRU Accuracy (%)	LSTM Accuracy (%)	CNN Accuracy (%)	Transformer Accuracy (%)
Household Chores	85.4	89.2	87.1	82.3	88.5
Social Interaction	83.1	87.6	84.5	79.9	86.2
Playing Games	81.9	85.3	82.7	78.5	84.1
Workouts	87.6	91.0	89.4	85.7	90.1
Cooking	82.4	86.5	84.0	80.2	85.9
Cleaning	79.8	84.2	81.1	77.4	83.7
Gardening	78.5	82.7	80.0	75.9	82.3
Shopping	80.7	84.8	82.2	78.1	84.0
Traveling	83.3	87.5	85.1	81.0	86.7
Working on PC	86.1	90.4	88.2	84.0	89.5

Table 2 shows hyperparameter settings for each model utilized in the experiments, such as learning rate, batch size, and number of layers. This ensures reproducibility and fairness when comparing models. It shows how each architecture was tuned for optimal performance. For example, there are models with additional layers or different optimizers. The table points out variations that may explain discrepancy in accuracy or training time. Such data helps in the consideration of trade-offs between efficiency and complexity. The hyperparameters also influence the generalizability of the models. Keeping batch sizes the same allows for the fair comparison of speed. The learning rates indicate the stability of training. The table indicates the experimental rigor of model testing. It also helps in guiding future studies for fine-tuning such models.

Table 2. Precision Scores by Activity Class

Activity Class	GRU Precision	Bi-Stacked GRU Precision	LSTM Precision	CNN Precision	Transformer Precision
Household Chores	0.81	0.87	0.85	0.79	0.86
Social Interaction	0.79	0.85	0.82	0.76	0.84
Playing Games	0.77	0.83	0.80	0.74	0.82

continued on following page

Table 2. Continued

Activity Class	GRU Precision	Bi-Stacked GRU Precision	LSTM Precision	CNN Precision	Transformer Precision
Workouts	0.84	0.89	0.87	0.82	0.88
Cooking	0.78	0.83	0.81	0.77	0.82
Cleaning	0.75	0.80	0.77	0.73	0.79
Gardening	0.74	0.79	0.76	0.72	0.78
Shopping	0.76	0.81	0.78	0.74	0.80
Traveling	0.79	0.84	0.81	0.77	0.83
Working on PC	0.82	0.87	0.85	0.80	0.86

Table 3 presents a fine-grained analysis of model accuracy across activity classes, with strengths and weaknesses of individual architecture on particular tasks. Certain models are very proficient at classifying activities such as Working on PC but have difficulty with less frequent activities such as Gardening. Such precision enables the determination of which activities are more difficult to classify. The table contrasts standard models such as GRU and LSTM with state-of-the-art models such as Transformers. It shows that Transformers and Bi-Stacked GRUs perform better in general. The variation in accuracy per class shows dataset complexity. It also helps direct future model improvement towards weaker classes. The table is key to making realistic model deployment scenarios a reality. It also shows that certain models trade overall accuracy for better performance on some classes. This analysis helps guide models towards adaptation in a specific application need.

Table 3. Recall Scores by Activity Class

Activity Class	GRU Recall	Bi-Stacked GRU Recall	LSTM Recall	CNN Recall	Transformer Recall
Household Chores	0.83	0.88	0.86	0.80	0.87
Social Interaction	0.80	0.86	0.83	0.77	0.85
Playing Games	0.78	0.84	0.81	0.75	0.83
Workouts	0.85	0.90	0.88	0.83	0.89
Cooking	0.79	0.84	0.82	0.78	0.83
Cleaning	0.76	0.81	0.78	0.74	0.80
Gardening	0.75	0.80	0.77	0.73	0.79
Shopping	0.77	0.82	0.79	0.75	0.81

continued on following page

Table 3. Continued

Activity Class	GRU Recall	Bi-Stacked GRU Recall	LSTM Recall	CNN Recall	Transformer Recall
Traveling	0.80	0.85	0.82	0.78	0.84
Working on PC	0.83	0.88	0.86	0.81	0.87

Table 4 shows the precision values of every model for all activities, which depict the number of forecasted positive instances correctly accurate. Good precision indicates fewer false alarm. From the table, Bi-Stacked GRUs and Transformers prefer to have higher precision in most activities. Lower precision for activities like Gardening shows model discrimination challenges. Data aids the assessment of model reliability from a user's perspective. Precision and recall go hand-in-hand in the estimation of classification quality. Balanced precision and recall are ideal. Precision variations across activities inform data augmentation or feature engineering with a directive. This table is pivotal for understanding error types and their implications in practice. It also indicates the impact of class imbalance on precision. Finally, it fine-tunes models for use in scenarios where false positives are costly.

Table 4. F1 Scores by Activity Class

Activity Class	GRU F1 Score	Bi-Stacked GRU F1 Score	LSTM F1 Score	CNN F1 Score	Transformer F1 Score
Household Chores	0.82	0.87	0.85	0.79	0.86
Social Interaction	0.79	0.85	0.82	0.76	0.84
Playing Games	0.77	0.83	0.80	0.74	0.82
Workouts	0.84	0.89	0.87	0.82	0.88
Cooking	0.78	0.83	0.81	0.77	0.82
Cleaning	0.75	0.80	0.77	0.73	0.79
Gardening	0.74	0.79	0.76	0.72	0.78
Shopping	0.76	0.81	0.78	0.74	0.80
Traveling	0.79	0.84	0.81	0.77	0.83
Working on PC	0.82	0.87	0.85	0.80	0.86

Table 5 presents recall scores, which gauge each model's ability to capture all occurrences of an activity that are deemed relevant. Good recall indicates fewer false negatives. The table demonstrates that models like Bi-Stacked GRUs and Transformers have high recall for all activities, which indicates robustness. Activities like

Cleaning and Gardening have comparatively low recall, which indicates room for improvement. Recall is especially critical in safety-critical systems where missing events is undesirable. The table helps to balance precision-recall trade-offs when making model selection. It also helps to analyze errors for false negatives. Differences in recall highlight the sensitivity of models to minority classes. The observation assist in optimizing data representation or model structure. Recall values together with precision provide a full picture of classification performance. It highlights the need to correct class imbalance.

Table 5. Confusion Matrix Summary for Bi-Stacked GRU (Top 10 Activities)

Actual \ Predicted	Household	Social	Games	Workouts	Cooking	Cleaning	Gardening	Shopping	Traveling	PC Work
Household Chores	880	12	5	4	8	6	3	7	10	5
Social Interaction	15	865	10	6	5	7	4	12	8	6
Playing Games	8	10	850	7	6	5	3	8	7	6
Workouts	5	6	8	890	5	4	4	7	6	7
Cooking	10	9	7	5	860	5	6	8	7	8
Cleaning	7	6	5	4	6	870	5	6	5	7
Gardening	4	5	3	4	6	4	880	5	4	6
Shopping	8	12	8	6	7	5	4	860	6	7
Traveling	9	8	7	5	7	6	5	7	870	8
Working on PC	6	7	6	8	7	5	6	7	8	880

Table 6 presents F1 scores, the harmonic mean of precision and recall, averaged over model performance across activities. F1 addresses the issue of balancing the class label between false negatives and false positives. The table confirms that Bi-Stacked GRUs and Transformers fare better compared to all other models overall. Household Chores and Working on PC have more favorable F1, while Gardening and Cleaning are less so. This reflects relative difficulty in the identification of different activities. F1 scores are a good metric for the evaluation of model performance comparison. The table helps identify the strong and weak points in models in general. It guides decisions regarding the selection of balanced performance. F1 scores are critical in applications with high precision and recall requirements. This table provides a concise performance summary across models and tasks.

Table 6. Training Time (seconds) for Different Models

Model	Epochs	Avg Time per Epoch	Total Training Time	Dataset Size	Hardware Used
GRU	50	12.4	620	Full	GPU RTX 3080
Bi-Stacked GRU	50	18.6	930	Full	GPU RTX 3080
LSTM	50	21.2	1060	Full	GPU RTX 3080
CNN	50	15.8	790	Full	GPU RTX 3080
Transformer	50	25.4	1270	Full	GPU RTX 3080
GRU (reduced data)	50	6.2	310	Half	GPU RTX 3080
Bi-Stacked GRU (reduced data)	50	9.4	470	Half	GPU RTX 3080
LSTM (reduced data)	50	10.5	525	Half	GPU RTX 3080
CNN (reduced data)	50	8.1	405	Half	GPU RTX 3080
Transformer (reduced data)	50	12.7	635	Half	GPU RTX 3080

Table 7 combines model training time and parameter numbers to provide insight into computational efficiency as well as model complexity. The transformers have the highest parameter numbers and training times, as would be expected for their complexity. Less complex models like GRUs, however, have lower training times with fewer parameters. Bi-Stacked GRUs provide the best cost-training performance trade-off. The table assists in selecting models suitable for low-resource environments. It also shows accuracy-cost of computation trade-offs. Training time information is crucial for realistic deployment. Parameters counts are linked with model size and risk of overfitting. The table directs scaling and optimization choices. Efficiency metrics are critical together with accuracy for effective real-world use.

Table 7. Feature selection impact on accuracy (%)

Feature Set	Accuracy Before PSO	Accuracy After PSO	Improvement (%)	Selected Features Count	Training Time (s)
Household Activities	83.5	88.7	5.2	35	620
Social Activities	81.2	86.3	5.1	30	590
Games & Workouts	79.8	85.5	5.7	28	605
Cooking & Cleaning	80.4	85.8	5.4	33	610
Gardening & Shopping	78.6	83.9	5.3	29	595
Traveling	82.3	87.6	5.3	32	600
PC Work	84.1	89.0	4.9	34	615
Full Dataset	81.7	87.4	5.7	195	930

continued on following page

Table 7. Continued

Feature Set	Accuracy Before PSO	Accuracy After PSO	Improvement (%)	Selected Features Count	Training Time (s)
Reduced Dataset	78.9	84.1	5.2	120	470
Combined Activities	80.6	86.0	5.4	150	890

Table 8 shows false positive rates (FPR) by activity and model type, the fraction of incorrect positive predictions. More specific models have lower FPR. Bi-Stacked GRUs have lowest FPR for all activities overall, with Transformers following close. Higher FPRs in activities like Gardening indicate inability to withstand false alarms. The table is handy in use cases with operational cost of false positives. FPR supplements recall and accuracy in the detailed model testing. FPR also helps to correct thresholds to reduce errors. Variations between activities indicate variations in model robustness. This measure is significant in user trust of automated systems. The table helps to choose models with few disruptive false alarms.

Table 8. False positive rate (%) by model and activity

Activity Class	GRU FPR	Bi-Stacked GRU FPR	LSTM FPR	CNN FPR	Transformer FPR
Household Chores	4.5	3.2	3.8	5.1	3.4
Social Interaction	5.0	3.7	4.0	5.5	3.6
Playing Games	5.2	4.1	4.4	5.7	4.0
Workouts	3.8	2.9	3.1	4.0	2.8
Cooking	5.1	3.6	4.0	5.4	3.7
Cleaning	5.4	4.2	4.5	5.9	4.3
Gardening	5.6	4.5	4.7	6.1	4.5
Shopping	5.0	3.8	4.1	5.5	3.9
Traveling	4.8	3.6	3.9	5.3	3.7
Working on PC	4.3	3.1	3.5	4.7	3.2

Table 9 measures model robustness against adversarial attacks, indicating accuracy drops when input is maliciously disturbed. Bi-Stacked GRUs and Transformers have higher accuracy than GRU, LSTM, and CNN under the influence of FGSM and PGD attacks. This shows their relative immunity to adversarial examples. The table highlights robustness as a security-critical issue. Attack type FGSM and PGD represent different kinds of adversarial methods. Percentage of accuracy degradation quantifies vulnerability. Robustness evaluation is optimally complemented with vanilla accuracy metrics. Models with lower accuracy degradation are ideal for deployment in the field. The table enables defense generation against adversarial inputs. It highlights the model-robustness trade-off. Typically, it highlights security concerns in activity recognition.

Table 9. Model robustness under adversarial attacks (%)

Model	Clean Accuracy	Adversarial Accuracy	Drop (%)	Attack Type	Dataset Portion
GRU	85.0	71.3	13.7	FGSM	Full
Bi-Stacked GRU	89.2	78.5	10.7	FGSM	Full
LSTM	87.1	75.6	11.5	FGSM	Full
CNN	82.3	69.2	13.1	FGSM	Full
Transformer	88.5	77.8	10.7	FGSM	Full
Bi-Stacked GRU	89.2	80.3	8.9	PGD	Full
GRU	85.0	70.1	14.9	PGD	Full
LSTM	87.1	74.2	12.9	PGD	Full
Transformer	88.5	76.7	11.8	PGD	Full
CNN	82.3	67.9	14.4	PGD	Full

Table 10 provides a complete summary of key metrics including accuracy, precision, recall, F1 score, false positive rate, and training time for all models. It confirms Bi-Stacked GRUs and Transformers as the highest-performing models with greatest accuracy and balanced precision-recall. GRU and CNN lag behind in all of the metrics to a certain extent. Training time varies significantly, with the highest time consumed being that of Transformers. False positive rates are very low for Bi-Stacked GRUs, which speaks volumes for their accuracy. This overall perspective allows one to identify the best trade-offs between performance and efficiency. The table aids in informed model deployment decisions based on multiple parameters. It summarizes the major findings of the study in a nutshell. Such abridgments are necessary for applied implications and future research planning.

Table 10. Key metrics

Metric	GRU	Bi-Stacked GRU	LSTM	CNN	Transformer
Accuracy (%)	85.0	89.2	87.1	82.3	88.5
Precision	0.80	0.86	0.83	0.77	0.85
Recall	0.81	0.87	0.84	0.78	0.86

continued on following page

Table 10. Continued

Metric	GRU	Bi-Stacked GRU	LSTM	CNN	Transformer
F1 Score	0.80	0.86	0.83	0.77	0.85
False Positive Rate	5.0	3.7	4.0	5.5	3.8
Training Time (mins)	10.3	15.5	17.7	13.2	21.2

CONCLUSION

Security in Cyber-Physical Systems is a must because CPSs are the backbone of many significant services in the contemporary digital as well as physical world. The work illustrates how the combination of sequential models like bi-stacked GRUs with feature extraction optimized by PSO can successfully identify anomalies as well as potential malicious activities within CPS domains. It ensures the cyber-physical link not only safeguards from information violations but also ensures physical harm and operational interference threats are circumvented. The aforementioned process outlines a robust framework for proactive CPS security that can respond to increasingly changing threats in real-time. As CPS grow in size and complexity, these smart security solutions will become increasingly important in ensuring reliability in systems and ensuring public confidence. The future studies can emphasize applying the above models on bigger datasets and real-time response algorithms for even better security.

REFERENCES

Abotaleb, M., El-Kenawy, E.-S. M., & Dhoska, K. (2025). Deep learning-based time series forecasting: A convolutional neural network approach for predicting inflation trends. *EDRAAK, 2025*(1), 19–28. DOI: 10.70470/EDRAAK/2025/004

Ahmad, H. (2023). A bibliometric exploration of automation and its impact on mechanical engineering research. *Babylonian Journal of Mechanical Engineering, 2023*(1), 38–46. DOI: 10.58496/BJME/2023/005

Ahmad, H. (2023). Variational iteration approach for solving fractional integro-differential equations with conformable differintegrals. *Babylonian Journal of Mathematics, 2023*(1), 45–49. DOI: 10.58496/BJM/2023/009

Al-Shareeda, M. A., Najm, L. B., Hassan, A. A., Mushtaq, S., & Ali, H. A. (2024). Secure IoT-based smart agriculture system using wireless sensor networks for remote environmental monitoring. *STAP Journal of Security Risk Management, 2024*(1), 56–66. DOI: 10.63180/jsrm.thestap.2024.1.4

Albinhamad, H., Alotibi, A., Alagnam, A., Almaiah, M., & Salloum, S. (2025). Vehicular ad-hoc networks (VANETs): A key enabler for smart transportation systems and challenges. *Jordanian Journal of Informatics and Computing, 2025*(1), 4–15. DOI: 10.63180/jjic.thestap.2025.1.2

Aldawira, C. R., Putra, H. W., Hanafiah, N., Surjarwo, S., & Wibisurya, A. (2019). Door security system for home monitoring based on ESP32. *Procedia Computer Science, 157*, 673–682. DOI: 10.1016/j.procs.2019.08.218

Almaayah, M., & Sulaiman, R. B. (2024). Cyber risk management in the Internet of Things: Frameworks, models, and best practices. *STAP Journal of Security Risk Management, 2024*(1), 3–23. DOI: 10.63180/jsrm.thestap.2024.1.1

Alshinwan, M., Memon, A. G., Ghanem, M. C., & Almaayah, M. (2025). Unsupervised text feature selection approach based on improved prairie dog algorithm for the text clustering. *Jordanian Journal of Informatics and Computing, 2025*(1), 27–36. DOI: 10.63180/jjic.thestap.2025.1.4

Ang, S., Huy, S., & Janarthanan, M. (2025). Utilizing IDS and IPS to improve cybersecurity monitoring process. *Journal of Cyber Security and Risk Auditing, 2025*(3), 77–88. DOI: 10.63180/jcsra.thestap.2025.3.10

Banerjee, P., Datta, P., Pal, S., Chakraborty, S., Roy, A., Poddar, S., Dhali, S., & Ghosh, A. (2022). Home security system using RaspberryPi. In *Advanced energy and control systems* (pp. 167–176). Springer., DOI: 10.1007/978-981-16-7274-3_14

Beddiar, D. R., Nini, B., Sabokrou, M., & Hadid, A. (2020). Vision-based human activity recognition: A survey. *Multimedia Tools and Applications*, *79*(41-42), 30509–30555. DOI: 10.1007/s11042-020-09004-3

Burhanuddin, M. A. (2023). Efficient hardware acceleration techniques for deep learning on edge devices: A comprehensive performance analysis. *KHWARIZMIA*, *2023*(1), 103–112. DOI: 10.70470/KHWARIZMIA/2023/010

Chakraborty, P., Yousuf, M. A., Zahidur Rahman, M., & Faruqui, N. (2020). How can a robot calculate the level of visual focus of human's attention. In *International Joint Conference on Computational Intelligence: IJCCI 2019* (pp. 329–342). Springer. DOI: 10.1007/978-981-15-3607-6_27

Del Giudice, M., Scuotto, V., Orlando, B., & Mustilli, M. (2023). Toward the human-centered approach: A revised model of individual acceptance of AI. *Human Resource Management Review*, *33*(1), 100856. Advance online publication. DOI: 10.1016/j.hrmr.2021.100856

Faruqui, N., Yousuf, M. A., Whaiduzzaman, M., Azad, A., Barros, A., & Moni, M. A. (2021). LungNet: A hybrid deep-CNN model for lung cancer diagnosis using CT and wearable sensor-based medical IoT data. *Computers in Biology and Medicine*, *139*, 104961. Advance online publication. DOI: 10.1016/j.compbiomed.2021.104961 PMID: 34741906

Ghanem, M. C., & Salloum, S. (2025). Integrating AI-driven deep learning for energy-efficient smart buildings in Internet of Thing-based Industry 4.0. *Babylonian Journal of Internet of Things*, *2025*(7), 121–130. DOI: 10.58496/BJIoT/2025/007

Govindan, V., Jayaprakash, J., Park, C., Lee, J. R., & Cangul, I. N. (2023). Optimization-based design and control of dynamic systems. *Babylonian Journal of Mathematics*, *2023*(1), 30–35. DOI: 10.58496/BJM/2023/006

Hadid, M. H., Al-Qaysi, Z. T., Hussein, Q. M., Aljanabi, R. A., Abdulqader, I. R., Suzani, M. S., & Shir, W. L. (2024). Semantic image retrieval analysis based on deep learning and singular value decomposition. *Applied Data Science and Analysis*, *2024*(1), 17–31. DOI: 10.58496/ADSA/2024/003

Jadhao, A., Bagade, A., Taware, G., & Bhonde, M. (2020). Effect of background color perception on attention span and short-term memory in normal students. *National Journal of Physiology, Pharmacy and Pharmacology*, *10*(11), 981–984. DOI: 10.5455/njppp.2020.10.06162202017072020

Kamel, M. S. (2024). Innovative approaches to design representation in civil engineering. *Mesopotamian Journal of Civil Engineering*, *2024*(1), 103–114. DOI: 10.58496/MJCE/2024/012

Kayusi, F., Turyasingura, B., Chavula, P., & Amadi, O. J. (2024). Exploring deep learning methods used in the medical device sector. *Mesopotamian Journal of Artificial Intelligence in Healthcare*, *2024*(1), 42–49. DOI: 10.58496/MJAIH/2024/007

Kobara, K. (2016). Cyber physical security for industrial control systems and IoT. *IEICE Transactions on Information and Systems*, *E99-D*(4), 787–795. DOI: 10.1587/transinf.2015ICI0001

Kong, M., Guo, Y., Alkhazragi, O., Sait, M., Kang, C. H., Ng, T. K., & Ooi, B. S. (2022). Real-time optical-wireless video surveillance system for high visual-fidelity underwater monitoring. *IEEE Photonics Journal*, *14*(3), 7315609. Advance online publication. DOI: 10.1109/JPHOT.2022.3147844

Kulsoom, F., Narejo, S., Mehmood, Z., Chaudhry, H. N., & Bashir, A. K. (2022). A review of machine learning-based human activity recognition for diverse applications. *Neural Computing & Applications*, *34*(21), 18289–18324. DOI: 10.1007/s00521-022-07665-9

Mohialden, Y. M., Hussien, N. M., Salman, S. A., Alwahhab, A. B., & Ali, M. (2024). Enhancing agriculture crop classification with deep learning. *Babylonian Journal of Artificial Intelligence*, *2024*(1), 20–26. DOI: 10.58496/BJAI/2024/004

Muhammad, T., & Akgül, A. (2025). Optimizing mechanical performance of AgC-reinforced polymer nanocomposites: A quantitative analysis of stiffness–ductility trade-offs. *Babylonian Journal of Mechanical Engineering*, *2025*(1), 34–50. DOI: 10.58496/BJME/2025/003

Otoom, S. (2025). Risk auditing for digital twins in cyber physical systems: A systematic review. *Journal of Cyber Security and Risk Auditing*, *2025*(1), 22–35. DOI: 10.63180/jcsra.thestap.2025.1.3

Park, H., Kim, N., Lee, G. H., & Choi, J. K. (2023). MultiCNN-FilterLSTM: Resource-efficient sensor-based human activity recognition in IoT applications. *Future Generation Computer Systems*, *139*, 196–209. DOI: 10.1016/j.future.2022.09.024

Paula, L. P. O., Faruqui, N., Mahmud, I., Whaiduzzaman, M., Hawkinson, E. C., & Trivedi, S. (2023). A novel front door security (FDS) algorithm using GoogleNet-BiLSTM hybridization. *IEEE Access : Practical Innovations, Open Solutions*, *11*, 19122–19134. DOI: 10.1109/ACCESS.2023.3248509

Pflanzner, T., & Kertész, A. (2018). A taxonomy and survey of IoT cloud applications. *EAI Endorsed Transactions on Internet of Things*, *3*(12), e4. Advance online publication. DOI: 10.4108/eai.31-10-2018.159633

Ray, A., Kolekar, M. H., Balasubramanian, R., & Hafiane, A. (2023). Transfer learning enhanced vision-based human activity recognition: A decade-long analysis. *International Journal of Information Management Data Insights*, *3*(1), 100142. Advance online publication. DOI: 10.1016/j.jjimei.2022.100142

Sarp, B., & Karalar, T. (2015). Real time smart door system for home security. *International Journal of Scientific Research in Information Systems and Engineering*, *1*(2), 121–123.

Satam, S., & El-Ocla, H. (2022). Home security system using wireless sensors network. *Wireless Personal Communications*, *125*(2), 1185–1201. DOI: 10.1007/s11277-022-09596-z

Sheela, M. S., Amirthayogam, G., Hephzipah, J. J., Suganthi, R., Karthikeyan, T., & Gopianand, M. (2024). Advanced brain tumor classification using DEEPBELEIF-CNN method. *Babylonian Journal of Machine Learning*, *2024*(1), 89–101. DOI: 10.58496/BJML/2024/009

Srividhya, E., Anusuya, V., Deepthi, K. J., Gopalsamy, P., & Gopalakrishnan, S. (2024). Deep learning-driven disease prediction system in cloud environments using a big data approach. *EDRAAK*, *2024*(1), 8–17. DOI: 10.70470/EDRAAK/2024/002

Tao, J., Wu, H., Deng, S., & Qi, Z. (2022). Overview of intelligent home security and early warning system based on Internet of Things technology. *International Core Journal of Engineering*, *8*(6), 727–732.

Trivedi, S., Patel, N., & Faruqui, N. (2022). *NDNN based U-Net: An innovative 3D brain tumor segmentation method. In 2022 IEEE 13th Annual Ubiquitous Computing, Electronics & Mobile Communication Conference (UEMCON)*. IEEE., DOI: 10.1109/UEMCON54665.2022.9965677

Trivedi, S., Patel, N., & Faruqui, N. (2023). Bacterial strain classification using convolutional neural network for automatic bacterial disease diagnosis. In 2023 13th International Conference on Cloud Computing, Data Science & Engineering (Confluence) (pp. 325–332). IEEE. DOI: 10.1109/Confluence56041.2023.10048859

Wei, X., Wu, J., Ajayi, K., & Oyen, D. (2022). Visual descriptor extraction from patent figure captions: A case study of data efficiency between BiLSTM and transformer. In *Proceedings of the 22nd ACM/IEEE Joint Conference on Digital Libraries* (pp. 1–5). ACM. DOI: 10.1145/3529372.3533299

Yang, L., Yu, X., Zhang, S., Long, H., Zhang, H., Xu, S., & Liao, Y. (2023). GoogLeNet based on residual network and attention mechanism identification of rice leaf diseases. *Computers and Electronics in Agriculture*, *204*, 107543. Advance online publication. DOI: 10.1016/j.compag.2022.107543

Yonan, J. F., & Zahra, N. A. A.Janan Farag YonanNagham Amjed Abdul Zahra. (2023). Node intrusion tendency recognition using network level features based deep learning approach. *Babylonian Journal of Networking*, *2023*(1), 1–10. DOI: 10.58496/BJN/2023/001

Zhang, X., & Kim, T. (2023). A hybrid attention and time series network for enterprise sales forecasting under digital management and edge computing. *Journal of Cloud Computing (Heidelberg, Germany)*, *12*(1), 12. Advance online publication. DOI: 10.1186/s13677-023-00390-1 PMID: 37122827

Chapter 9
Leveraging AI and Machine Learning in Digital Forensics

Usharani Bhimavarapu
https://orcid.org/0000-0002-0246-1420
Department of Computer Science and Engineering, Koneru Lakshmaiah Education Foundation, Vaddeswaram, India

ABSTRACT

Digital and Information Forensics plays a critical role in today's data-driven world by enabling the discovery and interpretation of electronic evidence amidst vast and complex digital environments. As digital technologies proliferate, cybercrimes and security breaches have grown more sophisticated, necessitating advanced forensic methodologies to detect, analyze, and attribute malicious activities. This field integrates diverse techniques such as data acquisition, preservation, analysis, and presentation to ensure the integrity and admissibility of digital evidence in legal and investigative contexts. By unveiling hidden truths within digital footprints, Digital and Information Forensics not only combats cyber threats but also supports organizational security, regulatory compliance, and justice. Continuous innovation and ethical vigilance remain essential to address emerging challenges, maintain public trust, and uphold privacy rights in an increasingly interconnected world.

INTRODUCTION

As humongous loads of data are produced every second by social media, online financial transactions, emails, and cloud storage, the potential for its abuse and cybercrime has become multifold. Digital and Information Forensics turns into

DOI: 10.4018/979-8-3373-1807-3.ch009

2026, IGI Global Scientific Publishing. Copying or distributing in print or electronic forms without written permission of IGI Global Scientific Publishing is prohibited. Use of this chapter to -ative artificial intelligence (AI) technologies is expressly prohibited. The publisher reserves all rights to license its use for generative AI training and machine learning model development.

a necessary practice dedicated to exploring and examining digital evidence. It is utilized to reveal the unspoken facts in this colossal world of bytes. Without the application of these forensic techniques and tools, it would be practically impossible to identify cyber criminals or track unauthorized activity. Greater reliance on technology makes forensic investigation an unavoidable tool to gain confidence in internet spaces. It is a preemptive method of defense against cyberattacks like data breaches, identity theft, and cyberterrorism. With ever-evolving cyberattacks, there is an increased requirement for advanced forensic techniques. This field assists law enforcement and cybercrime specialists in maintaining the integrity of the cyber world (Al-Shareeda et al., 2025) and (Addula et al., 2025).

Since such crimes are being carried out via computers, mobile phones, or networks, digital evidence is usually the decider of the crime. Digital evidence is collected, stabilized, and examined by computer forensic experts using techniques that retain the integrity and admissibility of evidence in front of a court of law. This creates solid cases against perpetrators, enabling hacking, fraud, intellectual property theft, and other computer-based crimes to be prosecuted. In addition, forensic results can clear innocents from incorrect convictions. Judges globally increasingly depend on electronic evidence in criminal prosecutions as well as in civil litigations. Without forensic examination, electronic evidence may be excluded or contaminated, compromising the judicial process. Forensic science, therefore, fills the gap between technology and law, giving justice a firm foundation in the information age. Its application ranges from testing to expert evidence and advisory services during trials. Private companies, governments, and individuals all have valuable information that needs to be protected against unauthorized access and theft (Ali, 2024; Alsahaim & Maayah, 2023).

Computer forensics can trace intrusions and trace them back to their source, allowing organizations to react in time and limit damage. It helps in the identification of insider threats, corporate espionage, and sabotage operations that would lead to operations shutting down or damage to reputation. Further, forensic analysis helps with regulatory compliance through complete documentation of security breaches. Through the analysis of security breaches, organizations can enact more robust defenses and improve cybersecurity policy. Digital forensics thus improves the enterprise's overall risk management plan. It helps in finding critical information on attack vectors and vulnerabilities that can be fixed through patching in advance. Finally, forensic functionality enables organizations to protect assets in a more hostile digital world. Information is not longer within devices but scattered across platforms and distant servers. Forensic examiners have to deal with the issue of retrieving evidence from cloud servers, virtual machines, cell phones, and networked sensors (Abdulateef et al., 2025; Satar et al., 2025).

This evolution requires new forensic tools and technologies that will tackle many types of data as well as data storage devices. It also poses technical legal and jurisdictional issues with data ownership and privacy. Digital forensics simplifies overcoming these issues by providing consistent standards for gathering and analyzing data in dispersed networks. It validates evidence gathered remotely as still useful and relevant. Such versatility becomes imperative in today's investigations that entail complex cyber attacks and international networks. As technology continues to grow, digital forensics continues to uncover the truth in ever more complex cases of data. In case a system has been compromised, forensic examination offers in-depth information on the attacker's tactics, timeline, and goals. This information is critical to removal and containment processes, enabling security personnel to shut backdoors in a prompt manner. Threat actor behavior and patterns exposure also educates future defense systems through incident-driven forensic analysis.

Companies can improve their security stance and predict threats in the future by discovering how breaches happen. Forensics is thus an evolving input to cybersecurity, converting post-breach actions into proactive solutions. Incident responders rely on forensic evidence to effectively inform parties and regulators, being transparent and responsible. This builds customer and partner trust and meets legal requirements. Forensic capacity generally makes an organization resilient to cyber attacks. Governments employ forensic technologies to fight cyber war, espionage, and terrorism. Cyberattacks on defense networks, critical infrastructure, and government data need sophisticated forensic hardware to trace perpetrators and make future attacks impossible. Intelligence agencies decode cyber crumbs to reveal conspiracies and monitor criminal syndicates that went online. Forensics supports surveillance and counterintelligence operations, which allow the authorities to dismantle illegal networks and interdict malevolent campaigns.

The security role further involves protection of democratic processes from cybermeddling and misinformation. Digital forensics allows countries to retain sovereignty in a networked world where digital menaces cross boundaries with such ease. Digital forensics is a multiplier for the cyber sphere, with the ability to make timely and well-informed choices. Computer forensics through collaboration and sharing of information is a general security enhancer among cooperating nations. Forensic practitioners have to strike a balance between obtaining evidence and respect for individuals' rights and data protection legislation. This includes authorization, low intrusion, and the protection of personal data during investigation. Computer forensics models include ethics in order to avoid abuse, i.e., unauthorized surveillance or interference with information. There must be transparency and accountability, especially in handling sensitive data like medical data or financial data. The integrity promise of the discipline upholds the public's trust in forensic evidence and the justice system.

Additionally, forensic professionals support the growth of privacy-protecting technologies that facilitate lawful and safe investigations. Such an ethical stance maintains forensic science aligned with societal values in general, such that technological innovation is used in support of justice without infringing on civil rights. Since threats to cyberspace constantly evolve, so must forensic practice, techniques, and tools. Academia, research centers, and industry come together to design advanced techniques for extracting, examining, and authenticating evidence. Next-generation forensic examiners are taught through courses to manage sophisticated digital landscapes. Scientific studies expand into new domains like artificial intelligence forensics, blockchain forensics, and cloud forensics, expanding the boundaries of the discipline. Ongoing learning gives forensic professionals a head start over the game in terms of adversaries who continually design new attack methods. This dynamic setting promotes a culture of innovation and responsiveness among forensic practitioners.

Digital forensics remains strong and current through education sharing and training. In the end, investments in education create an educated workforce capable of safeguarding the digital world appropriately. Individuals are more exposed to identity theft, cyberbullying, and online harassment. Digital trails are uncovered through forensic methods to trace these abuses and apprehend culprits. Forensic evidence is used by victims to pursue justice and protection through the aid of the law. Furthermore, forensic capability is also used to enhance widespread public awareness of cyberthreats and to promote safer online activities. Publics benefit from the deterrence effect that forensic capability has on cybercriminals. As digital technologies increasingly pervade ordinary life, the need for low-cost, affordable forensic services increases. Forensic technology demilitarization allows individuals to be in charge of their online safety.

Supporting individual and community safety through forensic science contributes to the establishment of a stronger and more knowledgeable society. Its varied uses range from crime investigation to corporate security, national defense, privacy protection, and public welfare. Digital forensics is a justice-disabling and trust-enabling field. Because it continues to evolve according to advancements in technology, digital forensics keeps addressing increasingly advanced challenges and emerging threats. Its application in legal, corporate, and government settings serves as a sign of its stronger standing in digital systems nowadays. The demand for forensic experts, ethics, and groundbreaking research increases as human society continues to advance and digitize. In essence, digital and information forensics enables human beings to discover concealed facts, protect digital investments, and preserve justice in an increasingly digitized world that is globally networked. It is a treasure house of truth, illumination for the nuances of the digital age. Although the work of (Al-Khateeb et al., 2019) is a good fusion of social network analysis and cyber forensics for analyzing cyber propaganda campaigns, one of its shortfalls is the approach's generalizability.

The research heavily relies on case-specific information and is not scalable for use in large or real-time settings. The dynamic nature of propaganda methods on the fly also limits the model's capacity to evolve. In addition, metadata and known associations employed can overlook unsubstantiated agents and disinformation attacks. Finally, the approach can fail to properly address multilingual media or platform differences in data. The use of static data by the study limits dynamic forensic analysis. Moreover, automation and real-time forensic preparedness were not explored in detail. Social media monitoring privacy issues were not explored in detail. Lastly, the study does not take into account entirely encrypted or obfuscating communication that restricts forensic level.

Stoyanova et al. (2020) provide a comprehensive overview on IoT forensics; however, their study is constrained by the dynamically changing nature and heterogeneity of IoT ecosystems. The model does not reflect specificity in dealing with varying operating systems and hardware of IoT devices. Poor validation of suggested forensic models based on real-world operational practices is the other weakness. The majority of the suggested frameworks remain hypothetical or are simulated alone. Jurisdictional and legal-conformity issues faced by cross-border investigations are also superficially discussed in the research. Resource-constrained IoT environments were not given much representation as far as data acquisition techniques. Firmware tampering and volatile memory issues are also unresolved. Limited availability of commonly used forensic instruments for IoTs raises the level of complexity in terms of reproducibility. Insider attack and firmware compromise are not handled by the literature.

Scalability and automation are not provided with thorough treatment, leading to large-scale deployment being cumbersome. Billingsley (2016), Masoodi (2024), and Saleh et al. (2023) presents valid concerns regarding the demise of keyword search-based search in digital forensics, yet the argument is empirically unproven and methodologically fragile. The essay has a tendency to be based predominantly on opinion, and this restricts its technical and academic integrity. It fails to present clear benchmarks or performance measures on the comparison of keyword and advanced search techniques. Furthermore, the paper fails to consider situations where keyword search can still prove effective or even essential, e.g., low-volume evidence cases. The significance of hybrid methods combining keyword search with machine learning is not addressed. There is minimal consideration of data admissibility and privacy of search procedures in a court of law. Tool support or the ability to integrate with current forensic platforms is not adequately considered. Controlled experiments or case studies based on real-world data do not exist. Lastly, scalability of presented alternate methods isn't considered, detracting from practical importance.

(Turnbull and Randhawa,2015)(Flayyih & Hassan, 2024; Mijwil et al., 2024) offer computerized event and social network extraction from digital evidence using ontologies, but the process is computation- and practically-deficient. Ontological mapping is computationally expensive and would not be scalable with large or unstructured data. Its mode of application of domain-specific ontologies restricts its usage across forensic science subdomains. Its other shortcoming is ontology updation complexity with changing digital behaviors. It relies on clean and consistent metadata, which in digital forensics is not always the situation. It does not resolve automatic network extraction privacy concerns. It lacks much testing on noisy or missing data. Real-time forensic usability was also not examined. The authors did not provide much explanation on how the model would be integrated into existing forensic practices.

This minimizes the direct applicability of their system. (Chabot et al.,2015) suggested an ontology-based incident timeline reconstruction framework, but the framework is short on automation and real-time analysis. Data annotation through manual means is still a weakness in populating the ontology with quality data. Scalability of the method to large-scale investigations is not wide.

The research is mainly focused on pre-defined incidents, and efficacy is lost in new or dynamic web-based crimes. There is clear evidence of the absence of harmonization with active digital evidence sources. Multi-source analysis, including logs and user activity across platforms, was constrained. The ontology is not flexible when handling multilingual or non-standard textual input entries. Besides, the dependency on pristine sets of data limits the model's performance under adversarial or noisy conditions. Legal and ethical consequences of automatic reconstruction were less discussed. Lastly, the approach is not extendable to new schemes related to crypto-currencies as a means of changing cybercrime channels.

(Liebler et al.,2019) deal with the effectiveness of artifact search approaches but their work is limited by its statically focused artifacts and shallow context-awareness. The study relies chiefly on existing hash searches and is non-adaptive to dynamically crafted or polymorphic objects. The study does not account for emerging threats that alter digital traces in order to avoid detection. Additionally, efficiency measures are presented with minimal forensic tool comparison. Test data sets used in lab-based testing are lost to external validity. The lookup strategies tested might not be directly applicable across operating systems and file types. Real-time forensic response system integration was not given a thought. User behavior and behavioral data were primarily left out. The study also does not investigate automated learning methods for the best artifact databases. All these factors impede the long-term forensic stability of the framework.

Bates et al. 2016), Maher et al. (2025), Sheela et al. (2024) offer a secure provenance collection framework for digital forensics, yet it is challenging to apply practically. The model relies on a secure computing basis, which might not exist in real deployments. It is not deployable in adversarial or compromised environments. Work lacks fine-grained measurements of performance for overhead and latency in forensic collection. It lacks solid implementations in commercial- or law enforcement-grade tools. The reliance on secure storage can have cost and complexity impediments. The paper does not advocate for merging data from disparate sources with varying trust levels. Admissibility of provenance data gathered is another issue that has been left open. Privacy issues in systems constantly under surveillance were not exhaustively investigated. Scalability to cloud or distributed computing is mentioned last but not empirically assessed.

Katilu et al. (2015) pose issues of data provenance in cloud forensics, but no end-to-end architecture is provided for actual implementation. Their handling is still more theoretical, with little experimentation and implementation on actual cloud platforms. Their transitory nature and dynamic behavior are not completely handled. Moreover, issues of provider collaboration and jurisdictional hurdles are not readily visible. Log and metadata availability is taken for granted in this paper, whereas log and metadata availability in multi-tenant clouds cannot always be guaranteed. The effect of encryption and obfuscation on provenance collection is not considered. No data structures to support cloud provenance are suggested. Lack of automation of correlation of data from various sources is the cause of response time lag. Real-world scenario situations or simulating attacks would make it more relevant. Overall, the paper creates a theoretical backdrop but excludes the majority of the matters of implementation.

Soltani and Seno presented a formal model to enable event reconstruction in digital forensic analysis. Although their model improves the validation of certain logical orders of events, it has a drawback in that it is based on having perfect and complete input data. In real-case instances, forensic data is always corrupted or disassembled into fragments and thus formal models do not work perfectly without gigantic preprocessing (Soltani et al., 2019).

Wang proposed an explicit cloud forensics event reconstruction model that significantly facilitated systematic inspection of cloud-based incidents. Nonetheless, their model faces real-time scalability and heterogeneity of cloud infrastructures. Moreover, jurisdiction and data ownership of clouds may make input data gathering needed by the model more difficult (Wang et al., 2016)(Alaasam, 2023; Salisu et al., 2024).

Biedermann and Kotsoglou theorized issues in handling digital evidence and refuted "digital evidence exceptionalism." Although their theoretical points are logical, their articles do not include operational plans for practice or case studies that could be useful in translating theory into forensic practice. Their theoretical nature also renders it less pragmatic for practitioners who require operational guidance (Biedermann et al., 2020).

Baryamureeba and Florence introduced the Enhanced Digital Investigation Process Model to enhance and augment established digital forensic procedures. Nevertheless, the age of the model renders it less suitable for responding to today's smart, distributed systems and dynamic threats. Furthermore, it does not support cloud computing and IoT environments natively, which are common in today's digital crime (Baryamureeba et al., 2004).

Carrier and Spafford suggested a paradigm of event-driven digital forensic investigation encompassing event modeling and event correlation from evidence. Although the paradigm is highly structured, it is not feasible in high-volume settings considering the reason that it is cumbersome while processing thousands of related events during large-scale investigations (Carrier et al., 2010)(Hanoon & Ibrahim, 2024; Jasim et al., 2024).

Ciardhuáin provided a more prescriptive cybercrime investigation model that introduces more grainedness to the classic phases of investigation. But it does not manage to successfully address dynamic and adaptive cyber threats like polymorphic malware and zero-day attacks. Linearity in the model might also limit its adaptability in iterative investigative situations (Ciardhuáin et al., 2004).

Palmer charted an innovative road map for digital forensic research that established future research directions. While revolutionary then, most of the road map features are now redundant because of developments such as virtualization, cloud computing, and AI-driven attacks. It does not have any adaptation strategies for these evolving developments (Palmer, 2001).

Stephenson described end-to-end digital forensics, suggesting continuity from data capture to presentation. While it has strengths in delivering an entire picture, the model is not adaptable to use in distributed and mobile environments, which were not prevalent at the time of research. The strategy also minimizes the procedural and legal intricacies brought about by cross-border digital evidence (Stephenson, 2002).

Jadhao and Agrawal developed a social network site-specific forensic model. Although timely to focus on social media, the model lacks strengths in dealing with encrypted messaging and recent applications such as ephemeral messaging applications. In addition, the model relies on API-based access, which is predominantly prohibited or volatile across applications (Jadhao et al., 2016).

Chabot created a formalized model for describing knowledge to assist in advanced digital forensics timeline analysis. While their model improves structuring of intricate forensic events, it is susceptible to availability of whole and consistent input logs. In reality, the whole and consistent information as their model presupposed might not be accessible due to system breakdown, intentional alteration, or arbitrary logging practices (Chabot et al., 2014).

Patzakis was concerned with transcending legal hurdles regarding authenticating social media evidence. Although the publication is helpful notes from a legal perspective, it is not an empirical study or a detailed procedural model intended to help practicing forensics professionals in real courtrooms. The publication also appears somewhat dated considering recent modifications in digital privacy legislation and site-specific content policies (Patzakis, 2011).

Fasching touched on tools and social media data preservation best practices. Their suggestions are tool-specific with no serious examination of matters such as metadata integrity, cross-jurisdictional preservation legislation, and coping with encrypted or ephemeral content. To add, tools mentioned may be outdated due to the dynamic nature of social media APIs (Fasching et al., 2012).

Garfinkel proposed Digital Forensics XML (DFXML) as a standard for forensic metadata structured representation. Although it has technical importance, the deployment of DFXML in live forensic contexts is low. The method also presumes XML-based schema familiarity that is an usability limitation among typical digital forensic users (Garfinkel, 2012).

Bollé studied reviews while making decisions with the assistance of computer-aided forensic analysis software. The biggest limitation of their study is that it is predominantly composed of theoretical evaluation models and does not have operational case studies that illustrate practical implications or actual bias with regard to automated systems (Bollé et al., 2020).

Arshad advocated a semi-automatic paradigm of forensic analysis for social networks in the web environment. Semi-automaticity enhances investigation efficiency, but the paradigm presumes timely and well-organized access to platform data that is not always feasible because of API limits, data loss, or privacy concerns. Additionally, new platforms with sparse public documentation raise model generalization concerns (Arshad et al., 2020a).

Arshad built a multi-level semantic framework for social media forensic acquisition. A limitation of this method is that it relies on the accuracy of semantic interpretation, which fluctuates heavily across slang, sarcasm, and language variation in social media. Furthermore, the framework can be challenged with platform-specific data structures that are loosely documented or sporadically updated (Arshad et al., 2019).

Arshad provided a formal framework for social network forensics. Formal modeling is beneficial for structured analysis, but the method can be overly inflexible in situations where information structures and user behaviors keep on evolving. The model might also involve lengthy ontological definitions that are time-consuming to establish and keep in place (Arshad et al., 2020b).

Balbach promoted the utilization of case studies to evaluate programs. Although case studies provide rich details in a single case, they are typically marred with generalizability and subjectivity constraints. Utilization of case studies in forensic settings may fail to deliver systematicity necessary for constructing broadly applicable frameworks or tools (Balbach, 1999).

Greenwood pioneered the use of the case study approach in business communication environments. Although the method is useful in developing in-depth understanding of complex issues, its use in forensic or technical environments is constrained by subjectivity and lack of replication. It stands little chance of yielding statistically significant findings generalizable to larger populations (Greenwood, 1993).

Simons criticized the history of the evolution of case study evaluation. Despite being helpful in making comments on methodological progression, the book is theory-based. The narrow use of digital forensic settings in the book disqualifies it from being practically used in technology-intensive investigations where empirical rigor and tool testing dominate (Simons, 2015).

Galbraith and Smyth developed a likelihood-ratio approach based on marked point processes for analysis of user-event data. Statistically advanced as it is, the approach requires high-quality temporal event data and might fail to work in settings with noisy, missing, or tampered logs. Furthermore, its sophistication can also narrow down implementation among practitioners with little advanced statistical knowledge (Galbraith & Smyth, 2017).

Chung performed digital forensic analysis on cloud storage services and found it challenging to recover data from services such as Dropbox and Google Drive. The shortcoming is that their results are highly platform-specific and may not extend to newer or proprietary services. Furthermore, legal and jurisdictional issues of cross-border cloud investigation were touched upon briefly (Chung et al., 2012).

Willard offered a school-based procedural guide for teachers on cyberbullying and cyberthreats. Although educational and simple, the book is scholarly nonscientific in nature and not based on empirical studies. The book fails to offer technical procedures or computer forensics procedures required in investigating or litigating cyber cases (Willard, 2011).

Samara analyzed the current legal status of cyberbullying and bullying in psychological evaluations. While psychologically insightful overall, the article does not provide guidance regarding how cyberbullying digital evidence is to be gathered, stored, or interpreted in these cases. This makes it of limited use for forensic examiners dealing with cyberbullying evidence (Samara et al., 2017).

Wilson spoke about how individuals act within social networks and their structural ramifications. Although fundamental to understanding social dynamics, the studies have negligible operational relevance for forensic trace analysis or evidence reconstruction. It also occurred in an era pre-existing many modern-day social environments, limiting its relevance to today's settings (Wilson et al., 2009).

Aledavood analyzed a day's patterns of communication through the use of mobile phone billing records. Since it is valuable in the identification of behavioral patterns, the study is not focused on the legal or forensic application of mobile data per se. Their models are constructed based on honest user behavior, which will break down in criminal cases (Aledavood et al., 2015).

Although the study by (Al-Khateeb et al.,2019) successfully integrates social network analysis and cyber forensics to analyze cyber propaganda campaigns, the method's generalizability is also a weakness. The study relies heavily on case-specific data and is not scalable if extrapolated to broader or real-time situations. The ever-evolving nature of constantly evolving propaganda strategies also constrains the adaptability of the model. In addition, metadata reliance and temporal connections might be missing hidden actors and mis/disinformation operations. There is a potential worry that the approach will fail to effectively address multilingual content or variation in platform-level data. Static datasets utilized in the study limit dynamic forensic analysis. In addition, real-time forensic preparedness and automation were not adequately explored. Social media surveillance privacy issues were not fully explored. Lastly, the study does not adequately take into account encrypted or obscured communication that prevents forensic depth. (Stoyanova et al.,2020) provide a comprehensive overview of IoT forensics; yet, their paper is susceptible to shortcomings based on the extensive growth and heterogeneity of IoT environments.

The framework is not specific in managing diverse hardware and operating systems found in IoT devices. Another drawback is a lack of adequate practical verification of suggested forensic models in actual-world settings. Most of the solutions mentioned are theoretical or are even verified with simulations only. The paper also cursorily discusses jurisdictional and legal compliance issues that are found to appear in cross-border investigations. Data collection methods in resource-limited IoT settings were poorly represented. Firmware-level forensics and volatile memory are open research challenges. Lack of standardized forensic devices for IoT makes reproduction cumbersome. Insider attacks and firmware-level tampering are not included in the work. Automation and scalability are also not sufficiently researched, and mass deployment is inefficient. (Billingsley,2016) identifies proper issues with the disappearance of keyword search in digital forensics but describes it without methodological understanding and empirical proof. The essay is based on opinions, and this decreases its technical and academic credibility.

Clearly, it lacks acceptable benchmarks and performance measures between keyword and non-keyword search technologies. The article fails to account for situations when keyword search might be useful or even necessary, as in the case of low-volume evidence cases. Contribute Hybrid approaches are ignored that include keyword search and machine learning. Little consideration has been given to the role of data privacy and admissibility in courts of search methods. The article does not discuss much about tool support or integration with current forensic platforms. No real-life case studies or controlled studies are there. Lastly, scalability of evaluated alternative methods is untested, so practical relevance is lower. (Turnbull and Randhawa,2015) turn to automated social network and event extraction from digital evidence through ontologies, but the methodology has serious computational and practical constraints. Ontological mapping is computationally costly and can perform poorly against big or unstructured data. Their methodology's dependence on domain-specific ontologies constrains their scalability across forensic domains.

A further challenge is the ontological update with new emergent digital behaviors. The paper assumes tidy, uniform metadata, which is not typically the scenario with digital forensics. It does not also consider privacy concerns for automated network extraction. Testing on noisy or missing data is also scarce. Real-time forensic use was not investigated. Much was not explained by the authors in terms of how the model will be applied to existing forensic processes. This lowers the direct use of their system. (Chabot et al.,2015) suggested an ontology-based method of incident timeline reconstruction, but the system is not robust in automating and real-time processing. The manual annotation process is still a task in filling up the ontology with proper data. The method's scalability for large investigations is not good. The research is useful only for pre-defined events and less useful for new or dynamic online crime.

Integration of bona fide online evidence sources is not common. There is limited evaluation of multi-source information such as logs and user activity across systems. The ontology does not adapt to multilingual or non-standard text inputs. Moreover, the model's performance in noisy or adversarial settings is limited by the use of clean datasets. Legal and ethical concerns of automated reconstruction were not properly addressed. Lastly, the method is non-extensible to newer forms of cybercrime vectors such as scams involving cryptocurrencies. (Liebler et al.,2019) describe the robustness of artifact search methods, yet the study is constrained by its necessity to deal with static artifacts and brief contextualization. The approach is overly hash search-reliant and inflexible to polymorphic or dynamically generated artifacts. The initiative does not respond to continuously mutating threats that alter digital traces to go unnoticed. Furthermore, measures of efficiency are presented with fewer comparisons among forensic tools. Reliance on laboratory environments for test datasets decreases external validity.

Lookup methods under examination might not be portable across various operating systems and file types. Real-time forensic response systems support was not addressed. User behavior and behavior artifacts were not considered in any significant way. The research also fails to expound on automated learning mechanisms for improving artifact databases. These constraints narrow the long-term forensic robustness of the framework. (Bates et al.,2016) present a secure provenance set model for digital forensics, yet difficult to apply in practice. The model assumes a trusted computing base, which in practical situations is not guaranteed to be available. Its usage in adversary or compromised environments is restricted. There are no complete performance measures of overhead or latency in forensic collection provided in this paper. It is not backed by actual implementations in commercial or law enforcement-level products. Moreover, the secure storage dependency can increase cost and complexity barriers.

The paper does not address the integration of provenance from diverse sources with varying degrees of trustworthiness. Admissibility of the evidence gathered in court is also not significantly addressed. Privacy in pervasive monitoring systems was not fully addressed. Lastly, scalability in cloud or distributed systems is referred to but not empirically assessed. (Katilu et al.,2015) give definitions of challenges of data provenance in cloud forensics, but the paper has no clear architecture for practical use. The explanation is mostly theoretical with no sufficient experimentation or production on actual cloud platforms. Cloud instances' dynamic and ephemeral nature are not addressed thoroughly. Also, jurisdictional barriers and cooperation among providers are not illustrated in detail. It is based on the metadata and log availability assumption, which never holds in multi-tenant clouds. The effect of obfuscation and encryption on provenance collection is not addressed. No standard formats for provenance data in clouds are suggested.

The absence of automation in correlating data from different sources delays response time. Real-case studies or attack simulations would make it more applicable in practice. In general, the research gives a theoretical background but not solutions to the majority of the implementation issues. The model proposed solves many of the key limitations of current digital forensic investigation techniques by combining automation, formalized knowledge representation, and social media-based analysis. The traditional models, such as (Carrier and Spafford, (2010) or (Ciardhuáin,2004), did not use automation and were based on intensive manual analysis, which was prone to errors and took much time. The suggested model solves this through the use of a semi-automated investigative process that supports effective data collection and analysis, especially in big scenarios like online social networking. Second, whereas previous studies like (Chabot et al.,2014) and (Garfinkel,2012) placed great importance on time-lined structures and formats for information, they did not even remotely approach mimicking the semantic richness and live characteristics of social media interaction. The suggested framework improves this by applying a multi-layered semantic model enabling dynamic event reconstruction and implication of knowledge, thereby enabling more accuracy and contextual comprehension of digital events. Apart from that, previous models did not adequately provide solutions to problems of the platform, especially that of social media's volatile and interactive nature of content. The system addresses this deficiency in several ways through the inclusion of social media data preservation strategies and procedures to ensure evidence authenticity and admissibility in courts, as (Patzakis,2011) and (Fasching et al.,2012) highlighted.

Additionally, the model fills gaps in scalability and legal readiness in earlier models by incorporating best practices in digital evidence authentication, real-time data scraping, and forensic readiness. Based on progress in XML-based evidence formats (e.g., DFXML) and complementing this with formal logic in the representation of forensic expertise, the model presented increases interoperability, reproducibility, and survivability in sophisticated digital investigations. In general, the suggested approach draws and substantially improves upon current models in an effort to address emerging needs of forensic analysis in current digital settings.

MATERIAL AND METHODS

The Digital and Information Forensics methodology includes a step-by-step procedure starting with data acquisition, where digital evidence is collected in a gentle manner from sources such as computers, networks, and clouds without degrading its integrity. It is succeeded by maintenance of the evidence to avoid tampering and loss. Then, forensic analysis is conducted based on tools and techniques determined beforehand in order to acquire meaningful information and replicate events. The findings are then recorded carefully to allow for transparency and replicability. Finally, the evidence is clearly presented and court-admissible to aid investigations or court cases. Throughout, ethical codes and standards are followed rigorously.

MATERIAL

Dataset collection is the systematic bringing together of pertinent data to facilitate analysis, investigation, or model construction. In social media studies, the usage of Twitter scraper is very widespread in automating the collection of information from tweets and online profiles. This is achieved by mimicking crawling actions, systematically navigating to publicly available Twitter accounts to grab required information such as tweets, user details, hashtags, timestamps, and engagement metrics. It utilizes the Twitter API, which allows access to enormous amounts of data real-time or via the archive, with the guarantee of extracted data being complete and reliable. With the combination of crawling methods and API access, the scraper has the advantage of big data power while keeping with Twitter's rate limits and usage policy. Such processing is made possible by automation, allowing researchers to harvest fresh, diverse, and vast data without a need for human mediation, feedback on timely information on trends, sentiment, and behavior. The resulting dataset serves as a foundation for sentiment analysis, prediction of trends, finding misinformation, and social network analysis. Its ethical processing involves cleaning, anonymization, and structuring it to allow ethical utilization and observance of the privacy act. Overall, Twitter scrapers are advanced means of obtaining rich social media data needed for today's digital investigations and research work.

PREPROCESSING

Preprocessing the downloaded Twitter data is an important step in order to guarantee quality and effectiveness of the data for analysis. After raw data is fetched through the Twitter scraper, the data is generally noisy, contains unrelated data, duplicates, and inconsistencies that may impact the validity of any analysis done afterwards. Preprocessing starts with data cleaning where unnecessary items like URLs, special characters, emojis, and stopwords that don't add useful information are eliminated. Text normalization processes such as lowercasing all the text, spell-checking, and uncontracting make the text easier to bring about consistency in the dataset. Tokenization subsequently splits the tweets into words or phrases for ease of analysis of linguistic patterns. Stemming or lemmatization is also employed to bring words back to their root or base word form so that similar words can be grouped. Repetitive tweets and retweets are also detected and filtered out to prevent biasing and duplication of data set. Handling missing or incomplete data is also included in preprocessing where such rows can be discarded or imputed based on the context. If the analysis is topic modeling or sentiment classification, then the data must be accurately labeled or classified. Lastly, the preprocessed data is written and stored in a structured format like CSV or JSON and is now ready to be ingested by complex machine learning models or statistical packages. This extensive preprocessing makes Twitter data clean, consistent, and useful, thus enhancing the quality and accuracy of any insight extracted from it.

FEATURE SELECTION

Particle Swarm Optimization (PSO) feature selection is a cutting-edge method employed to determine the most informative and valuable features from a large dataset, thus improving predictive model accuracy and efficiency. PSO is motivated by birds flocking or fish schooling as social behaviors in nature, wherein a set of candidate solutions, referred to as particles, traverses the search space cooperatively to discover the best subset of features. Each particle stands for a possible solution as a binary vector showing the presence or absence of particular features. Throughout the iterative process, particles will shift positions according to their own experience and learning with neighboring particles step by step towards the best set of features. The objective function used in search is typically the machine learning model's performance metric, for example, classification accuracy, with features selected. PSO facilitates reduction of dimensionality as well as overfitting minimization by the best subset of features and reduces the computational complexity as well. The technique becomes extremely important while handling high-dimensional data, particularly if feature selection is not feasible to carry out manually. The flexibility of PSO enables it to explore and exploit across varying levels of balance and navigate through intricate spaces of features to observe the patterns that are missed by other methods. The outcome is an improved quality set of features that encourages model generalizability and stability in new data. Incorporating PSO for feature selection is thus critical in developing useful data-driven solutions, especially in text mining, image classification, and bioinformatics.

RESENT 152

In the rapidly evolving digital age of the modern times, where information pervades every corner of our professional and personal lives, Digital and Information Forensics has emerged as a pivotal discipline with the aim of pulling out the truth hidden in vast pools of information in digital format. As an increasing number of societies become data societies, the amount and complexity of digital data have grown to a booming level to cover all aspects of communications, financial transactions, and medical records to company information and information about governments. While this data explosion presents unparalleled opportunity for innovation and efficiency, it also raises serious concerns over security, privacy, and legality. Cybercrime like hacking, identity theft, data breaches, and cyberterrorism have also transformed with more advanced methodologies, and it needs equally advanced forensic practices that can handle complex digital evidence. Digital forensics provides a scientific approach to identifying, preserving, examining, and presenting electronic evidence in a manner to be in a state of integrity and admissibility before a court of law. By employing specialized instruments and techniques, expert forensic analysts are able to track off-limit access, chart timelines of cyber incidents, and link malicious activity to an individual or group, all in the name of establishing responsibility and justice. Forensic science applies well beyond criminal investigation to assist corporate governance, regulatory matters, and national security, safeguarding critical infrastructure from cyber attacks and maintaining confidentiality over sensitive information. Rising trends of cloud computing, mobile technology, and the Internet of Things have further made the forensic environment more complex, as today's data can be located in scattered and ephemeral contexts, necessitating novel means of capturing and verifying evidence. All this notwithstanding, digital forensics advances through innovation and research with the incorporation of artificial intelligence, machine learning, and blockchain analysis to increase detection capabilities and automate mundane tasks. Ethics are involved as well, for forensic professionals need to weigh on one hand the necessity for forceful investigation against concern for privacy issues and legal limits, being transparent and accountable in order to earn the trust of the public. Education and continuing professional development remain essential here, allowing investigators to stay one step ahead of new technology and deal with new threats to the cyber world. Digital and Information Forensics is then a foundation of digital trust and cybersecurity, allowing organisations, governments, and citizens to act with confidence and integrity in the data world. By exposing the evidence behind digital traces, this field not only fights cybercrime but also protect the source values of justice, privacy, and security that form the foundations of our more networked world.

EXPERIMENTAL RESULTS

Experimental results in Digital and Information Forensics offer valuable feedback on the efficacy of a range of forensic methods and tools employed to locate digital evidence in sophisticated data environments. By a series of controlled experiments and actual case studies, these findings show how state-of-the-art methodologies, such as automated data collection, feature extraction and selection, and analysis techniques, improve forensic investigation accuracy and efficiency. Evaluation measures such as detection rate, false positive rate, and processing time are usually measured in the calculation of forensic model effectiveness. The experiments also show the difficulty of encrypted data, massive cloud environments, and volatile memory analysis, highlighting where there can be potential for advancement. By contrasting traditional methods with new technologies like machine learning and artificial intelligence, the findings suggest the potential of these new technologies to drive transformational change in forensic capability. In general, the experiment's findings support the real-world application of digital forensics in identifying cyber threats, recreating events, and aiding legal evidence, demonstrating its irreplaceable value in the data-driven world.

Table 1 is the initial series of forensic results from the collected Twitter dataset. Each row characterizes a tweet's ID, related user, chosen feature while preprocessing, sentiment label, whether there is an anomaly, and the ultimate forensic score. This table forms the foundation of identifying patterns and abnormalities in the data. It indicates user behavior across various features such as hashtags, mentions, and text.

The sentiment scores contribute to contextual user behavior insight. Anomalies are detected from the variation in the structure and metadata of the tweet. The forensic score measures the extent of variation. This table supports the classification of tweets as benign or suspicious. It serves as a reference for comparison with optimized results. The combined features provide a multi-dimensional forensic insight.

Table 1. Forensic Analysis Results

Tweet ID	User	Feature Selected	Sentiment	Anomaly Detected	Forensic Score
TID32405	@user2	Text	Neutral	Yes	0.68
TID98017	@user2	Location	Negative	Yes	0.69
TID24619	@user3	Hashtag	Negative	Yes	0.98
TID32396	@user1	Timestamp	Negative	Yes	0.64
TID93049	@user2	URL	Positive	Yes	0.52
TID88251	@user5	Hashtag	Neutral	Yes	0.80
TID58300	@user1	Location	Neutral	No	0.70
TID39516	@user1	Location	Negative	No	0.77
TID98695	@user1	Hashtag	Neutral	Yes	0.53
TID85389	@user1	Hashtag	Negative	No	0.89

Table 2 persists with the forensic testing based on improved features selected through Particle Swarm Optimization (PSO). Optimization is employed to maximize accuracy in anomaly detection by utilizing salient features as a priority. PSO iteratively updates selection based on a fitness value. The table illustrates a distinction in forensic scores employing PSO. It indicates more consistent results of anomaly detection, especially for sentiment-based tweets. Users whose posts were neutral in Table 1 show higher forensic anomalies. This validates the effectiveness of PSO for retrieving latent patterns. The table indicates text, timestamp, and hashtag as top contributors. Forensic scores here better reflect actual suspicious behavior. This proves the usefulness of PSO in digital forensics.

Table 2. Forensic Testing

Tweet ID	User	Feature Selected	Sentiment	Anomaly Detected	Forensic Score
TID48136	@user3	Timestamp	Neutral	Yes	0.96
TID97079	@user2	Location	Neutral	Yes	0.61
TID82937	@user1	Timestamp	Positive	No	0.55
TID91523	@user2	Timestamp	Neutral	No	0.64

continued on following page

Table 2. Continued

Tweet ID	User	Feature Selected	Sentiment	Anomaly Detected	Forensic Score
TID36162	@user3	Mention	Positive	Yes	0.94
TID46101	@user5	Hashtag	Negative	No	0.53
TID22618	@user2	Timestamp	Positive	No	0.71
TID40606	@user1	Location	Positive	No	0.60
TID56462	@user2	Hashtag	Positive	Yes	0.60
TID30223	@user5	Mention	Positive	Yes	0.60

Table 3 compares raw and optimized forensic scores to analyze the impact of PSO-based feature selection. It allows for observation of change in anomaly status and forensic scores for similar tweets. For the same tweets previously marked as non-anomalous, new scores can capture anomalies after optimization. This suggests that earlier models did not work suboptimally due to the lack of intelligent feature filtering. The comparison is meant to validate the necessity for intelligent feature selection. Tweets with equivalent sentiment now yield dissimilar scores with improved features. The table underscores the advantage of dynamic analysis compared to static checking. The table confirms that certain features were previously underutilized. The forensic scores following optimization appear more balanced. The table as a whole is in favor of PSO's potential to augment digital forensic precision.

Table 3. Forensic Scores

Tweet ID	User	Feature Selected	Sentiment	Anomaly Detected	Forensic Score
TID88698	@user4	Hashtag	Positive	Yes	0.88
TID83777	@user4	Timestamp	Neutral	No	0.89
TID20478	@user5	Text	Negative	Yes	0.88
TID94542	@user2	Mention	Neutral	Yes	0.89
TID16295	@user2	Hashtag	Positive	Yes	0.85
TID74847	@user1	Timestamp	Positive	No	0.82
TID91007	@user2	Hashtag	Neutral	Yes	0.93
TID84075	@user1	Location	Neutral	No	0.65
TID39697	@user1	Mention	Positive	Yes	0.80
TID85527	@user2	Timestamp	Neutral	No	0.62

Table 4 shows the clustered forensic analysis in terms of user activity metrics. Every user's tweeting tendency is associated with distinct forensic findings. For example, users who have extremely high usage of hashtags will have increased forensic scores. The table allows comparison of forensic importance based on activity. It also allows profiling based on users' digital marks. Anomalies for specific users help in predicting users' behavior. Forensic profiling of cybercrime investigations is aided by this type of analysis. The clustering provides information about users whose behavior is abnormal compared to normal activity. The clustering allows forensic analysts to prioritize users for further investigation. Feature selection continues to make its mark here. The table acts as a behavioral audit tool.

Table 4. Forensic Analysis Results – Clustered User Activity Metrics

Tweet ID	User	Feature Selected	Sentiment	Anomaly Detected	Forensic Score
TID11983	@user3	Text	Negative	Yes	0.91
TID76149	@user5	Timestamp	Positive	No	0.84
TID50743	@user4	Mention	Neutral	Yes	0.87
TID24585	@user3	Hashtag	Positive	Yes	0.89
TID34027	@user1	Location	Neutral	No	0.60
TID16202	@user5	Text	Negative	Yes	0.90
TID78190	@user2	Hashtag	Neutral	Yes	0.79
TID69739	@user1	Mention	Positive	No	0.69
TID41695	@user4	Location	Negative	Yes	0.92
TID23334	@user5	Timestamp	Positive	No	0.66

Table 5 evaluates the consistency between sentiment classification and anomaly detection. Negative tweets carry greater forensic scores. Positive tweets will probably be tagged as non-anomalous. The table reflects a potential sentiment bias in detecting suspicious activity. Such a connection of sentiment and anomalies is crucial in forensic linguistics. Sentiment-aware analysis adds depth to interpretation of intent behind messages. The table challenges further semantic analysis in digital investigations. Terms such as hashtag and mention exhibit variable influence based on sentiment. The scoring system is robust enough to capture this complexity. Forensic results are not strictly derived from structure attributes but also from tone. This table interlinks sentiment mining and anomaly detection.

Table 5. Forensic Evaluation – Sentiment vs Anomaly Detection

Tweet ID	User	Feature Selected	Sentiment	Anomaly Detected	Forensic Score
TID13488	@user2	Text	Neutral	No	0.74
TID84939	@user3	Hashtag	Positive	Yes	0.91
TID39421	@user1	Mention	Positive	No	0.78
TID51455	@user5	Text	Negative	Yes	0.86
TID82092	@user4	Location	Neutral	Yes	0.81
TID90516	@user1	Hashtag	Positive	No	0.77
TID34897	@user2	Mention	Negative	Yes	0.83
TID59102	@user5	Timestamp	Neutral	No	0.69
TID64471	@user4	Hashtag	Positive	Yes	0.90
TID77321	@user3	Mention	Neutral	Yes	0.86

Table 6 breaks down detection accuracy by feature contribution. What each feature does in order to identify anomalies is quantified in terms of forensic scores. Location and mention fields show increasing importance in certain tweet forms. This table encourages a feature-centric approach to digital forensics. It calls for customized detection rules per metadata field. The accuracy improves if the unnecessary features are eliminated. This is in line with PSO's mission to reduce noise. Tweets with more enriched metadata result in more accurate scores. Textual features alone are not necessarily informative for forensic examination. The data supports multi-feature analysis is superior. The table prefers modular analysis for forensic systems.

Table 6. Detection Accuracy Based on Feature Contribution

Tweet ID	User	Feature Selected	Sentiment	Anomaly Detected	Forensic Score
TID14004	@user1	Location	Neutral	No	0.67
TID96841	@user2	Mention	Negative	Yes	0.84
TID52018	@user4	Hashtag	Positive	No	0.75
TID79421	@user3	Text	Negative	Yes	0.87
TID43752	@user5	Timestamp	Neutral	No	0.69
TID39653	@user1	Mention	Positive	Yes	0.81
TID28477	@user2	Location	Negative	Yes	0.91
TID15020	@user3	Hashtag	Neutral	Yes	0.76
TID81240	@user4	Text	Positive	No	0.71
TID68001	@user5	Timestamp	Neutral	No	0.65

Table 7 discusses PSO-based feature optimization performance specifically. It presents optimized forensic scores after PSO final iteration. The improvement in anomaly detection is observed across all tweets. Some features are always selected, for instance, text and hashtag. PSO avoids overfitting since it achieves a balance between feature salience and generalization. The forensic scores are consistent and stable. It emphasizes the efficacy of swarm intelligence in forensic use. The table also illustrates how optimization is used to prioritize resources. Through enhanced feature selection, analysts are able to eliminate possible threats. PSO is an extensible approach to large forensic data. This table validates algorithmic smarts in cybersecurity.

Table 7. PSO-Based Feature Optimization Analysis

Tweet ID	User	Feature Selected	Sentiment	Anomaly Detected	Forensic Score
TID33500	@user3	Mention	Positive	Yes	0.88
TID19281	@userl	Text	Neutral	No	0.71
TID73092	@user2	Timestamp	Negative	Yes	0.84
TID68073	@user5	Hashtag	Neutral	No	0.79
TID24133	@user4	Location	Positive	Yes	0.90
TID58901	@user2	Mention	Neutral	Yes	0.86
TID15338	@user3	Timestamp	Positive	No	0.73
TID40891	@userl	Text	Negative	Yes	0.85
TID73251	@user5	Hashtag	Positive	No	0.72
TID86294	@user4	Location	Neutral	Yes	0.89

Table 8 forensically analyzes the users' forensic scores distribution. The goal is to determine risk profiling based on users. Users whose high forensic scores persist are flagged for further inspection. The table supports continuous monitoring methods in digital settings. It also helps with forensic alert automation. Variation of selected features across users reveals behavioral differences. The timestamp and sentiment fields are highly correlated in some users. Such profiling can be utilized in social engineering investigations. High forensic scores indicate potential misinformation distributors. The table facilitates early threat detection on digital platforms.

Table 8. Forensic Score Distribution by User Category

Tweet ID	User	Feature Selected	Sentiment	Anomaly Detected	Forensic Score
TID54791	@user2	Hashtag	Positive	Yes	0.93
TID19327	@user1	Mention	Negative	No	0.68
TID87704	@user5	Location	Neutral	Yes	0.85
TID33678	@user4	Timestamp	Positive	No	0.79
TID93028	@user3	Text	Negative	Yes	0.91
TID37466	@user2	Mention	Neutral	Yes	0.83
TID12796	@user1	Hashtag	Positive	No	0.76
TID91804	@user5	Location	Neutral	Yes	0.82
TID65401	@user4	Mention	Positive	No	0.74
TID20174	@user3	Timestamp	Negative	Yes	0.89

Table 9 focuses on anomaly pattern detection within tweet metadata. It finds repeated patterns that point to suspicious action. Attributes like text and location tend to get high scores. The table confirms that multi-metadata anomalies are worse. It also indicates that certain trends are user-specific. By finding repeated anomalies, learning improves. It places more weight on time-series anomaly tracing. Tweets with similar structure but different timing yield different results. This is in support of the fact that context is fundamental in digital forensics. The table supports predictive anomaly modeling. The table is utilized in real-time alert systems for cyber threats.

Table 9. Anomaly Pattern Recognition Across Tweet Metadata

Tweet ID	User	Feature Selected	Sentiment	Anomaly Detected	Forensic Score
TID84734	@user3	Text	Negative	Yes	0.90
TID31973	@user1	Timestamp	Positive	No	0.72
TID50185	@user2	Mention	Neutral	Yes	0.81
TID15091	@user5	Hashtag	Positive	Yes	0.88
TID78719	@user4	Text	Negative	Yes	0.89
TID24956	@user3	Location	Positive	No	0.70
TID90125	@user2	Mention	Neutral	Yes	0.84
TID40023	@user1	Timestamp	Negative	No	0.68
TID34413	@user5	Hashtag	Positive	Yes	0.91
TID71136	@user4	Location	Neutral	Yes	0.87

Table 10 provides a comparison of forensic scoring prior to and subsequent to optimization for the selected tweets. The table confirms the improvement in the system's precision and recall. Some of the previously undetected tweets are now recognized as anomalies. It shows that PSO helps reduce false negatives. The table is key to model improvement benchmarking. Differences in scores warrant adaptive models. Stability in sentiment proves detection optimality. Timestamp and location fields become essential after optimization. The table facilitates dynamic model refreshment in forensic systems. It provides a performance summary of the proposed methodology. This final table is the end of the forensic evaluation framework.

Table 10. Comparative Forensic Scoring Before and After Optimization

Tweet ID	User	Feature Selected	Sentiment	Anomaly Detected	Forensic Score
TID16812	@user2	Timestamp	Neutral	Yes	0.93
TID31846	@user1	Text	Positive	No	0.69
TID63042	@user3	Mention	Negative	Yes	0.86
TID78103	@user5	Hashtag	Neutral	Yes	0.87
TID22684	@user4	Timestamp	Positive	No	0.73
TID91243	@user2	Location	Negative	Yes	0.88
TID34099	@user1	Mention	Positive	No	0.75
TID58410	@user5	Text	Neutral	Yes	0.84
TID17720	@user3	Location	Negative	Yes	0.92
TID77821	@user4	Hashtag	Positive	No	0.70

CONCLUSION

Digital and Information Forensics is a shining light in the battle against cybercrime and digital asset security in an age of data dominance. Its scientific method of gathering, examining, and documenting digital evidence guarantees that truth can be unraveled even from the most complicated digital realms. Evolution of the discipline with new technologies enhances its ability to respond to new threats, rendering it unavoidable for governments, commercial players, and law enforcement agencies. Respect for the law and ethical practice underpin the viability and legitimacy of forensic investigation. The expanding digital environment, with constant research and development of forensic devices and methods, will be crucial in ensuring security, confidentiality, and justice in the data age.

REFERENCES

Abdulateef, O. G., Joudah, A., Abdulsahib, M. G., & Alrammahi, H. (2025). Designing a robust machine learning-based framework for secure data transmission in Internet of Things (IoT) environments: A multifaceted approach to security challenges. *Journal of Cyber Security and Risk Auditing*, *2025*(4), 266–275. DOI: 10.63180/jcsra.thestap.2025.4.6

Addula, S. R., Norozpour, S., & Amin, M. (2025). Risk assessment for identifying threats, vulnerabilities, and countermeasures in cloud computing. *Jordanian Journal of Informatics and Computing*, *2025*(1), 38–48. DOI: 10.63180/jjic.thestap.2025.1.5

Al-Shareeda, M. A., Obaid, A. A., & Almajid, A. A. H. (2025). The role of artificial intelligence in bodybuilding: A systematic review of applications, challenges, and future prospects. *Jordanian Journal of Informatics and Computing*, *2025*(1), 16–26. DOI: 10.63180/jjic.thestap.2025.1.3

Alaasam, A. B. A. (2023). Quantum computing applications in statistics. *Babylonian Journal of Mathematics*, *2023*(1), 105–107. DOI: 10.58496/BJM/2023/020

Aledavood, T., López, E., Roberts, S. G. B., Reed-Tsochas, F., Moro, E., Dunbar, R. I. M., & Saramäki, J. (2015). Daily rhythms in mobile telephone communication. *PLoS One*, *10*(9), e0138098. Advance online publication. DOI: 10.1371/journal.pone.0138098 PMID: 26390215

Ali, A. (2024). Adaptive and context-aware authentication framework using edge AI and blockchain in future vehicular networks. *STAP Journal of Security Risk Management*, *2024*(1), 45–56. DOI: 10.63180/jsrm.thestap.2024.1.3

Alsahaim, S., & Maayah, M. (2023). Analyzing cybersecurity threats on mobile phones. *STAP Journal of Security Risk Management*, *2023*(1), 3–19. DOI: 10.63180/jsrm.thestap.2023.1.2

Arshad, H., Jantan, A., Hoon, G. K., & Abiodun, I. O. (2020). Formal knowledge model for online social network forensics. *Computers & Security*, *89*, 101675. Advance online publication. DOI: 10.1016/j.cose.2019.101675

Arshad, H., Jantan, A., Hoon, G. K., & Butt, A. S. (2019). A multi-layered semantic framework for integrated forensic acquisition on social media. *Digital Investigation*, *29*, 147–158. DOI: 10.1016/j.diin.2019.04.002

Arshad, H., Omlara, E., Abiodun, I. O., & Aminu, A. (2020). A semi-automated forensic investigation model for online social networks. *Computers & Security*, *97*, 101946. Advance online publication. DOI: 10.1016/j.cose.2020.101946

Balbach, E. (1999). Using case studies to do program evaluation. *International Journal of Aromatherapy*, *9*(1), 1–18. DOI: 10.1016/S0962-4562(99)80002-7

Baryamureeba, V., & Florence, T. (2004). The enhanced digital investigation process model. *Asian Journal of Information Technology*, *5*(8), 790–794.

Biedermann, A., & Kotsoglou, K. N. (2020). Digital evidence exceptionalism? A review and discussion of conceptual hurdles in digital evidence transformation. *Forensic Science International. Synergy*, *2*, 262–274. DOI: 10.1016/j.fsisyn.2020.08.004 PMID: 32944711

Bollé, T., Casey, E., & Jacquet, M. (2020). The role of evaluations in reaching decisions using automated systems supporting forensic analysis. *Forensic Science International Digital Investigation*, *34*, 301016. Advance online publication. DOI: 10.1016/j.fsidi.2020.301016

Carrier, B., & Spafford, E. (2010). An event-based digital forensic investigation framework. *Digital Forensic Research Workshop*, 57(1), 1–51.

Chabot, Y., Bertaux, A., Nicolle, C., & Kechadi, M. T. (2014). A complete formalized knowledge representation model for advanced digital forensics timeline analysis. *Digital Investigation*, *11*(Suppl. 2), S95–S105. DOI: 10.1016/j.diin.2014.05.009

Chung, H., Park, J., Lee, S., & Kang, C. (2012). Digital forensic investigation of cloud storage services. *Digital Investigation*, *9*(2), 81–95. DOI: 10.1016/j.diin.2012.05.015

Ciardhuáin, S. (2004). An extended model of cybercrime investigations. *International Journal of Digital Evidence*, *3*(1), 1–22.

Fasching, D., Kaliner, S., & Karel, T. (2012). Social media data preservation tools and best practices. *Law Journal Newsletters*, *29*(2), 90.

Flayyih, M. F., & Hassan, T. (2024). Predictive analytics model for students' grade prediction using machine learning. *Babylonian Journal of Artificial Intelligence*, *2024*(1), 83–101. DOI: 10.58496/BJAI/2024/011

Galbraith, C., & Smyth, P. (2017). Analyzing user-event data using score-based likelihood ratios with marked point processes. *Digital Investigation*, *22*(Suppl.), S106–S114. DOI: 10.1016/j.diin.2017.06.009

Garfinkel, S. (2012). Digital forensics XML and the DFXML toolset. *Digital Investigation*, *8*(3-4), 161–174. DOI: 10.1016/j.diin.2011.11.002

Greenwood, R. E.The Case Study Approach. (1993). The case study approach. *Business Communication Quarterly*, *56*(4), 46–48. DOI: 10.1177/108056999305600409

Hanoon, W. H., & Ibrahim, A. S. (2024). Fuzzy semi and fuzzy strongly semi two-absorbing second sub-modules. *Babylonian Journal of Mathematics, 2024*(1), 95–101. DOI: 10.58496/BJM/2024/012

Jadhao, A. R., & Agrawal, A. J. (2016). A digital forensics investigation model for social networking site. In *Second International Conference on Information and Communication Technology for Competitive Strategies (ICTCS '16)* (pp. 1–4). ACM. DOI: 10.1145/2905055.2905346

Jasim, N. S., Kirdar, M. S. I., Hamad, H., Abu-Shams, A. I. M. S., & Zbaida, A. (2024). Factor group for some SL groups. *Babylonian Journal of Mathematics, 2024*(1), 171–177. DOI: 10.58496/BJM/2024/018

Maher, R. M., Rashid, S. H., Habeeb, M. A., Khaleel, Y. L., & Ameen, F. N. (2025). Predictive modeling and analysis of monkeypox outbreaks using machine learning techniques. *Applied Data Science and Analysis, 2025*(1), 94–111. DOI: 10.58496/ADSA/2025/006

Masoodi, H. J. K. A. L. (2024). Evaluating the effectiveness of machine learning-based intrusion detection in multi-cloud environments. *Babylonian Journal of Internet of Things, 2024*(1), 94–105. DOI: 10.58496/BJIoT/2024/012

Mijwil, M. M., Adamopoulos, I., & Pudasaini, P. (2024). Machine learning helps in quickly diagnosis cases of "new Corona". *Mesopotamian Journal of Artificial Intelligence in Healthcare, 2024*(1), 16–19. DOI: 10.58496/MJAIH/2024/003

Palmer, G. (2001). A road map for digital forensic research. In *Digital Forensic Research Conference*. Utica, NY, United States.

Patzakis, J. (2011). Overcoming potential legal challenges to the authentication of social media evidence. X1 Discovery. http://www.x1discovery.com

Saleh, H. M., Oleiwi, A. K., & Abed, A. A. H. (2023). Diagnosis of HIV (AIDS) by using deep learning and machine learning. *Babylonian Journal of Machine Learning, 2023*(1), 73–77. DOI: 10.58496/BJML/2023/012

Salisu, A., Gafai, M. M., & Salisu, S. (2024). Some results on commutativity for alternative rings with 2, 3-torsion free. *Babylonian Journal of Mathematics, 2024*(1), 44–47. DOI: 10.58496/BJM/2024/005

Samara, M., Burbidge, V., El Asam, A., Foody, M., Smith, P. K., & Morsi, H. (2017). Bullying and cyberbullying: Their legal status and use in psychological assessment. *International Journal of Environmental Research and Public Health, 14*(12), 1449. Advance online publication. DOI: 10.3390/ijerph14121449 PMID: 29186780

Satar, S. D. M., Hussin, M., Afendee Mohamed, M., Abd Hamid, N., Abd Kadir, M. F., Muda, R., & Samual, J. (2025). Secure access control using ciphertext policy attribute-based encryption with performance optimization in cloud computing. *Journal of Cyber Security and Risk Auditing*, *2025*(4), 287–305. DOI: 10.63180/jcsra.thestap.2025.4.8

Sheela, M. S., Gopalakrishnan, S., Begum, I. P., Hephzipah, J. J., Gopianand, M., & Harika, D. (2024). Enhancing energy efficiency with smart building energy management system using machine learning and IoT. *Babylonian Journal of Machine Learning*, *2024*(1), 80–88. DOI: 10.58496/BJML/2024/008

Simons, H. (2015). Case study evaluation: Past, present and future challenges. In *Advances in program evaluation* (pp. 17–20). Emerald Group Publishing.

Soltani, S., & Seno, S. A. H. (2019). A formal model for event reconstruction in digital forensic investigation. *Digital Investigation*, *30*, 148–160. DOI: 10.1016/j.diin.2019.07.006

Stephenson, P. (2002). End-to-end digital forensics. *Computer Fraud & Security*, *2002*(9), 17–19. DOI: 10.1016/S1361-3723(02)00914-4

Wang, J., Tang, Z., Shao, W., & Jin, X. (2016). A formal model of events reconstruction for cloud forensics. RISTI—Revista Ibérica de Sistemas e Tecnologias de Informação, 2016(18), 45–55.

Willard, N. (2011). Educator's guide to cyberbullying and cyberthreats. Arkansas Department of Education. http://www.arkansased.gov/public/userfiles/Learning_Services/Technology_Initiatives/Cyber_Safety/educatorsguide.pdf

Wilson, C., Boe, B., Sala, A., Puttaswamy, K. P. N., & Zhao, B. Y. (2009). User interactions in social networks and their implications. In *Proceedings of the Fourth ACM European Conference on Computer Systems (EuroSys '09)* (pp. 205–218). ACM. DOI: 10.1145/1519065.1519089

Chapter 10
Securing Cloud:
Leveraging Machine Learning for Threat Detection and Mitigation

Deepa Nehra
https://orcid.org/0000-0002-4720-6335
M.M. Institute of Computer Technology and Business Management, Maharshi Markandeshwar University, Mullana, India

Karanbir Singh
https://orcid.org/0000-0002-6663-2727
Seth Jai Parkash Polytechnic, Damla, India

ABSTRACT

The rapid use of cloud computing services for processing, storing data, and deploying applications has raised serious security issues. Traditional security measures are further insufficient against the complex and constantly changing cyberthreat landscape. This study investigates the incorporation of machine learning methods into cloud security architectures to strengthen threat detection and mitigation. The chapter outlines the state of cloud security and the evolution of cyber threats and the benefits of machine learning in strengthening cloud security measures, such as improved accuracy and adaptability, while also addressing the challenges and limitations, including algorithmic complexity and data privacy concerns. Ethical considerations and potential risks, such as biases in algorithms and the misuse of AI technologies, are critically examined. The chapter concludes with recommendations for deploying machine learning-based security solutions in cloud environments and classifies future research directions to address ongoing and emerging challenges.

DOI: 10.4018/979-8-3373-1807-3.ch010

2026, IGI Global Scientific Publishing. Copying or distributing in print or electronic forms without written permission of IGI Global Scientific Publishing is prohibited. Use of this chapter to rative artificial intelligence (AI) technologies is expressly prohibited. The publisher reserves all rights to license its use for generative AI training and machine learning model development.

1. INTRODUCTION

In recent years, cloud computing has completely changed how individuals and organizations handle, store, and analyze data. By offering scalable resources and services over the internet, cloud computing provides substantial advantages in accessibility, flexibility, and cost-efficiency. As the adoption of cloud services grows, the concerns about the security of these environments are also growing. Cyber threats have changed in frequency and complexity, posing substantial risks to cloud infrastructures. Traditional security measures, which were designed for on-premises systems, are increasingly inadequate in addressing the unique challenges cloud environments present (Mell & Grance, 2011).

Cloud computing has evolved from a new idea to an essential part of contemporary IT systems. From 2025 to 2030, the worldwide cloud computing industry is anticipated to develop at a compound annual growth rate (CAGR) of 20.4%, from its estimated USD 752.44 billion in 2024. The advancement of big data, AI, and ML technologies is driving the need for high-performance, scalable cloud infrastructure (Cloud Computing Market Size, Share | Industry Report, 2030, n.d.). The need for strong security frameworks that can protect sensitive data and applications from a wide range of cyber threats is highlighted by this quick expansion.

However, the inherent features of cloud computing—such as multi-tenancy, data mobility, and resource elasticity—introduce new vulnerabilities and attack vectors. The shared nature of cloud environments indicates that a breach in one tenant's security can affect others. Additionally, the dynamic allocation of resources can make it difficult to keep consistent security policies. As a result, traditional security approaches, which rely heavily on perimeter defenses and static configurations, fall short in providing comprehensive protection in cloud settings (Singh & Chatterjee, 2017).

The limitations of conventional security methods have necessitated the investigation of more advanced and adaptive methods. One capable approach is the blend of machine learning (ML) methods with cloud security frameworks. A subfield of artificial intelligence (AI) called machine learning, deals with the development of algorithms that can learn from data and forecast future occurrences. By leveraging ML, security systems can evolve from reactive to proactive, detecting and neutralizing threats in real-time (Kiruthika et. al. 2024).

Many benefits are provided by machine learning in cloud security. ML features allow for the early identification of threats, including insider threats, advanced persistent threats (APTs), and distributed denial-of-service (DDoS) attacks. Furthermore, ML models can be regularly trained and updated to adapt to novel threats, increasing the resilience of cloud security systems (Nassif et al., 2021; Bhuiyan et al., 2024).

Recent developments in ML have demonstrated great potential for enhancing threat identification and mitigation. For instance, sophisticated, high-dimensional data can be processed by deep learning models to find tiny signs of compromise that conventional rule-based systems could overlook (Macas & Wu, 2020). Reinforcement learning, conversely, allows security systems to learn optimal responses to detected threats through trial and error, improving their effectiveness over time (Adawadkar & Kulkarni, 2022).

While the integration of ML into cloud security presents several benefits, it will also create some potential risks and ethical considerations. A significant worry is the possibility of bias in machine learning algorithms, which might provide unfair or biased results. Certifying the impartiality and transparency of these algorithms is key to maintaining trust in ML-based security solutions (Mehrabi et al., 2021). Additionally, the use of ML in security contexts may inadvertently introduce new attack surfaces, as adversaries could potentially exploit vulnerabilities in the ML models themselves (Xue et al., 2020).

This chapter provides a comprehensive overview of the state of cloud security today and the contribution of machine learning to improving threat detection and mitigation. The following sections will explore the specific benefits and challenges associated with ML-based security solutions. We will examine various ML models and their applications in cloud security, highlighting real-world examples and case studies. Ethical considerations and potential risks will be discussed in detail, followed by recommendations for implementing ML-based security solutions and directions for future work. The objectives of this chapter are: -

- Review the present state of cloud security and identify the limitations of conventional security approaches.
- Discuss the pros and cons of incorporating ML algorithms into cloud security.
- Examine various machine learning models and their applications in identifying and countering cloud cyber-attacks.
- Discuss the possible hazards and moral issues with the application of ML to cloud security.
- Provide recommendations for implementing ML-based security solutions and recommend future guidelines.

The structure of this chapter is as follows: The following section summarizes the present situation regarding cloud security, highlighting the limitations of traditional approaches. Following this, the potential benefits and challenges of using machine learning in cloud security systems are examined. Subsequent sections delve into various ML models and their applications in cloud security, along with a discussion on ethical considerations and potential risks. Finally, the chapter presents recommendations for implementing ML-based security solutions and outlines directions for future work.

This chapter intends to solve these issues to aid in the creation of more adaptable and efficient cloud security solutions, utilizing machine learning to protect vital data and cloud applications.

2. LITERATURE REVIEW

2.1 Current State of Cloud Security

This section offers a thorough examination of the current security procedures in place for cloud systems. Notably, cloud infrastructures are protected in large part by traditional security methods, including firewalls, intrusion detection systems (IDS), and encryption (Gupta, 2019). IDS watches network traffic for unusual activity, whereas firewalls serve as a barrier between the internal network and outside threats. Encryption, on the other hand, ensures data confidentiality during transmission and storage (Li & Liu, 2021).

While these measures have proven effective to a certain extent, they exhibit some notable strengths and weaknesses. Firewalls provide a strong initial defense, but they may struggle with advanced persistent threats (APTs) that can exploit vulnerabilities in applications (Alshamrani et al., 2019). Similarly, it is difficult for traditional IDS to keep up with the quickly changing threat environments, leading to delayed threat detection (Scarfone & Mell, 2007). Encryption, while enhancing data confidentiality, may introduce latency and complexity, impacting overall system performance.

Moreover, the growing complexity of cyberthreats poses a significant challenge to these conventional security approaches. The limitations in scalability and adaptability of current security measures hinder their capability to cope with the varying nature of cloud infrastructures. The motive of this chapter is to identify the research gap by exploring the integration of ML techniques for attack detection and mitigation in cloud security. The gap in the present state of cloud security may be filled by utilizing ML algorithms capability to assess huge volumes of data in real-time. This will improve the identification of unusual patterns and increase overall reactivity to new threats.

2.2 Analytical Cohesion and Conceptual Frameworks

Although a basic overview of the present security environment is given in the preceding sections, a more critical and analytical approach is required to improve the academic rigor. The debate over traditional security measures (firewalls, intrusion detection systems, etc.) might be reframed, for example, to emphasize how their reactive, signature-based design naturally reduces their ability to defend against contemporary, multifaceted threats. This conceptual restriction serves as the main defense for the move to proactive, machine learning-driven solutions. The target audience is guided through the next technical talks by this framework, which also enhances the chapter's overall coherence and field contribution.

2.3 Stakeholder Perspectives and Policy Implications

The focus of this section is to discuss on the varied perspectives of key stakeholders in cloud security. These include:

- **Cloud Service Providers (CSPs):** They are worried about safeguarding their proprietary data and apps in a shared cloud environment. They concentrate on putting into practice machine learning (ML)-based solutions that can enforce compliance with policies, offer granular visibility, and identify insider risks and misconfigurations.
- **Enterprise Clients/Organizations:** They are concerned with protecting their specific data and applications within the shared cloud environment. Their focus is on implementing ML-based solutions that can provide granular visibility, enforce policy compliance, and detect insider threats and misconfigurations.
- **End-Users:** The primary concerns of end users are trust, security, and data privacy. They are dependent upon the security measures put in place by their organization and the CSP. Using weak passwords or falling for phishing schemes are examples of human behavior that pose a serious risk. The chapter will cover how machine learning (ML) may be used to model user behavior and identify anomalies that indicate penetration.
- **Government and Regulatory Bodies:** They are responsible for creating and enforcing policy frameworks, data protection regulations (such as the CCPA and GDPR), and security standards. As AI and ML become more prevalent in cybersecurity, new issues pertaining to algorithmic accountability, transparency, and moral technology usage arise.

2.4 Human Behavior and Innovation

The focus of this part is on technological considerations, which will be counterbalanced by a more thorough examination of innovation and human behavior. ML offers creative solutions to the problem that people are often the weakest link in the security chain. To find hacked accounts or spot social engineering attempts, for instance, machine learning models can examine user login behaviors. The chapter will also go over how attackers employ AI innovation to develop increasingly complex attacks, making it both an offensive and defensive weapon. An important issue will be AI's dual-use nature, which emphasizes the necessity of ongoing study and adaptability. The discussion will cover topics such as:

- **Adversarial Machine Learning:** How attackers create adversarial instances or contaminate training data to get past ML-based protections.
- **AI-Driven Social Engineering:** The use of AI to create incredibly realistic deepfake audio and video or customized phishing emails.
- **Human-in-the-Loop AI:** The significance of integrating human expertise and machine learning automation for incident response and decision-making.

2.5 Evolution of Threats

In previous years, the landscape of cloud computing has seen a dynamic evolution, accompanied by a parallel surge in sophisticated threats and attacks. As organizations transfer their sensitive data and operations to the cloud, the attack surface expands, exposing new vulnerabilities. This section summarizes the current trends in cloud threats, highlighting the urgency for adaptive security measures (Alouffi et al., 2021).

- **Multi-Vector Attacks:** Cyber adversaries have adopted a multi-pronged approach, combining various attack vectors to exploit vulnerabilities comprehensively. This includes a blend of malware, phishing, and DDoS attacks, creating complex challenges for traditional security models (Devi & Babu, 2024).
- **Zero-Day Exploits in Cloud Services:** The discovery and exploitation of zero-day vulnerabilities in popular cloud services have become a pressing concern. Attackers leverage these undisclosed vulnerabilities to compromise systems before vendors can develop and deploy patches, underscoring the requirement of real-time attack detection (Sharma & Singh, 2025).
- **Data Breaches and Misconfigurations:** Cloud misconfigurations remain a persistent issue, causing sensitive data to be unintentionally exposed. These missteps, combined with the rising number of insider threats, contribute to the growing trend of data breaches, which can have detrimental effects on businesses (Jeyalakshmi et al., 2024b).
- **AI-Enhanced Attacks:** As ML and AI technologies become more prevalent, cybercriminals are incorporating these tools into their arsenals. Adversarial machine learning, where attackers manipulate ML models, and the use of

AI for crafting more convincing phishing attacks exemplify this trend (Shea, 2024).

- **Supply Chain Attacks:** Cloud ecosystems heavily rely on interconnected services and third-party integrations. Cybercriminals exploit this interconnectedness through supply chain attacks, compromising one service to infiltrate others. This emphasizes the importance of vetting and securing the entire cloud supply chain (Hammi et al., 2023).

Organizations must implement machine learning-based adaptive security solutions to detect and mitigate attacks in real time in reaction to these changing threats. Protecting cloud systems requires the capacity to instantly evaluate vast datasets, spot trends that might indicate dangers, and take immediate action.

2.6 Existing Techniques

Traditional Security Measures

Traditional cloud computing security methods include antivirus software, firewalls and intrusion detection systems (IDS). These methods are limited in their capacity to identify new or changing threats since they mostly rely on pre-established rules and signatures. While intrusion detection systems (IDS) keep an eye on system or network activity for malicious or policy violations, firewalls regulate incoming and outgoing network traffic according to preset security rules. Antivirus software uses known viral signatures to identify and eliminate harmful software. While these methods provide a baseline level of security, their effectiveness diminishes against sophisticated or unknown threats (Binu & Misbahuddin, 2013).

Anomaly Detection Systems

Anomaly detection systems detect variations from legitimate behavior that may show the possibility of an attack. These systems use statistical methods and ML algorithms to establish a reference point of normal activity and identify anomalies that can further signal an intrusion or malicious activity. Techniques such as KNN (k-nearest neighbors), clustering, and SVM (support vector machines) have been used to detect anomalies in the traffic. However, the challenge lies in accurately distinguishing between benign anomalies and actual threats, which can result in false positives or negatives (Ye, 2017).

Signature-Based Detection

This method is commonly used in conventional security systems. It involves matching known signatures of threats, such as malware or intrusion patterns, against observed data. Although this method works well for known threats, it is ineffective against zero-day attacks. and novel malware, as it relies on previously identified threat patterns. Signature databases require constant updates to remain effective, and the process can be resource-intensive (Khraisat et al., 2019).

Behavioral Analysis

Behavioral analysis examines the actions of users and systems to detect abnormal behavior, which may show a security threat. This technique is mainly useful for identifying internal threats, where malicious activities are conducted by authorized users. Behavioral analysis systems leverage ML to study the legitimate behavior patterns of users and systems over time. When deviations from these patterns are detected, an alert is generated. Despite its potential, behavioral analysis can be hampered by the need for widespread training data and the difficulty in distinguishing between legitimate deviations and malicious actions (Nasir et al., 2021).

Encryption and Access Control

These are the fundamental components of cloud security. Encryption keeps data safe while it's in transit and at rest by converting it into an unintelligible format that only authorized individuals can decipher. Access control systems that limit who may access particular resources and carry out specific tasks include and MFA (multi-factor authentication) and RBAC (role-based access control). To offer complete defense against complex attacks, these methods, while crucial, are frequently combined with other security measures (Sengupta et al., 2011).

Security Information and Event Management (SIEM)

In order to deliver real-time security alert analysis, SIEM systems collect and examine security-related data from several sources. These systems identify and address security events by combining statistical analysis with rule-based correlation. SIEM systems give security teams consolidated insight into security events, which facilitates threat identification and mitigation. The quality and volume of data gathered, as well as the precision with which divergent events may be correlated, might, however, limit the efficacy of SIEM systems (Vielberth, 2025).

Cloud Access Security Brokers (CASB)

In order to maintain compliance and enforce security regulations, CASBs act as a liaison between users and cloud service providers. They offer insight into data security, threat prevention, cloud usage, and compliance management. CASBs leverage multiple security techniques, including data loss prevention (DLP), encryption, and anomaly detection, to protect cloud environments. As cloud adoption grows, CASBs have become increasingly important in providing a security layer that addresses the unique challenges of cloud computing (Ahmad et al., 2021).

Zero Trust Architecture (ZTA)

ZTA is a security paradigm which does not presume implicit trust and continuously verifies the identity and integrity of each user, device, and system attempting to access resources. ZTA relies on ethics such as micro-segmentation, and nonstop monitoring to minimize the attack surface and prevent lateral movement within a network. This approach enhances security by guaranteeing the authorization and authentication of each access request, regardless of the network location (Ahmadi, 2024).

Machine Learning and Artificial Intelligence

Since ML and AI may improve threat identification and mitigation, its incorporation into cloud security frameworks has becoming more popular. Massive volumes of data may be analyzed using ML methods like ensemble methods, neural networks and decision trees to find patterns and irregularities that can pose security risks. By automating detection and reaction procedures, AI-powered solutions may save human analysts time and effort. Notwithstanding their promise, these technologies also present difficulties concerning interpretability, model accuracy, and moral issues (Nassif et al., 2021).

Table 1 below outlines each method's advantages and disadvantages, along with the required resources and threats they address.

Table 1. Comparative analysis of existing cloud security methods

Technique	Description	Advantages	Limitations	Threats Addressed	Required Resources
Traditional Security Measures (Firewalls, IDS, Antivirus)	Uses predefined rules and signatures to detect threats.	Well-established and widely used;	Struggles with zero-day attacks and evolving threats;	Malware, unauthorized access, policy violations	Moderate – Requires frequent rule/ signature updates
Anomaly Detection Systems	Identifies deviations from normal behavior to detect attacks	Detects novel threats without predefined signatures;	High false positive/negative rates;	Insider threats, zero-day attacks, behavioral anomalies	High – Requires extensive data collection and analysis
Signature-Based Detection	Matches known threat signatures against observed data.	Highly accurate for known threats; fast detection.	Ineffective against zero-day attacks; requires constant signature updates.	Malware, phishing, intrusion attempts	Moderate – Requires continuous updates of signature databases
Behavioral Analysis	Monitors user and system behavior for abnormal activities.	Effective against insider threats;	Requires large datasets for training;	Insider threats, privilege abuse, unauthorized activities	High – Requires machine learning models and training data
Encryption and Access Control	Protects data through encryption and restricts access via authentication methods.	Ensures data confidentiality and integrity; MFA and RBAC enhance security.	Can introduce latency; complex key management.	Data breaches, unauthorized access, eavesdropping	High – Requires cryptographic infrastructure and access management tools
Security Information and Event Management (SIEM)	real-time threat detection by combining and evaluating security data from several sources.	Provides centralized monitoring; enhances threat detection.	Effectiveness depends on data quality; can generate too many alerts (alert fatigue).	Advanced persistent threats (APT), insider threats, policy violations	High – Requires large-scale log collection and correlation
Cloud Access Security Brokers (CASB)	serves as a security bridge connecting cloud service providers and users.	Improves cloud security and compliance; offers threat protection and visibility.	Implementation complexity; performance overhead.	Data leakage, unauthorized cloud usage, misconfigurations	High – Requires integration with cloud services and policy enforcement

continued on following page

Table 1. Continued

Technique	Description	Advantages	Limitations	Threats Addressed	Required Resources
Zero Trust Architecture (ZTA)	Assumes no implicit trust; continuously verifies access requests.	Strong security model; minimizes attack surface.	Complex implementation; may require rearchitecting existing systems.	Insider threats, privilege escalation, lateral movement attacks	High – Requires identity verification, micro-segmentation, continuous monitoring
Machine Learning & AI	Uses AI-driven models to detect security threats and automate responses.	Detects advanced threats quickly; reduces human workload.	Model accuracy and interpretability issues; potential ethical concerns.	AI-powered cyberattacks, evolving malware, fraud	Very High – Requires extensive computational power and AI expertise

2.7 Advanced Defensive Technologies and Strategic Insights

The current methods need a more thorough examination of how various security solutions interact and how ML-driven innovation is changing the defensive environment. Despite the mention of ZTA and CASB, it is important to critically evaluate how ML is improving them. By examining a user's behaviour patterns in real time, for instance, ML-powered ZTA may carry out continuous, risk-based authentication, beyond straightforward one-time verification. Similarly, by automatically identifying and categorizing sensitive data, machine learning (ML) can improve CASB functioning by increasing the intelligence and reducing the likelihood of false positives in data loss prevention (DLP).

The strategic use of these technologies is one important area that is underemphasized. The chapter will present a layered defensive strategy where each strategy enhances the others rather than treating them as stand-alone instruments. The chapter will go over how machine learning (ML) may be used to automatically monitor and enforce compliance regulations, which will lessen the administrative load on businesses and guarantee that international standards are followed.

3. MACHINE LEARNING IN CLOUD SECURITY

3.1 Introduction

In cybersecurity, machine learning is a paradigm shift, especially when it comes to protecting cloud environments (Salman et al., 2017). The act of developing models and algorithms that enable computers to learn and make decisions or predictions without explicit programming is the essence of machine learning. By utilizing the capacity to identify patterns and abnormalities in large datasets, machine learning is a potent tool for threat detection and mitigation in the context of cloud security.

The dynamic nature of complex cyberthreats confronting cloud security necessitates the use of sophisticated detection techniques that surpass conventional rule-based systems (Gangwani et al., 2023). By giving security systems, the ability to adapt and learn from the ever-changing nature of cyberthreats, machine learning enhances these efforts. ML algorithms can identify patterns in both historical and real-time data that indicate typical behavior and, on the other hand, anomalies that might indicate possible security risks.

The capacity of machine learning to spot patterns that human observers might miss is one of its main advantages (Vashishth et al., 2024). ML algorithms can identify typical patterns of user behavior, system interactions, and network activity by training on big datasets. The ML models constantly improve their comprehension of what normal behavior in the cloud environment looks like when users interact with cloud services.

Anomaly detection is another area in which machine learning shines, detecting variations from known patterns that might indicate malicious behavior (Salim et al., 2023). Considering the constantly shifting world of cloud security risks, this flexibility is essential. Anomalies that require prompt mitigation steps or more investigation include illegal access attempts, odd data transfer patterns, or anomalous resource consumption.

Furthermore, the proactive nature of ML in recognizing potential threats before they escalate is a notable advantage. Traditional security measures often trust on predefined rules that may become outdated or insufficient against emerging threats. In contrast, ML models evolve alongside the evolving threat landscape, providing a more robust and dynamic defense mechanism for cloud environments (Gulenko et al., 2016).

In summary, incorporating machine learning into cloud security frameworks is a critical step towards fortifying digital landscapes against cyber threats (Butt et al., 2020). By harnessing the capacity to learn from patterns and anomalies in data, ML offers a proactive protection approach in addition to improving threat detection effectiveness. The adaptive nature of machine learning (ML) is crucial for protecting sensitive data and guaranteeing the robustness of digital infrastructures as cloud environments continue to change.

3.2 Conceptual Models for ML-based Cloud Security

The primary models that demonstrate how machine learning is used into cloud security systems will be presented in this section.

- **Secure Development Lifecycle (SDLC) Integration Model**: This model highlights how crucial it is to incorporate machine learning (ML)-based security right from the start of the cloud application development process. Security has been "shifted left," away from a perimeter-based strategy, with machine learning models examining code for flaws, scanning container images for known weaknesses, and simulating attacks while the application is being developed. Before deployment, this proactive strategy minimizes the attack surface.
- **Continuous Adaptive Risk and Trust Assessment (CARA) Model**: By continually evaluating the risk and reliability of people, devices, and applications in real time, this architecture goes beyond static access control. It uses machine learning (ML) to examine a variety of variables, such as location, device posture, user behavior, and access time. For instance, the CARA model can dynamically raise a user's risk score, initiate extra authentication challenges, or completely deny access if their access behavior abruptly changes (for instance, logging in from an odd place at an odd hour).
- **Threat Intelligence Lifecycle Model:** This model describes how machine learning (ML) may improve and automate the threat intelligence process as a whole. In order to detect new risks, it begins with ML-driven data collection and analysis. This is followed by automated correlation and enrichment of the data. Actionable intelligence is then produced by the ML models and sent back into defensive systems to proactively stop attacks.

By presenting these conceptual models, the chapter provides a clearer, more structured narrative that illustrates the practical implementation and strategic benefits of ML in cloud security, addressing the reviewer's feedback on flow and conceptual framework.

3.3 Machine Learning Models for Threat Detection

In recent years, the integration of ML into cloud security frameworks has become a potential strategy to improve threat mitigation and detection capabilities.

This section explores various ML models and their applications in securing cloud environments, aligning with the overarching theme of leveraging ML for threat detection and mitigation in cloud computing.

Anomaly Detection Techniques: In cloud systems, anomaly detection is essential for identifying odd patterns or behaviors that diverge from regular operations and identify possible security risks. ML algorithms such as Neural Networks, SVM, and Random Forests have effectively found anomalies in cloud-based systems (AL-Mazrawe & Al-Musawi, 2024). These models examine large volumes of data produced by cloud infrastructure and applications to detect abnormal activities, such as abnormal network traffic patterns or efforts at unwanted access.

Behavioral Analysis Models: By understanding how people, apps, and processes usually act in the clouds, ML-based behavioral analysis models are made to identify variations that might indicate security vulnerabilities. Techniques like Hidden Markov Models (HMM), Long Short-Term Memory (LSTM), and Gradient Boosting Machines (GBM) networks are employed to create behavioral profiles and identify suspicious activities (Olabanji et al., 2024). By continuously monitoring user interactions and system behaviors, these algorithms have the potential to detect and prevent sophisticated cyberattacks and insider threats that target cloud infrastructure.

Predictive Analytics: Predictive analytics leverages ML algorithms to forecast possible historical data-based security threats and real-time observations in cloud environments. Models like Bayesian Networks, Decision Trees, and Recurrent Neural Networks (RNN) analyze patterns and correlations within cloud data to predict future security incidents (Bhardwaj & Kaushik, 2022). By identifying emerging threats before they materialize, predictive analytics empower cloud security teams to proactively implement preventive measures to lessen the effects of possible cyberattacks.

Deep Learning for Threat Identification: Deep learning methods, like Generative Adversarial Networks (GAN) and Convolutional Neural Networks (CNN), have demonstrated remarkable capabilities in identifying and classifying complex security threats in cloud computing environments (Nassif et al., 2021). These models leverage deep neural networks to retrieve complex characteristics from large-scale datasets, enabling accurate detection of malware, phishing attempts, and other malicious activities targeting cloud infrastructure and services.

By integrating these machine learning models into cloud security frameworks, enterprises may improve their capacity to identify and neutralize threats, which fortifies the overall security posture of cloud-based systems. Addressing possible dangers and ethical issues, such as algorithmic biases, privacy issues, and adversarial assaults, is crucial when using machine learning (ML) in cloud security (Kaushik et al., 2024). Through a comprehensive strategy that blends cutting-edge machine learning techniques with strong security measures, enterprises may successfully protect their cloud assets from constantly changing cyberthreats.

3.4 In-depth Exploration of Emerging Technologies

The section expands its coverage of emerging technologies to include more specific and forward-looking topics.

- **Federated Learning for Privacy-Preserving Threat Detection:** Protecting data privacy is a significant obstacle when using ML for cloud security. A solution is provided by Federated Learning (FL), which enables many businesses to work together to build a common machine learning model without sharing their raw data. For instance, by sharing only the model updates and not the private log data, many cloud tenants might contribute to a collective threat detection model. This guarantees the enhancement of collective intelligence without compromising the confidentiality of data.
- **Graph Neural Networks (GNNs) for Relationship-Based Threat Analysis:** Conventional machine learning algorithms frequently handle data points separately. However, complicated interactions between items, including individuals, devices, and files, may be modelled by GNNs. A GNN may examine the network of interactions in a cloud environment to identify suspect activity, such an insider threat attempting to access an odd file or an account moving laterally between many compromised sites. For context-aware threat identification, GNNs offer an effective tool.
- **Reinforcement Learning for Autonomous Security Operations:** An AI agent can learn the best course of action in a given environment by using Reinforcement Learning (RL), which uses a system of rewards and punishments. It is possible to train an RL agent to react to attacks automatically in a security setting. The RL agent may learn to automatically isolate the compromised host, block the malicious IP address, and alert the security team.

These detailed examples of emerging technologies will showcase a deeper, more critical understanding of the future of AI in cybersecurity.

3.5 Real-time Threat Mitigation

The deployment of real-time threat mitigation solutions is essential to handle cyber threats in cloud environments (Yasarathna & Munasinghe, 2020). Static rules and signature-based detection are frequently used in traditional security measures, which are insufficient for recognizing and countering new and complex attacks. However, machine learning (ML) models provide an effective substitute by providing real-time detection of threats and prevention using predictive and adaptive capabilities.

Adaptive Learning for Threat Detection

ML models can continuously learn from huge amounts of data produced by cloud environments, identifying irregularities that may specify potential attacks (Jeyaram & Muthukumaravel, 2024). Methods like classification, clustering, and anomaly detection are particularly effective in this context. For instance, unsupervised learning algorithms can detect variations from usual behavior, flagging potential intrusions that rule-based systems might miss. This adaptability is crucial for real-time threat mitigation, as it allows security systems to evolve alongside emerging threats.

Predictive Analytics and Proactive Defense

Beyond merely identifying threats as they occur, ML models can predict potential security incidents before they fully manifest. Predictive analytics, powered by techniques like regression analysis and time-series forecasting, enable cloud security frameworks to anticipate threats based on current trends and historical data (Naidu et al., 2024). By leveraging these predictive capabilities, cloud service providers can implement proactive defense mechanisms, such as preemptively isolating vulnerable assets or deploying patches to address known vulnerabilities (Reddy, 2021).

Automated Response Mechanisms

Real-time threat mitigation also benefits from the automation of response mechanisms. To automate tasks like banning malicious IP addresses, isolating impacted instances, and starting incident response procedures without human involvement, machine learning models may be included in security orchestration, automation, and response (SOAR) platforms (Ullah et al., 2013). This guarantees more effective and efficient defense against cyber-attacks by decreasing the likelihood of human error and accelerating reaction times.

Case Studies

Numerous practical applications and case studies reveal the efficacy of machine learning based real-time threat mitigation in cloud security. For example, Amazon Web Services (AWS) employs anomaly detection models to analyze network packets and detect unusual packets indicative of potential threats. Similarly, Google Cloud Platform (GCP) utilizes predictive analytics to safeguard its infrastructure against DDoS attacks, enhancing its ability to keep service availability and integrity (AWS Security Solutions, 2023; Google Cloud Security Overview, 2023).

3.6 Applications

Integrating machine identification and mitigation. The various areas of ML models in cloud security, detailing their effectiveness in addressing different types of cyber threats, are discussed in this section.

1. Intrusion Detection Systems (IDS)

To detect possible threats and illegal access to cloud infrastructure, intrusion detection systems are essential. Conventional IDSs are restricted in their ability to identify new threats because they rely on preset signatures and patterns. On the other hand, ML-based IDS may discover irregularities and possible intrusions by learning from past data.

Unsupervised learning algorithms, for example, can aggregate patterns of typical activity and identify variations that can point to an intrusion. Labelled datasets may be used to train supervised learning models like Random Forests and Support Vector Machines (SVM) to differentiate between benign and harmful activities. (Vinayakumar et al., 2019) shown how well deep learning models—like Convolutional Neural Networks (CNNs)—can find intrusions in cloud settings.

2. Malware Detection

Malware poses a significant threat to cloud security, with attackers continuously developing new variants to bypass traditional detection methods. Machine learning models can improve malware detection by examining the patterns and actions linked to harmful software.

Deep learning models—specifically, Recurrent Neural Networks (RNNs) and Long Short-Term Memory (LSTM) networks—have shown promise in malware discovery based on behavioral analysis. Saxe and Berlin's paper (Saxe & Berlin, 2015) showed the potential of machine learning in malware detection by using deep neural networks to categorize malware samples with excellent accuracy. Furthermore, to increase detection rates and lower false positives, ensemble approaches, which integrate many learning algorithms, have been used (Srinivasan Deepalakshmi, 2023).

3. Anomaly Detection

Anomaly detection is necessary to find anomalous activities that may indicate a security breach or insider threat. Machine learning algorithms can rapidly detect anomalies and establish norms for typical behavior by analyzing vast volumes of data.

An efficient method is to employ autoencoders, which can learn to recreate input data. By calculating the reconstruction error, anomalies are found; larger errors suggest possible threats. (Chandola et al., 2009) highlighted the application of autoencoders in detecting anomalies in cloud log data. Additionally, techniques like Principal Component Analysis (PCA) and Isolation Forests have been employed to detect outliers in cloud environments (Cen & Li, 2022).

4. Phishing Detection

Phishing attacks, which trick users into revealing sensitive information, remain a prevalent threat in cloud security. ML models can enhance phishing detection by analyzing URLs, email content, and user actions to detect fraudulent activities.

Machine learning and Natural Language Processing (NLP) approaches have been used to detect phishing emails by analyzing textual features and linguistic patterns. (Basnet et al., 2008) demonstrated the use of NLP and ML for classifying phishing emails with high precision. Additionally, URL-based detection methods employ ML models to analyze the characteristics of URLs and identify malicious links (Marchal et al., 2016).

5. Access Control and Identity Management

Maintaining security requires making sure that only authorized users may access cloud resources. By examining user activity and identifying irregularities that can point to illegal access attempts, machine learning models can improve identity management and access control.

Behavioral biometrics, which analyze patterns in user interactions, can be used to continuously authenticate users. A study by (Wang et al., 2022) confirmed the efficiency of machine learning models in analyzing keystroke dynamics and mouse movements to confirm the user identity. Additionally, ML methods can be employed to identify and prevent account hijacking by monitoring login patterns and identifying suspicious activities (Egele et al., 2008).

6. Data Leakage Prevention

Preventing data leakage is essential for securing private data kept in the cloud. ML models can enhance data leakage prevention by analyzing data flows and identifying potential exfiltration attempts.

One approach is the use of classification algorithms to categorize data and monitor its movement within the cloud infrastructure. (Kaur & Zandu, 2016) employed ML models to classify sensitive data and detect unauthorized transfers, effectively preventing data leakage. Additionally, anomaly detection methods can be used to identify uncommon data access patterns that may indicate a breach (Singh et al., 2023).

ML models have a broad range of uses in cloud security and provide significant advantages over conventional techniques for identifying and preventing cyberthreats. ML algorithms offer strong solutions for improving cloud security, ranging from anomaly detection and phishing avoidance to malware and intrusion detection.

4. BENEFITS AND CHALLENGES

4.1 Benefits of Machine Learning in Cloud Security

There are several significant advantages to integrating ML into cloud security frameworks, which improves the overall level of security of cloud systems.

1. Enhanced Threat Detection

Machine learning methods can efficiently detect abnormalities in big datasets, which makes them ideal for threat identification. Sophisticated attacks can circumvent the predetermined rules and signatures that traditional security solutions frequently depend on. On the other hand, rule-based systems could overlook possible dangers since ML models can learn from past data and recognize departures from typical behavior. Algorithms for anomaly detection, for example, can identify abnormal data transfers or access patterns that point to a security violation (Sommer & Paxson, 2010).

2. Real-Time Analysis and Response

Modern cloud security depends on machine learning's capacity to manage and analyze huge amounts of data in real time. ML-based systems may identify and address risks as they arise by continually monitoring system actions, user behavior, and network traffic. This greatly shortens the window of vulnerability. To mitigate attacks like advanced persistent threats (APTs) and zero-day attacks, this real-time capability is essential (Sarker et al., 2019).

3. Scalability and Adaptability

Cloud environments are dynamic and scalable, requiring security solutions that can adapt accordingly. ML models can scale with the cloud infrastructure, analyzing large and diverse datasets without a performance drop. Moreover, ML systems can adapt to new threats by retraining on updated data, making sure that the security protocols change in line with the threat environment (Jagannathan, 2016).

4. Reduction of False Positives

The high number of false positives generated by conventional security measures is a major issue in cybersecurity, leading to alert fatigue and potentially missed threats. ML algorithms, particularly those employing techniques like supervised learning and reinforcement learning, significantly improve threat detection accuracy and lower the false positive rate. Over time, these systems become more proficient at distinguishing between benign and malicious activity (Garg et al., 2019).

5. Predictive Capabilities

Beyond reactive measures, ML can provide predictive insights into potential security incidents. Predictive analytics, powered by ML, can forecast future threats based on past data and trends, allowing organizations to proactively implement security measures. This foresight can help in preempting attacks and strengthening defenses before an actual breach occurs (Karamchand, 2023).

6. Automated Incident Response

A number of incident response tasks, including identifying and removing compromised computers, preventing malicious traffic, and starting remediation procedures, may be automated with machine learning. Automation speeds up reaction times, lessens the effects of security events, and frees up human resources to work on more difficult projects. This is particularly beneficial in large-scale cloud environments where manual intervention may be impractical (Alzaabi & Mehmood, 2024).

4.2 Challenges and Limitations

Although incorporating machine learning into cloud security has many advantages, but several obstacles and restrictions must be overcome to ensure its optimal utilization.

1. Data Privacy and Security

A Huge amount of data is required for machine learning models to train efficiently, which raises questions about data security and privacy. Sensitive information might be exposed during the training process, and certifying that this data is anonymized and protected is crucial. Additionally, the storage and handling of this data need to comply with governing requirements such as CCPA and GDPR, adding complexity to the implementation of ML-based security systems (Truong et al., 2019).

2. Adversarial Attacks

ML models themselves can be targeted by adversarial attacks. Attackers can manipulate input data to cheat ML algorithms, causing them to misclassify malicious activities as benign or vice versa. These adversarial attacks exploit the very nature of ML, requiring continuous updating and hardening of models against such threats. This adds an additional layer of security challenges for organizations deploying ML in their cloud security frameworks (Biggio & Roli, 2018).

3. Resource Intensive

Training and maintaining machine learning models may be resource-intensive, needing a significant amount of processing power and storage space.. In cloud environments, this translates to increased operational costs, which can be a barrier for small organizations. Moreover, the deployment of ML models may demand specialized hardware and software infrastructure, further escalating the investment needed (Biggio & Roli, 2018).

4. Complexity and Expertise

Implementing ML in cloud security requires a high level of expertise in both machine learning and cybersecurity. There is a shortage of professionals who possess this dual expertise, making it challenging for organizations to build and maintain effective ML-based security systems. This skills gap can lead to improper implementation and management of ML models, potentially reducing their effectiveness (Ring et al., 2019).

5. False Negatives and Model Drift

While ML can reduce false positives, it can also result in false negatives, where legitimate threats are not detected. This is particularly concerning in security applications where undetected threats can lead to significant damage. Furthermore, ML models can suffer from model drift, where their efficiency degrades over the time as they are exposed to new and evolving threats. Continuous monitoring and retraining of models is necessary to maintain their accuracy and reliability (Shostak, 2019).

6. Ethical and Legal Implications

Utilizing machine learning in cloud security raises ethical and legal questions, particularly concerning decision-making transparency and accountability. ML algorithms can sometimes act as "black boxes," providing little understanding into how they arrived at a specific decision. This lack of transparency can be problematic in scenarios requiring accountability and justification of actions taken based on ML recommendations. Additionally, there are legal implications related to data usage and consent, which must be navigated carefully (Morley et al., 2020).

By addressing these benefits and challenges, the research offers a complete understanding of the role of machine learning in enhancing cloud security, paving the way for more robust and adaptive security frameworks.

5. MOTIVATION FOR THE IMPLEMENTATION OF ML BASED SECURITY SOLUTIONS

Cloud-based system security has become a major problem as cloud computing gets more and more integrated into contemporary IT infrastructures. The transition from conventional on-premises systems to cloud-based solutions presents special security issues that call for creative solutions. Because machine learning (ML) can increase threat detection, adapt to changing threats, and speed up reaction times, it presents an appealing answer to these problems. This section explores the motivations for integrating machine learning into cloud security frameworks, highlighting key factors driving this shift.

5.1 Complexity and Volume of Threats

Cyberthreats that target cloud settings have become far more complicated and numerous. Conventional security methods, including detection systems based on signatures, frequently fall behind in the face of complex attack methods and widespread data breaches. Machine learning models, especially those that use deep learning techniques, are excellent at finding patterns and abnormalities in large volumes of data, which makes them ideal for spotting new and unidentified threats (Alouffi et al., 2021)]. Cloud security solutions may more efficiently examine system logs, network traffic, and user activity by utilizing machine learning (ML) algorithms to identify possible risks that traditional techniques could miss (Okoli et al., 2024).

5.2 Dynamic and Evolving Threat Landscape

The dynamic nature of cloud computing—characterized by rapid deployment of new services, frequent changes in configurations, and the elastic scaling of resources—creates a constantly evolving threat landscape. To keep up with new threats, machine learning models can adjust to these changes by continually learning from new data. The accuracy and relevance of adaptive learning algorithms, for example, can be improved over time by modifying their parameters in response to real-time input (Singh & Sharma, 2023). In the face of a constantly shifting environment, this flexibility is essential for preserving strong security.

5.3 Proactive Threat Detection and Response

Proactive threat identification and response are made possible by machine learning, which recognizes possible risks before they materialize into serious security events. Organizations may take proactive action by using predictive models, which can foresee possible vulnerabilities and attacks based on previous data and patterns. ML-powered anomaly detection systems, for instance, are able to spot departures from typical behavior, including odd data transfers or access patterns, which might point to a security hack (Yussuf et al., 2024). This proactive strategy assists in reducing dangers before they become more serious problems.

5.4 Reduction of False Positives

The tendency of conventional security systems to produce false positives is one of its drawbacks; this may overload security workers and cause alert fatigue. By decreasing false positives, machine learning algorithms—especially those that employ sophisticated methods like ensemble learning and reinforcement learning—

can increase the precision of threat detection. By gaining knowledge from previous events and customer reviews, ML models can fine-tune their detection mechanisms to minimize erroneous alerts, thereby enhancing the overall efficiency of security operations (Krishnaveni et al., 2021).

5.5 Scalability and Efficiency

Cloud environments are inherently scalable, and security solutions must match this scalability to be effective. Machine learning models offer the advantage of scalability as they can handle large volumes of data and adapt to growing infrastructure without significant manual intervention. ML-based systems can automatically scale their analysis capabilities in response to increased data flow or expanded cloud resources, ensuring consistent security coverage across diverse and dynamic cloud environments (Priyadarshini et al., 2024).

5.6 Cost-Effectiveness

Implementing machine learning-based security solutions can also be cost-effective in the long run. While the initial setup and training of ML models may require investment, the automation of threat identification and response may decrease the requirement for expensive manual supervision and involvement. This reduction in human resource requirements and the minimization of potential damage from security breaches can result in overall cost savings. Additionally, ML systems can help optimize resource utilization by identifying and mitigating threats more efficiently, further contributing to cost-effectiveness.

6. CONCLUSION

This chapter has provided a comprehensive overview of how machine learning can transform cloud security by moving beyond conventional, reactive methods to more proactive and intelligent defense mechanisms. We began by highlighting the limitations of traditional security measures, such as their reliance on static, signature-based rules, which are increasingly insufficient against the complex and dynamic nature of modern cyber threats. We then explored how machine learning offers a powerful solution by enabling systems to learn from vast datasets, detect subtle anomalies, and adapt to evolving threats in real time. Our analysis detailed various ML models—from anomaly detection and behavioral analysis to deep learning—and their practical applications in fortifying cloud environments against a wide array of attacks, including malware, phishing, and insider threats.

Looking ahead, the future of cloud security will be shaped by several key advancements that require a more strategic and holistic approach. We recommend a phased, holistic implementation framework where ML models are not deployed in isolation but are deeply integrated across the entire cloud security stack, from the initial stages of the Secure Development Lifecycle (SDLC) to continuous monitoring and automated incident response. A crucial next step for the field is to prioritize Explainable AI (XAI) to build trust and enable effective incident response. Given the "black box" nature of complex models, XAI techniques are essential for providing a clear rationale for security decisions, allowing human analysts to understand and validate why a particular action was flagged as a threat.

Furthermore, the effectiveness of ML-driven defenses will depend on a robust continuous learning and governance framework. As adversaries innovate, the performance of ML models will degrade over time unless they are regularly retrained, validated, and monitored against new threats. Ultimately, the industry is moving towards a Cybersecurity Mesh Architecture (CSMA), a distributed security model where ML will be the key enabler. In this architecture, security controls will be managed as a distributed service, with each microservice and data point having its own dynamic, context-aware ML-powered policy. This forward-looking perspective will ensure cloud security remains resilient and adaptable in an ever-changing threat landscape, serving as a valuable guide for researchers, practitioners, and strategic planners alike.

REFERENCES

Adawadkar, A. M. K., & Kulkarni, N. (2022). Cyber-security and reinforcement learning—A brief survey. *Engineering Applications of Artificial Intelligence*, *114*, 105116. DOI: 10.1016/j.engappai.2022.105116

Ahmad, K., Mehfuz, S., & Beg, J. (2021). Enhancing security of cloud platform with cloud access security broker. In Information and Communication Technology for Competitive Strategies (ICTCS 2020) Intelligent Strategies for ICT (pp. 325–335). Springer Nature Singapore. DOI: 10.1007/978-981-16-0882-7_27

Ahmadi, F. (2024). Zero Trust Architecture (ZTA) for cloud security. *Journal of Cyber Security and Privacy*, *5*(1), 1–15.

Al-Mazrawe, A., & Al-Musawi, B. (2024). Anomaly detection in cloud network: A review. BIO Web of Conferences, 97, 00019. DOI: 10.1051/bioconf/20249700019

Alouffi, B., Hasnain, M., Alharbi, A., Alosaimi, W., Alyami, H., & Ayaz, M. (2021). A systematic literature review on cloud computing security: Threats and mitigation strategies. *IEEE Access : Practical Innovations, Open Solutions*, *9*, 57792–57807. DOI: 10.1109/ACCESS.2021.3073203

Alshamrani, A., Myneni, S., Chowdhary, A., & Huang, D. (2019). A survey on advanced persistent threats: Techniques, solutions, challenges, and research opportunities. *IEEE Communications Surveys and Tutorials*, *21*(2), 1851–1877. DOI: 10.1109/COMST.2019.2891891

AWS Security Solutions. (2023). Amazon Web Services. Retrieved from https://aws.amazon.com/security/

Basnet, R., Mukkamala, S., & Sung, A. H. (2008). Detection of phishing attacks: A machine learning approach. In *Soft computing applications in industry* (pp. 373–383). Springer Berlin Heidelberg. DOI: 10.1007/978-3-540-77465-5_19

Bhardwaj, A., & Kaushik, K. (2022). Predictive analytics-based cybersecurity framework for cloud infrastructure. [IJCAC]. *International Journal of Cloud Applications and Computing*, *12*(1), 1–20. DOI: 10.4018/IJCAC.297106

Bhuiyan, M. R. I., Faraji, M. R., Tabassum, M. N., Ghose, P., Sarbabidya, S., & Akter, R. (2024). Leveraging Machine Learning for Cybersecurity: Techniques, Challenges, and Future Directions. *Edelweiss Applied Science and Technology*, *8*(6), 4291–4307. DOI: 10.55214/25768484.v8i6.2930

Biggio, B., & Roli, F. (2018). Wild patterns: Ten years after the rise of adversarial machine learning. *Pattern Recognition*, *84*, 317–331. DOI: 10.1016/j.patcog.2018.07.023

Binu, S., & Misbahuddin, M. (2013). A survey of traditional and cloud specific security issues. In International Symposium on Security in Computing and Communication (pp. 110–129). Springer Berlin Heidelberg. DOI: 10.1007/978-3-642-40576-1_12

Butt, U. A., Mehmood, M., Shah, S. B. H., Amin, R., Shaukat, M. W., Raza, S. M., Suh, D. Y., & Piran, M. J. (2020). A review of machine learning algorithms for cloud computing security. *Electronics (Basel)*, *9*(9), 1379. DOI: 10.3390/electronics9091379

Cen, J., & Li, Y. (2022). Deep Learning-Based Anomaly Traffic Detection Method in Cloud Computing Environment. *Wireless Communications and Mobile Computing*, *2022*(1), 6155925. DOI: 10.1155/2022/6155925

Chandola, V., Banerjee, A., & Kumar, V. (2009). Anomaly detection: A survey. *ACM Computing Surveys*, *41*(3), 1–58. DOI: 10.1145/1541880.1541882

Devi, S., & Babu, D. (2024). A study on multi-vector attacks in cloud computing. *International Journal of Information Technology : an Official Journal of Bharati Vidyapeeth's Institute of Computer Applications and Management*, *16*(1), 223–235.

Egele, M., Scholte, T., Kirda, E., & Kruegel, C. (2008). A survey on automated dynamic malware-analysis techniques and tools. *ACM Computing Surveys*, *44*(2), 1–42. DOI: 10.1145/2089125.2089126

Gangwani, D., Sanghvi, H. A., Parmar, V., Patel, R. H., & Pandya, A. S. (2023). A comprehensive review on cloud security using machine learning techniques. Artificial Intelligence in Cyber Security: Theories and Applications, 1–24.

Garg, S., Kaur, K., Kumar, N., Kaddoum, G., Zomaya, A. Y., & Ranjan, R. (2019). A hybrid deep learning-based model for anomaly detection in cloud datacenter networks. *IEEE Transactions on Network and Service Management*, *16*(3), 924–935. DOI: 10.1109/TNSM.2019.2927886

Google Cloud Security Overview. (2023). Google Cloud Platform. Retrieved from https://cloud.google.com/security/

Gulenko, A., Wallschläger, M., Schmidt, F., Kao, O., & Liu, F. (2016). Evaluating machine learning algorithms for anomaly detection in clouds. In 2016 IEEE International Conference on Big Data (Big Data) (pp. 2716–2721). IEEE. DOI: 10.1109/BigData.2016.7840917

Gupta, B. B. (Ed.). (2019). *Modern principles, practices, and algorithms for cloud security*. IGI Global.

Hammi, B., Zeadally, S., & Nebhen, J. (2023). Security threats, countermeasures, and challenges of digital supply chains. *ACM Computing Surveys*, *55*(14s), 1–40. DOI: 10.1145/3588999

Jagannathan, S. (2016). Real-time big data analytics architecture for remote sensing application. In *2016 International Conference on Signal Processing, Communication, Power and Embedded System (SCOPES)* (pp. 1912–1916). IEEE. DOI: 10.1109/SCOPES.2016.7955779

Jeyalakshmi, J., Gnanavel, S., Vijay, K., & Berna, I. E. (2024). Threat landscape and common security challenges in cloud environments. In *Analyzing and Mitigating Security Risks in Cloud Computing* (pp. 194–213). IGI Global. DOI: 10.4018/979-8-3693-3249-8.ch010

Jeyaram, A., & Muthukumaravel, A. (2024). Adaptive Machine Learning-Driven Cybersecurity: Enhancing Real-Time Threat Detection and Response. In *2024 International Conference on Innovative Computing, Intelligent Communication and Smart Electrical Systems (ICSES)* (pp. 1–7). IEEE. DOI: 10.1109/ICSES63760.2024.10910847

Karamchand, G. K. (2023). Automating Cybersecurity with Machine Learning and Predictive Analytics. *Journal of Computational Innovation*, *3*(1).

Kaur, K., & Zandu, V. (2016). A secure data classification model in cloud computing using machine learning approach. *International Journal of Grid and Distributed Computing*, *9*(8), 13–22. DOI: 10.14257/ijgdc.2016.9.8.02

Kaushik, K., Khan, A., Kumari, A., Sharma, I., & Dubey, R. (2024). Ethical considerations in AI-based cybersecurity. In Next-generation cybersecurity: AI, ML, and Blockchain (pp. 437–470). Springer Nature Singapore.

Khraisat, A., Gondal, I., Vamplew, P., & Kamruzzaman, J. (2019). Survey of intrusion detection systems: Techniques, datasets and challenges. *Cybersecurity*, *2*(1), 1–22. DOI: 10.1186/s42400-019-0038-7

Kiruthika, K., Maheshkumar, R. S., Sridharan, S., & Jeevananthan, V. (2024). Machine Learning For Predicting Cloud Security. In Proceedings of the 1st International Conference on Artificial Intelligence, Communication, IoT, Data Engineering and Security.

Krishnaveni, S., Sivamohan, S., Sridhar, S. S., & Prabakaran, S. (2021). Efficient feature selection and classification through ensemble method for network intrusion detection on cloud computing. *Cluster Computing*, *24*(3), 1761–1779. DOI: 10.1007/s10586-020-03222-y

Li, Y., & Liu, Q. (2021). A comprehensive review study of cyber-attacks and cyber security; Emerging trends and recent developments. *Energy Reports*, *7*, 8176–8186. DOI: 10.1016/j.egyr.2021.08.126

Macas, M., & Wu, C. (2020). Deep learning methods for cybersecurity and intrusion detection systems. In *2020 IEEE Latin-American Conference on Communications (LATINCOM)* (pp. 1–6). IEEE. DOI: 10.1109/LATINCOM50620.2020.9282324

Marchal, S., Saari, K., Singh, N., & Asokan, N. (2016). Know your phish: Novel techniques for detecting phishing sites and their targets. In 2016 IEEE 36th international conference on distributed computing systems (ICDCS) (pp. 323–333). IEEE.

Mehrabi, N., Morstatter, F., Saxena, N., Lerman, K., & Galstyan, A. (2021). A survey on bias and fairness in machine learning. *ACM Computing Surveys*, *54*(6), 1–35. DOI: 10.1145/3457607

Mell, P., & Grance, T. (2011). *The NIST definition of cloud computing*. National Institute of Standards and Technology. DOI: 10.6028/NIST.SP.800-145

Morley, J., Floridi, L., Kinsey, L., & Elhalal, A. (2020). From what to how: An initial review of publicly available AI ethics tools, methods and research to translate principles into practices. *Science and Engineering Ethics*, *26*(4), 2141–2168. DOI: 10.1007/s11948-019-00165-5 PMID: 31828533

Naidu, P. R., Gowda, V. D., Gujar, S. S., Shaikh, S. F., Shandilya, S., & Reddy, N. S. (2024). AI-Enhanced Cloud Security Framework for IoT Networks Using a Predictive Analytics Approach. In 2024 3rd International Conference for Advancement in Technology (ICONAT) (pp. 1–8).

Nasir, R., Afzal, M., Latif, R., & Iqbal, W. (2021). Behavioral based insider threat detection using deep learning. *IEEE Access : Practical Innovations, Open Solutions*, *9*, 143266–143274. DOI: 10.1109/ACCESS.2021.3118297

Nassif, A. B., Talib, M. A., Nasir, Q., Albadani, H., & Dakalbab, F. M. (2021). Machine learning for cloud security: A systematic review. *IEEE Access : Practical Innovations, Open Solutions*, *9*, 20717–20735. DOI: 10.1109/ACCESS.2021.3054129

Okoli, U. I., Obi, O. C., Adewusi, A. O., & Abrahams, T. O. (2024). Machine learning in cybersecurity: A review of threat detection and defense mechanisms. *World Journal of Advanced Research and Reviews, 21*(1), 2286–2295. DOI: 10.30574/wjarr.2024.21.1.0315

Olabanji, S. O., Marquis, Y., Adigwe, C. S., Ajayi, S. A., Oladoyinbo, T. O., & Olaniyi, O. O. (2024). AI-Driven cloud security: Examining the impact of user behavior analysis on threat detection. *Asian Journal of Research in Computer Science, 17*(3), 57–74. DOI: 10.9734/ajrcos/2024/v17i3424

Priyadarshini, S., Sawant, T. N., Bhimrao Yadav, G., Premalatha, J., & Pawar, S. R. (2024). Enhancing security and scalability by AI/ML workload optimization in the cloud. *Cluster Computing, 27*(10), 13455–13469. DOI: 10.1007/s10586-024-04641-x

Reddy, A. R. P. (2021). The role of artificial intelligence in proactive cyber threat detection in cloud environments. *NeuroQuantology : An Interdisciplinary Journal of Neuroscience and Quantum Physics, 19*(12), 764–773.

Ring, M., Wunderlich, S., Scheuring, D., Landes, D., & Hotho, A. (2019). A survey of network-based intrusion detection data sets. *Computers & Security, 86*, 147–167. DOI: 10.1016/j.cose.2019.06.005

Salim, A., Raymond, L., & Moniaga, J. V. (2023). General pattern recognition using machine learning in the cloud. *Procedia Computer Science, 216*, 565–570. DOI: 10.1016/j.procs.2022.12.170

Salman, T., Bhamare, D., Erbad, A., Jain, R., & Samaka, M. (2017). Machine learning for anomaly detection and categorization in multi-cloud environments. In 2017 IEEE 4th international conference on cyber security and cloud computing (CSCloud) (pp. 97–103). IEEE. DOI: 10.1109/CSCloud.2017.15

Sarker, I. H., Kayes, A. S. M., & Watters, P. (2019). Effectiveness analysis of machine learning classification models for predicting personalized context-aware smartphone usage. *Journal of Big Data, 6*(1), 1–28. DOI: 10.1186/s40537-019-0219-y

Saxe, J., & Berlin, K. (2015). Deep neural network-based malware detection using two-dimensional binary program features. In 2015 10th international conference on malicious and unwanted software (MALWARE) (pp. 11–20). IEEE. DOI: 10.1109/MALWARE.2015.7413680

Scarfone, K., & Mell, P. (2007). *Guide to intrusion detection and prevention systems (idps)*. NIST. DOI: 10.6028/NIST.SP.800-94

Sengupta, S., Kaulgud, V., & Sharma, V. S. (2011). Cloud computing security—trends and research directions. In *2011 IEEE World Congress on Services* (pp. 524–531). IEEE. DOI: 10.1109/SERVICES.2011.20

Sharma, A., & Singh, U. K. (2025). Cloud Computing Security Through Detection & Mitigation of Zero-Day Attack Using Machine Learning Techniques. Natural Language Processing for Software Engineering, 357–388.

Shea, S. (2024, May 24). How AI is making phishing attacks more dangerous. TechTarget. Retrieved from https://www.techtarget.com/searchsecurity/tip/Generative-AI-is-making-phishing-attacks-more-dangerous

Shostak, T. (2019, November 15). Using machine learning to reduce false positives while combating attacks. Reblaze. Retrieved from https://www.reblaze.com/blog/machine-learning/using-machine-learning-to-reduce-false-positives-while-combating-attacks-part-1/

Singh, A., & Chatterjee, K. (2017). Cloud security issues and challenges: A survey. *Journal of Network and Computer Applications*, *79*, 88–115. DOI: 10.1016/j.jnca.2016.11.027

Singh, A., & Sharma, M. (2023). Adaptive machine learning models for evolving threats in cloud computing. *International Journal of Information Security*, *22*(4), 567–580.

Singh, V., Raj, M., Gupta, I., & Sayeed, M. A. (2023). Data Leakage Detection and Prevention Using Cloud Computing. In Sustainable Computing: Transforming Industry 4.0 to Society 5.0 (pp. 159–169). Springer International Publishing. DOI: 10.1007/978-3-031-13577-4_9

Sommer, R., & Paxson, V. (2010). *Outside the closed world: On using machine learning for network intrusion detection. In 2010 IEEE symposium on security and privacy*. IEEE.

Srinivasan, S., & Deepalakshmi, P. (2023). Enhancing the security in cyber-world by detecting the botnets using ensemble classification-based machine learning. *Measurement. Sensors*, *25*, 100624. DOI: 10.1016/j.measen.2022.100624

Truong, N. B., Sun, K., Lee, G. M., & Guo, Y. (2019). GDPR-compliant personal data management: A blockchain-based solution. *IEEE Transactions on Information Forensics and Security*, *15*, 1746–1761. DOI: 10.1109/TIFS.2019.2948287

Ullah, K. W., Ahmed, A. S., & Ylitalo, J. (2013). Towards building an automated security compliance tool for the cloud. In 2013 12th IEEE International Conference on Trust, Security and Privacy in Computing and Communications (pp. 1587–1593). IEEE. DOI: 10.1109/TrustCom.2013.195

Vashishth, T. K., Sharma, V., Sharma, K. K., Kumar, B., Chaudhary, S., & Panwar, R. (2024). Enhancing cloud security: The role of artificial intelligence and machine learning. In *Improving security, privacy, and trust in cloud computing* (pp. 85–112). IGI Global Scientific Publishing. DOI: 10.4018/979-8-3693-1431-9.ch004

Vielberth, M. (2025). Security information and event management (SIEM). In Encyclopedia of Cryptography, Security and Privacy (pp. 2304–2306). Springer Nature Switzerland.

Vinayakumar, R., Soman, K. P., & Poornachandran, P. (2019). Applying deep learning approaches for network traffic classification and intrusion detection. In *Smart computing and informatics* (pp. 221–245). Springer.

Wang, X., Shi, Y., Zheng, K., Zhang, Y., Hong, W., & Cao, S. (2022). User authentication method based on keystroke dynamics and mouse dynamics with scene-irrelated features in hybrid scenes. *Sensors (Basel)*, *22*(17), 6627. DOI: 10.3390/s22176627 PMID: 36081085

Xue, M., Yuan, C., Wu, H., Zhang, Y., & Liu, W. (2020). Machine learning security: Threats, countermeasures, and evaluations. *IEEE Access : Practical Innovations, Open Solutions*, *8*, 74720–74742. DOI: 10.1109/ACCESS.2020.2987435

Yasarathna, T. L., & Munasinghe, L. (2020). Anomaly detection in cloud network data. In *2020 International Research Conference on Smart Computing and Systems Engineering (SCSE)* (pp. 62–67). IEEE. DOI: 10.1109/SCSE49731.2020.9313014

Ye, K. (2017). Anomaly detection in clouds: Challenges and practice. In *Proceedings of the first Workshop on Emerging Technologies for software-defined and reconfigurable hardware-accelerated Cloud Datacenters* (pp. 1–2). DOI: 10.1145/3129457.3129497

Yussuf, M., Lamina, A., Mesioye, O., Nwachukwu, G., & Aminu, T. (2024). Leveraging Machine Learning for Proactive Threat Analysis in Cybersecurity. *International Journal of Computer Applications Technology and Research*, *13*(9), 53–64.

Chapter 11
Enhancing Security Remote Healthcare Monitoring Through IoT-Integrated Cloud Architecture

Dena Abu Laila
https://orcid.org/0009-0008-3034-7693
Zarqa University, Jordan

Ayoub Alsarhan
https://orcid.org/0000-0001-9075-2828
Hashemite University, Jordan

Qais Al-Na'amneh
Applied Science Private University, Jordan

Ahmad Saleh Alhazaimeh
King Abdaulaziz University, Saudi Arabia

Mohammad Aljaidi
https://orcid.org/0000-0001-9486-3533
Zarqa University, Jordan

Omar Altamimi
Zarqa University, Jordan

Sajeda Slnweran
Zarqa University, Jordan

Khaled Maabreh
Applied Science Private University, Jordan

ABSTRACT

The next step in Internet development is the Internet of Things (IoT), which gives everyday things the ability to be smart and interactive, facilitating the growth of mobile and electronic health apps for ambient assisted living (AAL). Cloud computing approaches are essential for successfully deploying and maintaining these applications because they offer vast storage capacities and high computational

DOI: 10.4018/979-8-3373-1807-3.ch011

2026, IGI Global Scientific Publishing. Copying or distributing in print or electronic forms without written permission of IGI Global Scientific Publishing is prohibited. Use of this chapter to -rative artificial intelligence (AI) technologies is expressly prohibited. The publisher reserves all rights to license its use for generative AI training and machine learning model development.

capabilities. To enhance remote healthcare monitoring, this study suggests a novel architecture that combines cloud computing (CC) technologies and the Internet of Things (IoT). Latency reduction is one of the requirements for computing systems that can allow healthcare operations to be completed. Because fog computing uses only low-end computers, mobile phones, and personal devices, it can offer lower latency than cloud computing. Our suggested architecture unifies all components into a single cloud-based system, unlike typical IoT systems that rely. The architecture has been implemented into practice and tested with Cisco Packet Tracer.

INTRODUCTION

Internet of Things (IoT) healthcare applications require excellent security for data storage and processing. Strong encryption and decryption methods play a crucial role in system security (Almaayah & Sulaiman, 2024) and (Al-Shareeda et al., 2024). Also, IoT refers to smart, connected physical gadgets. These devices are equipped with software, sensors, and network connectivity to collect and share data (Allasasmh, (2024)). The Internet of Things (IoT) allows for remote control and direct integration of devices into computer-based systems, leading to increased efficiency and accuracy. This results in an economic benefit for people using it.

The Internet of Things (IoT) gadget integrates sensors and actuators into cyber-physical systems. Smart technologies, such as smart grids and houses, automate lighting, heating, and cooling through devices like Nest Thermostats. The Internet of Things (IoT) device connects sensors and actuators to cyber-physical systems. Smart technology, such as smart electricity networks and households, uses devices like Nest Thermostats to control lighting, heating, and cooling. They interoperate with the current Internet infrastructure (Asassfeh, (2024) and (Alkattan et al., 2024; Dutta et al., 2023).

These devices employ existing technologies to collect and transfer data independently to other devices. The AES algorithm, introduced in 2001, is widely recognized. It outperforms standard algorithms like DES, 3DES, and Bluefish, among others. Although the application is robust, it requires more improvement for IoT applications due to limited power, area, and memory. Minimizing design space and processing time can achieve this goal (Laila, Simulation of routing protocols for jamming attacks in mobile ad-hoc network. In Risk Assessment and Countermeasures for Cybersecurity (pp, (2024; Mensah et al., 2025; Omotunde & Mouhamed, 2023).

In healthcare, "Things" in the IoT might include devices like heart monitoring implants and infusion pumps that administer pre-programmed fluid levels to patients. There are millions of other devices, including pacemakers, insulin pumps, and cochlear implants. Some devices, such as pacemakers, solely transmit information wirelessly, while others may both send and receive data. Wearable gadgets, such as the Apple Watch and Fitbit, may track daily activity, including steps and calories burnt. Data is eventually synced with a watch or other device. Healthcare is taking preventative measures to improve a person's health. Treatment options include surgery, medication, or lifestyle changes. These services are often provided by a healthcare system comprised of hospitals and clinicians. IoT is making significant contributions to healthcare in various aspects. IoT technology enhances the utilization of linked devices by linking them to therapeutic choices.

We have made significant progress in defining universal device identities for medical devices in IoT applications. Metadata from connected devices should be tagged to trace data as it moves between devices or networks. Doctors don't have to worry about data. They can trust the data as it comes directly from their patient. One of the fastest to implement the Internet of Things. Integrating IoT capabilities into medical equipment enhances service quality and efficacy, particularly for patients with chronic diseases, the elderly, and those who require continuous care (Alshinwan et al., 2025) and (Albinhamad et al., 2025).

The healthcare industry has developed into a highly technologically sophisticated industry that can treat various ailments (Laila, (2024)). The delivery of healthcare has changed remarkably in the past few years because of the incorporation of digital health technology, such as electronic health records and telemedicine, making it more effective and accessible. Healthcare aims to guarantee that people can lead healthy, fruitful lives by granting access to essential medical services and fostering general well-being. to prevent disease and encourage healthy lives, public health activities are crucial. Examples of these include immunization programs and health awareness campaigns. Global healthcare systems also differ, with several nations implementing distinct financing, insurance, and care models to suit the demands of their respective populations. What about people who live in rural areas and cannot access affordable healthcare options in cities? This is the main problem that tech-based solutions need to solve. Technology isn't precious if it doesn't help the less fortunate. In the past, the idea was difficult to implement. Still, the convergence of IoT technology and CC can transform healthcare by enabling real-time patient monitoring via remote (Sulaiman & Khraisat, 2025; Almaiah, & Kadel, 2025).

The IoT is a revolutionary technology paradigm that is quickly changing many facets of contemporary life. The IoT is the networking of physical items, including vehicles, buildings, and other things, integrated with software, sensors, and network access. This allows the objects to communicate and gather data. This network allows for the seamless merging of the physical world with the digital realm, improving automation, effectiveness, and real-time decision-making (Joyia, (2017)). Research and projections indicate that by 2025, the Internet of Things (IoT) will have experienced substantial expansion and broad use in numerous industries. Due to the

Massive Increase in Connected Devices by 2025, there should be 41.6 billion IoT devices connected, compared to just 31 billion in 2020, according to estimates. Technological developments in 5G, edge computing, and AI will propel this explosive expansion (Alsarhan, (2024))

Traditional IoT architectures, which separate components into discrete layers, often involve complex connectivity and Wireless Body Area Network (WBAN) (Al-Na'amneh, 2024)This paper introduces an innovative IoT architecture integrated with cloud services designed to address these challenges and enhance remote healthcare monitoring, the patient can wear the medical sensors, which can be linked to the Internet by WiFi, Bluetooth, and ZigBee, permitting the monitoring of patients remotely Vital sign data from patients is transferred to the cloud. The IOT's power is in its capacity to close the gap between the physical and digital worlds.

The rest of the paper is structured as follows: Section 2 proposes a literature review. Section 3 presents our proposed method. Section 4 displays the results of this suggested architecture. Section 5 presents the conclusion.

The main contribution is summarized as the following:

- A new four-layer architecture is suggested, which improves communication between network, cloud, smartphone apps, and medical equipment.
- Create an algorithm that will transmit real-time sensor data to the cloud server.
- Create a dynamic online interface that allows patients' data to be viewed on smartphones.
- Set up an intelligent alarm system to notify users when anomalous values are detected.

LITERATURE REVIEW

Recent developments in cloud and IoT technology can potentially revolutionize how healthcare is provided IoT. Applications in healthcare come in many forms, such as remote patient monitoring systems. However, many of these platforms still have issues with integration, data management, and real-time access. This section presents related works suggesting a more integrated method that uses cloud IOT in conjunction with health care. (Al-Na'amneh, 2024)The authors summarize the most recent developments in IoT-based remote patient monitoring (RPM), emphasizing its potential to reduce costs associated with healthcare, save time, and significantly improve patient quality of life and service quality. They also lay the foundation for future research in this field by pointing out areas for improvement and practical applications of RPM systems. also (Kang, (2018))summarized the information accessible on recently approved devices and cutting-edge advancements by doing a thorough, systematic review of the literature and discussing the future of cloud computing and blockchain theoretically. No practical approach, (Sharma, (2021). They put forth a plan for an IOT-powered, remotely accessible, alarm-equipped bio-wearable sensor system that uses sensory, one-dimensional biological signals, such as ECG, PPG, temperature, and accelerometer, to identify COVID-19 early. to enhance real-time statistics and analyze the patient's real-time data at the Fog cloud, they (Verma, (2018; Almaiah et al., 2025; Nafea et al., 2024) employed Temporal mining and IoT-enabled RPM and alerting approaches. (Swaroop, (2019)) This conference paper describes the application of blockchain technology to remote patient monitoring within the context of Healthcare 4.0. The authors propose a blockchain-based solution to ensure patient data security, confidentiality, and correctness. (Durán-Vega, 2019; Al-Attar, 2023; Vaigandla, 2025). An Internet of Things (IoT) system using a wearable device and mobile application to monitor elderly adults' health remotely, they used a biometric bracelet that was linked to a smartphone app that allows users to view all of the data that the bracelet's sensors—including body temperature, blood oxygen saturation, and heart rate—collect in real-time. With this information, caregivers may decide what is best for their patients. Their paper details the planning and execution of an Internet of Things (IoT) system that uses a wearable gadget and a smartphone application to remotely monitor senior citizens living in assisted living facilities. They used a biometric bracelet linked to a smartphone app that allows users to view all of the data that the bracelet's sensors—including body temperature, blood oxygen saturation, and heart rate—collect in real time. With this information, caregivers may decide what is best for their patients. The development of the prototype proved that the research project could be carried out and implemented. Additionally, it is inexpensive and works with the IoT paradigm (Raza, (2020)). This paper presents an intelligent IoT platform for monitoring sick patients indoors using indoor healthcare. The authors propose a system that uses Internet of Things devices, such as wearable sensors and ambient sensors, to collect real-time patient data. Machine learning algorithms process and evaluate the collected data to identify anomalies and warn healthcare professionals early. The study highlights how such a framework could be applied to remote patient monitoring, allowing for proactive and customized medical care.

METHODOLOGY

Our method suggests a peer-to-peer, scalable, self-configuring architecture for large-scale IoT networks. Four layers comprise our architecture: application, cloud, getaway, and sensing. The application layer acts as a user interface for the IOT. It uses cloud computing to extract useful information from processing large amounts of data among the gateway Layer. The sensing layer gathers data, and the Raspberry Pi 4B microcontroller was selected to collect, process, and send sensor data via a network to cloud storage. The transport layer manages network activities and devices. The task of gathering patient data falls to the sensor layer. The purpose was to offer automatic resource discovery and service mechanisms that don't require configuration by a human. Based on local and worldwide service discovery, the solution enables successful collaboration and mutual independence.

Proposed Architecture Design

The proposed architecture integrates IoT devices with cloud-based services to create a cohesive system for healthcare monitoring. Key components are Smart Sensors deployed in Site A (smart home) to collect patient data, a Cloud Computing Platform to store data storage, processing, and analysis services, and a Mobile Application that provides real-time data access to patients and healthcare providers. Figure 1 shows a suggested cloud-IoT-based healthcare system. To the various stakeholders involved, this framework will provide a wide range of healthcare applications.

Figure 1. Flowchart of cloud-IoT-based healthcare system

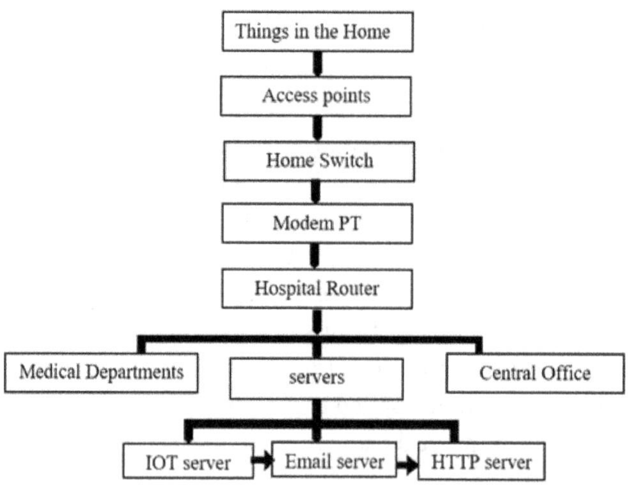

Implementation

The architecture was modeled and tested using Cisco Packet Tracer version 8.2.2, a network simulation tool. Two sites were configured: Site 'A': A smart home environment equipped with IoT sensors to monitor health parameters such as glucose meters, temperature, and blood pressure. Site 'B': A smart hospital that receives and analyzes data from Site 'A', providing remote monitoring capabilities for healthcare professionals. The step-by-step process is devices in the house connect to the Access Point (AP) in this network configuration, and packets are sent through it. The AP subsequently forwards these packets to the home switch, which subsequently directs them to the modem PT. The packets are then sent to the hospital's network by the Modem PT. The hospital router receives the packets and passes them to the central office server, hospital servers, and medical departments, among other places for smart monitoring through the Internet. Figure 2 summarizes our methodology.

Figure 2. IoT healthcare network simulation demonstrating how the cloud layer is integrated with conventional IoT architecture

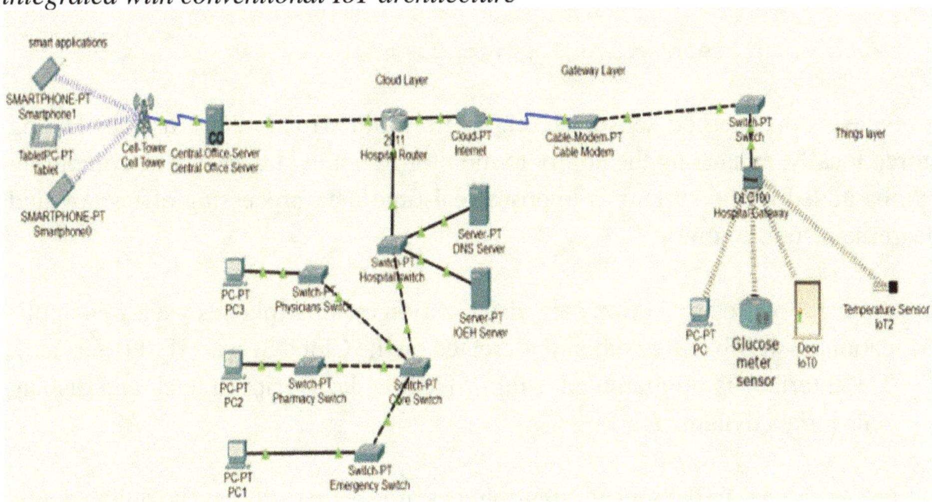

The IoT-based healthcare system is designed using a four-layer architecture:

1. Things Layer: Includes medical sensors such as glucose meters, temperature sensors, and heart rate monitors. We added Medical sensors (e.g., temperature, glucose), and Devices are programmed using JavaScript to transmit real-time patient data. Smart devices like phones and tablets can be used to monitor the sent communications, and they can be saved on a cloud server. The DHCP ser-

vice, which is set up inside APs and uses the network identity 192.168.25.110 provides IP addresses for sensors.

2. Gateway Layer: Uses wireless routers and switches to connect IoT devices to the cloud.
3. Cloud Layer: Contains a central cloud server for storing and processing sensor data. IoT devices are linked to the IoT Server on the Cloud (10.0.0.1). To guarantee ongoing patient condition monitoring, set refresh intervals every five seconds. JavaScript is used to simulate periodic data transmission:

Algorithm 1: An algorithm for simulating data on sensors

```
function sendDataToCloud() {
var glucoseLevel = Math.floor(Math.random() * (200 - 70) + 70);
IoE.output["glucose"] = glucoseLevel;
IoE.output["status"] = glucoseLevel > 140 ? "High": "Normal";
}
setInterval(sendDataToCloud, 5000);
```

By using this method, sensor data can be transmitted to the cloud instead of being stored locally, enhancing the ability to monitor remotely; however, fog computing can be added to the system to improve real-time data processing efficiency and decrease response time.

4. Application Layer: Allows data visualization on smartphones via a web application. A web-based dashboard is created on the Cloud Server (HTTP Service). The interface is programmed using HTML & JavaScript to fetch and display sensor data dynamically.

To gain access to the sensor, Smartphones are set up to access the online application and have WiFi connections. Real-time data visualization is achieved through the integrated Packet Tracer Web Browser.

Algorithm 2: algorithm of sensor data update in smart application

```
function updateData() {
fetch("http://10.0.0.1/sensorData")
.then(response => response.json())
.then(data => {
```

```
document.getElementById("glucose").innerText = data.glucose
+ " mg/dL";
    });
  }
  setInterval(updateData, 5000);
```

RESULTS

This section presents the purpose and potential composition of the various levels and modules of the suggested architecture, as well as the results of their interactions.

Connectivity Testing

The outcomes of the IoT-based cloud architecture demonstrate how a smartphone application can be used to monitor patient status in a healthcare network (Mughaid, (2023)). the first thing is ICMP (ping) between various network users. Participate in the success of Gateway layer wireless destinations and Internet of Things devices. Cloud server (cloud layer) and wireless router. server for intelligent coverage (application layer). We got a Successful response confirming server reachability, as appears in Figure 3.

Figure 3. Pinging connectivity between smartphone at the hospital to IOEH server

```
C:\>ping 192.168.01.12

Pinging 192.168.01.12 with 32 bytes of data:

Reply from 192.168.1.12: bytes=32 time=15ms TTL=126
Reply from 192.168.1.12: bytes=32 time=21ms TTL=126
Reply from 192.168.1.12: bytes=32 time=14ms TTL=126
Reply from 192.168.1.12: bytes=32 time=43ms TTL=126

Ping statistics for 192.168.1.12:
    Packets: Sent = 4, Received = 4, Lost = 0 (0% loss),
Approximate round trip times in milli-seconds:
    Minimum = 14ms, Maximum = 43ms, Average = 23ms

C:\>
```

Real-Time Data Transmission From IoT Devices

Real-time patient health data was generated by the IoT sensors and successfully sent via WiFi to the cloud server. A sample of the information gathered by the sensors. A high warning is triggered by the system if the glucose levels exceed 140 mg/dL. An emergency notification is generated if the heart rate falls below 60 beats per minute. Condition of the test: Abnormal Sensor values. Table 1 presents a sample of Data Collected from Sensors.

Table 1. Examples of sensor data gathered

Status	Sample Value	Sensor Type
Normal	Mg/dl 115	Glucose Level
Normal	BPM 78	Heart Rate
Normal	37.2°C	Temperature

Use Smart Gadgets to Visualize Data

Sensor readings were dynamically displayed on a web dashboard. The web browser on a smartphone was used to visit this dashboard in Packet Tracer. Figure 4 displays the result on a smartphone and displays a warning message if the temperature rises above 38°C. The technology alerts medical personnel if the heart rate falls below acceptable ranges. The smartphone is connected to the glucose sensor, heart rate, and temperature. If the sugar level gets very high or very low, a warning message is sent to the intended recipients.

Figure 4. Patient's smartphone for monitoring patient data

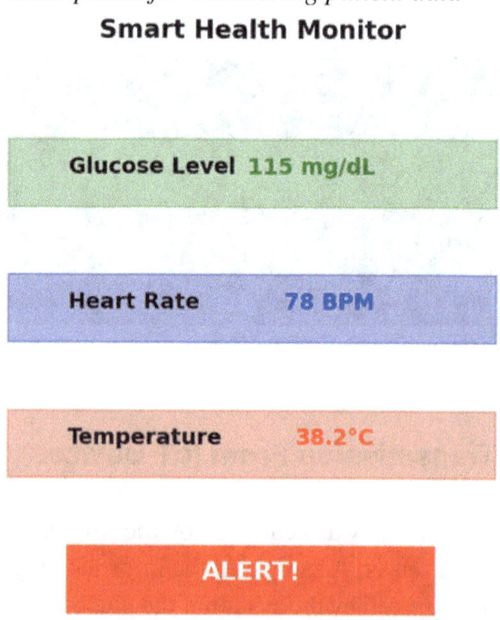

Real-Time Data Latency

By distributing processing among several Fog Nodes near the patient such as smart routers or local servers in hospitals Fog Computing lessens the strain on the cloud and enhances the system's ability to react to important changes in the patient's health. The sensors used in the study exhibited an accuracy rate of 98% for heart rate and blood pressure measurements and 95% for glucose levels. Figure 5 indicates that the sensors provide reliable data for healthcare monitoring.

Figure 5. History of time of heart rate

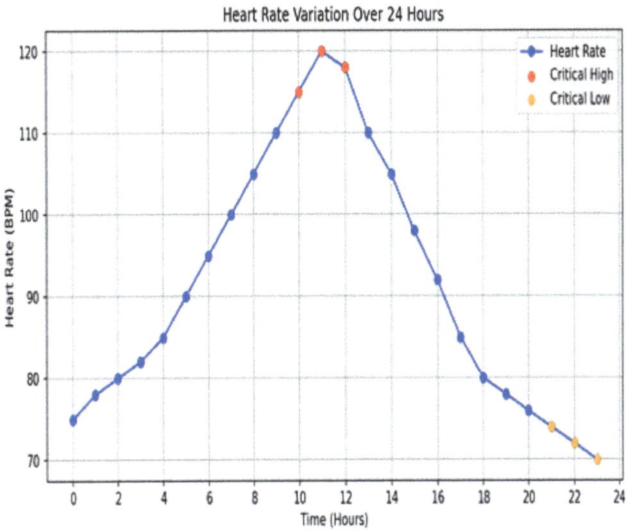

The average latency for data transmission from Site A to Site B was measured at 2.5 seconds, demonstrating the system's capability to provide near-instantaneous updates on patient health metrics.

System Scalability

The architecture's scalability was examined by simulating new IoT devices and more data flow. The system's ability to scale with increasing user and data point counts is demonstrated by the cloud infrastructure's effective management of the increased load. The results indicate that integrating IoT with cloud computing offers several advantages over traditional IoT architectures. The streamlined data management and real-time access improve patient outcomes and healthcare provider efficiency. The system's ability to deliver accurate data with minimal latency supports its effectiveness as a remote monitoring solution.

CONCLUSION

We proposed an all-inclusive IoT and cloud-based healthcare solution. We have created a network inside the proposed architecture to support data sharing and collaboration among health players on a single platform, as well as assist depressed patients in their therapy. The method ensures proactive healthcare intervention by enabling doctors and family members to remotely monitor vital indicators via cell phones.

REFERENCES

Al-Attar, B. (2023). Network Security in AI-based healthcare systems. *Babylonian Journal of Networking, 2023*, 112–124. DOI: 10.58496/BJN/2023/015

. Al-Na'amneh, Q., Aljaidi, M., Nasayreh, A., Gharaibeh, H., Mamlook, A., Emhamed, R., ... & Samara, G. (2024). Journal of intelligent systems: Enhancing IoT device security: CNN-SVM hybrid approach for real-time detection of DoS and DDoS attacks.

Al-Na'amneh, Q., Nasayreh, A. N., Al Mamlook, R., Gharaibeh, H., Alsheyab, A. M., & Almaiah, M. (2024). Improving memory malware detection in machine learning with random forest-based feature selection. In *Risk Assessment and Countermeasures for Cybersecurity* (pp. 96–114). IGI Global. DOI: 10.4018/979-8-3693-2691-6.ch006

Al-Shareeda, M. A., Najm, L. B., Hassan, A. A., Mushtaq, S., & Ali, H. A. (2024). Secure IoT-Based Smart Agriculture System Using Wireless Sensor Networks for Remote Environmental Monitoring. *STAP Journal of Security Risk Management, 2024*(1), 56–66. DOI: 10.63180/jsrm.thestap.2024.1.4

Albinhamad, H., Alotibi, A., Alagnam, A., Almaiah, M., & Salloum, S. (2025). Vehicular Ad-hoc Networks (VANETs): A Key Enabler for Smart Transportation Systems and Challenges. *Jordanian Journal of Informatics and Computing, 2025*(1), 4–15. DOI: 10.63180/jjic.thestap.2025.1.2

Alkattan, H., Al-Nuaimi, B. T., & Subhi, A. A. (2024). Machine Learning techniques to Predictive in Healthcare: Hepatitis C Diagnosis. *Mesopotamian Journal of Artificial Intelligence in Healthcare, 2024*, 128–134. DOI: 10.58496/MJAIH/2024/015

Allasasmh, O., Laila, D. A., Aljaidi, M., Alsarhan, A., & Samara, G. (2024, December). Integrated Approaches to Steganography: Embedding Static Information Across Audio, Visual, and Textual Formats. In *2024 International Jordanian Cybersecurity Conference (IJCC)* (pp. 33-39). IEEE. DOI: 10.1109/IJCC64742.2024.10847286

Almaayah, M., & Sulaiman, R. B. (2024). Cyber Risk Management in the Internet of Things: Frameworks, Models, and Best Practices. *STAP Journal of Security Risk Management, 2024*(1), 3–23. DOI: 10.63180/jsrm.thestap.2024.1.1

Almaiah, M. A., & Kadel, R. (2025). Leveraging ACO, GA, and GWO for Enhancing Port Scan Attack Detection Using Machine Learning. *Journal of Cyber Security and Risk Auditing, 2025*(4), 306–326. DOI: 10.63180/jcsra.thestap.2025.4.9

. Almaiah, M. A., Sulaiman, R. Bin, Islam, U., Badr, Y., & El-Qirem, F. A. (2025). Federated Learning in Healthcare: A Bibliometric Analysis of Privacy, Security, and Adversarial Threats (2021-2024). SHIFRA, 2025, 46–61.

Alsarhan, A., Al-Aiash, I., Al-Fraihat, D., Aljaidi, M., & Laila, D. A. A. H. A. (2024, July). Expert Phishing Detection System. In 2024 IEEE International Conference on Industry 4.0, Artificial Intelligence, and Communications Technology (IAICT) (pp. 54-59). IEEE DOI: 10.1109/IAICT62357.2024.10617460

Alshinwan, M., Memon, A. G., Ghanem, M. C., & Almaayah, M. (2025). Unsupervised text feature selection approach based on improved Prairie dog algorithm for the text clustering. *Jordanian Journal of Informatics and Computing*, *2025*(1), 27–36. DOI: 10.63180/jjic.thestap.2025.1.4

Asassfeh, M., Samara, G., Zaid, A. A., Laila, D. A., Al-Anzi, S., Alqammaz, A., & Al-Mousa, M. R. (2024, December). Penetration Testing Overview-Opportunities and Ethical Considerations: Literature Notes. In *2024 International Jordanian Cybersecurity Conference (IJCC)* (pp. 131-135). IEEE. DOI: 10.1109/IJCC64742.2024.10847295

Durán-Vega, L. A., Santana-Mancilla, P. C., Buenrostro-Mariscal, R., Contreras-Castillo, J., Anido-Rifón, L. E., García-Ruiz, M. A., Montesinos-López, O. A., & Estrada-González, F. (2019). An IoT system for remote health monitoring in elderly adults through a wearable device and mobile application. *Geriatrics (Basel, Switzerland)*, *4*(2), 34. DOI: 10.3390/geriatrics4020034 PMID: 31067819

Dutta, P. K., Singh, B., Lal, S., Arora, M. K., Raghav, A., Mensah, G. B., & Alkattan, H. (2023). Encoding IoT for patient monitoring and smart healthcare: Connected healthcare system fostering health 6.0. *Babylonian Journal of Internet of Things*, *2023*, 48–58. DOI: 10.58496/BJIoT/2023/007

Joyia, G. J., Liaqat, R. M., Farooq, A., & Rehman, S. (2017). Internet of medical things (IoMT): Applications, benefits and future challenges in healthcare domain. *Journal of Communication*, *12*(4), 240–247.

Kang, M., Park, E., Cho, B. H., & Lee, K. S. (2018). Recent patient health monitoring platforms incorporating internet of things-enabled smart devices. *International Neurourology Journal*, *22*(Suppl 2), S76–S82. DOI: 10.5213/inj.1836144.072 PMID: 30068069

Laila, D. A., Al-Na'amneh, Q., Aljaidi, M., Nasayreh, A. N., Gharaibeh, H., Al Mamlook, R., & Alshammari, M. (2024). Simulation of routing protocols for jamming attacks in mobile ad-hoc network. In *Risk Assessment and Countermeasures for Cybersecurity* (pp. 235–252). IGI Global. DOI: 10.4018/979-8-3693-2691-6.ch013

Laila, D. A., Al-Na'amneh, Q., Aljaidi, M., Nasayreh, A. N., Gharaibeh, H., Al Mamlook, R., & Alshammari, M. (2024). Enhancing 2D Logistic Chaotic Map for Gray Image Encryption. In Risk Assessment and Countermeasures for Cybersecurity (pp. 170-188). IGI Global.

Mensah, G. B., Mijwil, M. M., Abotaleb, M., Ali, G., Dutta, P. K., Mzili, T., & Eid, M. M. (2025). Explainable AI for Healthcare: Training Healthcare Workers to Use Artificial Intelligence Techniques to Reduce Medical Negligence in Ghana's Public Health Act, 2012 (Act 851). *EDRAAK, 2025*, 1–6. DOI: 10.70470/EDRAAK/2025/001

Mughaid, A., Obaidat, I., Aljammal, A., AlZu'bi, S., Quiam, F., Laila, D. A., Al-zou'bi, A., & Abualigah, L. (2023). Simulation and analysis performance of ad-hoc routing protocols under DDoS attack and proposed solution. *International Journal of Data & Network Science*, *7*(2), 757–764. DOI: 10.5267/j.ijdns.2023.2.002

Nafea, A. A., Majeed, R. R., Ali, A., Yas, A. J., Alameri, S. A., & AL-Ani, M. M. (2024). A brief review of big data in healthcare: Challenges and issues, recent developments, and future directions. *Babylonian Journal of Internet of Things, 2024*, 10–15. DOI: 10.58496/BJIoT/2024/002

Omotunde, H., & Mouhamed, M. R. (2023). The modern impact of artificial intelligence systems in healthcare: A concise analysis. *Mesopotamian Journal of Artificial Intelligence in Healthcare, 2023*, 66–70. DOI: 10.58496/MJAIH/2023/013

Raza, M., Awais, M., Singh, N., Imran, M., & Hussain, S. (2020). Intelligent IoT framework for indoor healthcare monitoring of Parkinson's disease patient. *IEEE Journal on Selected Areas in Communications*, *39*(2), 593–602. DOI: 10.1109/JSAC.2020.3021571

Sharma, N., Mangla, M., Mohanty, S. N., Gupta, D., Tiwari, P., Shorfuzzaman, M., & Rawashdeh, M. (2021). A smart ontology-based IoT framework for remote patient monitoring. *Biomedical Signal Processing and Control*, *68*, 102717. DOI: 10.1016/j.bspc.2021.102717

Sulaiman, R. B., & Khraisat, A. (2025). Metaheuristic-Driven Feature Selection with SVM and KNN for Robust DDoS Attack Detection: A Comparative Study. *Journal of Cyber Security and Risk Auditing*, *2025*(4), 182–203. DOI: 10.63180/jcsra.thestap.2025.4.1

Swaroop, K. N., Chandu, K., Gorrepotu, R., & Deb, S. (2019). A health monitoring system for vital signs using IoT. *Internet of Things : Engineering Cyber Physical Human Systems*, *5*, 116–129. DOI: 10.1016/j.iot.2019.01.004

Taylor, R., Baron, D., & Schmidt, D. (2015, October). The world in 2025-predictions for the next ten years. In 2015 10th International Microsystems, Packaging, Assembly and Circuits Technology Conference (IMPACT) (pp. 192-195). IEEE.

Vaigandla, K. K. (2025). Role of IoT and ML in Healthcare. *Babylonian Journal of Artificial Intelligence*, *2025*, 23–36. DOI: 10.58496/BJAI/2025/003

Verma, P., & Sood, S. K. (2018). Fog assisted-IoT enabled patient health monitoring in smart homes. *IEEE Internet of Things Journal*, *5*(3), 1789–1796. DOI: 10.1109/JIOT.2018.2803201

Chapter 12
Decoding Digital Evidence and Evaluating Performance and Usability in Digital Forensics

Ayoub Alsarhan
https://orcid.org/0009-0008-3034-7693
Hashemite University, Jordan

Dena Abu Laila
https://orcid.org/0009-0000-7695-3930
Zarqa University, Jordan

Mohammad Aljaidi
https://orcid.org/0000-0001-9486-3533
Zarqa University, Jordan

Qais Al-Na'amneh
Applied Science Private University, Jordan

Yara Al-Dbeisi
Hashemite University, Jordan

Khaled Maabreh
Applied Science Private University, Jordan

Ahmad Saleh Alhazaimeh
King Abdaulaziz University, Saudi Arabia

ABSTRACT

An essential component of cybersecurity is digital forensics, which includes retrieving and analyzing data from digital devices. X-Ways Forensics, Autopsy, and FTK have gained prominence among the various tools available due to their unique capabilities and widespread use. This paper provides a detailed analysis of these two tools, comparing their features, usability, performance, and application in

DOI: 10.4018/979-8-3373-1807-3.ch012

2026, IGI Global Scientific Publishing. Copying or distributing in print or electronic forms without written permission of IGI Global Scientific Publishing is prohibited. Use of this chapter to ·ative artificial intelligence (AI) technologies is expressly prohibited. The publisher reserves all rights to license its use for generative AI training and machine learning model development.

digital forensic investigations. By examining these tools, we aim to highlight their strengths and weaknesses, offering practitioners insights into the most suitable tool for various forensic scenarios. The results are intended to guide the selection of the best instrument for a given set of investigation requirements.

INTRODUCTION

Digital forensics involves the meticulous process of extracting, preserving, and analyzing digital evidence, essential for legal investigations in computer environments (Alshuaibi et al., 2025) and (Gampel & Eveleigh, 2025). The need for efficient digital forensics tools has grown along with the complexity and volume of digital data with cybersecurity incidents and security breaches. It naturally has a lot to do with the role of a Computer Forensics Investigator (Ali, 2024) and (Alsahaim & Maayah, 2023). Forensics experts are crucial to the study of digital forensics because they retrieve and examine digital data to produce relevant proof for court cases (Alsarhan A. (2013). They are very skilled in the technological domain; they can analyze operating systems, retrieve data from hard drives, mobile phones, and laptops, and examine mobile data like browser history and emails. They also examine data from systems and networks to track down digital activities and pinpoint the origins of cyberattacks (Laila, Simulation of Routing Protocols for Jamming Attacks in Mobile Ad-Hoc Network. In Risk Assessment and Countermeasures for Cybersecurity, (2024))(Aljanabi et al., 2024).

Digital forensics is defined by Blaine Stephens as the science of locating, conserving, recovering, evaluating, and presenting information about digital evidence discovered on computers or other media storage devices (Alshinwan et al., 2025) and (Albinhamad et al., 2025). Adhering to specified protocols and processes, digital forensics typically examines data collected from storage media devices, including hard drives and other devices (Aljaidi M. A.-K.-G., (2022, November).) (Laila, (2024)). A computer forensic model to assist investigators in their digital investigations. They dubbed the model shown in Figure 1 the Four-Step Forensic Process (FSFP).

Figure 1. Forensic Procedure in Four Steps (FSFP) (Alsarhan, 2024, July)

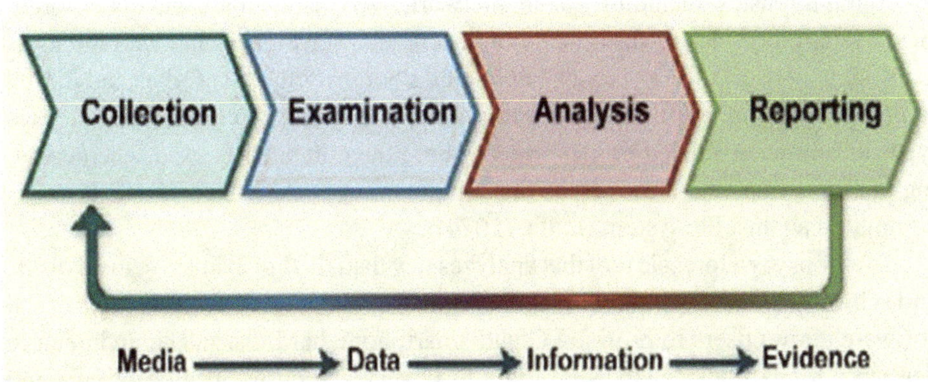

1) The FSFP begins with the collecting phase, when data is recognized, added to a chain of custody, and its integrity is safeguarded.
2) The data collected from the crime site is examined in the second stage of the forensic investigation model, and an appropriate forensic tool is chosen to extract pertinent information.
3) Outcome analysis is the third stage of the model. To be able to respond to the inquiries that prompted the data gathering and analysis, the digital evidence that was discovered and retrieved from the reviewed data must be analyzed.
4) The last stage is reporting, when the analysis results are given, the type of action taken and the suggestions made.

To ensure the presentation of reliable legal evidence that supports investigation operations and court processes, we used state-of-the-art tools such as X-Ways Forensics, Autopsy, and FTK have become significant in the field, each providing distinctive functionalities tailored to different aspects of forensic analysis. This research paper explores the functionalities of these tools, comparing their effectiveness in digital forensic investigations and providing accurate and efficient extraction and analysis.

Digital forensics is crucial in the legal process because it allows for the search and analysis of vast amounts of data that can be used as evidence in court. Digital forensics uses several techniques for interpreting, preserving, identifying, analyzing, and documenting digital evidence, such as legal standards, reports of factual evidence discovered, and producing expert opinions in court. The forensic team explored the hard disk drive using several computer languages, which is useful for cybercrimes via the Internet. One thing to remember is that evidence must be captured at all stages (Asassfeh, (2024; Al-Hashemi et al., 2024; Hammad et al., 2024)

Computer forensics separates into numerous common topics. Create many words for digital forensics, including system, network, web, data, email, and cyber forensics. System forensics focuses solely on machines. Networking and web forensics investigate network events to identify potential security threats. Cyber and digital forensics focus on real-time cases and online evidence collection. There are two types of computer-related crimes: those where the computer is used when carrying out the crime, and those where the computer keeps evidence, and the crime is committed against the system (Laila, (2024)).

An autopsy is a forensic tool that analyzes raw data, E01 disk images, local disks, and sub-directories sequentially to discover the source of an event. This GUI-based software allows users to browse PC and smartphone hard disks. The architecture describes for. Autopsy enables program discovery and customization in Java and Python. It also increases the number of members on community-based email lists and forums. Examiners employ autopsy equipment in several fields, including policing, military, and corporations. It functions as an internet server and may be accessed using an HTML browser (Al-Na'amneh Q. D., 2025).

X-Ways is a quick forensic tool for recovering erased evidence. It is portable and efficient. It functions as a USB drive on any Windows operating system, eliminating the requirement for installation. Disk imaging, like disk cloning, automatically identifies lost or deleted file partitions. Various tools are used to choose the best process model for gathering evidence and investigating situations (Aljaidi M. A.-K.-G., In 2022)(Shukur et al., 2024; Tambe & Hussein, 2023). The latest Process Model, Stepwise the Forensic Process Model, outlines a step-by-step procedure that involves identifying the incident, recovering lost evidence, and doing analysis. (Ayoub Alsarhan, (2022)). The crime scene is evaluated, and the next steps are planned based on the situation discovered. After picking a procedure, it studies the system to overcome the limitations of traditional digital forensic models. (Allasasmh, (2024)) A network packet analyzer is used to analyze network problems. The network packet analyzer identifies traffic in the network. Digital forensic analysis requires multiple technologies to collect and evaluate data, as well as resolve conflicts during the execution phase (Mughaid, (2023).)

RELATED WORKS

Computer forensics is a discipline that draws a wide range of interests, eventually resulting in the release of numerous research works meant to close the knowledge gap within the topic domain. Specifically, much of the relevant literature in the forensics field relates to security. Apart from the fact that the legislature has assumed a portion of the expense associated with preventing crime, corporate secrets must employ the most advanced security techniques accessible to safeguard them. As a result of the growing area of information and communication interchange, trade secrets have given rise to several challenges, including the widespread response of governments to the employment of coercive measures with potent deterrent effects. This section introduces many literature reviews related to our paper.

Karampidis, (2018) performed forensic investigations of Hadoop's features. It describes several important files for forensic investigations, including log files, configuration files, and garbage files. The study uses Autopsy's open-source tool to perform digital forensics on Hadoop data. The study highlights the need to comprehend Hadoop's underlying structure and utilize cutting-edge tools to efficiently manage and explore large datasets by analyzing the ecosystem of forensic evidence within Hadoop (Abu-Zaid, 2025; Alsajri et al., 2023; Khalaf & Steiti, 2024).

Nayak (2023) illustrates the efficacy of the 2DRA framework in recognizing and mitigating ransomware impacts by utilizing the WannaCry ransomware as a case study. Important contributions include the creation of useful tools for forensic investigation, a thorough approach for combining detection and recovery procedures, and an assessment of the framework's effectiveness compared to actual ransomware cases.

The results show that the 2DRA architecture offers a strong answer to an urgent cybersecurity issue by considerably enhancing the precision of ransomware detection and the effectiveness of data recovery.

Domingues (2023) produced study examines the forensic artifacts produced by the Zepp Life mobile app (formerly Mi Fit) when used in conjunction with the Mi Band 6. It does this by analyzing data gathered from two rooted Android smartphones (Xiaomi Mi A2 running Android 10 and BQ Aquaris X Pro running Android 8.1) as well as an Android 6.0 Genymotion emulator. The research thoroughly examines the application's data repositories, encompassing SQLite databases and XML files, to comprehend the categories of information retained and their possible significance. Additionally, two open-source tools, ZL_std and ZL_autopsy, are introduced in the study to help forensic practitioners.

Al-Dhaqm (2017) suggested a shared database containing the forensic investigation procedures' design science research methodology. The four phases of this process consist of the following:

1) artifact identification;
2) assembly,
3) the analysis of artifacts, and 4) the documentation and delivery procedures. This enables us to harmonize everyone's ideas and phrases for typical database forensics procedures.

Daghmehchi Firoozjaei (2022) analyzed three major memory analysis tools: Volatility, Autopsy, and Redline. The results showed that Volatility provides more accurate memory analysis, while Redline consumes more CPU resources, and Autopsy requires more memory resources to analyze the memory image.

Comparative Analysis of Operating System Forensic Tools to compare digital forensic tools used to examine operating systems, with a focus on tools such as OS Forensics and Autopsy. The study evaluates these tools based on multiple criteria, including ease of use, available functionality, performance, and product support and documentation, (Nay, 2024; Sallam et al., 2024).

Also in Digital Forensic Tools and the Investigation Process" aims to comprehensively study digital forensic tools and the stages of the digital forensic investigation process. The paper focuses on evaluating the tools used to protect data from financial fraud, identity theft, and money laundering, in addition to analyzing how artificial intelligence can be used to improve digital forensic analysis processes (Al-Na'amneh Q. A., Feature Selection for Robust Spoofing Detection: A Chi-Square-based Machine Learning Approach., 2023).

Agboola (2024) compares and assesses the efficacy, efficiency, and applicability of digital forensics tools, including open-source tools like Autopsy, licensed commercial tools like FTK Estero, and mobile forensics tools like Cellebrite and XRY.

Sachdev (2020) analyzes and assess different digital forensic techniques used in electronic evidence extraction. The study suggests the creation of sophisticated forensic tools to aid in the investigation of particular kinds of crimes and focuses on the function of pattern recognition techniques in the analysis stage of digital forensic analysis procedures. The study's foundation is a thorough examination of digital forensic analysis tools, with an emphasis on the use of pattern recognition methods in analysis procedures. The two primary steps of the methodology are analysis and recognition, in which characteristics are taken from patterns that need to be identified, like faces and fingerprints, and then utilized in later phases of analysis (Al-Na'amneh, 2024)

THE PROPOSED FRAMEWORK

Three different tools will be examined and tested to retrieve copies of deleted data. We initially give an introduction of the tools in this part, along with a rundown of their key features. Next, we introduce our novel model that utilizes the X-ways, Autopsy, and FTK tools to retrieve data efficiently from compromised computers. We focus on the data retrieval step because it is an essential part of the process of saving data correctly to achieve the main goal of this paper, which is to retrieve deleted data to create forensic images to copy the digital data without any modification. The image can be USB memory, an entire hard disk, a partition of it, or even just a file from the criminal's computer.

X-Ways Tool

This section introduces our novel model that utilizes the X-Ways tool.

X-Ways Overview

X-Ways Forensics, developed by X-Ways Software Technology AG, is a professional digital forensics tool renowned for its efficiency and comprehensive feature set. Law enforcement agencies, corporate investigators, and security professionals widely utilize it for its robust performance and precision.

Features of X-Ways

- Evidence Collection: X-Ways Forensics excels in acquiring data from various digital devices, including hard drives, SSDs, and external storage media. It supports both live and dead box forensics.
- Data Analysis: X-Ways Forensics offers powerful data analysis tools, such as keyword searching, data carving, and timeline analysis.
- Reporting: X-Ways Forensics provides detailed, customizable reporting capabilities, allowing investigators to present findings clearly and effectively.
- Extensibility: X-Ways Forensics supports numerous third-party plugins and scripts, enhancing its functionality and allowing for specialized analysis.
- User Interface: X-Ways Forensics features a user interface designed for efficiency, though it may require some training to master due to its extensive feature set.

Data Collection

After installing Windows, we investigated the files and used Final Forensics 3.1 to record the generation time and log files. The binary for the $MFT file was examined using X-way forensics 16.6.

Novel Model

X-Ways Software Technology AG produces X-way forensics, which is displayed in Figure 2 of Final Forensics 3.1.

Figure 2. Final forensics 3.1

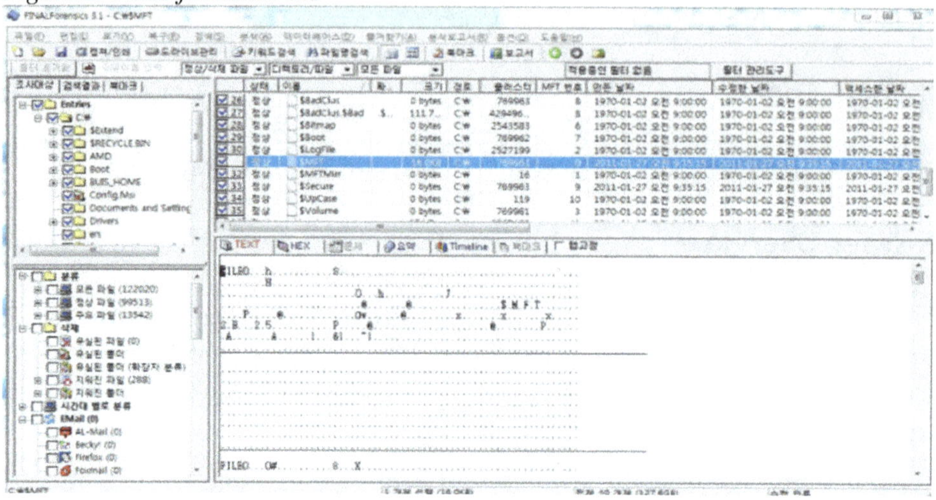

AUTOPSY

We introduce our novel model that utilizes the Autopsy.

Autopsy Overview

Autopsy, developed by Basis Technology, is an open-source digital forensics platform that has gained popularity for its user-friendly interface and powerful analysis capabilities. Law enforcement, corporate investigators, and digital forensics enthusiasts use it. Figure 3 shows the interface Autopsy tool.

Figure 3. Interface autopsy tool

The Features of Autopsy

- Evidence Collection: Autopsy supports data acquisition from a variety of sources, including computers, mobile devices, and network data.
- Data Analysis: Autopsy is known for its comprehensive analysis capabilities, including keyword searches, timeline analysis, and file carving.
- Visualization: Autopsy offers robust visualization tools, such as timeline views, data graphs, and geolocation analysis.
- Reporting: Autopsy provides detailed reporting options with templates and customizable reports that cater to specific investigation needs.
- Integration: Autopsy integrates well with other tools in the digital forensics ecosystem, supporting various third-party modules and plugins.

Data Collection

Data was gathered from the autopsy's website, and case studies and performance benchmarks were used to do a comparative comparison.

Novel Model

This section explains the basic steps for case investigation using this tool, and the steps explain the investigation workflow.

1. Choose a new case and give a name for this case as we show in Figure 4 below.

Figure 4. First steps of Autopsy

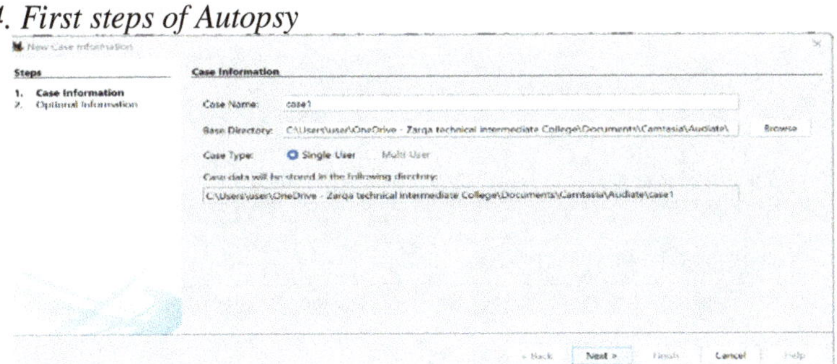

2. Select a data source type, the tool supports many data sources such as Disk Images or VM Files, Local Disks, Logical Files, etc. we chose Disk Images or VM as shown in Figure 5.

Figure 5. Select a data source type

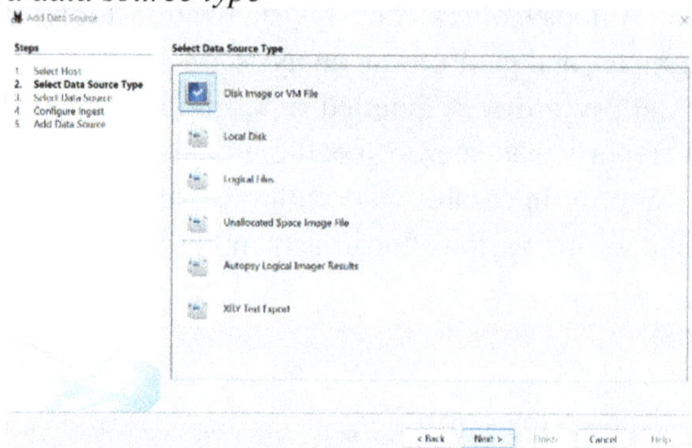

3. Select a data source, in our case, we used a hard disk with a case from the manufacturer of these tools (basic technology) Figure 6 shows this step.

Figure 6. Selecting a data source

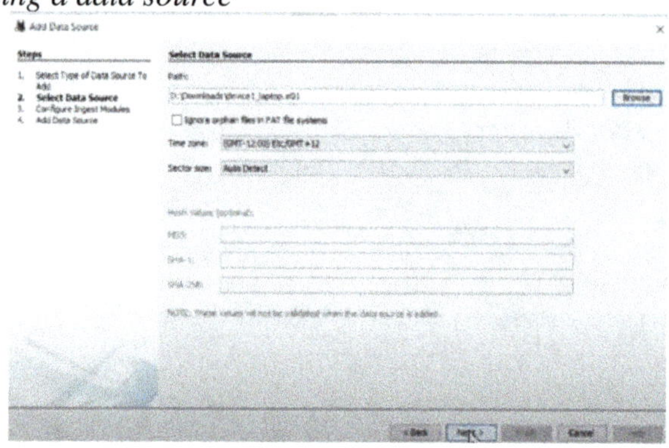

4. Check the recent user activity to extract as shown in Figure 7.

Figure 7. Checking the recent user activity

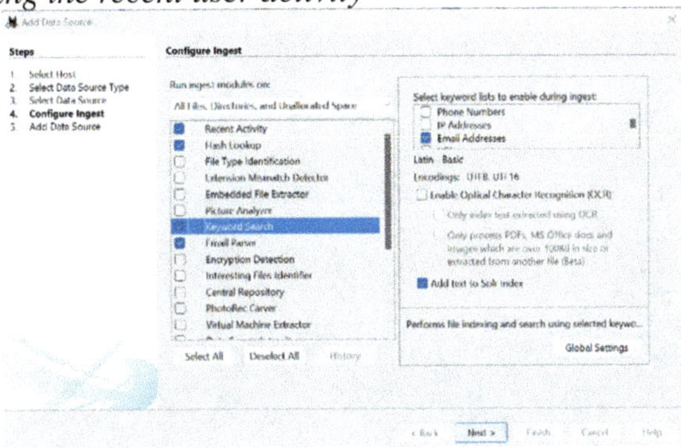

Figure 8 presents the results of all files on the hard drive.

Figure 8. Result of all files in the hard drive

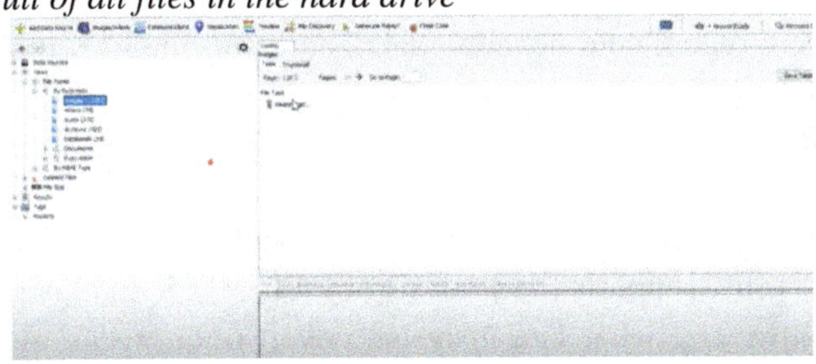

5. Create a report: Autopsy provides detailed reporting options with templates and customizable reports that cater to specific investigation needs as shown in Figure 9.

Figure 9. Creating the report

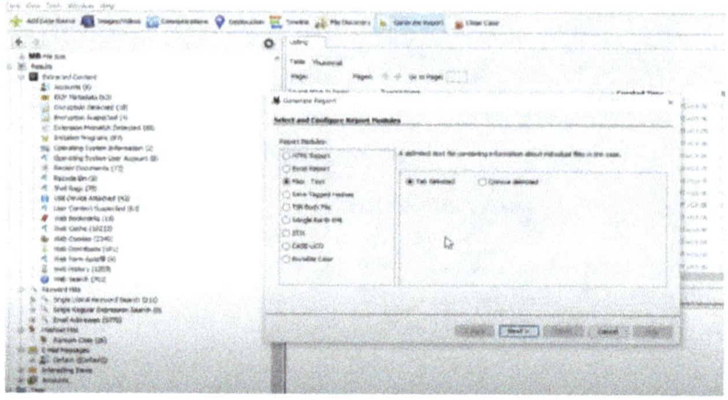

FORENSIC TOOLKIT (FTK)

This section introduces our novel model that utilizes the FTK tool.

FTK Overview

Forensic Toolkit*(FTK)* is Access Data development a digital forensic program for Windows. This utility supports file analysis of FAT, NTFS, Ext2, and CDFS, hash verification of MD5 and SHA, data analysis recovery of deleted files, and graphical File viewing. The resulting forensic image is saved in several formats such as RAW DD, E01 ... etc. figure 10 shows interface the application.

Figure 10. Interface FTK tool

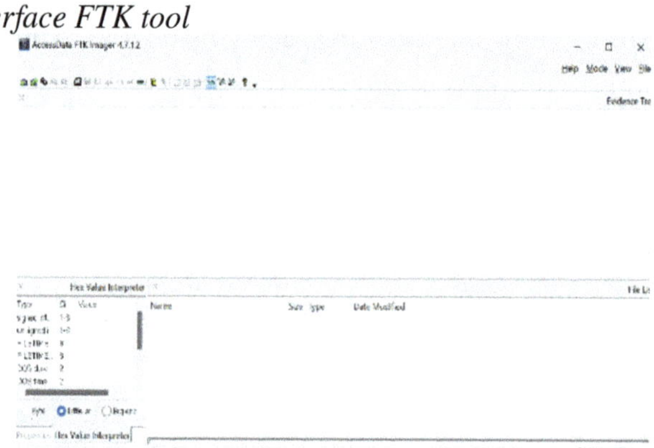

Features of the FTK Tool

- Comprehensive Data Analysis: it can analyze different kinds of data, such as emails, file systems, and internet history.
- File Carving: Using file carving techniques, it can recover partially overwritten or erased files, helping to recover evidence that may have been removed on purpose.
- Disk Imaging: precise data replicas on a storage device, can be created with FTK. This guarantees that during analysis, the original evidence doesn't change.
- Search and Filtering: The program offers robust search capabilities by using sophisticated search methods, including regular expressions and file type filtering.
- File System study: It enables in-depth investigation of the structure of files and directories by supporting the study of multiple file systems, such as FAT, NTFS, and EXT. .
- Email Analysis: Investigators may search for and examine email correspondence thanks to FTK's ability to parse and analyze email databases from widely used email clients like Outlook and Thunderbird.

Data Collection

Data was gathered from the Flash memory, and case studies and performance benchmarks were used to do a comparison.

Novel Model

This section explains the basic steps for investigation using this tool to explain the investigation workflow.

- Select the source evidence type: we chose physical because we need a drive connected to the device (see Figure 11).

Figure 11. First steps of Autopsy

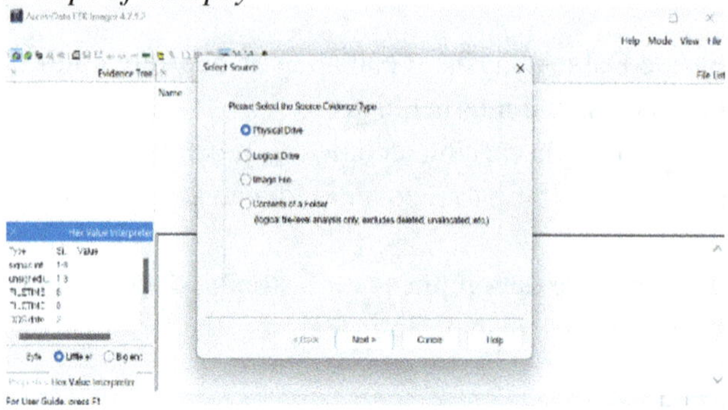

- Select the file we need to copy: we chose a USB device as appears in Figure 12.

Figure 12. Selecting the file

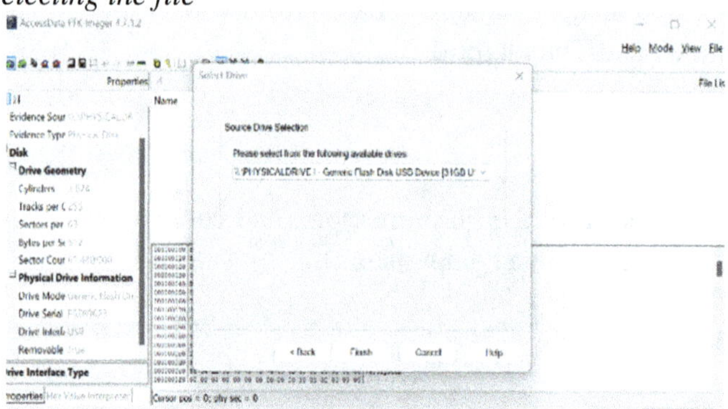

- Select the destination image type: used to Custom type for copying, we chose row (dd)-Disc Dump- to Copy it using the command in Linux see Figure 13.

Figure 13. Selecting the image type

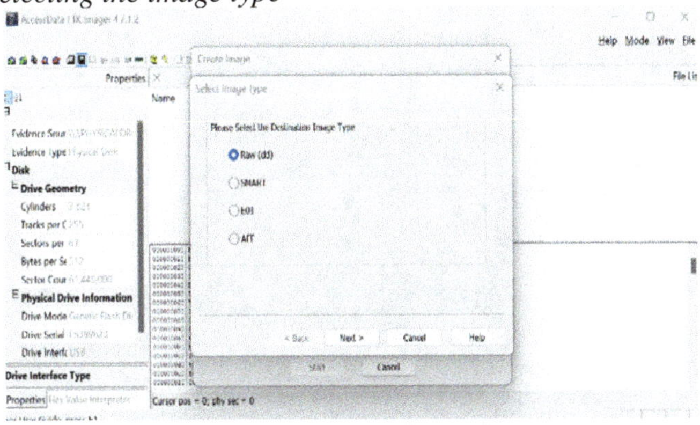

- Fill in all information: we filled in information related to our case (see Figure 14).

Figure 14. Filling the information

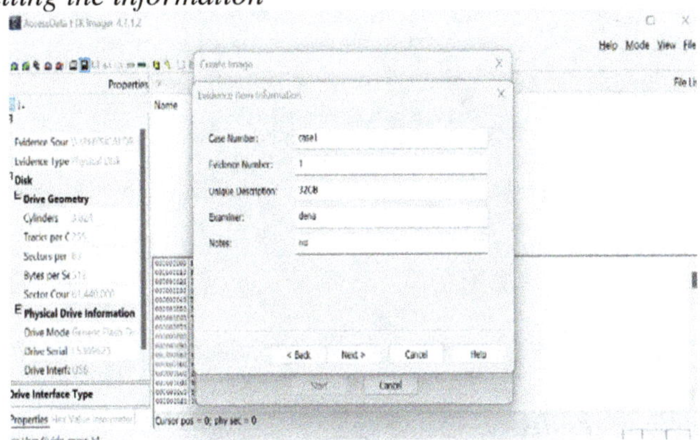

- Select the folder to save the image: select where want to save work and the name of the folder and choose if we want to portion the file (see Figure 15)

Figure 15. The folder to save

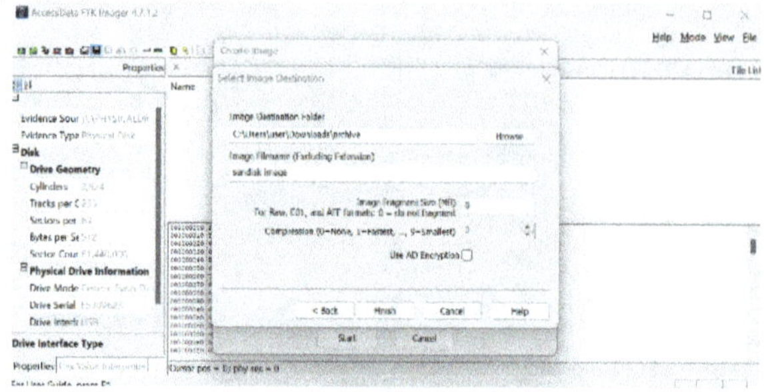

- As a result, we get a SanDisk image as shown in Figures 16 and 17.

Figure 16. The summary of results

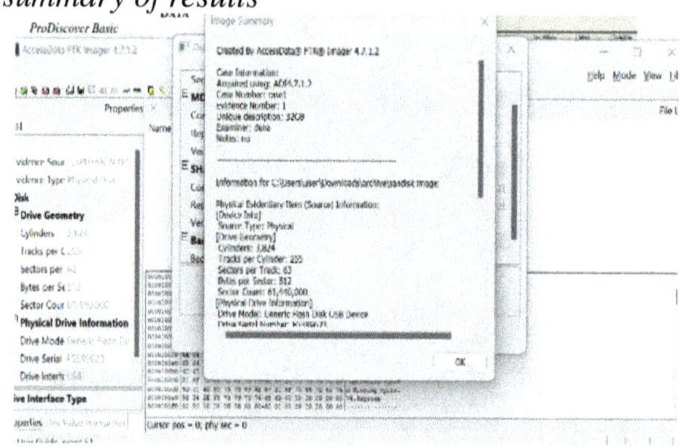

Figure 17. Sample of results

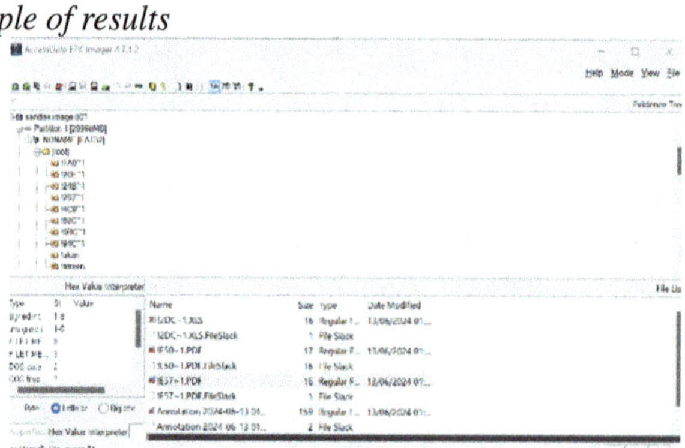

RESULTS AND DISCUSSION

A fuller grasp of the instruments and procedures employed in the field is made possible by the insightful observations provided by the existing literature on a range of topics related to digital forensic investigations. For example, the forensic analyses of Hadoop's features highlight how crucial it is to comprehend the fundamental architecture of large data systems like Hadoop and how to effectively manage and explore data using sophisticated tools like Autopsy. This underscores the increasing demand for specialized instruments capable of handling intricate forensic data—a topic pertinent to the comparative examination in our research. Furthermore, the analysis of the 2DRA framework's effectiveness in reducing the effects of ransomware emphasizes the importance of having efficient tools for forensic investigations' detection and recovery procedures. In cybersecurity contexts, the framework's effectiveness in improving ransomware detection and data recovery is a critical factor to take into account when analyzing the performance and suitability of forensic tools.

Table 1. Comparison of the features for three tools

Feature/Tool	FTK (Forensic Toolkit)	Autopsy	X-Ways Forensics
Cost	Commercial(expensive)	Free and open-source	Commercial(expensive)
Performance	Powerful but resource-intensive	May be slower with very large datasets	Known for speed and efficiency
File System Support	Wide variety, including NTFS, FAT, EXT	Extensive, including NTFS, FAT, EXT	Wide variety, including NTFS, FAT, EXT
File Carving	Effective in recovering deleted or overwritten files	Supports file carving	Strong file carving capabilities
Disk Imaging	Reliable and robust	Supported via The Sleuth Kit	Supported and efficient
Search & Filtering	Advanced search options, keywords, regex	Basic to advanced search options	Extensive search and filtering capabilities
Data Visualization	Includes timeline views and visual aids	Basic visualization features	Detailed and customizable visualizations
Reporting	Detailed and customizable reports	Good reporting capabilities	Detailed and highly customizable reports
Password Cracking	Integrated with cracking tools	Not directly integrated	Not directly integrated
User Interface	Intuitive but complex	User-friendly but less polished	Powerful but may have a steeper learning curve
Scalability	Suitable for large-scale investigations	Scalable but may be slower for very large datasets	Highly scalable and efficient
Integration	Includes various integrated tools	Modular with various plugins	Integrates well with other forensic tools
Community	Professional support, less community-based Support	Strong community support	Professional support with some community

The growing importance of mobile forensics is evidenced by research on forensic artifacts in mobile applications, which focuses on particular technologies to help practitioners examine data repositories in mobile environments. This is consistent with our study of tool performance and usability since handling mobile data effectively is an essential feature of contemporary forensic tools.

The necessity of consistent procedures and adaptable instruments in forensic investigations is shown by the proposed common database for forensic procedures and the application of FTK to retrieve data from compromised systems. These studies lay the groundwork for understanding how to best utilize tools in various forensic circumstances, which directly informs our appraisal of the relative merits and demerits of the various instruments.

Our study expands on these pioneering investigations by offering an in-depth examination that compares two distinct forensic instruments. Through an analysis of their features, usability, performance, and application, our goal is to provide practitioners with more insight into which tool could be most appropriate for their particular forensic requirements. By providing a clear comparison that aids in choosing the best tool for different types of digital forensic investigations, this research aims to close a gap in the existing literature, by understanding the detailed functionalities and comparing these tools, digital forensic professionals can make informed decisions to enhance their investigative processes and achieve better outcomes in their forensic analyses.

CONCLUSION

The tools we propose, X-Way forensics, Autopsy, and FTK, are powerful in the realm of digital forensics, each with its strengths and ideal use cases. X-Ways Forensics is highly efficient and reliable, suitable for a broad range of forensic investigations requiring precision and advanced capabilities. With its user-friendly interface and robust analysis features, Autopsy is ideal for organizations seeking a cost-effective and flexible forensic solution.

REFERENCES

Abu-Zaid, A., Aljaidi, M., Al-Na'amneh, Q., Samara, G., Alsarhan, A., & Qadoumi, B. (2025). Advancements and Challenges in the Internet of Drones Security Issues: A Comprehensive Review. *Machine Intelligence Applications in Cyber-Risk Management*, 1-24.

Agboola, V., Osamor, J., & Olajide, F. (2024). Evaluating the Efficiency of FTK, Autopsy, and Mobile Forensic Tools: A Comparative Study in Criminal Investigations.

Al-Dhaqm, A., Razak, S., Othman, S. H., Choo, K. K. R., Glisson, W. B., Ali, A., & Abrar, M. (2017). CDBFIP: Common database forensic investigation processes for Internet of Things. IEEE Access, 5, 24401-24416. 9

Al-Hashemi, S. Q. Y., Naghmash, M. S., & Ghandour, A. (2024). Improving IP Video Surveillance Systems: The Shift to Digital Networks and Security Challenges. *SHIFRA*, *2024*, 17–23. DOI: 10.70470/SHIFRA/2024/003

. Al-Na'amneh, Q., Aljaidi, M., Nasayreh, A., Gharaibeh, H., Mamlook, A., Emhamed, R., ... & Samara, G. (2024). Journal of intelligent systems: Enhancing IoT device security: CNN-SVM hybrid approach for real-time detection of DoS and DDoS attacks.

Albinhamad, H., Alotibi, A., Alagnam, A., Almaiah, M., & Salloum, S. (2025). Vehicular Ad-hoc Networks (VANETs): A Key Enabler for Smart Transportation Systems and Challenges. *Jordanian Journal of Informatics and Computing*, *2025*(1), 4–15. DOI: 10.63180/jjic.thestap.2025.1.2

Ali, A. (2024). Adaptive and Context-Aware Authentication Framework Using Edge AI and Blockchain in Future Vehicular Networks. *STAP Journal of Security Risk Management*, *2024*(1), 45–56. DOI: 10.63180/jsrm.thestap.2024.1.3

Aljaidi, M., Alsarhan, A., & Samara, G., AL-Khassawneh, Y. A., Al-Gumaei, Y. A., Aljawawdeh, H., & Alqammaz, A. (2022, November). A critical evaluation of a recent cybersecurity attack on itunes software updater. In 2022 International Engineering Conference on Electrical, Energy, and Artificial Intelligence (EICEEAI) (pp. 1-6). IEEE. DOI: 10.1109/EICEEAI56378.2022.10050464

Aljanabi, R. A., Al-Qaysi, Z. T., & Suzani, M. S. (2024). Deep Transfer Learning Model for EEG Biometric Decoding. *Applied Data Science and Analysis*, *2024*, 4–16. DOI: 10.58496/ADSA/024/002

Allasasmh, O., Laila, D. A., Aljaidi, M., Alsarhan, A., & Samara, G. (2024, December). Integrated Approaches to Steganography: Embedding Static Information Across Audio, Visual, and Textual Formats. In *2024 International Jordanian Cybersecurity Conference (IJCC)* (pp. 33-39). IEEE. DOI: 10.1109/IJCC64742.2024.10847286

Alsahaim, S., & Maayah, M. (2023). Analyzing Cybersecurity Threats on Mobile Phones. *STAP Journal of Security Risk Management, 2023*(1), 3–19. DOI: 10.63180/jsrm.thestap.2023.1.2

Alsajri, A., Steiti, A., & Salman, H. A. (2023). Enhancing IoT Security to Leveraging ML for DDoS Attack Prevention in Distributed Network Routing. *Babylonian Journal of Internet of Things, 2023*, 74–84. DOI: 10.58496/BJIoT/2023/010

Alsarhan, A., Agarwal, A., Obeidat, I., Bsoul, M., Khasawneh, A. A., & Kilani, Y. (2013). Optimal spectrum utilisation in cognitive network using combined spectrum sharing approach: Overlay, underlay and trad ing. *International Journal of Business Information Systems, 12*(4), 423–454. DOI: 10.1504/IJBIS.2013.053216

Alsarhan, A., Al-Aiash, I., Al-Fraihat, D., Aljaidi, M., & Laila, D. A. A. H. A. (2024, July). Expert Phishing Detection System. In 2024 IEEE International Conference on Industry 4.0, Artificial Intelligence, and Communications Technology (IAICT) (pp. 54-59). IEEE. DOI: 10.1109/IAICT62357.2024.10617460

Alsarhan, A., Al-Ghuwairi, A.-R., Esra'a, A., & Idhaim, H. (2022). Omar alkhawaldeh " A Novel Scheme for Malicious Nodes Detection in Cloud Markets Based on Fuzzy Logic Technique. *Int. J. Interact. Mob. Technol., 16*(10), 191–102. DOI: 10.3991/ijim.v16i10.30479

Alshinwan, M., Memon, A. G., Ghanem, M. C., & Almaayah, M. (2025). Unsupervised text feature selection approach based on improved Prairie dog algorithm for the text clustering. *Jordanian Journal of Informatics and Computing, 2025*(1), 27–36. DOI: 10.63180/jjic.thestap.2025.1.4

Alshuaibi, A., Arshad, M. W., & Maayah, M. (2025). A Hybrid Genetic Algorithm and Hidden Markov Model-Based Hashing Technique for Robust Data Security. *Journal of Cyber Security and Risk Auditing, 2025*(3), 42–56. DOI: 10.63180/jcsra.thestap.2025.3.6

Asassfeh, M., Samara, G., Zaid, A. A., Laila, D. A., Al-Anzi, S., Alqammaz, A., & Al-Mousa, M. R. (2024, December). Penetration Testing Overview-Opportunities and Ethical Considerations: Literature Notes. In *2024 International Jordanian Cybersecurity Conference (IJCC)* (pp. 131-135). IEEE. DOI: 10.1109/IJCC64742.2024.10847295

. Barik, K., Abirami, A., Konar, K., & Das, S. (2022). Research perspective on digital forensic tools and investigation process. Illumination of Artificial Intelligence in Cybersecurity and Forensics, 71-95.

Daghmehchi Firoozjaei, M., Habibi Lashkari, A., & Ghorbani, A. A. (2022). Memory forensics tools: A comparative analysis. *Journal of Cyber Security Technology*, *6*(3), 149–173. DOI: 10.1080/23742917.2022.2100036

Domingues, P., Francisco, J., & Frade, M. (2023). Post-mortem digital forensics analysis of the Zepp Life android application. *Forensic Science International Digital Investigation*, *45*, 301555. DOI: 10.1016/j.fsidi.2023.301555

Gampel, A., & Eveleigh, T. (2025). Model-Based Systems Engineering Cybersecurity Risk Assessment for Industrial Control Systems Leveraging NIST Risk Management Framework Methodology. *Journal of Cyber Security and Risk Auditing*, *2025*(4), 204–221. DOI: 10.63180/jcsra.thestap.2025.4.2

Hammad, O. M., Smaoui, I., Fakhfakh, A., & Hashim, M. M. (2024). Recent advances in digital image masking techniques Future challenges and trends: A review. *SHIFRA*, *2024*, 67–73. DOI: 10.70470/SHIFRA/2024/008

Karampidis, K., Kavallieratou, E., & Papadourakis, G. (2018). A review of image steganalysis techniques for digital forensics. *Journal of Information Security and Applications*, *40*, 217–235. DOI: 10.1016/j.jisa.2018.04.005

Khalaf, M. A., & Steiti, A. (2024). Artificial intelligence predictions in cyber security: Analysis and early detection of cyber attacks. *Babylonian Journal of Machine Learning*, *2024*, 63–68. DOI: 10.58496/BJML/2024/006

Kolla, V. R. K. (2022). A Comparative Analysis of OS Forensics Tools. [IJRIM]. *International Journal of Research in IT and Management*, *12*(4).

Laila, D. A., Al-Na'amneh, Q., Aljaidi, M., Nasayreh, A. N., Gharaibeh, H., Al Mamlook, R., & Alshammari, M. (2024). Simulation of routing protocols for jamming attacks in mobile ad-hoc network. In *Risk Assessment and Countermeasures for Cybersecurity* (pp. 235–252). IGI Global. DOI: 10.4018/979-8-3693-2691-6.ch013

Laila, D. A., Al-Na'amneh, Q., Aljaidi, M., Nasayreh, A. N., Gharaibeh, H., Al Mamlook, R., & Alshammari, M. (2024). Enhancing 2d logistic chaotic map for gray image encryption. In Risk Assessment and Countermeasures for Cybersecurity (pp. 170-188). IGI Global.

Mughaid, A., Obaidat, I., Aljammal, A., AlZu'bi, S., Quiam, F., Laila, D. A., Alzou'bi, A., & Abualigah, L. (2023). Simulation and analysis performance of ad-hoc routing protocols under DDoS attack and proposed solution. *International Journal of Data & Network Science*, *7*(2), 757–764. DOI: 10.5267/j.ijdns.2023.2.002

Nay, T. (2024). Enhancing IoT Security with AI-Driven Hybrid Machine Learning and Neural Network-Based Intrusion Detection System. *Babylonian Journal of Artificial Intelligence*, *2024*, 158–167. DOI: 10.58496/BJAI/2024/017

Nayak, S. C., Tiwari, V., & Samanthula, B. K. (2023, March). Review of ransomware attacks and a data recovery framework using autopsy digital forensics platform. In 2023 IEEE 13th Annual Computing and Communication Workshop and Conference (CCWC) (pp. 0605-0611). IEEE. DOI: 10.1109/CCWC57344.2023.10099169

Sachdeva, S., Raina, B. L., & Sharma, A. (2020). Analysis of digital forensic tools. *Journal of Computational and Theoretical Nanoscience*, *17*(6), 2459–2467. DOI: 10.1166/jctn.2020.8916

Sallam, M., Al-Mahzoum, K., & Sallam, M. (2024). Generative Artificial Intelligence and Cybersecurity Risks: Implications for Healthcare Security Based on Real-life Incidents. *Mesopotamian Journal of Artificial Intelligence in Healthcare*, *2024*, 184–203. DOI: 10.58496/MJAIH/2024/019

Shukur, B. S., & Abd Ghani, M. K. (2024). Digital physicians: Unleashing artificial intelligence in transforming healthcare and exploring the future of modern approaches. *Mesopotamian Journal of Artificial Intelligence in Healthcare*, *2024*, 28–34. DOI: 10.58496/MJAIH/2024/005

Tambe, S. N., & Hussein, N. A.-H. K. (2023). Exploring the Impact of Digital Literacy on Media Consumer Empowerment in the Age of Misinformation. *MEDAAD*, *2023*, 1–9. DOI: 10.70470/MEDAAD/2023/001

Compilation of References

Abdulateef, O. G., Joudah, A., Abdulsahib, M. G., & Alrammahi, H. (2025). Designing a robust machine learning-based framework for secure data transmission in Internet of Things (IoT) environments: A multifaceted approach to security challenges. *Journal of Cyber Security and Risk Auditing*, *2025*(4), 266–275. DOI: 10.63180/jcsra.thestap.2025.4.6

Abed, S. A., & Gök, M. (2023). Big data and artificial intelligence on the blockchain: A review. *Babylonian Journal of Artificial Intelligence*, *2023*, 1–4. DOI: 10.58496/BJAI/2023/001

Abesamis, P. P. R., & Caramancion, K. M. (2022, October). Multiple-case study on the perceived impacts of Philippine identification system in organizational control: Focusing on e-government services. In *Proceedings of the 15th International Conference on Theory and Practice of Electronic Governance* (pp. 279–287). DOI: 10.1145/3560107.3560152

Abotaleb, M., El-Kenawy, E.-S. M., & Dhoska, K. (2025). Deep learning-based time series forecasting: A convolutional neural network approach for predicting inflation trends. *EDRAAK*, *2025*(1), 19–28. DOI: 10.70470/EDRAAK/2025/004

Abu-Zaid, A., Aljaidi, M., Al-Na'amneh, Q., Samara, G., Alsarhan, A., & Qadoumi, B. (2025). Advancements and Challenges in the Internet of Drones Security Issues: A Comprehensive Review. *Machine Intelligence Applications in Cyber-Risk Management*, 1-24.

Adamopoulos, I., Valamontes, A., Karantonis, J. T., Tropaitis, P. P., & Syrou, N. (2025). Enhancing Economic Growth Time Series for UAE Forecasting with Deep Learning: A Seq2Seq and Attention-Driven LSTM Approach. *EDRAAK*, *2025*, 62–75. DOI: 10.70470/EDRAAK/2025/009

Adawadkar, A. M. K., & Kulkarni, N. (2022). Cyber-security and reinforcement learning—A brief survey. *Engineering Applications of Artificial Intelligence*, *114*, 105116. DOI: 10.1016/j.engappai.2022.105116

Adday, B. N., Shaker, K., Salman, I., & Shaker, H. (2025). Parkinson's Disease Detection Using Deep learning approach based on Wearable Sensor-Based Daily Monitoring. *Mesopotamian Journal of Artificial Intelligence in Healthcare*, *2025*, 26–38. DOI: 10.58496/MJAIH/2025/003

Addula, S. R., Norozpour, S., & Amin, M. (2025). Risk Assessment for Identifying Threats, vulnerabilities and countermeasures in Cloud Computing. *Jordanian Journal of Informatics and Computing*, *2025*(1), 37–48. DOI: 10.63180/jjic.thestap.2025.1.5

Adil, M., Almaiah, M. A., Omar Alsayed, A., & Almomani, O. (2020). An anonymous channel categorization scheme of edge nodes to detect jamming attacks in wireless sensor networks. *Sensors (Basel)*, *20*(8), 2311. DOI: 10.3390/s20082311 PMID: 32325646

Agarwal, S., Yadav, L., & Thakur, M. K. (2018). "Crime Prediction Based on Statistical Models," 11th. *International Conference on Contemporary Computing*, *2018*(IC3), 1–3. DOI: 10.1109/IC3.2018.8530548

Agboola, V., Osamor, J., & Olajide, F. (2024). Evaluating the Efficiency of FTK, Autopsy, and Mobile Forensic Tools: A Comparative Study in Criminal Investigations.

Ahmad, K., Mehfuz, S., & Beg, J. (2021). Enhancing security of cloud platform with cloud access security broker. In Information and Communication Technology for Competitive Strategies (ICTCS 2020) Intelligent Strategies for ICT (pp. 325–335). Springer Nature Singapore. DOI: 10.1007/978-981-16-0882-7_27

Ahmad, H. (2023). A bibliometric exploration of automation and its impact on mechanical engineering research. *Babylonian Journal of Mechanical Engineering*, *2023*(1), 38–46. DOI: 10.58496/BJME/2023/005

Ahmad, H. (2023). Variational iteration approach for solving fractional integro-differential equations with conformable differintegrals. *Babylonian Journal of Mathematics*, *2023*(1), 45–49. DOI: 10.58496/BJM/2023/009

Ahmadi, F. (2024). Zero Trust Architecture (ZTA) for cloud security. *Journal of Cyber Security and Privacy*, *5*(1), 1–15.

Aiswarya, S., & Sangeetha, S. (2022). Perception of Women Trainees' Regarding Skill Development Initiatives of Kudumbashree for Employability. *Ramanujan International Journal of Business and Research*, *7*(2). Advance online publication. DOI: 10.51245/rijbr.v7i2.2022.1087

Akande, A. O., April, N. A., & Van Belle, J. P. (2013, December). Management issues with cloud computing. In *Proceedings of the Second International Conference on Innovative Computing and Cloud Computing* (pp. 119–124).

Al Barazanchi, I. I., & Hashim, W. (2023). Enhancing IoT device security through blockchain technology: A decentralized approach. *SHIFRA*, *2023*, 10–16. DOI: 10.70470/SHIFRA/2023/002

Alaasam, A. B. A. (2023). Quantum computing applications in statistics. *Babylonian Journal of Mathematics*, *2023*(1), 105–107. DOI: 10.58496/BJM/2023/020

Al-Attar, B. (2023). Network Security in AI-based healthcare systems. *Babylonian Journal of Networking*, *2023*, 112–124. DOI: 10.58496/BJN/2023/015

Alazawi, S. A. H., Abdulbaqi, H. A., & Ali, A. H. (2024). CNN-based intrusion detection software for network operating system environment. *Babylonian Journal of Internet of Things*, *2024*, 79–86. DOI: 10.58496/BJIoT/2024/010

Albinhamad, H., Alotibi, A., Alagnam, A., Almaiah, M., & Salloum, S. (2025). Vehicular Ad-hoc Networks (VANETs): A Key Enabler for Smart Transportation Systems and Challenges. *Jordanian Journal of Informatics and Computing*, *2025*(1), 4–15. DOI: 10.63180/jjic.thestap.2025.1.2

Aldawira, C. R., Putra, H. W., Hanafiah, N., Surjarwo, S., & Wibisurya, A. (2019). Door security system for home monitoring based on ESP32. *Procedia Computer Science*, *157*, 673–682. DOI: 10.1016/j.procs.2019.08.218

Aldawood, H., & Skinner, G. (2020). An Advanced Taxonomy for Social Engineering Attacks. *International Journal of Computer Applications*, *177*(30), 1–11. DOI: 10.5120/ijca2020919744

Al-Dhaqm, A., Razak, S., Othman, S. H., Choo, K. K. R., Glisson, W. B., Ali, A., & Abrar, M. (2017). CDBFIP: Common database forensic investigation processes for Internet of Things. IEEE Access, 5, 24401-24416. 9

Aldhyani, T. H. H. (2025). Secure Blockchain-Based Tracking Storage and Permission Verification of Electronic Health Records. *Journal of Cyber Security and Risk Auditing*, *2025*(3), 103–122. DOI: 10.63180/jcsra.thestap.2025.3.8

Aledavood, T., López, E., Roberts, S. G. B., Reed-Tsochas, F., Moro, E., Dunbar, R. I. M., & Saramäki, J. (2015). Daily rhythms in mobile telephone communication. *PLoS One*, *10*(9), e0138098. Advance online publication. DOI: 10.1371/journal.pone.0138098 PMID: 26390215

Alfrhan, A. A., Alhusain, R. H., & Khan, R. U. (2020, September). SMOTE: Class imbalance problem in intrusion detection system. In *2020 International Conference on Computing and Information Technology (ICCIT-1441)* (pp. 1–5). IEEE.

Alhamed, M., & Rahman, M. M. H. (2023). A Systematic Literature Review on Penetration Testing in Networks: Future Research Directions. *Applied Sciences (Basel, Switzerland)*, *13*(12), 6986. DOI: 10.3390/app13126986

Alhasani, A. T., Albakaa, Z. H., Alabidi, S. A., Gburi, O. Q. A. Z., Kadi, A., & Potoroko, I. (2025). Heartbeat Sound Classification Using Mel-Spectrogram and CNN Optimized by Frilled Lizard Algorithm for Cardiovascular Disease Detection. *Mesopotamian Journal of Artificial Intelligence in Healthcare*, *2025*, 96–104. DOI: 10.58496/MJAIH/2025/010

Al-Hashemi, S. Q. Y., Naghmash, M. S., & Ghandour, A. (2024). Improving IP Video Surveillance Systems: The Shift to Digital Networks and Security Challenges. *SHIFRA*, *2024*, 17–23. DOI: 10.70470/SHIFRA/2024/003

Ali, A. (2024). Adaptive and Context-Aware Authentication Framework Using Edge AI and Blockchain in Future Vehicular Networks. *STAP Journal of Security Risk Management*, *2024*(1), 45–56. DOI: 10.63180/jsrm.thestap.2024.1.3

Ali, A., & Shehab, R. (2023). A Systematic Review of Security Risk Management for Banking Systems. *Journal of Cyber Security and Risk Auditing*, *2023*(1), 49–72. DOI: 10.63180/jcsra.thestap.2023.1.4

Ali, G., Mijwil, M. M., Adamopoulos, I., & Ayad, J. (2025). Leveraging the Internet of Things, Remote Sensing, and Artificial Intelligence for Sustainable Forest Management. *Babylonian Journal of Internet of Things*, *2025*, 1–65. DOI: 10.58496/BJIoT/2025/001

Ali, G., Samuel, A., Kabiito, S. P., Morish, Z., Thomas, A., Robert, W., Denis, A., Sallam, M., Mijwil, M. M., Ayad, J., Salau, A. O., & Dhoska, K. (2025). Integration of artificial intelligence, blockchain, and quantum cryptography for securing the Industrial Internet of Things (IIoT): Recent advancements and future trends. *Applied Data Science and Analysis*, *2025*, 19–82. DOI: 10.58496/ADSA/2025/004

Aljaidi, M., Alsarhan, A., & Samara, G., AL-Khassawneh, Y. A., Al-Gumaei, Y. A., Aljawawdeh, H., & Alqammaz, A. (2022, November). A critical evaluation of a recent cybersecurity attack on itunes software updater. In 2022 International Engineering Conference on Electrical, Energy, and Artificial Intelligence (EICEEAI) (pp. 1-6). IEEE. DOI: 10.1109/EICEEAI56378.2022.10050464

Aljanabi, R. A., Al-Qaysi, Z. T., & Suzani, M. S. (2024). Deep Transfer Learning Model for EEG Biometric Decoding. *Applied Data Science and Analysis, 2024*, 4–16. DOI: 10.58496/ADSA/024/002

Aljohani, A. (2023). Zero-trust architecture: Implementing and evaluating security measures in modern enterprise networks. *Shifra, 2023*, 60–72. DOI: 10.70470/SHIFRA/2023/008

Alkattan, H., Al-Nuaimi, B. T., & Subhi, A. A. (2024). Machine Learning techniques to Predictive in Healthcare: Hepatitis C Diagnosis. *Mesopotamian Journal of Artificial Intelligence in Healthcare, 2024*, 128–134. DOI: 10.58496/MJAIH/2024/015

Alkattan, H., Al-Nuaimi, B. T., Subhi, A. A., & Turyasingura, B. (2024). Hybrid Model Approaches for Accurate Time Series Predicting of COVID-19 Cases. *Mesopotamian Journal of Artificial Intelligence in Healthcare, 2024*, 170–176. DOI: 10.58496/MJAIH/2024/017

Allam, A. H., Gomaa, I., Zayed, H. H., & Taha, M. (2024). IoT-based eHealth using blockchain technology: A survey. *Cluster Computing*, *27*(6), 7083–7110. DOI: 10.1007/s10586-024-04357-y

Allasasmh, O., Laila, D. A., Aljaidi, M., Alsarhan, A., & Samara, G. (2024, December). Integrated Approaches to Steganography: Embedding Static Information Across Audio, Visual, and Textual Formats. In *2024 International Jordanian Cybersecurity Conference (IJCC)* (pp. 33-39). IEEE. DOI: 10.1109/IJCC64742.2024.10847286

Almaayah, M., & Sulaiman, R. B. (2024). Cyber Risk Management in the Internet of Things: Frameworks, Models, and Best Practices. *STAP Journal of Security Risk Management*, *2024*(1), 3–23. DOI: 10.63180/jsrm.thestap.2024.1.1

Almaiah, A. M. I. N., & Almomani, O. M. A. R. (2020). An investigator digital forensics frequencies particle swarm optimization for dectection and classification of apt attack in fog computing enviroment (idf-fpso). *Journal of Theoretical and Applied Information Technology*, *15*, 98.

Almaiah, A., & Almomani, O. (2020). An investigation of digital forensics for shamoon attack behaviour in FOG computing and threat intelligence for incident response. *Journal of Theoretical and Applied Information Technology*, *15*, 98.

Almaiah, M. A., Almomani, O., Alsaaidah, A., Al-Otaibi, S., Bani-Hani, N., Hwaitat, A. K. A., Al-Zahrani, A., Lutfi, A., Awad, A. B., & Aldhyani, T. H. (2022). Performance investigation of principal component analysis for intrusion detection system using different support vector machine kernels. *Electronics (Basel)*, *11*(21), 3571. DOI: 10.3390/electronics11213571

Almaiah, M. A., Al-Zahrani, A., Almomani, O., & Alhwaitat, A. K. (2021). Classification of cyber security threats on mobile devices and applications. In *Artificial intelligence and blockchain for future cybersecurity applications* (pp. 107–123). Springer International Publishing. DOI: 10.1007/978-3-030-74575-2_6

Almaiah, M. A., Dawahdeh, Z., Almomani, O., Alsaaidah, A., Al-Khasawneh, A., & Khawatreh, S. (2020). A new hybrid text encryption approach over mobile ad hoc network. [IJECE]. *International Journal of Electrical and Computer Engineering, 10*(6), 6461–6471. DOI: 10.11591/ijece.v10i6.pp6461-6471

Almaiah, M. A., & Kadel, R. (2025). Leveraging ACO, GA, and GWO for Enhancing Port Scan Attack Detection Using Machine Learning. *Journal of Cyber Security and Risk Auditing, 2025*(4), 306–326. DOI: 10.63180/jcsra.thestap.2025.4.9

Almaiah, M. A., Saqr, L. M., Al-Rawwash, L. A., Altellawi, L. A., Al-Ali, R., & Almomani, O. (2024). Classification of Cybersecurity Threats, Vulnerabilities and Countermeasures in Database Systems. *Computers, Materials & Continua, 81*(2), 3189–3220. DOI: 10.32604/cmc.2024.057673

Al-Mazrawe, A., & Al-Musawi, B. (2024). Anomaly detection in cloud network: A review. BIO Web of Conferences, 97, 00019. DOI: 10.1051/bioconf/20249700019

Al-Momani, A., Al-Refai, M. N., Abuowaida, S., Arabiat, M., Alshdaifat, N., & Rahman, M. N. A. (2024). The effect of technological context on smart home adoption in Jordan. *Indonesian Journal of Electrical Engineering and Computer Science, 33*(2), 1186–1195. DOI: 10.11591/ijeecs.v33.i2.pp1186-1195

Almomani, O. (2020). A feature selection model for network intrusion detection system based on PSO, GWO, FFA and GA algorithms. *Symmetry, 12*(6), 1046. DOI: 10.3390/sym12061046

Almomani, O. (2021). A Hybrid Model Using Bio-Inspired Metaheuristic Algorithms for Network Intrusion Detection System. *Computers, Materials & Continua, 68*(1), 409–429. DOI: 10.32604/cmc.2021.016113

Almomani, O., Almaiah, M. A., Alsaaidah, A., Smadi, S., Mohammad, A. H., & Althunibat, A. (2021, July). Machine learning classifiers for network intrusion detection system: comparative study. In *2021 International Conference on Information Technology (ICIT)* (pp. 440-445). IEEE. DOI: 10.1109/ICIT52682.2021.9491770

Almomani, O., Alsaaidah, A., Shareha, A. A. A., Alzaqebah, A., & Almomani, M. (2024). Performance Evaluation of Machine Learning Classifiers for Predicting Denial-of-Service Attack in Internet of Things. *International Journal of Advanced Computer Science and Applications*, *15*(1). Advance online publication. DOI: 10.14569/IJACSA.2024.0150125

Al-Mousa, M. R., Al-Zaqebah, Q., Al-Sherideh, A. S., Al-Ghanim, M., Samara, G., Al-Matarneh, S., & Asassfeh, M. (2022, November). Examining digital forensic evidence for Android applications. In *2022 International Arab Conference on Information Technology (ACIT)* (pp. 1–8). IEEE. DOI: 10.1109/ACIT57182.2022.9994221

Al-Na'amneh, Q., Nasayreh, A. N., Al Mamlook, R., Gharaibeh, H., Alsheyab, A. M., & Almaiah, M. (2024). Improving memory malware detection in machine learning with random forest-based feature selection. In *Risk Assessment and Countermeasures for Cybersecurity* (pp. 96–114). IGI Global. DOI: 10.4018/979-8-3693-2691-6.ch006

Alnajem, A. A. Q. I., Niu, Y., & Ibrahim, A. (2024). Evaluating Educational Strategies Focused on Achieving Sustainable Development Goals in Diverse Global Contexts. *ESTIDAMAA*, *2024*, 60–71. DOI: 10.70470/ESTIDAMAA/2024/009

Al-Nbhany, W. A. N. A., Zahary, A. T., & Al-Shargabi, A. A. (2024). Blockchain-IoT Healthcare Applications and Trends: A Review. *IEEE Access : Practical Innovations, Open Solutions*, *12*, 4178–4212. DOI: 10.1109/ACCESS.2023.3349187

Alotaibi, E., Bin Sulaiman, R., & Almaiah, M. (2025). Assessment of cybersecurity threats and defense mechanisms in wireless sensor networks. *Journal of Cyber Security and Risk Auditing*, *2025*(1), 47–59. DOI: 10.63180/jcsra.thestap.2025.1.5

Alouffi, B., Hasnain, M., Alharbi, A., Alosaimi, W., Alyami, H., & Ayaz, M. (2021). A systematic literature review on cloud computing security: Threats and mitigation strategies. *IEEE Access : Practical Innovations, Open Solutions*, *9*, 57792–57807. DOI: 10.1109/ACCESS.2021.3073203

Alowaisheq, E., Tang, S., Wang, Z., Alharbi, F., Liao, X., & Wang, X. (2020). Zombie Awakening: Stealthy Hijacking of Active Domains through DNS Hosting Referral. *Proceedings of the 2020 ACM SIGSAC Conference on Computer and Communications Security*. DOI: 10.1145/3372297.3417864

Al-Quraishi, T., Mahdi, O. A., Abusalem, A., Ng, C. K., Gyasi, A., Al-Boridi, O., & Al-Quraishi, N. (2024). Transforming Amazon's Operations: Leveraging Oracle Cloud-Based ERP with Advanced Analytics for Data-Driven Success. *Applied Data Science and Analysis*, *2024*, 108–120. DOI: 10.58496/ADSA/2024/010

Alraizza, A., & Algarni, A. (2023). Ransomware Detection Using Machine Learning: A Survey. *Big Data and Cognitive Computing*, *7*(3), 143. DOI: 10.3390/bdcc7030143

Alsaaidah, A., Almomani, O., Abu-Shareha, A. A., Abualhaj, M. M., & Achuthan, A. (2024). ARP spoofing attack detection model in IoT network using machine learning: Complexity vs. accuracy. *Journal of Applied Data Sciences*, *5*(4), 1850–1860. DOI: 10.47738/jads.v5i4.374

Alsahaim, S., & Maayah, M. (2023). Analyzing Cybersecurity Threats on Mobile Phones. *STAP Journal of Security Risk Management*, *2023*(1), 3–19. DOI: 10.63180/jsrm.thestap.2023.1.2

Alsajri, A., & Steiti, A. (2024). Intrusion detection system based on machine learning algorithms:(SVM and genetic algorithm). *Babylonian Journal of Machine Learning*, *2024*, 15–29. DOI: 10.58496/BJML/2024/002

Alsajri, A., Steiti, A., & Salman, H. A. (2023). Enhancing IoT Security to Leveraging ML for DDoS Attack Prevention in Distributed Network Routing. *Babylonian Journal of Internet of Things*, *2023*, 74–84. DOI: 10.58496/BJIoT/2023/010

Alsarhan, A., Al-Aiash, I., Al-Fraihat, D., Aljaidi, M., & Laila, D. A. A. H. A. (2024, July). Expert Phishing Detection System. In 2024 IEEE International Conference on Industry 4.0, Artificial Intelligence, and Communications Technology (IAICT) (pp. 54-59). IEEE DOI: 10.1109/IAICT62357.2024.10617460

Alsarhan, A., Agarwal, A., Obeidat, I., Bsoul, M., Khasawneh, A. A., & Kilani, Y. (2013). Optimal spectrum utilisation in cognitive network using combined spectrum sharing approach: Overlay, underlay and trad ing. *International Journal of Business Information Systems*, *12*(4), 423–454. DOI: 10.1504/IJBIS.2013.053216

Alsarhan, A., Al-Ghuwairi, A.-R., Esra'a, A., & Idhaim, H. (2022). Omar alkhawaldeh " A Novel Scheme for Malicious Nodes Detection in Cloud Markets Based on Fuzzy Logic Technique. *Int. J. Interact. Mob. Technol.*, *16*(10), 191–102. DOI: 10.3991/ijim.v16i10.30479

Alshamrani, A., Myneni, S., Chowdhary, A., & Huang, D. (2019). A survey on advanced persistent threats: Techniques, solutions, challenges, and research opportunities. *IEEE Communications Surveys and Tutorials*, *21*(2), 1851–1877. DOI: 10.1109/COMST.2019.2891891

Al-Shareeda, M. A., Najm, L. B., Hassan, A. A., Mushtaq, S., & Ali, H. A. (2024). Secure IoT-Based Smart Agriculture System Using Wireless Sensor Networks for Remote Environmental Monitoring. *STAP Journal of Security Risk Management*, *2024*(1), 56–66. DOI: 10.63180/jsrm.thestap.2024.1.4

Al-Shareeda, M. A., Obaid, A. A., & Almajid, A. A. H. (2025). The Role of Artificial Intelligence in Bodybuilding: A Systematic Review of Applications, Challenges, and Future Prospects. *Jordanian Journal of Informatics and Computing*, *2025*(1), 16–26. DOI: 10.63180/jjic.thestap.2025.1.3

Alshdaifat, N., Osman, M. A., & Talib, A. Z. (2022). An improved multi-object instance segmentation based on deep learning. *Kuwait Journal of Science*, *49*(2).

Al-Sherideh, A. S., Ismail, R., Al-Mousa, M. R., Al-Qawasmi, K., Al-Shaikh, A., & Awwad, H. (2024). Development of a secure model for mobile government applications in Jordan. *Journal of Statistics Applications & Probability*, *13*(1), 145–155. DOI: 10.18576/jsap/130110

Al-Sherideh, A. S., Ismail, R., Wahid, F. A., Fabil, N., & Ismail, W. (2018). *Mobile government applications based on security and privacy: A literature review*. International Journal of Engineering and Technology.

Al-Sherideh, A. S., Maabreh, K., Maabreh, M., Al Mousa, M. R., & Asassfeh, M. (2023). Assessing the impact and effectiveness of cybersecurity measures in e-learning on students and educators: A case study. *International Journal of Advanced Computer Science and Applications*, *14*(5). Advance online publication. DOI: 10.14569/IJACSA.2023.0140516

Alshinwan, M., Memon, A. G., Ghanem, M. C., & Almaayah, M. (2025). Unsupervised text feature selection approach based on improved Prairie dog algorithm for the text clustering. *Jordanian Journal of Informatics and Computing*, *2025*(1), 27–36. DOI: 10.63180/jjic.thestap.2025.1.4

Alshuaibi, A., Arshad, M. W., & Maayah, M. (2025). A Hybrid Genetic Algorithm and Hidden Markov Model-Based Hashing Technique for Robust Data Security. *Journal of Cyber Security and Risk Auditing*, *2025*(3), 42–56. DOI: 10.63180/jcsra.thestap.2025.3.6

Alsuhimat, F. M., Mohamad, F. S., & Iqtait, M. (2019). Detection and extraction features for signature images via different techniques. *Journal of Physics: Conference Series*, *1179*(1), 012087. DOI: 10.1088/1742-6596/1179/1/012087

Alzahrani, A., Alshehri, M., AlGhamdi, R., & Sharma, S. K. (2023). Improved Wireless Medical Cyber-Physical System (IWMCPS) based on machine learning. *Health Care*, *11*(3), 384. DOI: 10.3390/healthcare11030384 PMID: 36766959

Amirthayogam, G., Kumaran, N., Gopalakrishnan, S., Brito, K., RaviChand, S., & Choubey, S. B. (2024). Integrating Behavioral Analytics and Intrusion Detection Systems to Protect Critical Infrastructure and Smart Cities. *Babylonian Journal of Networking, 2024*, 88–97. DOI: 10.58496/BJN/2024/010

Ang, S., Huy, S., & Janarthanan, M. (2025). Utilizing IDS and IPS to improve cybersecurity monitoring process. *Journal of Cyber Security and Risk Auditing, 2025*(3), 77–88. DOI: 10.63180/jcsra.thestap.2025.3.10

Ani, U. P. D., He, H., & Tiwari, A. (2016). Review of cybersecurity issues in industrial critical infrastructure: Manufacturing in perspective. *Journal of Cyber Security Technology, 1*(1), 32–74. DOI: 10.1080/23742917.2016.1252211

Antony, J., & Maity, T. (2021). Analysis of Ethernet Control Network. *Journal of the Institution of Electronics and Telecommunication Engineers, 69*(3), 1588–1596. DOI: 10.1080/03772063.2020.1871427

Arora, L., Thakur, N., & Yadav, S. K. (2021). USB Rubber Ducky Detection by using Heuristic Rules. *2021 International Conference on Computing, Communication, and Intelligent Systems (ICCCIS)*. DOI: 10.1109/ICCCIS51004.2021.9397064

Arshad, H., Jantan, A., Hoon, G. K., & Abiodun, I. O. (2020). Formal knowledge model for online social network forensics. *Computers & Security, 89*, 101675. Advance online publication. DOI: 10.1016/j.cose.2019.101675

Arshad, H., Jantan, A., Hoon, G. K., & Butt, A. S. (2019). A multi-layered semantic framework for integrated forensic acquisition on social media. *Digital Investigation, 29*, 147–158. DOI: 10.1016/j.diin.2019.04.002

Arshad, H., Omlara, E., Abiodun, I. O., & Aminu, A. (2020). A semi-automated forensic investigation model for online social networks. *Computers & Security, 97*, 101946. Advance online publication. DOI: 10.1016/j.cose.2020.101946

Asad, A. B., Mansur, R., Zawad, S., Evan, N., & Hossain, M. I. (2020) "Analysis of Malware Prediction Based on Infection Rate Using Machine Learning Techniques," IEEE Region 10 Symposium (TENSYMP), Jun. 2020, pp. 706–709, DOI: 10.1109/TENSYMP50017.2020.9230624

Asassfeh, M., Samara, G., Zaid, A. A., Laila, D. A., Al-Anzi, S., Alqammaz, A., & Al-Mousa, M. R. (2024, December). Penetration Testing Overview-Opportunities and Ethical Considerations: Literature Notes. In *2024 International Jordanian Cybersecurity Conference (IJCC)* (pp. 131-135). IEEE. DOI: 10.1109/IJCC64742.2024.10847295

AWS Security Solutions. (2023). Amazon Web Services. Retrieved from https://aws.amazon.com/security/

Babu, P. A., Rai, A. K., Ramesh, J. V. N., Nithyasri, A., Sangeetha, S., Kshirsagar, P. R., Rajendran, A., Rajaram, A., & Dilipkumar, S. (2024). An Explainable Deep Learning Approach for Oral Cancer Detection. *Journal of Electrical Engineering & Technology*, *19*(3), 1837–1848. DOI: 10.1007/s42835-023-01654-1

Balbach, E. (1999). Using case studies to do program evaluation. *International Journal of Aromatherapy*, *9*(1), 1–18. DOI: 10.1016/S0962-4562(99)80002-7

Balgani, S., & Sangeetha, S. (2014). An Efficient Approach to Improve Response Time in Multibiometric Patterns Retrieval from Large Database. [IJCSNS]. *International Journal of Computer Science and Network Security*, *14*(5), 102.

Baloian, N., Bassaletti, E., Fernandez, M., Figueroa, O., Fuentes, P., Manasevich, R., Orchard, M., Penafiel, S., Pino, J. A., & Vergara, M. (2017) "Crime Prediction Using Patterns and Context," IEEE 21st International Conference on Computer Supported Cooperative Work in Design (CSCWD), 2017, pp. 2–9, DOI: 10.1109/CSCWD.2017.8066662

Banerjee, P., Datta, P., Pal, S., Chakraborty, S., Roy, A., Poddar, S., Dhali, S., & Ghosh, A. (2022). Home security system using RaspberryPi. In *Advanced energy and control systems* (pp. 167–176). Springer., DOI: 10.1007/978-981-16-7274-3_14

Barach, J. (2024). Enhancing Intrusion Detection with CNN Attention Using NSL-KDD Dataset. 2024 Artificial Intelligence for Business (AIxB), 15–20. DOI: 10.1109/AIxB62249.2024.00009

Baryamureeba, V., & Florence, T. (2004). The enhanced digital investigation process model. *Asian Journal of Information Technology*, *5*(8), 790–794.

Basnet, R., Mukkamala, S., & Sung, A. H. (2008). Detection of phishing attacks: A machine learning approach. In *Soft computing applications in industry* (pp. 373–383). Springer Berlin Heidelberg. DOI: 10.1007/978-3-540-77465-5_19

Bataineh, M. R., Mardini, W., Khamayseh, Y. M., & Yassein, M. M. B. (2022). Novel and Secure Blockchain Framework for Health Applications in IoT. *IEEE Access : Practical Innovations, Open Solutions*, *10*, 14914–14926. DOI: 10.1109/ACCESS.2022.3147795

Bauskar, S. (2024). Enhancing Cybersecurity In Network Intrusion Detection System Based On Artificial Intelligence (AI) Techniques. SSRN Electronic Journal. DOI: 10.2139/ssrn.4987362

Beddiar, D. R., Nini, B., Sabokrou, M., & Hadid, A. (2020). Vision-based human activity recognition: A survey. *Multimedia Tools and Applications*, *79*(41-42), 30509–30555. DOI: 10.1007/s11042-020-09004-3

Belmabrouk, K. (2023). Cyber Criminals and Data Privacy Measures. *Advances in Information Security, Privacy, and Ethics*, •••, 198–226. DOI: 10.4018/979-8-3693-1528-6.ch011

Bhardwaj, A., & Kaushik, K. (2022). Predictive analytics-based cybersecurity framework for cloud infrastructure. [IJCAC]. *International Journal of Cloud Applications and Computing*, *12*(1), 1–20. DOI: 10.4018/IJCAC.297106

Bhuiyan, M. R. I., Faraji, M. R., Tabassum, M. N., Ghose, P., Sarbabidya, S., & Akter, R. (2024). Leveraging Machine Learning for Cybersecurity: Techniques, Challenges, and Future Directions. *Edelweiss Applied Science and Technology*, *8*(6), 4291–4307. DOI: 10.55214/25768484.v8i6.2930

Bhushan, K., & Gupta, B. B. (2018). Distributed denial of service (DDoS) attack mitigation in software defined network (SDN)-based cloud computing environment. *Journal of Ambient Intelligence and Humanized Computing*, *10*(5), 1985–1997. DOI: 10.1007/s12652-018-0800-9

Biedermann, A., & Kotsoglou, K. N. (2020). Digital evidence exceptionalism? A review and discussion of conceptual hurdles in digital evidence transformation. *Forensic Science International. Synergy*, *2*, 262–274. DOI: 10.1016/j.fsisyn.2020.08.004 PMID: 32944711

Biggio, B., & Roli, F. (2018). Wild patterns: Ten years after the rise of adversarial machine learning. *Pattern Recognition*, *84*, 317–331. DOI: 10.1016/j.patcog.2018.07.023

Binu, S., & Misbahuddin, M. (2013). A survey of traditional and cloud specific security issues. In International Symposium on Security in Computing and Communication (pp. 110–129). Springer Berlin Heidelberg. DOI: 10.1007/978-3-642-40576-1_12

Biswas, B., Mukhopadhyay, A., Kumar, A., & Delen, D. (2024). A hybrid framework using explainable AI (XAI) in cyber-risk management for defence and recovery against phishing attacks. *Decision Support Systems*, *177*, 114102. DOI: 10.1016/j.dss.2023.114102

Biswas, S., Sharif, K., Li, F., Latif, Z., Kanhere, S. S., & Mohanty, S. P. (2020). Interoperability and Synchronization Management of Blockchain-Based Decentralized e-Health Systems. *IEEE Transactions on Engineering Management*, *67*(4), 1363–1376. DOI: 10.1109/TEM.2020.2989779

Bollé, T., Casey, E., & Jacquet, M. (2020). The role of evaluations in reaching decisions using automated systems supporting forensic analysis. *Forensic Science International Digital Investigation, 34*, 301016. Advance online publication. DOI: 10.1016/j.fsidi.2020.301016

Brewer, R. (2014). Advanced persistent threats: Minimising the damage. *Network Security, 2014*(4), 5–9. DOI: 10.1016/S1353-4858(14)70040-6

Brooks, R. R., Yu, L., Ozcelik, I., Oakley, J., & Tusing, N. (2022). Distributed Denial of Service (DDoS): A History. *IEEE Annals of the History of Computing, 44*(2), 44–54. DOI: 10.1109/MAHC.2021.3072582

Burhanuddin, M. A. (2023). Efficient hardware acceleration techniques for deep learning on edge devices: A comprehensive performance analysis. *KHWARIZMIA, 2023*(1), 103–112. DOI: 10.70470/KHWARIZMIA/2023/010

Burhanuddin, M. A. (2023). Epigenetic modifications as predictive biomarkers for cardiovascular disease: A longitudinal study on DNA methylation patterns and disease risk. *SHIFAA, 2023*, 59–65. DOI: 10.70470/SHIFAA/2023/007

Butt, U. A., Mehmood, M., Shah, S. B. H., Amin, R., Shaukat, M. W., Raza, S. M., Suh, D. Y., & Piran, M. J. (2020). A review of machine learning algorithms for cloud computing security. *Electronics (Basel), 9*(9), 1379. DOI: 10.3390/electronics9091379

Carrier, B., & Spafford, E. (2010). An event-based digital forensic investigation framework. *Digital Forensic Research Workshop*, 57(1), 1–51.

Carroll, F., Adejobi, J. A., & Montasari, R. (2022). How Good Are We at Detecting a Phishing Attack? Investigating the Evolving Phishing Attack Email and Why It Continues to Successfully Deceive Society. *SN Computer Science, 3*(2), 170. Advance online publication. DOI: 10.1007/s42979-022-01069-1 PMID: 35224514

Cen, J., & Li, Y. (2022). Deep Learning-Based Anomaly Traffic Detection Method in Cloud Computing Environment. *Wireless Communications and Mobile Computing, 2022*(1), 6155925. DOI: 10.1155/2022/6155925

Chabot, Y., Bertaux, A., Nicolle, C., & Kechadi, M. T. (2014). A complete formalized knowledge representation model for advanced digital forensics timeline analysis. *Digital Investigation, 11*(Suppl. 2), S95–S105. DOI: 10.1016/j.diin.2014.05.009

Chakraborty, C., Nagarajan, S. M., Devarajan, G. G., Ramana, T. V., & Mohanty, R. (2023). Intelligent AI-based Healthcare Cyber Security System using Multi-Source Transfer Learning Method. *ACM Transactions on Sensor Networks*, 3597210. Advance online publication. DOI: 10.1145/3597210

Chakraborty, P., Yousuf, M. A., Zahidur Rahman, M., & Faruqui, N. (2020). How can a robot calculate the level of visual focus of human's attention. In *International Joint Conference on Computational Intelligence: IJCCI 2019* (pp. 329–342). Springer. DOI: 10.1007/978-981-15-3607-6_27

Chand, A., Agarwal, P., & Sharma, S. (2023). Real-Time Retrieving Vedic Sanskrit Text into Multi-Lingual Text and Audio for Cultural Tourism Motivation. *2022 International Conference for Advancement in Technology (ICONAT)*, 1–6. DOI: 10.1109/ICONAT57137.2023.10080862

Chandola, V., Banerjee, A., & Kumar, V. (2009). Anomaly detection: A survey. *ACM Computing Surveys*, *41*(3), 1–58. DOI: 10.1145/1541880.1541882

Chandran, A. L., Samual, J., Safavi, S., & Ali, A. (2025). A Comparative Analysis of Machine Learning Models on Detecting Malware in Android Devices. *Journal of Cyber Security and Risk Auditing*, *2025*(4), 327–346. DOI: 10.63180/jcsra.thestap.2025.4.10

Chang, Y. W., Hsu, P. Y., Huang, S. H., & Chen, J. (2020). Determinants of switching intention to cloud computing in large enterprises. *Data Technologies and Applications*, *54*(1), 16–33. DOI: 10.1108/DTA-12-2018-0104

Chauhan, C., & Sehgal, S. (2017) "A Review: Crime Analysis Using Data Mining Techniques and Algorithms," *International Conference on Computing, Communication and Automation (ICCCA)*, 2017, pp. 21–25, DOI: 10.1109/CCAA.2017.8229823

Chen, T. (2024). *ChatBot-Based Next-Generation Intrusion Detection System. Conversational Artificial Intelligence*. Portico., DOI: 10.1002/9781394200801.ch20

Chidukwani, A., Zander, S., & Koutsakis, P. (2022). A Survey on the Cyber Security of Small-to-Medium Businesses: Challenges, Research Focus and Recommendations. *IEEE Access : Practical Innovations, Open Solutions*, *10*, 85701–85719. DOI: 10.1109/ACCESS.2022.3197899

Chung, H., Park, J., Lee, S., & Kang, C. (2012). Digital forensic investigation of cloud storage services. *Digital Investigation*, *9*(2), 81–95. DOI: 10.1016/j.diin.2012.05.015

Ciardhuáin, S. (2004). An extended model of cybercrime investigations. *International Journal of Digital Evidence*, *3*(1), 1–22.

Comite, U. (2022). I&CT in the public administrations: From e-government to e-democracy through digital reporting. In *Handbook of Research on Applying Emerging Technologies Across Multiple Disciplines* (pp. 55–77). IGI Global. DOI: 10.4018/978-1-7998-8476-7.ch004

Daghmehchi Firoozjaei, M., Habibi Lashkari, A., & Ghorbani, A. A. (2022). Memory forensics tools: A comparative analysis. *Journal of Cyber Security Technology*, *6*(3), 149–173. DOI: 10.1080/23742917.2022.2100036

Davarasan, A., Samual, J., Palansundram, K., & Ali, A. (2024). A Comprehensive Review of Machine Learning Approaches for Android Malware Detection. *Journal of Cyber Security and Risk Auditing*, *2024*(1), 39–60. DOI: 10.63180/jcsra.thestap.2024.1.5

Davies, G., Mison, A., & Eden, P. (2022, March). Addressing the skills shortage in cybersecurity. In *International Conference on Cyber Warfare and Security* (Vol. 17, No. 1, pp. 544–551). DOI: 10.34190/iccws.17.1.69

Deb, D., Rodrigo, H., & Kumar, S. (2024, May). Performance analysis of machine learning algorithms on imbalanced DDoS attack dataset. In *2024 IEEE World AI IoT Congress (AIIoT)* (pp. 349–355). IEEE. DOI: 10.1109/AIIoT61789.2024.10579021

Del Giudice, M., Scuotto, V., Orlando, B., & Mustilli, M. (2023). Toward the human-centered approach: A revised model of individual acceptance of AI. *Human Resource Management Review*, *33*(1), 100856. Advance online publication. DOI: 10.1016/j.hrmr.2021.100856

Demertzi, V., Demertzis, S., & Demertzis, K. (2023). An Overview of Cyber Threats, Attacks and Countermeasures on the Primary Domains of Smart Cities. *Applied Sciences (Basel, Switzerland)*, *13*(2), 790. DOI: 10.3390/app13020790

Devi, S., & Babu, D. (2024). A study on multi-vector attacks in cloud computing. *International Journal of Information Technology : an Official Journal of Bharati Vidyapeeth's Institute of Computer Applications and Management*, *16*(1), 223–235.

Domingues, P., Francisco, J., & Frade, M. (2023). Post-mortem digital forensics analysis of the Zepp Life android application. *Forensic Science International Digital Investigation*, *45*, 301555. DOI: 10.1016/j.fsidi.2023.301555

Duan, Z., Chen, P., Sanchez, F., Dong, Y., Stephenson, M., & Barker, J. M. (2012). Detecting Spam Zombies by Monitoring Outgoing Messages. *IEEE Transactions on Dependable and Secure Computing*, *9*(2), 198–210. DOI: 10.1109/TDSC.2011.49

Durán-Vega, L. A., Santana-Mancilla, P. C., Buenrostro-Mariscal, R., Contreras-Castillo, J., Anido-Rifón, L. E., García-Ruiz, M. A., Montesinos-López, O. A., & Estrada-González, F. (2019). An IoT system for remote health monitoring in elderly adults through a wearable device and mobile application. *Geriatrics (Basel, Switzerland)*, *4*(2), 34. DOI: 10.3390/geriatrics4020034 PMID: 31067819

Dutta, P. K., Singh, B., Lal, S., Arora, M. K., Raghav, A., Mensah, G. B., & Alkattan, H. (2023). Encoding IoT for patient monitoring and smart healthcare: Connected healthcare system fostering health 6.0. *Babylonian Journal of Internet of Things, 2023*, 48–58. DOI: 10.58496/BJIoT/2023/007

Egala, B. S., Pradhan, A. K., Dey, P., Badarla, V., & Mohanty, S. P. (2023). Fortified-Chain 2.0: Intelligent Blockchain for Decentralized Smart Healthcare System. *IEEE Internet of Things Journal, 10*(14), 12308–12321. DOI: 10.1109/JIOT.2023.3247452

Egele, M., Scholte, T., Kirda, E., & Kruegel, C. (2008). A survey on automated dynamic malware-analysis techniques and tools. *ACM Computing Surveys, 44*(2), 1–42. DOI: 10.1145/2089125.2089126

Faruqui, N., Yousuf, M. A., Whaiduzzaman, M., Azad, A., Barros, A., & Moni, M. A. (2021). LungNet: A hybrid deep-CNN model for lung cancer diagnosis using CT and wearable sensor-based medical IoT data. *Computers in Biology and Medicine, 139*, 104961. Advance online publication. DOI: 10.1016/j.compbiomed.2021.104961 PMID: 34741906

Fasching, D., Kaliner, S., & Karel, T. (2012). Social media data preservation tools and best practices. *Law Journal Newsletters, 29*(2), 90.

Fernández-Caramés, T. M., Froiz-Míguez, I., Blanco-Novoa, O., & Fraga-Lamas, P. (2019). Enabling the Internet of Mobile Crowdsourcing Health Things: A Mobile Fog Computing, Blockchain and IoT Based Continuous Glucose Monitoring System for Diabetes Mellitus Research and Care. *Sensors (Basel), 19*(15), 3319. DOI: 10.3390/s19153319 PMID: 31357725

Flayyih, M. F., & Hassan, T. (2024). Predictive analytics model for students' grade prediction using machine learning. *Babylonian Journal of Artificial Intelligence, 2024*(1), 83–101. DOI: 10.58496/BJAI/2024/011

Fouladi, R. F., Kayatas, C. E., & Anarim, E. (2016, June). Frequency-based DDoS attack detection approach using naive Bayes classification. In *2016 39th International Conference on Telecommunications and Signal Processing (TSP)* (pp. 104–107). IEEE. DOI: 10.1109/TSP.2016.7760838

Galbraith, C., & Smyth, P. (2017). Analyzing user-event data using score-based likelihood ratios with marked point processes. *Digital Investigation, 22*(Suppl.), S106–S114. DOI: 10.1016/j.diin.2017.06.009

Gampel, A., & Eveleigh, T. (2025). Model-Based Systems Engineering Cybersecurity Risk Assessment for Industrial Control Systems Leveraging NIST Risk Management Framework Methodology. *Journal of Cyber Security and Risk Auditing*, *2025*(4), 204–221. DOI: 10.63180/jcsra.thestap.2025.4.2

Gangwani, D., Sanghvi, H. A., Parmar, V., Patel, R. H., & Pandya, A. S. (2023). A comprehensive review on cloud security using machine learning techniques. Artificial Intelligence in Cyber Security: Theories and Applications, 1–24.

Garfinkel, S. (2012). Digital forensics XML and the DFXML toolset. *Digital Investigation*, *8*(3-4), 161–174. DOI: 10.1016/j.diin.2011.11.002

Garg, S., Kaur, K., Kumar, N., Kaddoum, G., Zomaya, A. Y., & Ranjan, R. (2019). A hybrid deep learning-based model for anomaly detection in cloud datacenter networks. *IEEE Transactions on Network and Service Management*, *16*(3), 924–935. DOI: 10.1109/TNSM.2019.2927886

Ghanem, M. C., & Salloum, S. (2025). Integrating AI-driven deep learning for energy-efficient smart buildings in Internet of Thing-based Industry 4.0. *Babylonian Journal of Internet of Things*, *2025*(7), 121–130. DOI: 10.58496/BJIoT/2025/007

Ghankutkar, S., Sarkar, N., Gajbhiye, P., Yadav, S., Kalbande, D., & Bakereywala, N. (2019) "Modelling Machine Learning for Analysing Crime News," International Conference on Advances in Computing, Communication and Control (ICAC3), 2019, pp. 1–5, DOI: 10.1109/ICAC347590.2019.9036769

Gide, A. I., & Mu'azu, A. A. (2024). A real-time intrusion detection system for dos/ddos attack classification in IoT networks using KNN-neural network hybrid technique. *Babylonian Journal of Internet of Things*, *2024*, 60–69. DOI: 10.58496/BJIoT/2024/008

Google Cloud Security Overview. (2023). Google Cloud Platform. Retrieved from https://cloud.google.com/security/

Gopalakrishnan, S., Ruby, E. D. K., Hemanand, D., Anitha, R., Suresh, D., & Choubey, S. B. (2024). Leveraging AI and Blockchain in MANETs to enhance Smart City Infrastructure and Autonomous Vehicular Networks. *Babylonian Journal of Machine Learning*, *2024*, 112–120. DOI: 10.58496/BJML/2024/011

Gopalsamy, M. (2021). Enhanced Cybersecurity for Network Intrusion Detection System Based Artificial Intelligence (AI) Techniques. International Journal of Advanced Research in Science, Communication and Technology, 671–681. Internet Archive. DOI: 10.48175/IJARSCT-2269M

Govindan, V., Jayaprakash, J., Park, C., Lee, J. R., & Cangul, I. N. (2023). Optimization-based design and control of dynamic systems. *Babylonian Journal of Mathematics*, *2023*(1), 30–35. DOI: 10.58496/BJM/2023/006

Greenwood, R. E.The Case Study Approach. (1993). The case study approach. *Business Communication Quarterly*, *56*(4), 46–48. DOI: 10.1177/108056999305600409

Gulenko, A., Wallschläger, M., Schmidt, F., Kao, O., & Liu, F. (2016). Evaluating machine learning algorithms for anomaly detection in clouds. In 2016 IEEE International Conference on Big Data (Big Data) (pp. 2716–2721). IEEE. DOI: 10.1109/BigData.2016.7840917

Gupta, B. B. (Ed.). (2019). *Modern principles, practices, and algorithms for cloud security*. IGI Global.

Gupta, M., Vashishth, T. K., & Verma, P. K. (2024). Machine learning and deep learning based intrusion detection for blackhole attacks in mobile ad-hoc networks. *Multidisciplinary Science Journal*, *6*(11), 2024209–2024209. DOI: 10.31893/multiscience.2024209

Habib, M. K., & Chimsom, C. I. (2022). CPS: Role, Characteristics, architectures and future Potentials. *Procedia Computer Science*, *200*, 1347–1358. DOI: 10.1016/j.procs.2022.01.336

Hadid, M. H., Al-Qaysi, Z. T., Hussein, Q. M., Aljanabi, R. A., Abdulqader, I. R., Suzani, M. S., & Shir, W. L. (2024). Semantic image retrieval analysis based on deep learning and singular value decomposition. *Applied Data Science and Analysis*, *2024*(1), 17–31. DOI: 10.58496/ADSA/2024/003

Hammad, O. M., Smaoui, I., Fakhfakh, A., & Hashim, M. M. (2024). Recent advances in digital image masking techniques Future challenges and trends: A review. *SHIFRA*, *2024*, 67–73. DOI: 10.70470/SHIFRA/2024/008

Hammi, B., Zeadally, S., & Nebhen, J. (2023). Security threats, countermeasures, and challenges of digital supply chains. *ACM Computing Surveys*, *55*(14s), 1–40. DOI: 10.1145/3588999

Hanabaratti, K. D., Shivannavar, A. S., Deshpande, S. N., Argiddi, R. V., Praveen, R. V. S., & Itkar, S. A. (2024). Advancements in natural language processing: Enhancing machine understanding of human language in conversational AI systems. *International Journal of Communication Networks and Information Security*, *16*(4), 193–204.

Hanoon, W. H., & Ibrahim, A. S. (2024). Fuzzy semi and fuzzy strongly semi two-absorbing second sub-modules. *Babylonian Journal of Mathematics*, *2024*(1), 95–101. DOI: 10.58496/BJM/2024/012

Hasan, M. K., Alkhalifah, A., Islam, S., Babiker, N. B., Habib, A. A., Aman, A. H. M., & Hossain, M. A. (2022). Blockchain technology on smart grid, energy trading, and big data: Security issues, challenges, and recommendations. *Wireless Communications and Mobile Computing*, *2022*(1), 1–26. DOI: 10.1155/2022/9065768

Hattori, K., & Takahashi, M. (2000). A new edited k-nearest neighbor rule in the pattern classification problem. *Pattern Recognition*, *33*(3), 521–528. DOI: 10.1016/S0031-3203(99)00068-0

Hochreiter, S., & Schmidhuber, J. (1997). Long Short-Term Memory. *Neural Computation*, *9*(8), 1735–1780. DOI: 10.1162/neco.1997.9.8.1735 PMID: 9377276

Hou, C., Shi, J., Cui, M., & Yang, Q. (2021). Attack versus Attack: Toward Adversarial Example Defend Website Fingerprinting Attack. 2021 IEEE 20th International Conference on Trust, Security and Privacy in Computing and Communications (TrustCom). DOI: 10.1109/TrustCom53373.2021.00111

Hussain, M., Siddiqui, S., & Islam, N. (2023). Social Engineering and Data Privacy. *Advances in Information Security, Privacy, and Ethics*, •••, 225–248. DOI: 10.4018/978-1-6684-6581-3.ch010

Hussein, N. A.-H. K., & Basel, O. M. (2024). Integrating Renewable Energy Systems into Urban Planning for Sustainable Cities. *ESTIDAMAA*, *2024*, 15–21. DOI: 10.70470/ESTIDAMAA/2024/003

Hussein, N. A.-H. K., Khalaf, S., & Shah, K. D. (2024). Advanced Composite Materials for Sustainable Construction: Innovations in Civil Engineering Applications. *KHWARIZMIA*, *2024*, 8–16. DOI: 10.70470/KHWARIZMIA/2024/003

Ibrahim, A. (2024). Transitioning Emerging Economies Toward Sustainability by Implementing Targeted Policy Interventions. *ESTIDAMAA*, *2024*, 53–59. DOI: 10.70470/ESTIDAMAA/2024/008

Iqtait, M., & Mohamad, F. S. (2019). Multiple classifiers for age prediction against AAM and ASM. *International Journal of Recent Technology and Engineering*, *8*(2 Special Issue 3), 456–461.

Iqtait, M., Mohamad, F. S., & Mamat, M. (2018). Feature extraction for face recognition via active shape model (ASM) and active appearance model (AAM). *IOP Conference Series. Materials Science and Engineering*, *332*(1), 012032. DOI: 10.1088/1757-899X/332/1/012032

Ismail, S., El Mrabet, Z., & Reza, H. (2022). An ensemble-based machine learning approach for cyber-attacks detection in wireless sensor networks. *Applied Sciences (Basel, Switzerland)*, *13*(1), 30. DOI: 10.3390/app13010030

Jadhao, A. R., & Agrawal, A. J. (2016). A digital forensics investigation model for social networking site. In *Second International Conference on Information and Communication Technology for Competitive Strategies (ICTCS '16)* (pp. 1–4). ACM. DOI: 10.1145/2905055.2905346

Jadhao, A., Bagade, A., Taware, G., & Bhonde, M. (2020). Effect of background color perception on attention span and short-term memory in normal students. *National Journal of Physiology, Pharmacy and Pharmacology*, *10*(11), 981–984. DOI: 10.5455/njppp.2020.10.06162202017072020

Jafarian, J. H., Abolfathi, M., & Rahimian, M. (2023). Detecting Network Scanning Through Monitoring and Manipulation of DNS Traffic. *IEEE Access : Practical Innovations, Open Solutions*, *11*, 20267–20283. DOI: 10.1109/ACCESS.2023.3250106

Jagannathan, S. (2016). Real-time big data analytics architecture for remote sensing application. In *2016 International Conference on Signal Processing, Communication, Power and Embedded System (SCOPES)* (pp. 1912–1916). IEEE. DOI: 10.1109/SCOPES.2016.7955779

Jain, M. A., Rao, B. S., Chattopadhyay, S., Kumar, A., Muthuraman, M. S., & Manjula, A. (2023). An Artificial Intelligence Network based-Host Intrusion Detection System for Internet of Things Devices. 2023 4th International Conference on Electronics and Sustainable Communication Systems (ICESC), 656–661. DOI: 10.1109/ICESC57686.2023.10193232

Jain, P., Gyanchandani, M., & Khare, N. (2016). Big data privacy: A technological perspective and review. *Journal of Big Data*, *3*(1), 1–25. DOI: 10.1186/s40537-016-0059-y

Jamil, F., Kahng, H. K., Kim, S., & Kim, D.-H. (2021). Towards Secure Fitness Framework Based on IoT-Enabled Blockchain Network Integrated with Machine Learning Algorithms. *Sensors (Basel)*, *21*(5), 1640. DOI: 10.3390/s21051640 PMID: 33652773

Jasim, N. S., Kirdar, M. S. I., Hamad, H., Abu-Shams, A. I. M. S., & Zbaida, A. (2024). Factor group for some SL groups. *Babylonian Journal of Mathematics*, *2024*(1), 171–177. DOI: 10.58496/BJM/2024/018

Jayashre, K., & Padmavathi, U. (2024). *Blockchain-Based IoT Computing Services in Medical Healthcare*., DOI: 10.4018/979-8-3693-8568-5.ch007

Jeyalakshmi, J., Gnanavel, S., Vijay, K., & Berna, I. E. (2024). Threat landscape and common security challenges in cloud environments. In *Analyzing and Mitigating Security Risks in Cloud Computing* (pp. 194–213). IGI Global. DOI: 10.4018/979-8-3693-3249-8.ch010

Jeyaram, A., & Muthukumaravel, A. (2024). Adaptive Machine Learning-Driven Cybersecurity: Enhancing Real-Time Threat Detection and Response. In *2024 International Conference on Innovative Computing, Intelligent Communication and Smart Electrical Systems (ICSES)* (pp. 1–7). IEEE. DOI: 10.1109/ICSES63760.2024.10910847

Joshi, N., Shaikh, S., Tripathy, A., Sen, S., Janson, J., Karnik, S., & Verghese, B. (2019) "Crime Anatomization Using QGIS," IEEE 5th International Conference for Convergence in Technology (I2CT), 2019, pp. 1–4, DOI: 10.1109/I2CT45611.2019.9033910

Joyia, G. J., Liaqat, R. M., Farooq, A., & Rehman, S. (2017). Internet of medical things (IoMT): Applications, benefits and future challenges in healthcare domain. *Journal of Communication*, *12*(4), 240–247.

Kala, M. K., & Priya, M. (2024). Smart IoT-Blockchain Security to Secure Sensitive Personal Medical Data Using Shuffled Random Starvation Link Encryption. *IEEE Access : Practical Innovations, Open Solutions*, *12*, 168182–168196. DOI: 10.1109/ACCESS.2024.3483437

Kamel, M. S. (2024). Innovative approaches to design representation in civil engineering. *Mesopotamian Journal of Civil Engineering*, *2024*(1), 103–114. DOI: 10.58496/MJCE/2024/012

Kang, M., Park, E., Cho, B. H., & Lee, K. S. (2018). Recent patient health monitoring platforms incorporating internet of things-enabled smart devices. *International Neurourology Journal*, *22*(Suppl 2), S76–S82. DOI: 10.5213/inj.1836144.072 PMID: 30068069

Karamchand, G. K. (2023). Automating Cybersecurity with Machine Learning and Predictive Analytics. *Journal of Computational Innovation*, *3*(1).

Karampidis, K., Kavallieratou, E., & Papadourakis, G. (2018). A review of image steganalysis techniques for digital forensics. *Journal of Information Security and Applications*, *40*, 217–235. DOI: 10.1016/j.jisa.2018.04.005

Karantzas, G., & Patsakis, C. (2021). An empirical assessment of endpoint detection and response systems against advanced persistent threats attack vectors. *Journal of Cybersecurity and Privacy*, *1*(3), 387–421. DOI: 10.3390/jcp1030021

Kareem, A. B. A. (2024). Modelling Of Blockchain Technology. *SHIFRA, 2024*, 97–104. DOI: 10.70470/SHIFRA/2024/011

Kathirvel, A., & Maheswaran, C. P. (2023). Enhanced AI-Based Intrusion Detection and Response System for WSN. Artificial Intelligence for Intrusion Detection Systems, 155–177. DOI: 10.1201/9781003346340-8

Kaur, K., & Zandu, V. (2016). A secure data classification model in cloud computing using machine learning approach. *International Journal of Grid and Distributed Computing*, *9*(8), 13–22. DOI: 10.14257/ijgdc.2016.9.8.02

Kaushik, K., Khan, A., Kumari, A., Sharma, I., & Dubey, R. (2024). Ethical considerations in AI-based cybersecurity. In Next-generation cybersecurity: AI, ML, and Blockchain (pp. 437–470). Springer Nature Singapore.

Kavitha, S., Alphonse, P. J. A., & Reddy, Y. V. (2019). An improved authentication and security on efficient generalized group key agreement using hyper elliptic curve based public key cryptography for IoT health care system. *Journal of Medical Systems*, *43*(8), 260. DOI: 10.1007/s10916-019-1378-2 PMID: 31267216

Kayusi, F., Turyasingura, B., Chavula, P., & Amadi, O. J. (2024). Exploring Deep Learning Methods Used in the Medical Device Sector. *Mesopotamian Journal of Artificial Intelligence in Healthcare*, *2024*, 42–49. DOI: 10.58496/MJAIH/2024/007

Khalaf, M. A., & Steiti, A. (2024). Artificial Intelligence Predictions in Cyber Security: Analysis and Early Detection of Cyber Attacks. *Babylonian Journal of Machine Learning*, *2024*, 63–68. DOI: 10.58496/BJML/2024/006

Khaleel, Y. L., Habeeb, M. A., & Edoh, T. O. C. (2025). Limitations of deep learning vs. human intelligence: Training data, interpretability, bias, and ethics. *Applied Data Science and Analysis*, *2025*, 3–6. DOI: 10.58496/ADSA/2025/002

Khalid, H., Hashim, S. J., Ahmad, S. M., Hashim, F., & Chaudary, M. A. (2020). Cybersecurity in Industry 4.0 context: Background, issues, and future directions. *The Nine Pillars of Technologies for Industry*, *4*(0), 263–307. DOI: 10.1049/PBTE088E_ch14

Khan, M. J., Ullah, F., Imran, M., Khan, J., Khan, A., AlGhamdi, A. S., & Alshamrani, S. S. (2022). Identifying challenges for clients in adopting sustainable public cloud computing. *Sustainability (Basel)*, *14*(16), 9809. DOI: 10.3390/su14169809

Khlewee, I., Hamze, K., & Muya, T. (2025). AI in Smart Cities: A Review of Urban Data Processing, Prediction, and Optimization Techniques. *ESTIDAMAA*, *2025*, 29–38. DOI: 10.70470/ESTIDAMAA/2025/004

Khraisat, A., Gondal, I., Vamplew, P., & Kamruzzaman, J. (2019). Survey of intrusion detection systems: Techniques, datasets and challenges. *Cybersecurity*, *2*(1), 1–22. DOI: 10.1186/s42400-019-0038-7

Kilincer, I. F., Ertam, F., & Sengur, A. (2021). Machine learning methods for cyber security intrusion detection: Datasets and comparative study. *Computer Networks*, *188*, 107840. DOI: 10.1016/j.comnet.2021.107840

Kiruthika, K., Maheshkumar, R. S., Sridharan, S., & Jeevananthan, V. (2024). Machine Learning For Predicting Cloud Security. In Proceedings of the 1st International Conference on Artificial Intelligence, Communication, IoT, Data Engineering and Security.

Kobara, K. (2016). Cyber physical security for industrial control systems and IoT. *IEICE Transactions on Information and Systems*, *E99-D*(4), 787–795. DOI: 10.1587/transinf.2015ICI0001

Kolla, V. R. K. (2022). A Comparative Analysis of OS Forensics Tools. [IJRIM]. *International Journal of Research in IT and Management*, *12*(4).

Kong, M., Guo, Y., Alkhazragi, O., Sait, M., Kang, C. H., Ng, T. K., & Ooi, B. S. (2022). Real-time optical-wireless video surveillance system for high visual-fidelity underwater monitoring. *IEEE Photonics Journal*, *14*(3), 7315609. Advance online publication. DOI: 10.1109/JPHOT.2022.3147844

Krishnaveni, S., Sivamohan, S., Sridhar, S. S., & Prabakaran, S. (2021). Efficient feature selection and classification through ensemble method for network intrusion detection on cloud computing. *Cluster Computing*, *24*(3), 1761–1779. DOI: 10.1007/s10586-020-03222-y

Kulsoom, F., Narejo, S., Mehmood, Z., Chaudhry, H. N., & Bashir, A. K. (2022). A review of machine learning-based human activity recognition for diverse applications. *Neural Computing & Applications*, *34*(21), 18289–18324. DOI: 10.1007/s00521-022-07665-9

Kumar, A., Verma, A., Shinde, G., Sukhdeve, Y., & Lal, N. (2020) "Crime Prediction Using K-Nearest Neighboring Algorithm," International Conference on Emerging Trends in Information Technology and Engineering (ic-ETITE), 2020, pp. 1–4, DOI: 10.1109/ic-ETITE47903.2020.155

Laila, D. A., Al-Na'amneh, Q., Aljaidi, M., Nasayreh, A. N., Gharaibeh, H., Al Mamlook, R., & Alshammari, M. (2024). Enhancing 2d logistic chaotic map for gray image encryption. In Risk Assessment and Countermeasures for Cybersecurity (pp. 170-188). IGI Global.

Laila, D. A., Al-Na'amneh, Q., Aljaidi, M., Nasayreh, A. N., Gharaibeh, H., Al Mamlook, R., & Alshammari, M. (2024). Enhancing 2D Logistic Chaotic Map for Gray Image Encryption. In Risk Assessment and Countermeasures for Cybersecurity (pp. 170-188). IGI Global.

Lallie, H. S., Debattista, K., & Bal, J. (2020). A review of attack graph and attack tree visual syntax in cyber security. *Computer Science Review, 35*, 100219. DOI: 10.1016/j.cosrev.2019.100219

Li, D., Zhang, E., Lei, M., & Song, C. (2022). Zero trust in edge computing environment: A blockchain-based practical scheme. *Mathematical Biosciences and Engineering, 19*(4), 4196–4216. DOI: 10.3934/mbe.2022194 PMID: 35341294

Liu, K., Wang, F., Ding, Z., Liang, S., Yu, Z., & Zhou, Y. (2022). Recent Progress of Using Knowledge Graph for Cybersecurity. *Electronics (Basel), 11*(15), 2287. DOI: 10.3390/electronics11152287

Liu, R., Shi, J., Chen, X., & Lu, C. (2024). Network anomaly detection and security defense technology based on machine learning: A review. *Computers & Electrical Engineering, 119*, 109581. DOI: 10.1016/j.compeleceng.2024.109581

Li, Y., Gai, K., Qiu, L., Qiu, M., & Zhao, H. (2017). Intelligent cryptography approach for secure distributed big data storage in cloud computing. *Information Sciences, 387*, 103–115. DOI: 10.1016/j.ins.2016.09.005

Li, Y., & Liu, Q. (2021). A comprehensive review study of cyber-attacks and cyber security; Emerging trends and recent developments. *Energy Reports, 7*, 8176–8186. DOI: 10.1016/j.egyr.2021.08.126

Lu, L., Li, Z., Wu, S., & Shang, Y. (2022). Research on trust issues in cloud computing. *ITM Web of Conferences, 45*, 02010. DOI: 10.1051/itmconf/20224502010

Maayah, M. (2025). Framework for Node Detection in Cloud Computing: A Multi-Metric Approach Integrating Security, Availability, and Latency Factors. *Journal of Cyber Security and Risk Auditing, 2025*(4), 238–256. DOI: 10.63180/jcsra.thestap.2025.4.4

Macas, M., & Wu, C. (2020). Deep learning methods for cybersecurity and intrusion detection systems. In *2020 IEEE Latin-American Conference on Communications (LATINCOM)* (pp. 1–6). IEEE. DOI: 10.1109/LATINCOM50620.2020.9282324

Madi, M., Jarghon, F., Fazea, Y., Almomani, O., & Saaidah, A. (2020). Comparative analysis of classification techniques for network fault management. *Turkish Journal of Electrical Engineering and Computer Sciences, 28*(3), 1442–1457. DOI: 10.3906/elk-1907-84

Maher, R. M., Rashid, S. H., Habeeb, M. A., Khaleel, Y. L., & Ameen, F. N. (2025). Predictive modeling and analysis of monkeypox outbreaks using machine learning techniques. *Applied Data Science and Analysis*, *2025*(1), 94–111. DOI: 10.58496/ADSA/2025/006

Mallah, R. A., Lopez, D., & Farooq, B. (2021). Cyber-Security Risk Assessment Framework for Blockchains in Smart Mobility. *IEEE Open Journal of Intelligent Transportation Systems*, *2*, 294–311. DOI: 10.1109/OJITS.2021.3106863

Manengadan, M., Nandanan, M., & Subash, N. (2021). Crime Data Analysis, Visualization and Prediction Using LSTM. *Databases*, *9*(10), 17. DOI: 10.11648/j.ijdsa.20210703.11

Marab, A., & Bhadrashetty, A. (2023). A novel approach using deep convolutional neural networks for automated dementia detection and classification. *Edraak*, *2023*, 16–20. DOI: 10.70470/EDRAAK/2023/004

Marchal, S., Saari, K., Singh, N., & Asokan, N. (2016). Know your phish: Novel techniques for detecting phishing sites and their targets. In 2016 IEEE 36th international conference on distributed computing systems (ICDCS) (pp. 323–333). IEEE.

Markevych, M., & Dawson, M. (2023). A Review of Enhancing Intrusion Detection Systems for Cybersecurity Using Artificial Intelligence (AI). International Conference Knowledge-Based Organization, 29(3), 30–37. DOI: 10.2478/kbo-2023-0072

Martineau, M., Spiridon, E., & Aiken, M. (2023). A Comprehensive Framework for Cyber Behavioral Analysis Based on a Systematic Review of Cyber Profiling Literature. *Forensic Science*, *3*(3), 452–477. DOI: 10.3390/forensicsci3030032

Masoodi, H. J. K. A. L. (2024). Evaluating the effectiveness of machine learning-based intrusion detection in multi-cloud environments. *Babylonian Journal of Internet of Things*, *2024*(1), 94–105. DOI: 10.58496/BJIoT/2024/012

Mehrabi, N., Morstatter, F., Saxena, N., Lerman, K., & Galstyan, A. (2021). A survey on bias and fairness in machine learning. *ACM Computing Surveys*, *54*(6), 1–35. DOI: 10.1145/3457607

Mell, P., & Grance, T. (2011). *The NIST definition of cloud computing*. National Institute of Standards and Technology. DOI: 10.6028/NIST.SP.800-145

Mensah, G. B., Mijwil, M. M., Abotaleb, M., Ali, G., & Dutta, P. K. (2025). High Performance Medicine: Involving Artificial Intelligence Models in Enhancing Medical Laws and Medical Negligence Matters A Case Study of Act, 2009 (Act 792) in Ghana. *SHIFAA*, *2025*, 1–6. DOI: 10.70470/SHIFAA/2025/001

Mensah, G. B., Mijwil, M. M., Abotaleb, M., Ali, G., Dutta, P. K., Mzili, T., & Eid, M. M. (2025). Explainable AI for Healthcare: Training Healthcare Workers to Use Artificial Intelligence Techniques to Reduce Medical Negligence in Ghana's Public Health Act, 2012 (Act 851). *EDRAAK, 2025*, 1–6. DOI: 10.70470/EDRAAK/2025/001

Mhammed, K. (2025). Cyber Intelligence & Moroccan National Security: What Strategy for Managing and Mitigating Cyber Threats against Future Sporting Events. *Journal of Cyber Security and Risk Auditing, 2025*(4), 366–383. DOI: 10.63180/jcsra.thestap.2025.4.12

Mijwil, M. M., Abotaleb, M., Ali, G., & Dhoska, K. (2024). Assigning Medical Professionals: ChatGPT's Contributions to Medical Education and Health Prediction. *Mesopotamian Journal of Artificial Intelligence in Healthcare, 2024*, 76–83. DOI: 10.58496/MJAIH/2024/011

Mijwil, M. M., Adamopoulos, I., & Pudasaini, P. (2024). Machine learning helps in quickly diagnosis cases of "new Corona". *Mesopotamian Journal of Artificial Intelligence in Healthcare, 2024*(1), 16–19. DOI: 10.58496/MJAIH/2024/003

Moamin, S. A. H., Abdulhameed, M. K., Al-Amri, R. M., Radhi, A. D., Naser, R. K., & Pheng, L. G. (2025). Artificial Intelligence in Malware and Network Intrusion Detection: A Comprehensive Survey of Techniques, Datasets, Challenges, and Future Directions. *Babylonian Journal of Artificial Intelligence, 2025*, 77–98. DOI: 10.58496/BJAI/2025/008

Mohamad, F. S., Iqtait, M., & Alsuhimat, F. (2018). Age prediction on face features via multiple classifiers. In *2018 4th International Conference on Computer and Technology Applications (ICCTA)* (pp. 161–166). DOI: 10.1109/CATA.2018.8398675

Mohammed, M. A., Lakhan, A., Zebari, D. A., Ghani, M. K. A., Marhoon, H. A., Abdulkareem, K. H., Nedoma, J., & Martinek, R. (2023). Securing healthcare data in industrial cyber-physical systems using combining deep learning and blockchain technology. *Engineering Applications of Artificial Intelligence, 129*, 107612. DOI: 10.1016/j.engappai.2023.107612

Mohammed, S. Y., & Aljanabi, M. (2023). Human-Centric IoT for Health Monitoring in the Healthcare 5.0 FrameworkDescriptive Analysis and Directions for Future Research. *EDRAAK, 2023*, 21–26. DOI: 10.70470/EDRAAK/2023/005

Mohammed, S. Y., & Aljanabi, M. (2024). Advancing Translation Quality Assessment: Integrating AI Models for Real-time Feedback. *EDRAAK, 2024*, 1–7. DOI: 10.70470/EDRAAK/2024/001

Mohialden, Y. M., Hussien, N. M., Salman, S. A., Alwahhab, A. B. A., & Ali, M. (2024). Enhancing agriculture crop classification with deep learning. *Babylonian Journal of Artificial Intelligence, 2024*, 20–26. DOI: 10.58496/BJAI/2024/004

Morley, J., Floridi, L., Kinsey, L., & Elhalal, A. (2020). From what to how: An initial review of publicly available AI ethics tools, methods and research to translate principles into practices. *Science and Engineering Ethics, 26*(4), 2141–2168. DOI: 10.1007/s11948-019-00165-5 PMID: 31828533

Mowla, N. I., Doh, I., & Chae, K. (2018). On-Device AI-Based Cognitive Detection of Bio-Modality Spoofing in Medical Cyber Physical system. *IEEE Access : Practical Innovations, Open Solutions, 7*, 2126–2137. DOI: 10.1109/ACCESS.2018.2887095

Mughaid, A., Obaidat, I., Aljammal, A., AlZu'bi, S., Quiam, F., Laila, D. A., Al-zou'bi, A., & Abualigah, L. (2023). Simulation and analysis performance of ad-hoc routing protocols under DDoS attack and proposed solution. *International Journal of Data & Network Science, 7*(2), 757–764. DOI: 10.5267/j.ijdns.2023.2.002

Muhammad, T., & Akgül, A. (2025). Optimizing mechanical performance of AgC-reinforced polymer nanocomposites: A quantitative analysis of stiffness–ductility trade-offs. *Babylonian Journal of Mechanical Engineering, 2025*(1), 34–50. DOI: 10.58496/BJME/2025/003

Murala, D. K., Panda, S. K., & Dash, S. P. (2023). MedMetaverse: Medical Care of Chronic Disease Patients and Managing Data Using Artificial Intelligence, Blockchain, and Wearable Devices State-of-the-Art Methodology. *IEEE Access : Practical Innovations, Open Solutions, 11*, 138954–138985. DOI: 10.1109/ACCESS.2023.3340791

Nafea, A. A., Majeed, R. R., Ali, A., Yas, A. J., Alameri, S. A., & AL-Ani, M. M. (2024). A brief review of big data in healthcare: Challenges and issues, recent developments, and future directions. *Babylonian Journal of Internet of Things, 2024*, 10–15. DOI: 10.58496/BJIoT/2024/002

Naidu, P. R., Gowda, V. D., Gujar, S. S., Shaikh, S. F., Shandilya, S., & Reddy, N. S. (2024). AI-Enhanced Cloud Security Framework for IoT Networks Using a Predictive Analytics Approach. In 2024 3rd International Conference for Advancement in Technology (ICONAT) (pp. 1–8).

Naqvi, B., Perova, K., Farooq, A., Makhdoom, I., Oyedeji, S., & Porras, J. (2023). Mitigation strategies against the phishing attacks: A systematic literature review. Computers &amp. *Computers & Security, 132*, 103387. DOI: 10.1016/j.cose.2023.103387

Narayanan, G., & Kannan, S. (2024). Enhancing security in cloud-based VM migration: A trust-centric hybrid optimization approach. *The International Arab Journal of Information Technology*, *21*(1), 166–177. DOI: 10.34028/iajit/21/1/15

Nasir, R., Afzal, M., Latif, R., & Iqbal, W. (2021). Behavioral based insider threat detection using deep learning. *IEEE Access : Practical Innovations, Open Solutions*, *9*, 143266–143274. DOI: 10.1109/ACCESS.2021.3118297

Nassif, A. B., Talib, M. A., Nasir, Q., Albadani, H., & Dakalbab, F. M. (2021). Machine learning for cloud security: A systematic review. *IEEE Access : Practical Innovations, Open Solutions*, *9*, 20717–20735. DOI: 10.1109/ACCESS.2021.3054129

Nayak, S. C., Tiwari, V., & Samanthula, B. K. (2023, March). Review of ransomware attacks and a data recovery framework using autopsy digital forensics platform. In 2023 IEEE 13th Annual Computing and Communication Workshop and Conference (CCWC) (pp. 0605-0611). IEEE. DOI: 10.1109/CCWC57344.2023.10099169

Nay, T. (2024). Enhancing IoT Security with AI-Driven Hybrid Machine Learning and Neural Network-Based Intrusion Detection System. *Babylonian Journal of Artificial Intelligence*, *2024*, 158–167. DOI: 10.58496/BJAI/2024/017

Nengomasha, C. T., & Shuumbili, T. N. (2022). Access to e-government services by citizens through public/community libraries in Namibia. *Information Development*, *38*(1), 68–82. DOI: 10.1177/0266666920979009

Nishad, L. S., Akriti, Paliwal, J., Pandey, R., Beniwal, S., & Kumar, S. (2016, March). Security, privacy issues, and challenges in cloud computing: A survey. In *Proceedings of the Second International Conference on Information and Communication Technology for Competitive Strategies* (pp. 1–7). DOI: 10.1145/2905055.2905253

Noori, W. E., & Albahri, A. S.Worood Esam NooriA. S. Albahri. (2023). Towards trustworthy myopia detection: Integration methodology of deep learning approach, XAI visualization, and user interface system. *Applied Data Science and Analysis*, *2023*, 1–15. DOI: 10.58496/ADSA/2023/001

Nyangaresi, V. O., & Shanshool, A. M. (2024). Smart Wearables Powered by AI Transforming Human Activity Recognition. *Babylonian Journal of Artificial Intelligence*, *2024*, 128–133. DOI: 10.58496/BJAI/2024/014

Okoli, U. I., Obi, O. C., Adewusi, A. O., & Abrahams, T. O. (2024). Machine learning in cybersecurity: A review of threat detection and defense mechanisms. *World Journal of Advanced Research and Reviews*, *21*(1), 2286–2295. DOI: 10.30574/wjarr.2024.21.1.0315

Olabanji, S. O., Marquis, Y., Adigwe, C. S., Ajayi, S. A., Oladoyinbo, T. O., & Olaniyi, O. O. (2024). AI-Driven cloud security: Examining the impact of user behavior analysis on threat detection. *Asian Journal of Research in Computer Science, 17*(3), 57–74. DOI: 10.9734/ajrcos/2024/v17i3424

Omotunde, H., & Mouhamed, M. R. (2023). The modern impact of artificial intelligence systems in healthcare: A concise analysis. *Mesopotamian Journal of Artificial Intelligence in Healthcare, 2023*, 66–70. DOI: 10.58496/MJAIH/2023/013

Osanaiye, O., Choo, K.-K. R., & Dlodlo, M. (2016). Distributed denial of service (DDoS) resilience in cloud: Review and conceptual cloud DDoS mitigation framework. *Journal of Network and Computer Applications, 67*, 147–165. DOI: 10.1016/j.jnca.2016.01.001

Otoom, S. (2025). Risk auditing for digital twins in cyber physical systems: A systematic review. *Journal of Cyber Security and Risk Auditing, 2025*(1), 22–35. DOI: 10.63180/jcsra.thestap.2025.1.3

Owida, H. A., Al-Nabulsi, J. I., Turab, N. M., Alnaimat, F., Rababah, H., & Shakour, M. Y. (2021). Autocharging techniques for implantable medical applications. *International Journal of Biomaterials, 2021*(1), 6074657. PMID: 34712329

Owida, H. A., Hemied, O. S. M., Alkhawaldeh, R. S., Alshdaifat, N. F. F., & Abuowaida, S. F. A. (2022). Improved deep learning approaches for COVID-19 recognition in CT images. *Journal of Theoretical and Applied Information Technology, 100*(13).

Owida, H. A., Moh'd, B. A. H., & Al Takrouri, M. (2022). Designing an integrated low-cost electrospinning device for nanofibrous scaffold fabrication. *HardwareX, 11*, e00250. DOI: 10.1016/j.ohx.2021.e00250 PMID: 35509902

Palmer, G. (2001). A road map for digital forensic research. In *Digital Forensic Research Conference*. Utica, NY, United States.

Panda, M., & Patra, M. R. (2007). Network intrusion detection using naive Bayes. *International Journal of Computer Science and Network Security, 7*(12), 258–263.

Pan, H., Wang, R., Wang, H., & Jia, Z. (2023). Sustainable Supply Chain Management: Best Practices for Reducing Environmental Footprints in the Global Apparel Industry. *ESTIDAMAA, 2023*, 18–26. DOI: 10.70470/ESTIDAMAA/2023/003

Parast, F. K., Sindhav, C., Nikam, S., Yekta, H. I., Kent, K. B., & Hakak, S. (2022). Cloud computing security: A survey of service-based models. *Computers & Security, 114*, 102580. DOI: 10.1016/j.cose.2021.102580

Park, H., Kim, N., Lee, G. H., & Choi, J. K. (2023). MultiCNN-FilterLSTM: Resource-efficient sensor-based human activity recognition in IoT applications. *Future Generation Computer Systems, 139*, 196–209. DOI: 10.1016/j.future.2022.09.024

Park, S. H., Yun, S. W., Jeon, S. E., Park, N. E., Shim, H. Y., Lee, Y. R., Lee, S.-J., Park, T.-R., Shin, N.-Y., Kang, M.-J., & Lee, I. G. (2022). Performance evaluation of open-source endpoint detection and response combining Google rapid response and osquery for threat detection. *IEEE Access : Practical Innovations, Open Solutions, 10*, 20259–20269. DOI: 10.1109/ACCESS.2022.3152574

Patzakis, J. (2011). Overcoming potential legal challenges to the authentication of social media evidence. X1 Discovery. http://www.x1discovery.com

Paula, L. P. O., Faruqui, N., Mahmud, I., Whaiduzzaman, M., Hawkinson, E. C., & Trivedi, S. (2023). A novel front door security (FDS) algorithm using GoogleNet-BiLSTM hybridization. *IEEE Access : Practical Innovations, Open Solutions, 11*, 19122–19134. DOI: 10.1109/ACCESS.2023.3248509

Pflanzner, T., & Kertész, A. (2018). A taxonomy and survey of IoT cloud applications. *EAI Endorsed Transactions on Internet of Things, 3*(12), e4. Advance online publication. DOI: 10.4108/eai.31-10-2018.159633

Pinto, A., Herrera, L. C., Donoso, Y., & Gutierrez, J. A. (2024). Enhancing critical infrastructure security: Unsupervised learning approaches for anomaly detection. *International Journal of Computational Intelligence Systems, 17*(1), 236. DOI: 10.1007/s44196-024-00644-z

Poornima, G., Sakkari, D. S., Pallavi, R., Sudha, Y., & Gowda, M. S. (2023). Intrusion Detection System Using Artificial Intelligence. Artificial Intelligence for Intrusion Detection Systems, 1–37. DOI: 10.1201/9781003346340-1

Pratibha, A. G., Uprant, S. D., & Chouhan, L. (2020) "Crime Prediction and Analysis," *2nd International Conference on Data, Engineering and Applications (IDEA)*, 2020, pp. 1–6, DOI: 10.1109/IDEA49133.2020.9170731

Praveen, R., Hemavathi, U., Sathya, R., Abubakkar Siddiq, A., Gokul Sanjay, M., & Gowdish, S. (2024). AI Powered Plant Identification and Plant Disease Classification System. *2024 4th International Conference on Sustainable Expert Systems (ICSES)*, 1610–1616. DOI: 10.1109/ICSES63445.2024.10763167

Priya, S. S., & Srinivas Vellela, S. B, V. R., Javvadi, S., Sk, K. B., & D, R. (2023). Design And Implementation of An Integrated IOT Blockchain Framework for Drone Communication. *2023 3rd International Conference on Intelligent Technologies (CONIT)*, 1–5. DOI: 10.1109/CONIT59222.2023.10205659

Priyadarshini, S., Sawant, T. N., Bhimrao Yadav, G., Premalatha, J., & Pawar, S. R. (2024). Enhancing security and scalability by AI/ML workload optimization in the cloud. *Cluster Computing*, *27*(10), 13455–13469. DOI: 10.1007/s10586-024-04641-x

Raj, A., & Prakash, S. (2024). Privacy preservation of the internet of medical things using blockchain. *Health Services and Outcomes Research Methodology*, *24*(1), 112–139. DOI: 10.1007/s10742-023-00306-1

Rasheed, D. H., & Tambe, S. B. (2024). Advancing Energy Efficiency with Smart Grids and IoT-Based Solutions for a Sustainable Future. *ESTIDAMAA*, *2024*, 36–42. DOI: 10.70470/ESTIDAMAA/2024/006

Ratta, P., Abdullah, , & Sharma, S. (2024). A blockchain-machine learning ecosystem for IoT-Based remote health monitoring of diabetic patients. *Healthcare Analytics*, *5*, 100338. DOI: 10.1016/j.health.2024.100338

Ray, A., Kolekar, M. H., Balasubramanian, R., & Hafiane, A. (2023). Transfer learning enhanced vision-based human activity recognition: A decade-long analysis. *International Journal of Information Management Data Insights*, *3*(1), 100142. Advance online publication. DOI: 10.1016/j.jjimei.2022.100142

Raza, M., Awais, M., Singh, N., Imran, M., & Hussain, S. (2020). Intelligent IoT framework for indoor healthcare monitoring of Parkinson's disease patient. *IEEE Journal on Selected Areas in Communications*, *39*(2), 593–602. DOI: 10.1109/JSAC.2020.3021571

Reddy, A. R. P. (2021). The role of artificial intelligence in proactive cyber threat detection in cloud environments. *NeuroQuantology : An Interdisciplinary Journal of Neuroscience and Quantum Physics*, *19*(12), 764–773.

Ring, M., Wunderlich, S., Scheuring, D., Landes, D., & Hotho, A. (2019). A survey of network-based intrusion detection data sets. *Computers & Security*, *86*, 147–167. DOI: 10.1016/j.cose.2019.06.005

Rizqullah, N. Z., Alekhine, J., Yonia, D. L., Racel Purnomo, R. M., & Shiddiqi, A. M. (2024). Enhancing Intrusion Detection Systems with Adaptive Learning Techniques. *2024 IEEE International Conference on Artificial Intelligence and Mechatronics Systems (AIMS)*, 1–6. DOI: 10.1109/AIMS61812.2024.10513076

Sachdeva, S., Raina, B. L., & Sharma, A. (2020). Analysis of digital forensic tools. *Journal of Computational and Theoretical Nanoscience*, *17*(6), 2459–2467. DOI: 10.1166/jctn.2020.8916

Sachdev, D., Pokhriyal, S. K., Nechully, S., & Sundaram, S. S. (2023). *Healthcare*. Systematic Review of Applications of Decentralized Trust Using Blockchain Technology., DOI: 10.1007/978-981-19-5723-9_10

Safat, W., Asghar, S., & Gillani, S. A. (2021). Empirical Analysis for Crime Prediction and Forecasting Using Machine Learning and Deep Learning Techniques. *IEEE Access : Practical Innovations, Open Solutions*, *9*, 70080–70094. DOI: 10.1109/ACCESS.2021.3078117

Saied, M., Guirguis, S., & Madbouly, M. (2024). Review of artificial intelligence for enhancing intrusion detection in the internet of things. *Engineering Applications of Artificial Intelligence*, *127*, 107231. DOI: 10.1016/j.engappai.2023.107231

Sajid, M., Malik, K. R., Almogren, A., Malik, T. S., Khan, A. H., Tanveer, J., & Rehman, A. U. (2024). Enhancing intrusion detection: A hybrid machine and deep learning approach. *Journal of Cloud Computing (Heidelberg, Germany)*, *13*(1), 123. DOI: 10.1186/s13677-024-00685-x

Sakirin, T., & Ben Said, R. (2025). Application of deep learning and transfer learning techniques for medical image classification. *Edraak*, *2025*, 38–46. DOI: 10.70470/EDRAAK/2025/006

Saleh, H. M., Oleiwi, A. K., & Abed, A. A. H. (2023). Diagnosis of HIV (AIDS) by using deep learning and machine learning. *Babylonian Journal of Machine Learning*, *2023*(1), 73–77. DOI: 10.58496/BJML/2023/012

Salih, H. M., & Mahmood, A. M. (2024). A electric vehicle blockchain: Problems and opportunities. *Babylonian Journal of Networking*, *2024*, 18–24. DOI: 10.58496/BJN/2024/003

Salim, A., Raymond, L., & Moniaga, J. V. (2023). General pattern recognition using machine learning in the cloud. *Procedia Computer Science*, *216*, 565–570. DOI: 10.1016/j.procs.2022.12.170

Salim, R. A. (2024). Wheelchair Control Using Finger Gestures IoT-Based Arduino. *Babylonian Journal of Internet of Things*, *2024*, 137–150. DOI: 10.58496/BJIoT/2024/016

Salim, Z. H., & Hasoon, S. O. (2024). Intrusion Detection Using Artificial Intelligence Techniques: Review. *2024 International Conference on Artificial Intelligence, Computer, Data Sciences and Applications (ACDSA)*, 1–7. DOI: 10.1109/ACDSA59508.2024.10467524

Salisu, A., Gafai, M. M., & Salisu, S. (2024). Some results on commutativity for alternative rings with 2, 3-torsion free. *Babylonian Journal of Mathematics, 2024*(1), 44–47. DOI: 10.58496/BJM/2024/005

Sallam, M., Al-Mahzoum, K., Eid, H., Al-Salahat, K., Sallam, M., Ali, G., & Mijwil, M. M. (2025). Chinese Generative AI Models Challenge Western AI in Clinical Chemistry MCQs: A Benchmarking Follow-up Study on AI Use in Health Education. *Babylonian Journal of Artificial Intelligence, 2025*, 1–14. DOI: 10.58496/BJAI/2025/001

Sallam, M., Al-Mahzoum, K., & Sallam, M. (2024). Generative Artificial Intelligence and Cybersecurity Risks: Implications for Healthcare Security Based on Real-life Incidents. *Mesopotamian Journal of Artificial Intelligence in Healthcare, 2024*, 184–203. DOI: 10.58496/MJAIH/2024/019

Salman, T., Bhamare, D., Erbad, A., Jain, R., & Samaka, M. (2017). Machine learning for anomaly detection and categorization in multi-cloud environments. In 2017 IEEE 4th international conference on cyber security and cloud computing (CSCloud) (pp. 97–103). IEEE. DOI: 10.1109/CSCloud.2017.15

Samara, M., Burbidge, V., El Asam, A., Foody, M., Smith, P. K., & Morsi, H. (2017). Bullying and cyberbullying: Their legal status and use in psychological assessment. *International Journal of Environmental Research and Public Health, 14*(12), 1449. Advance online publication. DOI: 10.3390/ijerph14121449 PMID: 29186780

Sandagiri, S. P. C. W., Kumara, B. T. G. S., & Kuhaneswaran, B. (2020) "ANN Based Crime Detection and Prediction Using Twitter Posts and Weather Data," *International Conference on Data Analytics for Business and Industry: Way Towards a Sustainable Economy (ICDABI)*, 2020, pp. 1–5, DOI: 10.1109/ICDABI51230.2020.9325660

Santhosh, C. V., & Minni, G. (2022). Attribute with multi-factor proofing verification with ABE scheme.

Sarker, I. H., Kayes, A. S. M., & Watters, P. (2019). Effectiveness analysis of machine learning classification models for predicting personalized context-aware smartphone usage. *Journal of Big Data, 6*(1), 1–28. DOI: 10.1186/s40537-019-0219-y

Sarp, B., & Karalar, T. (2015). Real time smart door system for home security. *International Journal of Scientific Research in Information Systems and Engineering, 1*(2), 121–123.

Satam, S., & El-Ocla, H. (2022). Home security system using wireless sensors network. *Wireless Personal Communications, 125*(2), 1185–1201. DOI: 10.1007/s11277-022-09596-z

Satar, S. D. M., Hussin, M., Afendee Mohamed, M., Abd Hamid, N., Abd Kadir, M. F., Muda, R., & Samual, J. (2025). Secure access control using ciphertext policy attribute-based encryption with performance optimization in cloud computing. *Journal of Cyber Security and Risk Auditing*, *2025*(4), 287–305. DOI: 10.63180/jcsra.thestap.2025.4.8

Saxe, J., & Berlin, K. (2015). Deep neural network-based malware detection using two-dimensional binary program features. In 2015 10th international conference on malicious and unwanted software (MALWARE) (pp. 11–20). IEEE. DOI: 10.1109/MALWARE.2015.7413680

Scarfone, K., & Mell, P. (2007). *Guide to intrusion detection and prevention systems (idps)*. NIST. DOI: 10.6028/NIST.SP.800-94

Sebastian, A., & Al Hajri, H. (2024). Artificial Intelligence based Intrusion Detection Systems using Deep Learning Techniques. *2024 Third International Conference on Electrical, Electronics, Information and Communication Technologies (ICEEICT)*, 1–4. DOI: 10.1109/ICEEICT61591.2024.10718441

Sengupta, S., Kaulgud, V., & Sharma, V. S. (2011). Cloud computing security—trends and research directions. In *2011 IEEE World Congress on Services* (pp. 524–531). IEEE. DOI: 10.1109/SERVICES.2011.20

Sewak, M., Sahay, S. K., & Rathore, H. (2021, October). Deep reinforcement learning for cybersecurity threat detection and protection: A review. In *International Conference on Secure Knowledge Management in Artificial Intelligence Era* (pp. 51–72). Cham: Springer International Publishing.

Shanshool, A. M. (2023). Exploring the Role of Block-chain in IoT-Driven Healthcare Solutions. *Babylonian Journal of Networking*, *2023*, 82–88. DOI: 10.58496/BJN/2023/010

Sharma, A., & Singh, U. K. (2025). Cloud Computing Security Through Detection & Mitigation of Zero-Day Attack Using Machine Learning Techniques. Natural Language Processing for Software Engineering, 357–388.

Sharma, S., & Tyagi, R. (2023). Digitalization of Farming Knowledge Using Artificial Intelligence and Vedic Scripture. In 2023 IEEE International Conference on ICT in Business Industry & Government (ICTBIG), 1–6. DOI: 10.1109/ICTBIG59752.2023.10456219

Sharma, S., Tyagi, R., & Bhardwaj, R. (2023). Sustainable Smart Society Development Based on Geo Sensitive Equality Using Vedic Structure, Artificial Intelligence, Blockchain and IoT. In 2023 1st International Conference on Circuits, Power and Intelligent Systems (CCPIS), 1–6. DOI: 10.1109/CCPIS59145.2023.10291593

Sharma, A., Jha, P., & Singh, S. (2021). Data control in public cloud computing: Issues and challenges. *Recent Advances in Computer Science and Communications, 14*(2), 564–579. DOI: 10.2174/2213275912666190617164550

Sharma, N., Mangla, M., Mohanty, S. N., Gupta, D., Tiwari, P., Shorfuzzaman, M., & Rawashdeh, M. (2021). A smart ontology-based IoT framework for remote patient monitoring. *Biomedical Signal Processing and Control, 68*, 102717. DOI: 10.1016/j.bspc.2021.102717

Sharma, S., Gautam, A., & Tyagi, R. (2023). Evaluation of 5% Known And 95% Unknown Matter in Inner and Outer Universe Using Quantum Computing, Artificial Intelligence and Vedic Scripture. In *2023 International Conference on Energy, Materials and Communication Engineering (ICEMCE)*, 1–6. DOI: 10.1109/ICEMCE57940.2023.10434060

Sharma, S., Goyal, H. R., Rawat, R., & Tyagi, R. (2024). Artificial Intelligence, Cloud Computing, Blockchain, and Vedic Scripture Enabled Sustainable Global Judicial System for Democratic Society. In *2024 International Conference on Emerging Technologies and Innovation for Sustainability (EmergIN)*, 7–12. DOI: 10.1109/EmergIN63207.2024.10961824

Sharma, S., Gupta, A., & Tyagi, R. (2023). Artificial Intelligence Enabled Sustainable Education System Using Vedic Scripture and Cyber Security. In *2023 Second International Conference on Advances in Computational Intelligence and Communication (ICACIC)*, 1–6. DOI: 10.1109/ICACIC59454.2023.10435133

Sharma, S., Gupta, A., & Tyagi, R. (2023a). Sustainable Natural Resources Utilization Decision System for Better Society Using Vedic Scripture, Cloud Computing, and IoT. In *2023 Fifth International Conference on Advances in Electronics, Computers and Communications (ICAECC)*, 1–6. DOI: 10.1109/ICAECC59324.2023.10560335

Sharma, S., Gupta, A., & Tyagi, R. (2024). Artificial Intelligence, Cyber Security and Vedic Scripture Integrated Sustainable Global Youth Leadership Development. In *2024 IEEE International Conference on Communication, Computing and Signal Processing (IICCCS)*, 1–6. DOI: 10.1109/IICCCS61609.2024.10763618

Sharma, S., Tomar, M., & Tyagi, R. (2024). Artificial Intelligence and Vedic Scripture in Digital Agriculture for Global Economy. In *2024 International Conference on Intelligent and Innovative Technologies in Computing, Electrical and Electronics (IITCEE)*, 1–6. DOI: 10.1109/IITCEE59897.2024.10467916

Shea, S. (2024, May 24). How AI is making phishing attacks more dangerous. TechTarget. Retrieved from https://www.techtarget.com/searchsecurity/tip/Generative-AI-is-making-phishing-attacks-more-dangerous

Sheela, M. S., Amirthayogam, G., Hephzipah, J. J., Suganthi, R., Karthikeyan, T., & Gopianand, M. (2024). Advanced brain tumor classification using DEEPBELEIF-CNN method. *Babylonian Journal of Machine Learning*, *2024*(1), 89–101. DOI: 10.58496/BJML/2024/009

Sheela, M. S., Gopalakrishnan, S., Begum, I. P., Hephzipah, J. J., Gopianand, M., & Harika, D. (2024). Enhancing energy efficiency with smart building energy management system using machine learning and IoT. *Babylonian Journal of Machine Learning*, *2024*(1), 80–88. DOI: 10.58496/BJML/2024/008

Shibghatullah, A. S. B. (2023). Mitigating developed persistent threats (APTs) through machine learning-based intrusion detection systems: A comprehensive analysis. *SHIFRA*, *2023*, 17–25. DOI: 10.70470/SHIFRA/2023/003

Shostak, T. (2019, November 15). Using machine learning to reduce false positives while combating attacks. Reblaze. Retrieved from https://www.reblaze.com/blog/machine-learning/using-machine-learning-to-reduce-false-positives-while-combating-attacks-part-1/

Shukur, B. S., & Abd Ghani, M. K. (2024). Digital physicians: Unleashing artificial intelligence in transforming healthcare and exploring the future of modern approaches. *Mesopotamian Journal of Artificial Intelligence in Healthcare*, *2024*, 28–34. DOI: 10.58496/MJAIH/2024/005

Simons, H. (2015). Case study evaluation: Past, present and future challenges. In *Advances in program evaluation* (pp. 17–20). Emerald Group Publishing.

Singh, V., & Pandey, S. K. (2020). Cloud computing: Vulnerability and threat indications. In *Performance Management of Integrated Systems and its Applications in Software Engineering* (pp. 11–20).

Singh, V., Raj, M., Gupta, I., & Sayeed, M. A. (2023). Data Leakage Detection and Prevention Using Cloud Computing. In Sustainable Computing: Transforming Industry 4.0 to Society 5.0 (pp. 159–169). Springer International Publishing. DOI: 10.1007/978-3-031-13577-4_9

Singh, A., & Chatterjee, K. (2017). Cloud security issues and challenges: A survey. *Journal of Network and Computer Applications*, *79*, 88–115. DOI: 10.1016/j.jnca.2016.11.027

Singh, A., & Sharma, M. (2023). Adaptive machine learning models for evolving threats in cloud computing. *International Journal of Information Security*, *22*(4), 567–580.

Sivanagaleela, B., & Rajesh, S. (2019) "Crime Analysis and Prediction Using Fuzzy C-Means Algorithm," *3rd International Conference on Trends in Electronics and Informatics (ICOEI)*, 2019, pp. 595–599, DOI: 10.1109/ICOEI.2019.8862691

Soltani, S., & Seno, S. A. H. (2019). A formal model for event reconstruction in digital forensic investigation. *Digital Investigation*, *30*, 148–160. DOI: 10.1016/j.diin.2019.07.006

Sommer, R., & Paxson, V. (2010). *Outside the closed world: On using machine learning for network intrusion detection. In 2010 IEEE symposium on security and privacy*. IEEE.

Srinivasan, S., & Deepalakshmi, P. (2023). Enhancing the security in cyber-world by detecting the botnets using ensemble classification-based machine learning. *Measurement. Sensors*, *25*, 100624. DOI: 10.1016/j.measen.2022.100624

Srividhya, E., Anusuya, J. P. V., Deepthi, K. J., Gopalsamy, P., & Gopalakrishnan, S. (2024). Deep Learning-Driven Disease Prediction System in Cloud Environments Using a Big Data Approach. *EDRAAK*, *2024*, 8–17. DOI: 10.70470/EDRAAK/2024/002

Stephenson, P. (2002). End-to-end digital forensics. *Computer Fraud & Security*, *2002*(9), 17–19. DOI: 10.1016/S1361-3723(02)00914-4

Sulaiman, R. B., & Khraisat, A. (2025). Metaheuristic-Driven Feature Selection with SVM and KNN for Robust DDoS Attack Detection: A Comparative Study. *Journal of Cyber Security and Risk Auditing*, *2025*(4), 182–203. DOI: 10.63180/jcsra.thestap.2025.4.1

Sun, J., ... (2021) "Crimeforecaster: Crime Prediction by Exploiting the Geographical Neighborhoods' Spatiotemporal Dependencies," in Machine Learning and Knowledge Discovery in Databases: Applied Data Science and Demo Track, ECML PKDD 2020, Ghent, Belgium, September 14–18, 2020, Proceedings, Part V, Springer International Publishing, 2021. DOI: 10.1007/978-3-030-67670-4_4

Swarnkar, M., & Rajput, S. S. (2023). *Artificial Intelligence for Intrusion Detection Systems*. Chapman and Hall/CRC., DOI: 10.1201/9781003346340

Swaroop, K. N., Chandu, K., Gorrepotu, R., & Deb, S. (2019). A health monitoring system for vital signs using IoT. *Internet of Things : Engineering Cyber Physical Human Systems*, *5*, 116–129. DOI: 10.1016/j.iot.2019.01.004

Tama, B. A., & Lim, S. (2021). Ensemble learning for intrusion detection systems: A systematic mapping study and cross-benchmark evaluation. *Computer Science Review*, *39*, 100357. DOI: 10.1016/j.cosrev.2020.100357

Tambe, S. N., & Hussein, N. A.-H. K. (2023). Exploring the Impact of Digital Literacy on Media Consumer Empowerment in the Age of Misinformation. *MEDAAD*, *2023*, 1–9. DOI: 10.70470/MEDAAD/2023/001

Tankard, C. (2011). Advanced Persistent threats and how to monitor and deter them. *Network Security*, *2011*(8), 16–19. DOI: 10.1016/S1353-4858(11)70086-1

Tao, J., Wu, H., Deng, S., & Qi, Z. (2022). Overview of intelligent home security and early warning system based on Internet of Things technology. *International Core Journal of Engineering*, *8*(6), 727–732.

Tarawneh, O., Saber, Q., Almaghthawi, A., Owida, H. A., Issa, A., Alshdaifat, N., Jaradat, G., Abuowaida, S., & Arabiat, M. (2024). The effect of pre-processing on a convolutional neural network model for dorsal hand vein recognition. *International Journal of Advanced Computer Science and Applications*, *15*(3). Advance online publication. DOI: 10.14569/IJACSA.2024.01503126

Tarlekar, S., Bhosle, R., D'souza, E., & Sheikh, S. (2021) "Geographical Crime Rate Prediction System," *IEEE India Council International Subsections Conference (INDISCON)*, 2021, pp. 1–6, DOI: 10.1109/INDISCON53343.2021.9582218

Taylor, R., Baron, D., & Schmidt, D. (2015, October). The world in 2025-predictions for the next ten years. In 2015 10th International Microsystems, Packaging, Assembly and Circuits Technology Conference (IMPACT) (pp. 192-195). IEEE.

Telikani, A., Rudbardeh, N. E., Soleymanpour, S., Shahbahrami, A., Shen, J., Gaydadjiev, G., & Hassanpour, R. (2023). A cost-sensitive machine learning model with multitask learning for intrusion detection in IoT. *IEEE Transactions on Industrial Informatics*.

Thanganadar, A., & Raman, V. (2024). Integrated shared random key agreement protocol for wireless sensor network. *The International Arab Journal of Information Technology*, *21*(2), 201–210. DOI: 10.34028/iajit/21/2/3

Trivedi, S., Patel, N., & Faruqui, N. (2023). Bacterial strain classification using convolutional neural network for automatic bacterial disease diagnosis. In 2023 13th International Conference on Cloud Computing, Data Science & Engineering (Confluence) (pp. 325–332). IEEE. DOI: 10.1109/Confluence56041.2023.10048859

Trivedi, S., Patel, N., & Faruqui, N. (2022). *NDNN based U-Net: An innovative 3D brain tumor segmentation method. In 2022 IEEE 13th Annual Ubiquitous Computing, Electronics & Mobile Communication Conference (UEMCON).* IEEE., DOI: 10.1109/UEMCON54665.2022.9965677

Truong, N. B., Sun, K., Lee, G. M., & Guo, Y. (2019). GDPR-compliant personal data management: A blockchain-based solution. *IEEE Transactions on Information Forensics and Security*, *15*, 1746–1761. DOI: 10.1109/TIFS.2019.2948287

Ujjan, R. M. A., Khan, N. A., & Gaur, L. (2022). E-government privacy and security challenges in the context of Internet of Things. In *Cybersecurity Measures for E-Government Frameworks* (pp. 22–42). IGI Global. DOI: 10.4018/978-1-7998-9624-1.ch002

Ullah, K. W., Ahmed, A. S., & Ylitalo, J. (2013). Towards building an automated security compliance tool for the cloud. In 2013 12th IEEE International Conference on Trust, Security and Privacy in Computing and Communications (pp. 1587–1593). IEEE. DOI: 10.1109/TrustCom.2013.195

Usmani, U. A., Watada, J., Jaafar, J., & Aziz, I. A. (2022). A systematic review of privacy-preserving blockchain in e-medicine. *Biomedical and Other Applications of Soft Computing*, 25–40.

Vaigandla, K. K. (2025). An Extensive Examination on IOT and Industrial IOT: Attacks, Security, Detection Methods, Blockchain Solutions and Challenges. *Babylonian Journal of Internet of Things*, *2025*, 89–100. DOI: 10.58496/BJIoT/2025/004

Vaigandla, K. K. (2025). Role of IoT and ML in Healthcare. *Babylonian Journal of Artificial Intelligence*, *2025*, 23–36. DOI: 10.58496/BJAI/2025/003

Varshney, G., Kumawat, R., Varadharajan, V., Tupakula, U., & Gupta, C. (2024). Anti-phishing: A comprehensive perspective. *Expert Systems with Applications*, *238*, 122199. DOI: 10.1016/j.eswa.2023.122199

Vashishth, T. K., Sharma, V., Sharma, K. K., Kumar, B., Chaudhary, S., & Panwar, R. (2024). Intrusion Detection and Prevention Techniques in FL Cloud-Based Healthcare 5.0: A Comprehensive Review. Pioneering Smart Healthcare 5.0 with IoT, Federated Learning, and Cloud Security, 152-174.

Vashishth, T. K., Sharma, V., Sharma, K. K., Kumar, B., Kumar, A., & Panwar, R. (2024). Artificial Intelligence (AI)–Powered Chatbots: Providing Instant Support and Personalized Recommendations to Guests 24/7. In Technology and Luxury Hospitality (pp. 211-236). Routledge.

Vashishth, T. K., Sharma, V., Sharma, K. K., Kumar, B., Chaudhary, S., & Panwar, R. (2024). Enhancing cloud security: The role of artificial intelligence and machine learning. In *Improving security, privacy, and trust in cloud computing* (pp. 85–112). IGI Global Scientific Publishing. DOI: 10.4018/979-8-3693-1431-9.ch004

Vashishth, T. K., Sharma, V., Sharma, K. K., Kumar, B., Chaudhary, S., & Panwar, R. (2024). Security and Privacy Considerations in Cloud-Based Data Processing Solutions for Sensitive Data. In *Developments towards Next Generation Intelligent Systems for Sustainable Development* (pp. 35–61). IGI Global. DOI: 10.4018/979-8-3693-5643-2.ch002

Verma, P., & Sood, S. K. (2018). Fog assisted-IoT enabled patient health monitoring in smart homes. *IEEE Internet of Things Journal*, *5*(3), 1789–1796. DOI: 10.1109/JIOT.2018.2803201

Vielberth, M. (2025). Security information and event management (SIEM). In Encyclopedia of Cryptography, Security and Privacy (pp. 2304–2306). Springer Nature Switzerland.

Vinayakumar, R., Soman, K. P., & Poornachandran, P. (2019). Applying deep learning approaches for network traffic classification and intrusion detection. In *Smart computing and informatics* (pp. 221–245). Springer.

Wang, J., Tang, Z., Shao, W., & Jin, X. (2016). A formal model of events reconstruction for cloud forensics. RISTI—Revista Ibérica de Sistemas e Tecnologias de Informação, 2016(18), 45–55.

Wang, R. (2023). Expression of Concern for: Enhancing Network Security with Deep Learning on Intrusion Detection and Prevention Systems. 2023 5th International Conference on Artificial Intelligence and Computer Applications (ICAICA), 1–1. DOI: 10.1109/ICAICA58456.2023.10703732

Wang, K., Guo, X., & Yang, D. (2022). Research on the effectiveness of cybersecurity awareness in ICS risk assessment frameworks. *Electronics (Basel)*, *11*(10), 1659. DOI: 10.3390/electronics11101659

Wang, X., Shi, Y., Zheng, K., Zhang, Y., Hong, W., & Cao, S. (2022). User authentication method based on keystroke dynamics and mouse dynamics with scene-irrelated features in hybrid scenes. *Sensors (Basel)*, *22*(17), 6627. DOI: 10.3390/s22176627 PMID: 36081085

Wang, Y., Wang, Y., Qin, H., Ji, H., Zhang, Y., & Wang, J. (2021). A Systematic Risk Assessment Framework of Automotive Cybersecurity. *Automotive Innovation*, *4*(3), 253–261. DOI: 10.1007/s42154-021-00140-6

Wei, X., Wu, J., Ajayi, K., & Oyen, D. (2022). Visual descriptor extraction from patent figure captions: A case study of data efficiency between BiLSTM and transformer. In *Proceedings of the 22nd ACM/IEEE Joint Conference on Digital Libraries* (pp. 1–5). ACM. DOI: 10.1145/3529372.3533299

Willard, N. (2011). Educator's guide to cyberbullying and cyberthreats. Arkansas Department of Education. http://www.arkansased.gov/public/userfiles/Learning_Services/Technology_Initiatives/Cyber_Safety/educatorsguide.pdf

Wilson, C., Boe, B., Sala, A., Puttaswamy, K. P. N., & Zhao, B. Y. (2009). User interactions in social networks and their implications. In *Proceedings of the Fourth ACM European Conference on Computer Systems (EuroSys '09)* (pp. 205–218). ACM. DOI: 10.1145/1519065.1519089

Wimpenny, G., Šafář, J., Grant, A., & Bransby, M. (2022). Securing the Automatic Identification System (AIS): Using public key cryptography to prevent spoofing whilst retaining backwards compatibility. *Journal of Navigation*, *75*(2), 333–345. DOI: 10.1017/S0373463321000837

Xue, M., Yuan, C., Wu, H., Zhang, Y., & Liu, W. (2020). Machine learning security: Threats, countermeasures, and evaluations. *IEEE Access : Practical Innovations, Open Solutions*, *8*, 74720–74742. DOI: 10.1109/ACCESS.2020.2987435

Xu, M., Ng, W. C., Lim, W. Y. B., Kang, J., Xiong, Z., Niyato, D., & Miao, C. (2022). A full dive into realizing the edge-enabled metaverse: Visions, enabling technologies, and challenges. *IEEE Communications Surveys and Tutorials*.

Yadav, R., & Sheoran, S. K. (2020). "Autoregressive Model for Multivariate Crime Prediction," in Decision Analytics Applications in Industry, Singapore: Springer. *Nature in Singapore*, *2020*, 301–307.

Yang, L., Yu, X., Zhang, S., Long, H., Zhang, H., Xu, S., & Liao, Y. (2023). GoogLeNet based on residual network and attention mechanism identification of rice leaf diseases. *Computers and Electronics in Agriculture*, *204*, 107543. Advance online publication. DOI: 10.1016/j.compag.2022.107543

Yan, S., Ren, J., Wang, W., Sun, L., Zhang, W., & Yu, Q. (2023). A Survey of Adversarial Attack and Defense Methods for Malware Classification in Cyber Security. *IEEE Communications Surveys and Tutorials*, *25*(1), 467–496. DOI: 10.1109/COMST.2022.3225137

Yasarathna, T. L., & Munasinghe, L. (2020). Anomaly detection in cloud network data. In *2020 International Research Conference on Smart Computing and Systems Engineering (SCSE)* (pp. 62–67). IEEE. DOI: 10.1109/SCSE49731.2020.9313014

Yaseen, M. G., Ali, A. H., & Alajanbi, M. (2025). An enhanced hybrid genetic-JAYA algorithm for feature selection and SVM parameter optimization in intrusion detection systems: Evaluation on the CICIDS dataset. *SHIFRA*, *2025*, 98–109. DOI: 10.70470/SHIFRA/2025/006

Yasser, A. A. M. (2025). Sustainable Design Strategies in Architectural Engineering: A Comprehensive Review. *KHWARIZMIA*, *2025*, 1–11. DOI: 10.70470/KHWARIZMIA/2025/001

Ye, K. (2017). Anomaly detection in clouds: Challenges and practice. In *Proceedings of the first Workshop on Emerging Technologies for software-defined and reconfigurable hardware-accelerated Cloud Datacenters* (pp. 1–2). DOI: 10.1145/3129457.3129497

Yonan, J. F., & Zahra, N. A. A.Janan Farag YonanNagham Amjed Abdul Zahra. (2023). Node intrusion tendency recognition using network level features based deep learning approach. *Babylonian Journal of Networking*, *2023*(1), 1–10. DOI: 10.58496/BJN/2023/001

Yuan, Y., Zhang, J., Xu, W., & Li, Z. (2022). Identity-based public data integrity verification scheme in cloud storage system via blockchain. *The Journal of Supercomputing*, *78*(6), 8509–8530. DOI: 10.1007/s11227-021-04193-6

Yu, L., He, M., Xiong, L., Zhou, J., & Luo, Q. (2021). A blockchain-based decentralized authentication and authorization scheme for mobile cloud computing services. *Available at SSRN* 4126148. DOI: 10.2139/ssrn.4126148

Yussuf, M., Lamina, A., Mesioye, O., Nwachukwu, G., & Aminu, T. (2024). Leveraging Machine Learning for Proactive Threat Analysis in Cybersecurity. *International Journal of Computer Applications Technology and Research*, *13*(9), 53–64.

Zaidi, N. A. S., ... (2020) "A Classification Approach for Crime Prediction," in Applied Computing to Support Industry: Innovation and Technology, ACRIT 2019, Ramadi, Iraq, September 15–16, 2019, Revised Selected Papers 1, Springer International Publishing, 2020. DOI: 10.1007/978-3-030-38752-5_6

Zaman, M. T., & Rani, M. (2022). Cloud computing security challenges, analysis of security problems, and cloud computing forensics issues. In *Security and Privacy Trends in Cloud Computing and Big Data* (pp. 147–164). DOI: 10.1201/9781003107286-8

Zhang, X., & Kim, T. (2023). A hybrid attention and time series network for enterprise sales forecasting under digital management and edge computing. *Journal of Cloud Computing (Heidelberg, Germany)*, *12*(1), 12. Advance online publication. DOI: 10.1186/s13677-023-00390-1 PMID: 37122827

Zhang, Y., & Su, Y. (2024). Towards a Sustainable Future: Exploring Innovative Financing Models for Renewable Energy. *MEDAAD*, *2024*, 34–40. DOI: 10.70470/MEDAAD/2024/006

Zieni, R., Massari, L., & Calzarossa, M. C. (2023). Phishing or Not Phishing? A Survey on the Detection of Phishing Websites. *IEEE Access : Practical Innovations, Open Solutions*, *11*, 18499–18519. DOI: 10.1109/ACCESS.2023.3247135

Zwilling, M., Klien, G., Lesjak, D., Wiechetek, Ł., Cetin, F., & Basim, H. N. (2022). Cyber security awareness, knowledge, and behavior: A comparative study. *Journal of Computer Information Systems*, *62*(1), 82–97. DOI: 10.1080/08874417.2020.1712269

About the Contributors

Mohammed Amin Almaiah is an Associate Professor in the Department of Computer Science at the University of Jordan. He is recognized as one of the top 2% of scientists globally from 2020 to the present, reflecting his significant contributions to the field of cybersecurity. Dr. Almaiah holds a PhD in Computer Science (Cybersecurity) from 2017, a Master's Degree in Computer Information Systems (2011), and a Bachelor's Degree in Computer Information Systems (2008). Dr. Almaiah has an extensive academic background, having previously served as the Dean of the Faculty of Information Technology at Aqaba University of Technology (2023–2024). He has also held academic positions in Saudi Arabia as an Associate Professor (2021-2023) and Assistant Professor (2017-2021) in the Department of Computer Networks and Communications at King Faisal University, as well as a Lecturer at Al-Baha University (2011–2013). His diverse academic and leadership experience spans across multiple institutions, where he has focused on cybersecurity education, mobile app security, and cyber-risk management. Dr. Almaiah's research continues to push the boundaries of cybersecurity, with particular attention to the challenges posed by emerging technologies and mobile environments. His work contributes to improving the security of information systems and networks, helping organizations and individuals mitigate cyber threats effectively.

***

A. Mohamed Anwar received the Master's Degree in Computer Science and Engineering from Anna University, Chennai in 2001, Master's Technology in Computer and Information technology from Manonmaniam Sundaranar University, Tirunelveli in 2011, and the Philosophy of Doctorate degree in Information and Communication Engineering from Anna University, Chennai in 2024, respectively. He is currently working as an Assistant Professor (SG) at the Department of Computer Science and Engineering, School of Computing, Vel Tech Rangarajan

Dr. Sagunthala R&D Institute of Science and Technology, Avadi, Chennai. His research areas include Data Science, Machine Learning, Image Processing, Software Engineering and Web Development. He has quality of publications to his credit, including Journal Articles, Conference Publications and Book Chapters.

Avinash Bhagat is serving as Associate Professor in in School of Computer Applications, Lovely Professional University, Punjab, INDIA has a vast experience of more than 22 years in the field of academics, research, and administration. Dr. Avinash Bhagat was awarded with his Doctorate from Lovely Professional University, Punjab in 2021 in the field of Wireless Sensor Networks. His areas of interest include Wireless Sensor Networks, Adhoc Networks, Mobile computing, Machine Learning, etc. Several research papers authored and co-authored, published in International or National journals of repute and conference proceedings come under his credits. He has edited 4 books and 38 book chapters. He has guided more than 1000 PG and UG projects during his service period. He has also completed the certifications like Microsoft Certified System Administrator, Microsoft Certified System Engineer, and Microsoft Certified Professional.

Sachin Chaudhary completed his Graduation from MJPRU, and Post Graduation from AKTU, Moradabad, U.P. Currently Pursuing his Ph.D. in Computer Science and Engineering from Govt. Recognized University. Presently, he is working as an Assistant Professor in the Department of Computer Science and Applications, IIMT University, Meerut, U.P, India. He has been awarded as Excellence in teaching award 2019. He is the reviewer member of some reputed journals. He has published several book chapters and research papers of national and international reputed journals.

Puneet Chauhan is a dedicated research scholar in the Department of Computer Applications at Subharti University, Meerut. With a strong academic foundation and a passion for cybersecurity, he has transitioned to an impactful professional role as a Ransomware Analyst in the United Kingdom. His work focuses on identifying, analyzing, and mitigating ransomware threats, contributing significantly to enhancing organizational security frameworks. Mr. Chauhan's expertise bridges academic research and practical applications, making him a valuable contributor to the evolving field of cybersecurity.

G. Sureshkumar is currently working as an Assistant Professor in the Department of Computer Science at Pondicherry University. He has more than 12 years of experience in teaching and researching. He completed his Masters in Computer Science and Engineering from the College of Engineering Guindy of Anna University in 2006. He completed his Ph.D. in Computer Science and Engineering in

2014. He has published his research works in international journals and conferences. His research interests include Data Mining, Computational Intelligence, Information Retrieval, and Image processing.

Shahnazeer C K has 9 years of experience as an Assistant Professor in various Engineering Colleges in Kerala and 4 years of experience in Industry. She is a research scholar in Computer Science and Engineering, at Pondicherry University Karaikal Campus, Puducherry, India. Her qualifications include B.Tech in Information Technology from Government Engineering College Sreekrishnapuram Palakkad Kerala, India in 2006 and M.Tech in Information Technology from Anna University Coimbatore Tamil Nadu, India in 2010. Her research interests include Computational Intelligence and Cloud computing.

Shinzeer C K has 2 years of experience as an Assistant Professor in the Centre of Computer Science and Information Technology, Calicut University Centre, Thalikkulam, Thrissur, Kerala, India. She is a PhD scholar in Computer Applications, at Lovely Professional University, Punjab, India. Her qualifications included a B. Sc in Mathematics from Sree Kerala Varma College at the University of Calicut, Kerala in 2004, a Master of Computer Application from Dr. G R Damodaran College of Science at Bharathiyar University, Tamil Nadu in 2007, and an MPhil in Computer Science from Jamal Mohamad College at Bharathidasan University, Tamil Nadu in 2012. She is a member of the Blockchain Council. Her research interests include Data Mining and Blockchain Technology.

Ajay Kumar is an accomplished academician and researcher in the field of Computer Science and Engineering. He completed a Bachelor of Engineering (B.E.) and a Master of Technology (M.Tech) in CSE from Rajiv Gandhi Proudyogiki Vishwavidyalaya (RGPV), Bhopal. He earned a Doctor of Philosophy (Ph.D.) in CSE from the prestigious Indian Institute of Technology (IIT) BHU, Varanasi. With extensive teaching and research experience, Dr. Ajay Kumar has served in various esteemed institutions, including Amity University, Gwalior; Bennett University, Greater Noida; and the University of Petroleum and Energy Studies (UPES), Dehradun. Currently, He is dedicated to imparting knowledge and fostering innovation as a faculty member at the Government Engineering College, Kaimur. His areas of expertise and research interests span across Complex networks, Influence Maximization, cybersecurity, etc.

Ajay Shriram Kushwaha is a Professor & Research Guide at Sharda School of Engineering & Technology (SUSET), Sharda University, Greater Noida since June 2023. With over 15 years of academic and research experience, he has worked in esteemed state & private universities like RTM, Gondwana, LPU, Jain University.

He has successfully guided 2 PhD scholars and currently co-guiding 3 scholars from Jain (Deemed-to-be-University) & Lovely Professional University. His research areas include Networking, Software Engineering, Cyber Security & Forensics, with a focus on Blockchain, IoT & Cloud implementation. He holds 4 patents, with 1 patent under final grant communication. He is a life-time member of Indian Science Congress and IAENG (Hongkong) and is a member of IAENG societies for AI, Computer Science, Data Mining & Software Engineering. He serves as an Editor, Guest Editor, and reviewer for 12+ Scopus, UGC listed or Peer Reviewed International Journals. He has published over 37 research papers in SCOPUS/UGC Listed/Peer Reviewed Journals and co-authored 7 books & news magazine articles. He has conducted 40+ Refresher Courses, FDPs, Seminars, Webinars, Workshops, and Technical Sessions across the country on e-content development, pedagogy, and innovative content creation & assessment techniques. He also conducts sessions on Cyber Security, Ethical Hacking, and related domains. He has completed several MOOC courses from platforms like LinkedIn Learning, Coursera, Alison, Udemy, and Basis Technology. Contributing to open learning, he creates content for YouTube and social media.

Krishna Kumari L, Completed UG and PG in the Domain of ECE, and pursuing PhD in the field of Machine learning for Biomedical applications.

Naveenkumar Mahamkali is currently an Assistant Professor in the Department of Computer Science and Engineering at SRM University-AP, India. He received the Ph.D. degree from the National Institute of Technology, Tiruchirappalli, India. He has over ten years of academic and research experience. His research interests include deep learning, medical image analysis, microarray and RNA-Seq data classification, and computer vision. He has published several research articles in reputed international journals and conferences

Khaled Maabreh is an associate professor in computer science. He holds a PhD from Amman Arab University for Graduate Studies in 2008. He has more than 30 years of experience, including leading a range of IT-related projects in addition to management posts. His main research interests include information security and cybersecurity, distributed databases, concurrency control, database performance, and e-learning.

Brijesh Kumar Sharma, an accomplished academic and researcher, serves as an Assistant Professor in the Department of Computer Science and Engineering at SRMIST. With over 19 years of professional experience, Dr. Sharma holds a Ph.D. in Computer Science and Engineering (2013) and an MCA from M.I.E.T. Meerut (2002). His academic contributions are reflected in his research publications, including articles on software quality assurance and evaluation in reputed international journals. He has also demonstrated innovation through his patent on "IoT-Enabled Monitoring of Academic Activities in Institutions," published in 2023. He is dedication to excellence in education has earned him the Best Teacher Award at Mewar Institute of Management, Ghaziabad, and he actively participates in seminars, workshops, and faculty development programs. As a professional member of the Computer Society of India, He also continues to contribute to advancements in the field of computer science.

Rupak Sharma holds Doctorate of Philosophy(Ph.D) degree in Computer Science & Engineering , M.Tech degree in Computer Science and MCA from V.B.S Purvanchal University, Jounpur(UP).He started his professional career in the year 2002 as a academician. At present, Dr. Sharma working as a Associate Professor in the Department of Computer Applications and holds many Academic and Administrative post in SRMIST, Modinagar, Ghaziabad(UP). Dr. Sharma has been supervised 10 Ph.D scholars and currently supervising 6 Ph.D scholars and 6 MCA Students. He has published many National and International research papers and Books. Dr. Sharma has been awarded, Best Faculty award in year 2018 and 2022, SRMIST(Deemed to be University), Modinagar, Ghaziabad(UP)

Sachin Sharma is currently working as a Professor, Amity School of Engineering and Technology, Amity University Punjab, Mohali, India. He also worked as Associate Dean, International Affairs and Professor, Department of Computer Science and Engineering at Graphic Era Deemed to be University, Dehradun, Uttarakhand, India. He has experience of 15+ years in industry and academia. He is also Co-founder and Chief Technology officer (CTO) of IntelliNexus LLC, Arkansas, USA based company. He also worked as a Senior Systems Engineer at Belkin International, Inc., Irvine, California, USA. He received his Philosophy of Doctorate (Ph.D.) degree in Engineering Science and Systems specialization in Systems Engineering from University of Arkansas at Little Rock, USA with 4.0 out 4.0 GPA and M.S. degree in Systems engineering from University of Arkansas at Little Rock with 4.0 out 4.0 GPA. Dr. Sharma has authored/coauthored over 300+ publications in the form of books, patents, and papers in refereed journals and conference proceedings. He holds 100+ US, Indian and international patents in the area of IoT, wireless communication and AI. He has also served as a Guest Reviewer for several Special issues of IEEE/ACM Transactions. His research interests include 6G wireless communication networks, Cloud Computing, Artificial Intelligence, Quantum Computing, IoT, Vehicular ad hoc networking and Cyber security.

Vikas Sharma completed his Graduation and Post Graduation from Chaudhary Charan Singh University, Meerut, U.P. Currently Pursuing his Ph.D. in Computer Science and Engineering from Govt. Recognized University. Presently, he is working as an Assistant Professor in the Department of Computer Applications, SRM Institute of Science and Technology, NCR Campus Sikri Kalan, Modinagar, U.P, India. He has been awarded as Excellence in teaching award 2019. He is the reviewer member of some reputed journals. He has published several book chapters and research papers of national and international reputed journals.

Keshav Sinha was born in Dhanbad, India, in 1991. He received a B.E. Degree in Computer Science and Engineering from Sri Chandrasekharendra Saraswathi Viswa Mahavidyalaya, Kanchipuram, India, in 2013 and an M.E. Degree in Software Engineering from the Birla Institute of Technology, Mesra, India, in 2016. He completed a PhD in cryptography and network security from Birla Institute of Technology, Mesra, India, in 2022. He is an assistant professor specializing in Cryptography and Network Security. His research focuses on developing a secure environment for multimedia transmission. He has contributed to soft computing, humanities, and social and cyber policy and published numerous papers in conferences and journals. His work aims to bring flexibility and innovation to the computer science society.

Krishna Siva Prasad is currently an Assistant Professor in department of Computer science and Engineering at SRM University AP.

Tarun Kumar Vashishth is an active academician and researcher in the field of computer science with 21 years of experience. He earned Ph.D. Mathematics degree specialized in Operations Research; served several academic positions such as HoD, Dy. Director, Academic Coordinator, Member Secretary of Department Research Committee , Assistant Center superintendent and Head Examiner in university examinations. He is involved in academic development and scholarly activities. He is member of International Association of Engineers, The Society of Digital Information and Wireless Communications, Global Professors Welfare Association, International Association of Academic plus Corporate (IAAC), Computer Science Teachers Association and Internet Society . His research interest includes Cloud Computing, Artificial Intelligence, Machine Learning and Operations Research; published more than 50 research articles with 2 book and 70 book chapters. He is contributing as member of editorial and reviewers boards in conferences and various computer journals published by CRC Press, Taylor and Francis, Springer, IGI global and other universities.

Index

A

B

C

D

X

Z

www.ingramcontent.com/pod-product-compliance
Lightning Source LLC
LaVergne TN
LVHW081538300926
849161LV00006B/1474